MORNING BY MORNING

To Erin,

May these devotions
deepen your sense
of God's sustaining presence
& bring fresh joy to your day!

Blessings in your ministry,

Love,
Dan

MORNING BY MORNING

Daily Meditations
from the Writings of Marva J. Dawn

MARVA J. DAWN

Edited by
Karen Dismer

William B. Eerdmans Publishing Company
Grand Rapids, Michigan / Cambridge, U.K.

Lime Grove House Publishing
Auckland, New Zealand / Sydney, Australia

© 2001 Wm. B. Eerdmans Publishing Co.

Published jointly 2001 by
Wm. B. Eerdmans Publishing Co.
255 Jefferson Ave. S.E., Grand Rapids, Michigan 49503 /
P.O. Box 163, Cambridge CB3 9PU U.K.
www.eerdmans.com
and by
Lime Grove House Publishing Ltd
P.O. Box 37-955
Parnell, Auckland, N.Z. /
P.O. Box 1704
Rozelle, N.S.W.
Sydney, Australia

Printed in the United States of America

06 05 04 03 02 01   7 6 5 4 3 2 1

Eerdmans ISBN 0-8028-4769-2

Lime Grove House ISBN 1 876798 66 1

Some of the selections in this book are adapted from *Joy in Our Weakness* by
Marva Dawn. © 1994 Concordia Publishing House. Used with permission of CPH.

*This book is dedicated to Michael, my husband and pastor, and to Marva,
my friend and teacher, in gratitude for all they have done
in nurturing my faith. —KAD*

*This book is dedicated to all those who have helped to keep me alive—
against expectations—so that I can keep writing.*

*I am immensely grateful to these:
Dr. Stephen Ebert and Dr. Harry Glauber,
for general and diabetic safekeeping;
Dr. Cathryn Wise, who watches over my failing kidneys;
Dr. Robert Buys, who helped me see again
and minds my functioning retina;
Dr. Hans Behrens, Dr. Joseph Low, and Dr. David Swan,
who care for ears and jaws;
Dr. Daniel Granville and David Varnau,
who enabled me to walk again;
Dr. J. Thomas Leimert, who treated my cancer and still stands guard;
Dr. Mark Rarick, whose cancer project treatment
still produces my red blood cells;
all my prayer partners through Christians Equipped for Ministry
and the Board of CEM, who pray and advise and counsel;
and especially Myron, who nurses and nurtures me constantly.*

*I also thank Karen Dismer for her extraordinary friendship
and work of love to compile this book!*
—MJD

Table of Contents

Editor's Introduction

If you have ever heard a keynote speech, a sermon, or a Bible study given by Marva Dawn, you will understand why I have, many times, traveled hundreds of miles to hear her speak. Marva's spiritual yet scholarly insights into biblical texts, shared in her speaking and writing, have taught, inspired, encouraged, comforted, challenged, and thrilled me for twenty-two years. This book is for all of you who have been similarly affected by Marva's ministry.

For those of you who have never heard Marva speak or have never read one of her books or magazine articles, this book is for you, too. I hope and pray that the passages I have selected will be a fair introduction to all that Marva has to say to you — that, morning by morning, you will find nourishment for your faith and encouragement for your daily life in Christ.

Now let me introduce this book to you. Passages have been chosen from ten of Marva's books (slight modifications have been made for their inclusion here). I have arranged them in a weekly pattern in this manner: the Sunday passages come almost exclusively from *Reaching Out without Dumbing Down* and *A Royal "Waste" of Time*, Marva's books on worship. They were chosen to help us reflect seriously on our own worship experiences and opportunities, so that what we choose to do in our worship honors God and forms our Christian character. Quotations from Scripture are from the New International Version, unless otherwise noted.

Monday's passages come from *Truly the Community* because our Sunday experiences in worship grow out of, and lead us more deeply into, our life in the community of believers.

The Tuesday passages come mainly from three books, focusing on three aspects of our daily life as members of the Christian community: how we (all of us, not just clergy) understand our ministry (why it is "unnecessary" and essential — *The Unnecessary Pastor*); how we nurture children in the Church (passing on the faith — *Is It a Lost Cause?*); and how we live decently, honestly, and faithfully as adults in relationships that reflect the relationship we have with God *(Sexual Character)*.

On Wednesdays the readings come from Marva's book *I'm Lonely, LORD — How Long?* No matter what our circumstances are, there are times when we each feel lost and alone, when we don't experience a sense of belonging or purpose in the community of believers. The passages from this book, based on the Psalms, address these trying times.

Passages from *Joy in Our Weakness,* based on the book of Revelation, will focus our Thursdays on the wonderful words of hope and encouragement written to Christians in a time of persecution — words that speak amazingly clearly to our day as well.

We will read selections primarily from *To Walk and Not Faint,* Marva's book on Isaiah 40, for our Friday meditations. After four days of focusing on God's direction for our lives within the community of believers, we will refocus our attention on God's character — God's loving, steadfast faithfulness.

On Saturday, meditations from, among other books, *Keeping the Sabbath Wholly* will help us respond to God's faithfulness by anticipating and preparing once again for the blessings of Sunday worship and rest.

In addition to this weekly cycle of readings, Marva has provided meditations for special days throughout the year, which you may choose to read on the appropriate days with, or in place of, the daily readings. These meditations, located at the back of the book, include a message for your birthday and a meditation for each of the major church festivals according to the church year calendar.

Several extra readings can also be found at the back of this book so that you may begin using it at once. Simply read one of these meditations each day until it is Sunday; then move to the main body of the book where the fifty-two weeks of selections begin.[1]

Each meditation ends with what is intended as a "prayer starter." I hope these will lead you into words of your own before the "Amen."

In each of Marva's books, her ideas are well illustrated by stories, examples, personal experiences, biblical passages, and supporting material from other scholars, making even difficult theological issues more understandable. If a particular topic from these meditations interests you, I can promise you that there is a whole, wonderful book awaiting you with much more in it than I was able to share in these brief selections. If you've ever seen a good movie and then read the book it was based on, you'll know what I mean.

1. If you know someone who would like to *hear* a daily meditation, this book will be available on tape from Dottie Davis, CEM Tape Ministry Coordinator, 10918 N.E. 152nd Avenue, Vancouver, WA 98682-1776; phone: 360-892-3618.

Editor's Introduction

It has been such a blessing for me to read straight through ten of Marva's books in as many months that I most sincerely encourage you to consider doing the same! Meanwhile, I pray that starting or ending each day with one of these selected meditations will richly bless your life and ministry in the community of believers.

Karen Dismer
American Falls, Idaho
November 2000

Notes on Words

Throughout this book we capitalize *Church* to signify the ideal as Christ would have his Body be and use lowercase *church* or *churches* to name concrete fallen (and seeking to be faithful) realities.

We join many other scholars and pastors in calling the first three-fourths of the Bible the "First Testament" or the "Hebrew Scriptures," to avoid our culture's negative connotations of the name *Old* Testament and to emphasize both the consistency of God's grace for all God's people and also the continuity of God's covenants in the Bible, first with Israel and then in addition with Christians.

The canonical tradition of the Jews and earliest Christians passed on psalms naming David as their author and various New Testament letters naming Paul as their author. Since the meditations in this book are not intended as commentary, but rather as devotional and pastoral helps, we don't debate here the historical accuracy of these or any other canonical ascriptions. Rather, because there are deep narrative and descriptive benefits from identifying the emotions and situations of the psalms or the letters with a particular poet or apostle, we will, throughout this book, accept the titles and names associated with these writings and honor them canonically.

The chief character of these pages is the LORD as he reveals himself to his people. We have followed the customary practice in Bibles of capitalizing all the letters in the words *LORD* and *GOD* when the Hebrew word to be translated is *YHWH*, often vocalized as *Yahweh* (formerly as *Jehovah*). The original Hebrew noun, composed of the four consonants Y H W H, was related to the root of the verb *to be*. At some places in this book we use *YHWH* and hope that this will cause you to reflect upon the name's mystery and God's unreachable majesty. Throughout the First Testament the name *YHWH*, the LORD, implies the faithfulness of GOD, especially as he delivers his people. We need to recover this image in our times, to learn the glory of the LORD's constant faithfulness to his covenant and his effective deliverance of his people from all their captivities.

It is Marva's practice, out of her concern to reach the widest possible audience, to refer to God (when necessary for literary flow) with the pronouns *he, his,* and *him,* which she has always understood as gender-neutral — and yet personal — if used in connection with God. Certainly God is neither masculine nor feminine, but more than all our inadequate words can ever connote.

It is also Marva's custom to capitalize characteristic words at points when she wants to call attention to the difference in these entities if they come directly from God and our relationship with him. Two words especially should be noted — "Hilarity" and "Joy." The former comes from the Greek word *hilarotēs,* which Paul selected in Romans 12:8 to invite those who have the gift of showing mercy to exercise that gift with "cheerfulness." The Greek term signifies a gladness that arises from a deep sense of well-being founded in trusting the Grace-Giver to work through his gifts to us. In this book the word *Hilarity* describes the spirit of the Christian community and names the glad hope that could characterize God's people, who know surely that they are profoundly loved by God, as manifested in the past by God's creation and in the life, death, resurrection, and ascension of Jesus Christ. Our present Hilarity is made possible by the empowering indwelling of the Holy Spirit in our lives. Our Hilarity is heightened when we look forward confidently to the wild ecstasy that will be ours at the end of time when all suffering is finished and we experience the eternal, incredible Joy of face-to-face communion with God.

Similarly, the word *Joy* is capitalized to distinguish the specific Joy of the Lord from mere (and fading) human happiness. We pray that you might experience that Joy as you read the pages that follow and meditate on the promises of God and their results in our lives of service to God's glory.

52 Weeks of Meditations

God of grace and God of glory, on your people pour your power;
Crown your ancient Church's story; bring its bud to glorious flow'r.
Grant us wisdom, grant us courage
For the facing of this hour,
For the facing of this hour.

Harry Emerson Fosdick, 1878-1969

We often don't ask enough questions or the right kind of questions about the foundations of what we are doing. Just as scientists sometimes begin to perform medical procedures before anyone has raised the necessary moral objections, so it seems that many congregations today are switching worship practices without investigating what worship means and how our worship relates to contemporary culture.

The Scriptures, the history of the Church, and my own faith, experience, and training convince me that the vitality and faithfulness of our personal and corporate Christian lives and the effectiveness of our outreach to the world around us depend on the character that is formed in us. What concerns me is whether our local parishes and denominations have thought thoroughly enough about worship and culture to function effectively in contemporary society. How can we best reach out to this society without "dumbing down" that essential character formation?

My major concern for the Church has to do with worship, because its character-forming potential is so subtle and barely noticed, and yet worship creates a great impact on the hearts and minds and lives of a congregation's members. Indeed, how we worship both reveals and forms our identity as persons and communities. . . .

In light of the "dumbing down" that happens in worship in some places, we might paraphrase Neil Postman: "When the congregation becomes an audience and its worship a vaudeville act, then the Church finds itself at risk; the death of faith and Christian character is a clear possibility." . . .

It is not too late to ask better questions as we seek to make worship meaningful for persons in our present culture. . . . Can the Church be a place of meaningful talking, attentive listening, and profound thinking? In short, can we develop a theology of worship for the Church to flourish and grow in a turn-of-the-century culture?

Prayer
   Before we adopt any worship practice, O Lord, guide our thinking . . .
   Amen.

Reaching Out, pp. 3-4, 13.

Rejoice in the Lord always. I will say it again: Rejoice!

Philippians 4:4

If [someone's gift] is showing mercy, let [that person] do it cheerfully.

Romans 12:8d

Paul selected the Greek word *hilarotēs* for Romans 12:8 to invite those who have the gift of showing mercy to exercise that gift with "cheerfulness."

The gladness Paul identifies by means of this word choice arises from a deep sense of well-being founded in trusting the Grace-Giver to work through his gifts to us. I use the word *Hilarity* to describe the spirit of the Christian community, . . . to name the glad hope that could characterize God's people.

The basis of our hope-full Hilarity encompasses all the dimensions of time. We experience glad Hilarity in the sure knowledge that we are loved by God, as manifested in the past by God's creation of us and in the life, death, resurrection, and ascension of Jesus Christ. Our present Hilarity is made possible by the empowering indwelling of the Holy Spirit in our lives. Our Hilarity is heightened when we look forward confidently to the . . . end of time when all suffering is finished and we experience the eternal, incredible Joy of face-to-face communion with God. . . .

Unfortunately, one of the most powerful reasons for our often evident lack of gladness is that ours is a culture of solo efforts. We live our Christian faith independently — not inextricably linked with other members of the Body of believers. Consequently, we do not experience the Hilarity of being enfolded in a moment-by-moment awareness of the good news of our hope and life in Jesus Christ. We don't experience the support that true community engenders. We aren't set free to be truly ourselves in the stewardship of our Spirit-given grace-gifts.

So I use the word *Hilarity* to describe the ideal Christian community, and my intention is to make us stop and think: what would it be like if the Christian Church were truly a community that thoroughly enjoyed being itself? It seems to me it could change the world!

Prayer

Grace-Giver, help us live in true community — in Hilarity — by which, rejoicing together always, we can change the world . . .   Amen.

Truly the Community, pp. ix-xi.

4

Bless all those who nurture children, sharing knowledge, showing love,
   who by faithful works and actions lead young lives to God above!
                                        John A. Dalles (1993, modified 1994)

How are our children being formed? Do they know themselves primarily as citizens of the kingdom of God? Do we and our offspring look, act, talk, and think like people who are shaped . . . by God's Revelation? . . .

   What do certain groups . . . do to cause their children to grow up with . . . integrity and faith? Is it possible to nurture children and develop adults so profoundly without retreating into an isolation that would keep us from ministering to the world around us? Obviously the answer is Yes. . . .

   But why is it not happening more often? . . .

   Our increasing postmodern world is, usually unconsciously, desperate for the gifts of the Christian faith. . . . Individuals without a home yearn for community; people without a story seek a framework for understanding; "boomers" who have rejected moral authority search for a reference point; "busters" without motivation long for meaning beyond the next entertainment; teenagers pursue love and ache for it to last; children crave attention and a reason to care about anything. . . . Are we raising our own children to live the substance and the presence of faith — and to pass God's love and their faith on to their friends, neighbors, and peers at school? Or are we letting them be sucked into the behavior patterns, the attitudes, the meaninglessness, and the despair of the world around them? . . .

   Is the raising of genuinely *Christian* children a lost cause in our post-Christian society? . . . It is not — if we wake up. . . . But the task is large. . . . In fact, it is a mortal combat with societal forces, cultural directions, and social institutions that contradict the purposes of God. . . .

   Christianity is no longer the dominant culture in the United States. If we want our children to grow up with Christian convictions, capacities, and choices, we must much more deliberately nurture the faith and its concomitant lifestyle. . . .

   We must be more deliberate in *thinking Christianly* about raising children.

Prayer
   Trustworthy God, help us raise our children in the faith, with a faith that will
   shape their characters for a lifetime of discipleship . . .   Amen.
                                        Is It a Lost Cause? pp. 1-7.

How long, O LORD? Will you forget me forever?
  How long will you hide your face from me? . . .
But I trust in your unfailing love;
  my heart rejoices in your salvation.

Psalm 13:1, 5

An overwhelming number of us are lonely. . . . Sometimes we are lonely for a specific reason. . . . Sometimes our loneliness is a general, pervasive alienation: we just don't feel as if we belong. . . . Maybe we don't have anyone with whom we can share the most important dimensions of our lives. . . .

We think that as soon as circumstances in our lives get put right, we can proceed. When they don't, we remain incapacitated and ask, "How long, LORD?"

In our loneliness especially, we join the psalmist in asking God if he is going to forget us forever. The original Hebrew text wonders if God will disregard us for "an everlastingness." God seems to have dropped us out of his plans. Nothing is changing. We have been abandoned. . . .

"But I trust in your unfailing love." . . . Suddenly the psalmist is writing words of hope and victory. Is such a change really possible? . . .

The key lies in one of my favorite Hebrew words, the noun *chesedh,* which is translated "unfailing love" in the New International Version of Psalm 13. The term describes the steadfast, covenant love of the LORD, the amazing grace of his infinite kindness and compassion toward us, his people. . . .

God has not forgotten us, not for a moment; nor will he ever. . . .

It may seem so when he does not grant us what we ask or take away our interminable sorrow, but his infinite wisdom and love are always present with us and on behalf of us.

Of course it will seem that we wrestle with our thoughts for too long. . . . Only when we are finally reduced to the point of helplessness, the realization that we will never be able to deal with our loneliness and grief by ourselves, will we give in to *chesedh* and let God bring to us the gifts of his love. When we finally let God be God-for-us and participate in his plans willingly, we can discover the Joy of them.

Prayer
  Steadfast LORD, you have not forgotten us; rather, we have forgotten that your love is unfailing — a waiting gift . . .   Amen.

I'm Lonely, LORD, pp. 1-2, 5-6.

The revelation of Jesus Christ, which God gave him to show his servants what must soon take place. He made it known by sending his angel to his servant John. . . .

Revelation 1:1

"The Revelation of Jesus Christ" . . . reminds us that by grace God revealed, through his servant John, the truth about the lordship of Jesus, to comfort people who were powerless against Roman persecution. Many people are uncomfortable with The Revelation for the very reason that it is filled with the paradox of weakness, in contrast to our world's stresses on efficiency and usefulness and power. We don't want to face the weaknesses in ourselves or cope with the weaknesses of others.

Furthermore, many people find The Revelation difficult because . . . we can hardly understand a book that is flooded with images, memories, symbols, and mysteries. Consequently, we miss some of God's best promises and the comfort that God would give us through this wonderful book of hope. . . .

Finally, some people avoid the book of Revelation because they are frightened by the grotesque stories of supernatural warfare that are sometimes over-accentuated or falsely elaborated in the anticipation of the end of time. . . .

The Revelation . . . invites everyone, Christian and non-Christian alike, to explore the value of its message for this century. . . . It contains questions that apply to that dimension of everyone's existence that is manifested in our allegiance to something — anything. . . .

Its value for everybody is that it portrays the lordship of the Christ. One of its great themes (often missed) is that Christ reigns especially in the midst of our suffering.

In my experience, some of the Christians who have understood best what that reign means have been disabled people or people with other limitations . . . who have learned to trust God in their physical challenges or other struggles, and therefore often render us all a great service by teaching us a theology of weakness. . . .

My major hope is that all of us in the body of Christ could learn that theology better, by receiving the teaching that our sufferings bring us and valuing more thoroughly the contributions that those who suffer bring to our communities.

Prayer
> *Jesus Christ our Lord, thank you for your word of hope to us through The Revelation . . .   Amen.*

Joy in Our Weakness, pp. 10-11.

"Comfort ye, O comfort my people,"
  says your God.

Isaiah 40:1 (composite translation)

At one time or another, we all feel so overwhelmed by our situations that we grope for any fragment of comfort to sustain us.

Where in the world can comfort be found?

The situations described in the book of Isaiah were no better. Isaiah himself rebuked the Israelites for losing sight of their purpose as the chosen people. Intrigue and rebellion, hypocritical worship and injustice, materialism and idolatries of all sorts — the same sins plagued the people in his time as plague the world today. Then the Israelites were taken into captivity; their temple was destroyed, and their capital city's walls were torn down. Now Abraham's descendants were overcome with despair. Were they still God's chosen people? How could the LORD have let this happen to them? How could they be delivered from the Babylonians? When would they return to their own land?

After many chapters filled with doom oracles for other nations and rebukes for Israel, the fortieth chapter of Isaiah suddenly ushers in an entirely different tone. In the midst of the darkness of sin and despair, God proclaims a new message of light and hope. Similarly, in the midst of the troubled times of our personal lives and into the shambles of postmodern culture (that in despair has given up the modern myth of progress), God calls to his people today to hear new assurance, a word of comfort and victory.

"Comfort, O comfort." God says it twice to the nameless audience. One call to comfort is not enough, for pain and suffering are deep and agony is long. The fact that the verb occurs twice implies that the comfort we are being offered is continuous. There IS comfort to be given, God declares. . . .

Not only is there a bounteous supply of comfort, but what we receive and give is truly comforting. . . . Society would comfort us with false hopes by feeding our egos or nursing our grudges or building our illusions. God, on the other hand, wants to give us the comfort of his Truth, the entire Truth concerning both our condition in relation to him and his gracious remedies for our brokenness.

Prayer

  Consoling God, in our need, teach us to turn to you for true comfort . . .
  Amen.

To Walk and Not Faint, pp. 1-3.

Come, let us welcome the Sabbath in joy and peace! Like a bride, radiant and joyous, comes the Sabbath. It brings blessings to our hearts; workday thoughts and cares are put aside. . . .

From the Kiddush ritual of a Reform home service for Sabbath eve

What a sad commentary it is on our spirituality that the delight of "keeping the Sabbath day" has degenerated into the routine and drudgery — even the downright oppressiveness — of "going to church." . . .

In the first place, how we talk affects how we live. To say "I am going to church" both reveals and promotes bad theology. In the earliest days of Christianity, "the church" was a living and vibrant gathering of God's *people,* who met together to be strengthened and then went out into the world to manifest the gospel in their actions and their very beings. Now the church has become a static *place. . . .* We are NOT "going to church"! We are going to a *sanctuary* to participate in an *order of worship* together with other *people of God* gathered in *community,* to be nourished by all that we do there together so that we can go out into the world and *be church.*

In the second place, the act of worship is only one small part (though an essential one) of the whole meaning of Sabbath keeping. To "keep the Sabbath holy" means to recognize that the rhythm of six days of work and one day of ceasing work is written into the very core of our beings. To observe that order week by week creates in us a wholeness that is possible only when we live in accordance with this pattern of being graciously commanded by God. . . .

To keep the Sabbath is not a legalistic duty. Rather, living in accordance with our own natural rhythm gives freedom, the delight of one whole day in every seven set apart as holy. . . .

In Jewish tradition the Sabbath is loved as a bride or a queen. Deep in our beings there is a longing for completion. . . . Only holy time, in which we experience the presence of God, can fill our emptiness.

Prayer
  Creator of the Sabbath, bless our efforts to keep the Sabbath holy, so that we may meet you in that holy time and learn more fully how to love and serve you . . .   Amen.

Keeping the Sabbath Wholly, pp. x-xv, 2.

Ascribe to the LORD the glory of his name;
*   worship the LORD in holy splendor.*

Psalm 29:2

To worship the LORD is — in the world's eyes — a waste of time. It is, indeed, a *royal* waste of time, but a waste nonetheless. By engaging in it, we don't accomplish anything useful in our society's terms.

Worship ought not to be construed in a utilitarian way. Its purpose is not to gain numbers nor for our churches to be seen as successful. Rather, the entire reason for our worship is that God deserves it. Moreover, it isn't even useful for earning points with God, for what we do in worship won't change one whit how God feels about us. We will always still be helpless sinners caught in our endless inability to be what we should be or to make ourselves better — and God will always still be merciful, compassionate, and gracious, abounding in steadfast love and ready to forgive us as we come to him.

Worship is a royal waste of time, but indeed it is royal, for it immerses us in the regal splendor of the King of the cosmos. The churches' worship provides opportunities for us to enjoy God's presence in corporate ways that take us out of time and into the eternal purposes of God's kingdom. As a result, we shall be changed — but not because of anything we do. God, on whom we are centered and to whom we submit, will transform us by his Revelation of himself.

To understand worship as a royal waste of time is good for us because that frees us to enter into the poverty of Christ. We worship a triune God who chose to rescue the world he created by means of the way of humility. God sent his Son into the world to empty himself in the obedience of a slave, humbling himself to suffer throughout his entire life and to die the worst of deaths on our behalf. He did not come to be "solving the world's problems in any sense that the world could understand," as Simon Tugwell puts it. Worship of such a God immerses us in such a way of life, empowered by a Spirit who does not equip us with means of power or control, accomplishment or success, but with the ability and humility to waste time in love of the neighbor.

Prayer
> *King of the cosmos, as we "waste" time worshiping you, change our lives! . . .*
> *Amen.*

A Royal "Waste" of Time, pp. 1-2.

I appeal to you, therefore, brothers and sisters, because of the mercies of God, to offer your bodies as a sacrifice, living and holy and acceptable — which is your spiritual worship.

Romans 12:1 (my translation)

The word *bodies* can be interpreted to signify both individuals and the various house churches of the Roman congregation. . . . Let us consider here the first interpretation.

The Greek word *sōma* is usually interpreted to signify our physical bodies. In that sense, Paul's plea is for each of us to put our whole selves into our relationship with God and, consequently, with each other. . . .

Offering our bodies has all sorts of practical implications. . . . We cannot be Christians merely intellectually; rather, we must respond to God's love by loving him with our words and attitudes, our emotions and actions.

To offer the Lord our bodies might mean doing physical work in his service. . . . It might mean mowing the lawn for our parents, going to the hospital to visit someone who is ill, or mopping the floor for someone disabled. . . .

When we offer our bodies, we want to give God the best that we can, to put our whole beings into the offering. Our motivation for doing that, of course, is the Hilarity created by the revelation of his immense love and grace expounded in the first eleven chapters of Romans.

This emphasis on the response of our lives to God's love is underscored by our English verb *offer.* That word connotes freedom. We are not coerced. Instead, an offering is the gift of our choice. God's love for us is so rich and inviting that we want with our whole beings to offer up our whole beings. . . .

The mystery of the Christian life is that we can truly offer ourselves to God only if we are willing to give up ourselves. Yet in that death to our limited human concerns, God uses us in ways that demonstrate powerful life at work within us. . . .

When our own needs or fears are put to death, then we discover a source of life in God that is unexplainable.

This is the challenge of Paul's invitation for us: . . . to be willing more and more to make such a complete offering.

Prayer

Merciful God, we offer ourselves — wholly — to you, in gratitude and willing service . . .   Amen.

Truly the Community, pp. 11-15.

I heard the voice of Jesus say, "Behold, I freely give
the living water; thirsty one, stoop down and drink and live."

Horatius Bonar (1846), alt.

It seems to me that pastors and parents, churches and communities don't understand what they are up against in their endeavor to form Christian character in young people. . . .

At root, our neighbors — and we ourselves — are driven by a profound, unquenchable yearning, and we all try various methods to deal with it. This burning longing, this powerful thirst, in its essence is a yearning for God and is part of what it means to have been created in God's image. . . .

There are a variety of inadequate goals by which persons in our culture try to appease or repress their spiritual hunger. These idolatries often begin with genuine concern for things that are important, but the devotion gets out of hand and usurps the place of the one true God. . . .

For example, why does money have such control over so many people? . . .

Powers of evil turn human beings, institutions, laws, rulers, cultural elements, or authorities away from their God-given roles into functioning for harm. . . . Thus, we must do battle against these forces of darkness (Eph. 6:10-18) and expose them, even as Christ did (Col. 2:15). . . .

What makes the battle so intense in the present world is that so much of life is becoming ambiguous, chaotic, fearsome, unmoored. Consequently, people cling more desperately to whatever idolatries seem to them capable of freeing them from pain, confusion, weariness, or meaninglessness. . . . Our neighbors in the world (and we, in spite of knowing better) wind up with ultimate concerns that are trite, violent, enslaving, or flimsy. These goals will never ultimately satisfy or repress our deepest longing. . . .

We need to think about the powers of evil with repentance, for we all must acknowledge how easily they turn us away from living as followers of Christ. Especially we can't expect our children to resist the gods of the world unless we equip them — and ourselves — with knowledge of, and trust in, a true God who is strong enough to be worth turning to, away from what fascinates their peers.

Prayer

Holy Spirit, inspire our faithfulness, for our sake and our children's . . .
Amen.

Is It a Lost Cause? pp. 15-22.

How long must I wrestle with my thoughts
  and every day have sorrow in my heart? . . .
But I trust in your unfailing love;
  my heart rejoices in your salvation.
I will sing to the LORD;
  for he has been good to me.

Psalm 13:2, 5-6

God, the promising I AM, has *always* been faithful to his promises. Surely he will not single us out as individuals to withhold from us his *chesedh* (unfailing love). In that fact we can trust, even before it has sunk into our feelings.

The essence of the matter is that we can't experience the truth of *chesedh* in the reality of our feelings until we know it first as a fact of faith.

Sometimes it helps, the psalmist points out, to look back to the past. The final verse of Psalm 13 says, "I will sing because the LORD has been good to me." Not only will we be able someday to sing because we will have learned how he has been good to us in this situation, but also right now we can sing because he has been good to us in the past. . . .

We can train our minds to turn to memories of those times in the moments when we are tempted to ask, "How long?" and thus be strengthened by the precious instances when the "how long?" came crashing to a halt in the wonder of God's *chesedh*.

That is why the psalmist can say, "My heart rejoices in your salvation." The Hebrew language doesn't have past, present, or future tense verbs as our English does. Its verbs indicate simply completed or uncompleted action. The verb here for rejoicing is in the imperfect, or incomplete, form. We could translate it, "My heart will rejoice in your salvation," or . . . "My heart rejoices" (the action is continually going on). If we are not experiencing Joy in God's deliverance yet, we can confidently look forward to the time when we will. . . .

The delightful irony is that usually the change of attitude is the deliverance. As soon as we stop asking "How long?" we are liberated from that question's bondage. Then we can rejoice instead in the memories of how God has been good to us or "how bountifully He has dealt" with us (the New American Standard Version).

Prayer
Bountiful God, we will rejoice in all you have done for us, and in rejoicing we will trust! . . .   Amen.

I'm Lonely, LORD, pp. 1, 6-7.

Blessed is the one who reads the words of this prophecy, and blessed are those who hear it and take to heart what is written in it, because the time is near.

Revelation 1:3

The lecturer had everything pinned down. . . . He knew exactly what events of world history were prophesied by which images in the book of Revelation so that he could plot on a timeline exactly how close we were to the end. . . .

However, a careful study of The Revelation will demonstrate that this is not the primary message of the book. Rather, its symbols and images affirm the truth that victory lies in weakness. . . . Such a perspective really offers profound comfort and hope. . . .

At the book's end, the one who is coming soon gives this promise: "Blessed is the one heeding the words of the prophecy in this book" (22:7). Certainly these promises at the beginning and end of The Revelation invite us to search for insight into this precious, mysterious book. Its visions will give us a new understanding of life and suffering and the significance of our religious yearnings. . . .

To read for insight, however, we must first remember that one rule for understanding any piece of literature is that we must know in what time period it was written to clarify what it meant originally for those who first read it. . . . Even though scholars disagree about many particulars of its external situation (such as whether the John who wrote the book was the disciple of Jesus and whether the author actually saw the visions or dreamed them), all scholars agree that the book was written during a time of persecution against the early Christians — perhaps the persecution of Nero, around A.D. 64, or of Domitian, between A.D. 81 and 96. . . .

To study the Scriptures with historical integrity means to judge them in their own time and place and to take literally their original message for the original readers.

Our approach . . . then should be to understand The Revelation as did the earliest Christians, to formulate from their situation the principles conveyed by the text, and only then to apply those principles to our times. . . . Such an interpretation invites us to turn to the last book of the Bible when things are hard.

Prayer

    Promising Lord, bless our reading of The Revelation that it might give us comfort and hope in our sufferings, too . . .   Amen.

Joy in Our Weakness, pp. 13-15.

"Comfort ye, O comfort my people,"
   says your God.

Isaiah 40:1 (composite translation)

The implications of these three phrases take two very important directions in our lives — one for ourselves and one for our relationships with others. Personally, we can look for the ways in which God will bring this word of consolation to us in whatever situations we might be confronting. Rooted in the authority of his Word and in God's call for us to be his own, we can be sure of his consolation in our trials, of his hope in our despair, of his peace in our confusion, and of his faithful presence in our bad times and good times.

For others, we have the capability, because of what we have learned from God, to offer deep and meaningful solace. We can assure them that God is a Father who speaks graciously to his children continuously. When we meet people who need hope and assurance, we do not have to settle for sentimental drivel or pious platitudes. We can give them solid comfort, consolations that are genuine and eternal — and free, out of the richness of God's most abundant grace.

What kind of comfort do you offer to those who need to hear consolation? What do you say, for example, to the good friend whose father just died, to the neighbor who can't keep up with the speed of life, to your wife who was bypassed for a promotion?

What kind of comfort do you carry with you into the uncomfortable situations of your life? What sustains you when circumstances beyond your control prevent your earning an adequate income, when you find yourself failing as a pastor, when you realize that your husband doesn't really love you anymore? . . .

We begin by simply recognizing that God's comfort is real and that it is really for us all. To you also this sure word is addressed: "'Comfort ye, O comfort my people,' says your God."

Prayer

God of true solace, into our uncomfortable lives bring us your truly comforting love . . . Amen.

To Walk and Not Faint, pp. 1, 5-6.

There are six days when you may work, but the seventh day is a Sabbath of rest [liter-ally, a ceasing], a day of sacred assembly. You are not to do any work; wherever you live, it is a Sabbath to the LORD.

Leviticus 23:3

To cease working on the Sabbath means to quit laboring at anything that is work. Activity that is enjoyable and freeing and not undertaken for the pur-pose of accomplishment . . . qualifies as acceptable for Sabbath time.

To advocate a complete day of ceasing from work . . . does not mean, of course, that work is wrong. Indeed, our work is worship when we do it to the glory of God. However . . . to cease working is the original meaning of Sab-bath. . . .

First of all, we must note that the day is "a Sabbath to the LORD"; in other words, it is a ceasing in order to honor the covenant God. Sacred as-semblies were held for the same reason — to gather the children of Israel to-gether to worship Yahweh. . . .

What God wants from us is a whole day that we set apart to honor him by gathering with a sacred assembly and by ceasing from work — a day that is a Sabbath ceasing unto Yahweh. Perhaps those people, such as nurses and pastors, who must labor on Sundays could form small groups to set aside another day to assemble for worship and to cease working for the entire day. . . .

God's design of the Sabbath was never meant to impose a legalistic duty. . . . We need to learn again the psalmists' delight in the law as God's in-struction for true blessing in our lives. . . .

Imagine what a glorious relief it can be *every week* to know that in the rhythm of our lives there is one day in every seven on which we can cease our working. That knowledge gives us all kinds of energy to keep at tasks for the other six days, since we know that soon it will be time to rest. Furthermore, ceasing from work for one day enables us to return to it with renewed vigor as the new week begins. Thus, the day of ceasing empowers us both as we an-ticipate and as we remember its benefits.

Prayer
> LORD *of the Sabbath, we thank you for the blessings of ceasing from our work one day each week . . .   Amen.*

Keeping the Sabbath Wholly, pp. 5-8.

God of grace and God of glory, on your people pour your power;
Crown your ancient Church's story; bring its bud to glorious flow'r.
Grant us wisdom, grant us courage
For the facing of this hour,
For the facing of this hour.

Harry Emerson Fosdick, 1878-1969

Knowing that Christians are saved totally by God's grace and not by any effort on our part, the Church throughout the ages has understood that its task as an institution is to provide opportunities for the worship and praise of God and the education and forming of its people for a life of caring for others in response to that grace. We might compare these two tasks to the two great commandments — to love God with all our heart, soul, mind, and strength and to become the kind of people who will love our neighbors as ourselves.

These tasks were more easily accomplished in the past when many elements in the structure of Western civilization contributed to the Church's goals. . . . We must see the vast difference between our present society and previous societies. . . .

For example, in the Reformation era, much of the best music and art was inspired by the Christian faith and used for its worship. Homes were undergirded by Christian principles. Whole communities helped to raise children to understand and participate in Christian practices. . . .

Can the Church counteract our culture's loss of family nurturing and training to moor children to the wisdom and values inherent in the faith? It is urgent that Christians understand more clearly their position in this present culture as a minority, an alternative society. Like the earliest Christians, we want to be a people formed not by the ethos of the world around us but by the narratives of Scriptures and by the community of believers. . . .

We must therefore consider not only the factors from the outside culture but also the voices from within that influence how the Church understands itself. . . . We must ask new questions about the meaning and means of worshiping and living in the family of faith and of welcoming our children and strangers to live there, too.

Prayer

God of grace and glory, call us to faithfulness in following your command to
love you and our neighbor, within, and in spite of, a culture that does not
share these goals . . .   Amen.

Reaching Out, pp. 3, 8-10.

I appeal to you, therefore, brothers and sisters, because of the mercies of God, to offer your bodies as a sacrifice, living and holy and acceptable — which is your spiritual worship.

Romans 12:1 (my translation)

A possible interpretation of *sōma*, besides that of our individual bodies, is . . . the Church as the corporate Body of Christ. . . . Then the term in the plural would refer to the various house churches into which the Christians in Rome were divided. . . . Paul thereby exhorts them to deepen their unity by offering their various small bodies, or parts of the Church, as one whole, living, and holy sacrifice to God. . . .

That interpretation offers exciting, practical applications to the churches of today — . . . for example, to the transdenominational efforts . . . to battle world hunger, the problems of refugees, government policies, the housing shortage, and the need for economic development in the poorer countries of the world. . . .

The readers of Paul's letters were aware of the way the apostle worked and the care he invested in the people whom he served. Paul did not stand at a distance from the Romans and tell them condescendingly how to offer their house groups to God. Rather, he joined them as a fellow member of the Christian community to urge them to participate together in a wholehearted offering of the Body.

The communal sense that Paul intended in Romans 12:1 is highlighted by his use of the term of affection *brothers and sisters*. . . .

Paul calls them by a special term of endearment in order to underscore the relationships they might have with each other in the different groups. All together the members of each house church — whether Jew or Gentile, slave or free — are brothers and sisters together with Paul. . . .

The Christian community has no hierarchy. In Romans 12 Paul invites us to the Hilarity of a thorough commitment to each other as brothers and sisters, in the deepest sense of those names, as we struggle to apply the challenges of the Scriptures to our lives.

Prayer

> *Unifying Lord, help us embrace each other as brothers and sisters, as we jointly struggle to present ourselves, and our churches, as a living, holy sacrifice of worship and service to you . . .   Amen.*

Truly the Community, pp. 11, 15-17.

Let us seek the courage needed, our high calling to fulfill,
  that the world may know the blessing of the doing of God's will.
                                        Thomas A. Jackson (1973), alt.

Postmodern notions . . . have hit the streets, our homes, and our children
and lead to a rejection of truth, authority, meaning, and hope. . . . We are
bombarded by — and young people especially believe — postmodern slogans
such as these:

 • life has no meaning — it's just a game;
 • you are the only one who cares about you;
 • there is no such thing as truth except what you create for yourself;
 • you only go around once, so do it with gusto. . . .

What is the result when . . . any claim to truth is seen as oppressive,
when people insist that truth cannot be known? We have to reckon with the
effects of such postmodern thinking on our children and on the average
person, on the attitudes of those to whom the Church seeks to minister.
Many of our children's friends and our neighbors have no reference point,
no guiding standard by which to assess life; many others concoct their own
"spirituality" by intermingling whatever appeals to them. . . .

Without authorities in the postmodern world to guide the formation of
their moral character, children today lack basic resources of principled disposition to know how to find joy in what is beautiful, to have compassion
for those who suffer, to develop goals for their work and lives. . . .

At every church I visit most members think the congregation is doing
fine — but then I talk with the youth or children and discover how little they
know about the faith, how negligibly it affects their daily lives. People agree
that certainly we need more adults to help with the youth group — or
Sunday school or whatever — but they themselves are too busy and don't
want to sacrifice. . . .

I don't think Christianity is powerless to influence (not control) the
culture around us and to enable our children to find a different way from its
madness and meaninglessness, violence and valuelessness. The problem is
that we have lost the heart of God and the heart of the Church. . . .

Prayer
  Lord of truth and mercy, we need your heart for our church's children and
  our own . . .   Amen.
                                        Is It a Lost Cause? pp. 13, 22-29.

But I trust in you, O Lord;
  I say, "You are my God."
My times are in your hands.

Psalm 31:14-15a

To which kind of friend will you turn in a crisis? Which one will you trust?

Exactly. You will turn to the one who is trustable, the one who is worthy of your confidence. Your trusting does not depend upon how good you are at trusting, but upon your knowledge that the one on whom you lean is stable and will certainly support you. . . .

The psalmist David declares that it is the Lord, *YHWH*, in whom he trusts. We must therefore, first of all, consider who *YHWH* is. . . .

On the basis of God's thorough revelation, we can . . . come back again and again to the fact that God is called by the name *YHWH*. He is the Covenant God, the One who has never broken any of his promises. He is the faithful, loving, holy, just, steadfast, compassionate, creative One whose infinite majesty and sovereignty we can never comprehend. Yet the more we search to know who he is, the more we will be able to trust him.

If we have learned that he is perfectly wise, then we can trust him for his purposes in our lives. If we know him to be unremittingly loving, then we can believe him even when something doesn't appear to be the product of his love.

That is why in Psalm 31, David, despite the apparent triumph of his enemies, can say . . . *"But I trust in you, O YHWH."* Greatly to the contrary of how others might react — in fear, because of who the foes are — the poet is able to trust *YHWH* because of who the "I AM" is.

The Hebrew verb *to trust* is related to the noun for "security." . . . When enemies of every sort are filling our lives with sadness or terror, it is the best of hope to remember that . . . again and again the Scriptures assure us that God's character can be trusted. Knowing that he loves us with the compassion of a father (Ps. 103:13) or a mother (Isa. 49:13-15) or a shepherd (John 10:1-3, 11-16), we can find the security for which we long.

Prayer
  Covenant God, because you are YHWH, we can trust that our times are in
  your hands . . .   Amen.

I'm Lonely, Lord, pp. 9-11.

I, John, your brother and companion in the suffering and kingdom and patient endurance that are ours in Jesus, was on the island of Patmos because of the word of God and the testimony of Jesus.

Revelation 1:9

If we are looking at The Revelation for what it said in a historical situation of persecution, we will search for why it was written and the way in which it was written. . . .

The writer addressed Christians confronting an agonizing situation. They were being persecuted — tortured, thrown to the lions, burned — because they clung to the lordship of Christ. How could they have the courage to go on in the face of such terror?

The writer of The Revelation responds carefully. He, too, is a prisoner for his faith. According to his testimony, he was imprisoned on the island of Patmos, where political captives worked in the mines. The Roman government was wise. . . . To make John a martyr would only have increased the influence of his witness. So he was sent away into slavery. His letters were most certainly censored.

How, then, could he communicate with the Christians back in Asia Minor? How could he offer them hope and comfort without his letters being destroyed by the officials who guarded him?

He wrote stories. They were crazy and bizarre stories — probably passed on as the work of a lunatic. However, they overflowed with images identifiable to the family, to those who knew the family history, for The Revelation is filled with stories and images from the First Testament and from the oral tradition of Jesus' teachings maintained in the early Christian community. Its pictures come from the traditions of Israel; they symbolize the ways in which God took care of the weak and despised Hebrews and made them his people.

The original readers of The Revelation would immediately recognize those images as well as the larger biblical passages from which they came . . . and would remember God's promises of protection and reconciliation and hope for a covenant land. . . .

This is the framework. . . . From these purposes we can draw applications for our times.

Prayer
> *Promising and protecting Lord, we rejoice in the wisdom of John, who found a way to share your word. May we learn from him both your word of comfort and a willingness to find a way to share it . . .   Amen.*

Joy in Our Weakness, pp. 15-17.

Speak to the heart of Jerusalem,
    and call out to her
that her warfare [hard service] has ended,
    that her penalty of iniquity [is] accepted as paid off,
that she has received of the LORD's hand
    double for all her sins.

                    Isaiah 40:2 (New American Standard Version, with sidenotes)

"Speak to the heart," verse 2 begins in the original Hebrew. The word connotes the will and conscience, the intentions, inner person, and desires that are a combination of knowledge, emotion, and the passion of commitment. In moments of crisis, it is not enough to react merely with feelings. This larger sense of the "heart" helps us know how to speak most tenderly, for it is more than emotions that need healing.

Sometimes anguish wells up so powerfully, the pain in us seems so overwhelming, that we are sure it will break us apart with grief. . . . We need to find the will to surmount our feelings, to forgive, to go on toward different goals.

For the people of Israel, the overwhelming anguish was their captivity in Babylon because of their injustice and pride and idolatries. They were a rebellious nation and repeatedly ignored the rebukes and warnings of Isaiah, Jeremiah, and other prophets. Yet the LORD now commands, "Speak to the heart" — the will and intentionality — "of Jerusalem." After the captivity, the Israelites needed words of hope, the will to return, promises to sustain them in the difficulties of beginning again. Consequently, *YHWH* addresses their minds and moral character.

Isaiah 40:1 commanded the unnamed listeners to "comfort my people." Now verse 2 adds the verbs "speak to the heart" and "call out" (also both plural) to complete the three-part command. Frequently in the book of Isaiah imperatives or descriptions are grouped in threes, a Hebrew means of underscoring the divinity of the set. These are tasks God himself summoned the Israelites to do, a trio of ministries to which God's people are still called in our times. We bring comfort, we speak to the wills and passions of others, and we cry out God's truths. We console others by addressing their inner person and by declaring to them the good news of grace that gives them the courage to go on.

Prayer
    Comforting God, help us to console and encourage others with your word of
    truth and the good news of your grace . . .   Amen.
                                        To Walk and Not Faint, pp. 8-10.

Blessed art Thou, O LORD our God, King of the Universe, who hast sanctified us by Thy commandments, and commanded us to kindle the Sabbath lights.

From the opening prayer of the traditional
Jewish home service for Sabbath eve

Jews begin the Sabbath at sundown on Friday in keeping with their notion of the day — that it lasts from sunset to sunset. Since I prefer the Jewish concept, but have not managed to be ready by sunset, my Sabbath observance begins when I lie down to sleep on Saturday night. That way my sleep is a Sabbath sleep before I enter the keeping of the whole day. . . .

The Jewish custom is to make all the preparations for the coming of the Sabbath Bride before sundown and then at that time to light the Kiddush (literally "sanctification") candles and to welcome the Sabbath Queen. Thus, blissful expectancy marks this ritual that begins the wedding celebration. I have adopted this practice because it decisively begins my Sabbath celebration and sanctifies the day as set apart for a special purpose. After I have completed all my bedtime preparations, the Kiddush ceremony of lighting the candles tangibly marks the moment of ceasing from work. I keep special candles beside my bed (or carry some with me when I travel) and enjoy the candles' glow as I pray an extended prayer beginning with the Jewish phrases quoted above. . . .

The Jews focus especially on creation in their Kiddush rituals, so I usually spend most of the time thanking God for all his creations in the week that is past and for the Joy of his creating now an opportunity to cease from its labors. I pray about the ways that I will spend the next day and ask that these activities will draw me closer to God and fill me more fully with a sense of his presence in my life. This is also a special time to pray for the Church and for pastors, musicians, and others who contribute to the worship services taking place throughout the world on Sundays. This prayer creates in me a global perspective and provides a weekly preparation so that I can be more ready to worship and less distracted by any thoughts or worries of work.

Prayer
King of the Universe, your command to keep the Sabbath holy is also a gift we wish to receive and honor . . .   Amen.

Keeping the Sabbath Wholly, pp. 10-11.

Thee we would be always blessing . . .
  Pray, and praise thee without ceasing . . .
  Lost in wonder, love, and praise.

Charles Wesley, 1707-1788

Surely one of the greatest problems of our times is that we have become so nonchalant about the Lord of the cosmos. Certainly if we were more immersed in God's splendor we would find ourselves thoroughly "lost in wonder, love, and praise." With all the amazing sights and sounds of our cyberspace world, however, many of us no longer recognize that if we but catch a glimpse of *GOD* — the imperial Lord of the cosmos, the almighty King of the universe — we will be compelled to fall on our faces. Our awareness of God's absolute otherness would give us the sense that we could die now because we have seen God. . . .

The awe and astonishment of God's presence so far beyond us is so immense that we could hardly react with anything less than fear and trembling and the sacrifice of all our lives. Our superhyped culture makes it difficult for us to take the immense sovereignty and preeminence of *GOD* seriously; we find it hard to realize that his infinite splendor would overwhelm us if he weren't so gracious as to give us samples of it in small morsels. As with Moses, we really see only God's "back" or the *glory* of where he has been and how he has worked (see Exod. 33:17-23).

Such taking God seriously is, however, decidedly countercultural. We live in an age and culture that want instead to turn the worship of God into a matter of personal taste and time, convenience and comfort. Consequently, we need the biggest dose of God we can get when we gather for worship on Sunday morning — to . . . summon us to behold God's splendor and respond with adoration and service and sacrifice.

Taking God seriously, being immersed in his splendor, unites us with a community that practices the alternative way of life of following Jesus, of participation in the kingdom of God. . . . When we come to belief or are baptized . . . the eternal reign of God begins in our life. Thus also begin both the transformation of our character and the responsibility for the whole community to nurture our eschatological life.

Prayer

Reigning God, may worship immerse us in your splendor and invite our adoration and service . . .   Amen.

A Royal "Waste" of Time, pp. 7-8.

Therefore, I appeal to you, brothers and sisters, because of the mercies of God, to present your bodies as a sacrifice, living and holy and acceptable to God — which is your spiritual worship.

Romans 12:1 (my translation)

This is the paradox of our sacrifice: only when we offer ourselves wholly to God can we thoroughly live, set apart and acceptable as a sacrifice. Earlier in Romans Paul has stressed that we can be set free for a new life that is godly and powerful only when in Christ we become dead to disobedience against God. . . .

When Paul throws his hands up in despair over the struggle and cries, "Wretched man that I am! Who will set me free from the body of this death?" he answers immediately with Hilarity: "Thanks be to God through Jesus Christ our Lord!" (Rom. 7:24-25, NASV). . . .

Though we have blown it, we need not despair. Forgiveness gives us new hope, . . . sets us apart as holy, . . . and sets us free to *do* pleasing things because we already know that we *are* pleasing to God. . . .

Paul summarizes these qualities by calling our sacrifice our "spiritual worship." The Greek noun that is used here, which can also be translated "service," . . . reminds us that our worship rites and Christian service are inextricably related. All of life is of a piece as we respond to God's love in . . . praise and action. . . .

Such a wholistic concept of worship pervading our congregations will lead to a better balance of true spirituality in the Church. We will recognize that sharing our faith (evangelism) is not something we do, but that a witness is something we are. . . .

When our churches become more aware of all the dimensions of spiritual worship . . . we will care more profoundly about one another's ministries in whatever places God has called us to serve. Then, also, our time in our churches will be spent more profitably to become equipped for those ministries. . . .

To give our bodies — individually and corporately — in response to God's love enables our worship to be spiritual, our service to be genuine, and our communities to be "Hilarious," filled with glad hope in God.

Prayer

Loving Lord, help us to worship you rightly, with praise and Christian service, as your witnesses . . .   Amen.

Truly the Community, pp. 19-28.

O make your church, dear Savior, a lamp of burnished gold
  to bear before the nations your true light as of old. . . .

William Walsham How (1867), alt.

For the sake both of our children's faith and life and also of our ministry to our neighbors, what must we be? . . . It is the narrative of faith — the Word, the Revelation of God — from which, around which, out of which the community must be formed. . . .

We need to recover our belief in Scripture as the highest authority for knowing the heart of God for ourselves and our children. . . .

To be true to the Hebrew/Christian Scriptures of the Church, first of all, we must reject the individualism of Western civilization, which causes us to read the Bible singularly and to think about our faith only in personal terms — which is exceedingly devastating for our children's faith. . . .

Our children need the entire community for their growth in the life of faith and, especially, for their learning the heart of God through his Revelation.

Second, the Christian community, to be true to our children and a genuine gift to the postmodern world, must deliberately be an *alternative society* that understands itself according to what God has revealed about his heart — that is, his will for us. We find God's heart in the Word, Christ, who displayed it in his earthly life, and in the Word of the Revelation. The Holy Spirit inspired the Church's process of preserving and passing on that Word and continues to inspire our interpretation of the Word in all its forms.

To faithfully be this alternative community of the Church, I believe we must work seriously and strenuously to understand the social forces of the culture that surrounds us and disavows Christianity. . . . For the sake of truly being the Church . . . pastors, leaders, and parents . . . must equip our congregations and our children with insights to answer the critiques of Christianity, . . . to know deeply that our belief in the triune God is justifiable, to celebrate the gift that the Bible is to us and to our world, to cherish the Revelation of God that we have been given to teach us God's heart and form us as his people.

Prayer
  Revealing God, form us as your people through your Word . . .   Amen.

Is It a Lost Cause? pp. 31-34.

But I trust in you, O Lord;
  I say, "You are my God."
My times are in your hands.

Psalm 31:14-15a

After we have released everything into God's hands, we will become more able to see his love in action and to feel his comfort in our lives. . . .

But we forget the fact of God's relationship with us at times, especially in the pain and despair of loneliness and rejection. When these times come, we must re-sort our priorities and deal with our doubts in order to come again to the declaration, "Yes. All other gods cannot be trusted. Everything else will pass away. My God is you, *YHWH*, Covenant God!"

In that declaration we join the psalmist in putting our times back into *YHWH*'s hands. And in such a committing of ourselves into God's care, we finally come to peace. . . .

It is not that God takes over our lives and controls everything arbitrarily. No; rather, in his hands he gives us the perfect freedom to be wholly ourselves, yet under his infinitely wise and loving care. . . . He will guide us through our very own desires, which are being newly formed as we grow in faith.

When we can rest enough to trust with our times the One who is trustable . . . we will be able to see that however long God allows certain processes to continue is partly the gift of his perfect wisdom. . . .

We can't become too simplistic in our demands for deliverance. We might not be delivered out of the hands of certain enemies. . . . Our times might not be changed, but *we* will be changed in those times. Furthermore, we will become more able to see some of God's purposes in them. . . .

We all are challenged by the need to grow in our ability to trust. We will sometimes fail to depend on God, because we will always be human — yet in those times the character of *YHWH* is all the more precious to us. . . . Just when we trust him the least, he is the most trustable, continuing to love us with perfect mercy. Therefore, we are set free to go on, feebly trusting, but learning, by means of the Psalms, to trust him more.

Prayer

Faithful Lord, when trusting is hardest, we nevertheless know that we can trust you . . .   Amen.

I'm Lonely, Lord, pp. 12-14.

The revelation of Jesus Christ, which God gave to him, to make manifest to his bond-servants the things which must necessarily take place shortly; and he communicated [these things] having sent [them] through his angel to his bond-servant John, who bore witness to the word of God and to the testimony of Jesus Christ, even to all that he saw.

Revelation 1:1-2 (literal translation of the original Greek)

I think that The Revelation (properly explained) is a good book for unbelievers to read in order to discover the character of God, who is the Lord of everything. . . .

We live in an age of subjectivism, in which how we are experiencing things determines their reality. Subjectivism is evident in such slogans as "If it feels good, do it." Not so evident is the way subjectivism distorts our society's approach to religious phenomenon. Modern interpretations of scriptural accounts center on the perceptions of the disciples rather than on what Jesus was teaching about his kingdom, or on the experience of the children of Israel rather than on what Yahweh was showing them about himself. Because the modern mind is characteristically inward-turned, this subjectivism has invaded our theology, as can be seen in much of contemporary ethics, as well as in Christian music. A large, dramatic Easter pageant shocked me when the words from Handel's *Messiah*, "and the glory of the Lord shall be revealed," were changed to "when we shall see his glory." That shift might not seem so drastic, but think of the dichotomous difference of perspectives it indicates. Now the emphasis is on how we, subjectively, are seeing God's glory, rather than on the objective fact of God's revelation of his glory.

In order to analyze properly a piece of literature, we simply must study it from the point of view from which it was written, and the Scriptures declare themselves to be God's revelation of himself. The Revelation (notice that the word is singular) literally begins by making that point. In one sentence the *theo*centric perspective (which includes the testimony of Jesus, clearly recognized in the book as divine) is mentioned four times. . . .

It seems to me that much of the flabbiness of contemporary Christianity derives precisely from this failure to approach things from God's perspective and to recognize the objectivity of his revelation.

Prayer
> *O Lord, we pray that we will learn to rely on who you are rather than what we feel . . .   Amen.*

Joy in Our Weakness, pp. 18-20.

Speak to the heart of Jerusalem,
     and call out to her
that her warfare [hard service] is ended,
     that her penalty of iniquity [is] accepted as paid off,
that she has received of the LORD's hand
     double for all her sins.

                                        Isaiah 40:2 (NASV, with sidenotes)

We are told that the warfare of the people of God is over. In the time of the book of Isaiah, this primarily promised a physical end to the long, hard term of captive service. However, as all the prophets of Israel show, a message of freedom from hard labor is needed for all the struggles of our lives. We turn many of our jobs and situations into harder service than necessary because we try to live apart from God's grace. . . .

     Our own guilt is one of the greatest barriers to enjoying the freedom of the gospel. That barrier is smashed, however, by the second of the three proclamations to be called out to Jerusalem — that is, that her iniquity has been removed. Her guilt has been pardoned and her punishment accepted because of the immensity of God's grace. We in New Testament times know better how that can be true, for we know the fullness of Christ's love for us through his life and work and death. . . .

     The last phrase in verse 2 is ambiguous. It does not tell us of *what* Israel has received double. . . . Since this is a message of comfort and since the previous phrases recorded God's forgiveness, perhaps this ambiguous phrase is meant to refer to the LORD's grace. Certainly it was purely by grace that Israel was released from captivity — and by grace that God delivers us from the bondages into which we place ourselves. . . .

     There doesn't have to be any doubt. The warfare is ended, the guilt is removed, the grace is doubled. What good news to speak tenderly to someone's heart and will!

Prayer
     Forgiving LORD, help us all to accept the release from our self-inflicted bondage, guilt, and remorse purchased for us by Christ's death and resurrection. Help us to receive gratefully a double measure of grace, for the formation of our Christian character . . .   Amen.

                                        To Walk and Not Faint, pp. 8-14.

*But now, this is what the L*ORD *says —*
  he who created you, O Jacob,
  he who formed you, O Israel:
"Fear not, for I have redeemed you;
  I have called you by name; you are mine. . . .
Since you are precious and honored in my sight
  and because I love you. . . .

Isaiah 43:1, 4a

Trying to accomplish a lot is one of the ways we seek to satisfy the deepest longing of our existence, but inevitably when we reach our goals we will not be satisfied. . . . As the great theologian Augustine acknowledged, "O Lord, thou hast made us, and our spirits are restless until we rest in thee." We will never satisfy the longing for God himself with the accomplishments of our own efforts, so why do we keep trying? And why do we judge the worth of others on the same basis that always leaves us feeling empty? . . .

Setting aside a holy Sabbath means that we can cease our productivity and accomplishments for one day in every seven. . . . This frees us up to worry less about how much we produce on the other days. . . .

One of my favorite passages on this topic, Isaiah 43:1-4a, focuses on God's overt declaration of what makes his people worthy. Over and over the text insists that Yahweh is the one who makes us valuable. He is the one who created, formed, redeemed, called his people by name, made them his, was with them, protected them, saved them, and made them precious and honored in his sight. The last phrase of this passage is absolutely incredible; the verb that we translate "love" is usually used to denote the love of a husband for his wife. With that kind of personal, intimate love God loves the sinful people of Israel. . . .

This is what we celebrate in the Sabbath day. We join the generations of believers — going all the way back to God's people, the Jews — who set aside a day to remember that we are precious and honored in God's sight and loved, profoundly loved, not because of what we produce.

To celebrate God's love on our Sabbath also transforms us so that we can more deeply value others in the same way.

Prayer
  *O L*ORD, *thank you for calling us by name as precious, honored, and loved,*
  with no requirements attached . . .   Amen.

Keeping the Sabbath Wholly, pp. 18-20.

God of grace and God of glory,
On your people pour your power;
Crown your ancient Church's story;
Bring its bud to glorious flow'r.
Grant us wisdom, grant us courage
For the facing of this hour,
For the facing of this hour.

Harry Emerson Fosdick, 1878-1969

I am primarily concerned about what is happening to the Church spiritually, so I plead with you for careful theological reflection concerning the meaning and practice of worship. . . .

We should have these four goals: to reflect upon the culture for which we want to proclaim the gospel; to expose the subtle powers that beckon us into idolatries . . . ; to stimulate better questions about if, why, and how we might be dumbing faith down in the ways we structure, plan, and participate in worship education and in worship itself; and to offer better means for reaching out to people outside the Church. It is my claim that we ought not to, and do not need to, conform to our culture's patterns, but that the Christian community must intentionally sustain its unique character and just as intentionally care about the culture around it in order to be able to introduce people genuinely to Christ and to nurture individuals to live faithfully. . . .

What we must realize is that the dumbing down of our society forces the Church to ask critical questions about its life and worship, its ministries to people in such a world, its ability to survive in post-Christian times. In what ways do we, too, lack the patience necessary for forming the intellect and faith? How has faith formation been disrupted by instant sensory gratification? What resources does Christian faith provide for renewing and sustaining churches in such a culture and for helping them reach beyond themselves to persons of that culture? . . .

Most of all, let us all together always be asking this basic question: Do our efforts in worship lead to genuine praise of God and the growth of character in the members and the whole body of this Christian community?

Prayer
> *God of grace and glory, grant us the wisdom and courage to face and deal*
> *with the difficult questions that must be asked for the sake of faithful worship*
> *and faith formation in the Church . . .   Amen.*

Reaching Out, pp. 3, 7, 11-12.

And do not be conforming to this age, but be [in the process of] being transformed by the renewing of your mind.

Romans 12:2a-b (my translation)

Once a little boy was trying to open a flower bud. Under his persistent efforts the blossom fell apart in his hands. In exasperation he looked up at his mother and asked, "Why does the bud fall apart when I try to open it, but when God opens it the flower is beautiful?" . . . Then he answered his own question, "Oh, I know! When God opens the flower, he opens it from the inside."

That story is a charming illustration of the difference between being conformed and being transformed. The former forces someone's personhood or a group's identity from the outside. The latter opens up the individual or the community from the inside. The difference in results is dramatic.

When God opens persons from the inside, they can truly be themselves, the uniquely gifted individuals they were created to be. Unfortunately, however, all sorts of influences obstruct God's opening processes. Oftentimes our society, our families, even our churches force us to conform. . . .

One extremely disturbing evidence of conformity is the way in which the culture around us has drawn Christians into its values. Our model, Jesus, taught us to sell our possessions and give to the poor, to be generous in our hospitality. But our society urges us to compete for possessions and to hoard them for ourselves. We struggle to choose intentionally a simpler lifestyle and to resist cultural pressures to crave, to buy, to own. . . . Too often we are dissatisfied with what we have and who we are. . . .

"Do not be conforming," Paul urges. We do not have to buy the values of this age. J. B. Phillips paraphrases the clause, "Don't let the world around you squeeze you into its mold." . . .

God wants each Christian and each community to be unique, opened up from the inside to reveal in a special way possible only for that person or group some of the dimensions of God's grace in a particular combination that no one else can reveal.

Prayer

> *Holy Spirit, transform our minds so that we choose to reveal the life you have placed within us, rather than conforming to the lifestyle our culture pressures us to adopt . . .   Amen.*

Truly the Community, pp. 29-31, 36.

O word of God incarnate, O wisdom from on high,
O truth unchanged, unchanging, O light of our dark sky:
  we praise you for the radiance that from the scripture's page,
  a lantern to our footsteps, shines on from age to age.

                                        William Walsham How (1867), alt.

We believe that the triune God has revealed himself potentially to the whole world through a Word that is entrusted to a faith community that passes it on, incarnated in the flesh in the person of Jesus Christ who lived among us, and transmitted through the centuries by the guidance and empowerment of the Holy Spirit. . . .

We recognize the reasonableness of Christian faith as the best answer to the existential questions of who we are and why we exist, of what is wrong with the world, and what can be done about it.

These are the insights our children need for postmodern times. . . .

It is crucial to teach our children that there are several reasons why the biblical narratives can be seen as universally applicable. God's Revelation knits all human beings together because all are equally created by God, because Christ died for all, and because the Spirit has been poured out upon "all flesh" — and the result of that outpouring originally was that each person heard the disciples speaking in his or her own language. The Revelation of the Trinity encompasses all human beings threefold.

Furthermore, the Revelation carries within it counterideological elements — that is, elements that prevent us from becoming fixed on certain ideas, political doctrines, or social systems as earthly solutions to human problems. . . . Jesus himself is the most obvious counter element, for his submission to suffering demonstrates most graphically that God does not work through the power structures and ideologies of the world. Furthermore, at the cross he exposed and triumphed over all the principalities and powers of politics, economics, and religious institutions.

Against the violence and oppression, the injustice and legalism of the society around us, it requires extra effort to nurture our children in the kind of alternative vision the Bible delineates.

Prayer

Triune God, help us commit ourselves to studying your Word, sharing it with
our children, and living in the alternative way of Jesus . . .   Amen.

                                        Is It a Lost Cause? pp. 31, 36-37.

In my alarm I said,
  "I am cut off from your sight!"
Yet you heard my cry for mercy
  when I called to you for help.

Psalm 31:22

How we perceive the surface reality and the deeper truths of our lives makes all the difference in the world. . . .

Panic prevents us from observing the truth; we think that we are cut off because, in our dread, that is the only reality we are able to see. However, handling our emotions more carefully might help us to assess the situation more accurately so that we can discover genuine truth. . . .

The Hebrew original shows much more clearly than our English translations how violent our alarm becomes. In its basic form the verb that we render "I am cut off" means to exterminate. It is related to the common noun for "ax," but this is the only use of the verb in the First Testament. Such a rare and violent word emphasizes that the poet's panic caused him to fear unduly that he had been obliterated from *YHWH*'s sight, axed out of his goodness forever.

We don't usually comprehend how violent panic is to us. It robs us of the truth and causes us to overaccentuate the negatives of our observable reality. That is why we say such extreme things as "nobody helps me" . . . or "there isn't anyone who loves me." Into such emotional extremism *YHWH* wants to bring the comfort of his loving truth.

In his summary conclusion, the psalmist remembers that God has ministered to his needs. He further recognizes the disparity between his perceptions and the truth of his situation. . . .

After the psalmist has shown us his dread alarm and how it caused him to misunderstand extremely the details of his situation, now he will tell us, greatly to the contrary, what the truth actually was. . . .

The poet proclaims that *YHWH*, true to his character, had "heard my cry for mercy when I called [to him] for help." . . .

Because of his strong memory of *YHWH*'s rescue, the psalmist can conclude his poem with a great exhortation to his readers to love the covenant God and to be strong because of their hope in him.

Prayer
  Covenant Lord, *when we believe we are cut off from you forever, help us remember your abiding love, and know that we can call to you and you will rescue us . . . Amen.*

I'm Lonely, Lord, pp. 16-20.

Do not be afraid of what you are about to suffer. I tell you, the devil will put some of you in prison to test you, and you will suffer persecution for ten days. Be faithful, even to the point of death, and I will give you the crown of life.

Revelation 2:10-11

God's message to us in the last book of the Bible is that in the present we are not always going to win; our lives will not always be characterized by triumph. That is a lesson hard to accept — in fact, impossible — except that it is balanced on the opposite side with this hope: eventually we will win. These poles stand in dialectical tension and cannot be brought together because of the intervening reality of satanic opposition.

These three parts — the ultimate, cosmic lordship of God in Christ; the present opposition of the powers of evil; and the resultant suffering on the part of God's people — lead to this other important aspect of the theology of The Revelation: that meanwhile we endure with patience our weakness. The hope of God's ultimate reign sustains our longsuffering.

Many Christians these days find that almost impossible to accept. Instead they have espoused a theology of "victory, healing, luxury, and blessedness" that The Revelation does *not* teach. God does not promise us a rose garden — at least not one without thorns. And though there are, of course, many roses in life, they fade, too — with the promise that they will come again next season. . . .

We have to get our facts straight. We cannot ignore that we live in a world dominated by sin and not by the purposes of God. All the talk about the progress of the human race is really an illusion, as we discover when we correctly read the Scriptures and human history. We see over and over again that power corrupts, leaders deceive, persons hurt each other for their own gains, dreams die — or, perhaps more precisely, are usually killed. This is not just gloomy pessimism. In fact, Christian realism is much more optimistic than shallow illusions about humankind's goodness because this genuine realism recognizes that God is working still in spite of evidence to the contrary, . . . a message we could more easily embrace if we paid better attention to those in our midst who understand the grace of weakness.

Prayer

Holy Spirit, help us face life both realistically and hopefully . . . Amen.

Joy in Our Weakness, pp. 21-22.

A voice cries out:
"In the wilderness prepare the way of the LORD,
  make straight in the desert a highway for our God."

Isaiah 40:3 (New Revised Standard Version)

How can we prepare the way for *YHWH?* How do we make straight a highway for our God?

How do we prepare our minds and souls for God to enter them more deeply now? The way was prepared for Jesus to come the first time when John the Baptizer stirred up Jewish listeners to repent and to long for the kingdom of God. . . .

The graphic imagery of this text challenged the Israelites to remove those obstructions that stood in the way and prevented the LORD's coming. Certainly our hearts are often like a barren and stony wilderness. The image suggests the driest desert, an apt characterization of a life withered in its self-centeredness. To that emptiness God wants to come . . . but is often prevented by the obstructions we keep building or by our failure to open ourselves to his gifts.

What kinds of things obstruct God's way? For some, the path is blocked by fears; for others, the obstruction is pride or our illusions of our own importance, deceptive opinions of our own ability to handle things by ourselves. The path might be blocked by our mistaken anger at God — when we blame him inaccurately for not interrupting life's natural processes and consequences. . . .

We can take the imagery of this verse a step further. Not only do we allow things to block God's coming, but also, neglecting our spiritual lives, we let ourselves become scorched and made dry and barren. Our hearts have become a wilderness because they have not been cultivated. . . . The cry to make a highway invites us to the disciplines of cultivation — nourishing our minds with God's Word, watering the stoniness with worship, raking away the rocks by the admonition of fellow Christians, . . . engaging in prayer. . . . Our disciplines cannot earn us his presence, but they cultivate the way for him to come.

Prayer

  O LORD, *open our eyes to the obstructions and the barrenness that hinder*
  your coming . . .   Amen.

To Walk and Not Faint, pp. 15-19.

Do not be anxious about anything, but in everything, by prayer and petition, with thanksgiving, present your requests to God. . . . [I]f anything is excellent or praiseworthy — think about such things. . . . And the God of peace will be with you.

Philippians 4:6, 8b, 9b

One of the main causes of modern stress is that we have too much to do. Consequently, Sabbath days — when we don't *have* to do anything — can release us from the anxiety that accompanies our work. . . .

However, it is also necessary to concentrate specifically on ceasing to worry as part of our Sabbath-keeping habits. Several practices help me to set anxiety aside in order to celebrate the Sabbath more thoroughly and to be set free thereby from anxiety during the other days of the week.

One helpful practice is getting my house ready for "Queen Sabbath." . . . Thus, the Sabbath release from tension begins to happen already on Saturday evenings when I stack up all the business papers and writing projects and books.

The tension drains away more fully as I commit all the things I do for my work into the Lord's hands during the Kiddush prayer at bedtime. . . .

Another especially important practice to help me cease worrying is to focus on relationships — particularly my relationship with God — during my Sabbath observance. Instead of status seeking, the day promotes friendship building. In the love of the Christian community we cease being anxious. . . .

You might be thinking that it doesn't do any good to set worries aside for just one day. . . . However, the Sabbath is not a running away from problems, but the opportunity to receive grace to face them. . . .

To celebrate the Sabbath is to rejoice in God's presence. Our practices for the day include extra moments of thanksgiving and special times of prayer and petition, by which we can lay our anxieties and worries before God so that his peace, which both bypasses and surpasses our understanding, can guard and keep our hearts and minds in Christ Jesus. Finally, to think about constructive things rather than our concerns — about beautiful and noble things, that which is excellent and praiseworthy — ushers us into the presence of the God of peace himself.

Prayer

> *Heavenly Father, may our Sabbath observances be days of peace — peace that can enfold us all week long . . .   Amen.*

Keeping the Sabbath Wholly, pp. 23-25.

I love to tell the story, for some have never heard
The message of salvation from God's own holy Word.

Katherine Hankey, 1834-1911

A wealthy Scottish nobleman . . . came beside a poor peasant . . . kneeling in the mud and praying. "You must be close to God," the lord scoffed. "Aye," the peasant responded with unmistakable bliss, "He is very fond of me." What Joy worship bestows when it conveys this identity! . . .

One great challenge for people in our time is the lack of a genuine story, one that is coherent and gives meaning to their lives in relation to God. . . .

I believe Christians can be at the forefront in offering the world around us a . . . genuine story of community and faith. . . .

We can offer to people in the postmodern world an introduction to the God who loves them and wants to reconcile them to himself. We can tell them the story of a faithful, promising God who demonstrated his devotion by always remembering his covenant with Israel. The dependability of the Revelation is established most profoundly in the resurrection of Jesus, for in the empty tomb we see the culmination of God's work on our behalf, the fulfillment of all the prophecies concerning the Messiah, the down payment on all God's promises for the future.

The Revelation, then, offers a convincing story of hope for people in our postmodern times. It proclaims a God of compassion and gracious mercy, who gives meaning and focus to lives. . . . It announces forgiveness and atonement and reconciliation to those torn by guilt and lacking skills for re-lationships. It describes the Trinity whom our neighbors genuinely need — a loving Creator for those who think they have to create their own identity, a perfect Model for those who have no mentors, and an empowering Spirit for those who think they have to do everything on their own.

The Revelation is not a book of rules that gives us step-by-step proce-dures for life. . . . Rather, . . . the Scriptures must be understood as a master story with multiple narratives that form us as we are immersed in them. We become part of this genuine story as we then live out of the character shaped by all of God's Revelation.

Prayer

Revealing God, thank you for your thrilling, empowering Word — which is our story to live by and share . . .   Amen.

A Royal "Waste" of Time, pp. 24, 39, 48-49, 52-53.

. . . but be [in the process of] being transformed by the renewing of your mind.
Romans 12:2b (my translation)

In his magnificent creativity, God, the Designer, has fashioned us each into a unique personality; moreover, he has given each of our communities a unique identity. Then, when the Spirit dwells in us and fills us with his power, we take the form that we were created to manifest. . . . This offers a tremendous potential for freedom and the glad Hilarity of being truly ourselves. . . .

Especially our sense of self-worth is strengthened when we know that we are each uniquely fashioned by God's infinite care. . . . As the psalmist says, "I will give thanks to thee for I am fearfully and wonderfully made; / Wonderful are Thy works, and my soul knows it very well" (Ps. 139:14).

Now this second verse from Romans 12 invites us to be . . . constantly transformed into the person or community God delights for us to be. How appropriate is the button that says . . . "Please be patient; God is not finished with me yet." . . . Members of the Christian community . . . can afford to be patient with one another — knowing that God is still changing each of us and the whole of us corporately. We need not have the world's expectations of perfection or productivity concerning brothers and sisters in the community.

As we grow in Christian faith and life, we are always becoming who we are meant to be. That continual process, however, gets aborted (a proper word choice since it is death to God's creation) when we allow ourselves to be crammed by our society, ourselves, or even our churches into a mold that violates his original design for us.

Specifically, people of God have a unique freedom to take the shape of their possibilities. Not under any "performance principles," we don't have to conform to society's values and become like everyone else, futilely chasing after false gods of success or prestige that produce nothing but emptiness. Nor do we have to prove our worth to one another; rather, we can . . . explore our unique possibilities within the affirmation of the completely accepting love of God and the consequent love of the community.

Prayer
Transforming God, thank you for creating us wonderfully, uniquely, and full of possibilities as we live by your perfect design . . .   Amen.
Truly the Community, pp. 38-40.

Church of God, elect and glorious . . .
know the purpose of your calling,
show to all God's mighty deeds;
tell of love which knows no limits,
grace which meets all human needs.

James E. Seddon (1982)

What gifts do we have in the Church for forming our offspring with the life of faith revealed in the Scriptures? . . .

Because we take our direction from the Trinity and the Revelation, because we are citizens first of heaven, God's people are a society parallel to the world surrounding us. When we gather for worship and education, we tell the narratives of the faith, sing our hymns, and say our prayers until we know the truth so well that we and our children can go out to our neighbors and offer alternatives to the lies of the principalities and powers that dominate U.S. society. As royal priests, . . . we offer to the world around us the gifts of the One who is the Truth, the Way, and the Life. . . .

Rather than becoming enculturated and entrapped by the world's values of materialistic consumerism, of narcissistic self-aggrandizement, of solitary superficiality, and of ephemeral satisfaction, members of Christ's Body choose his simple lifestyle of sharing, his willingness to suffer for the sake of others, his communal vulnerability, and his eternal purposes. By continual hearing and study of God's Word we and our children are equipped with new visions of God's heart for our mission and ministry of communicating the Christian story, of enfolding our neighbors in God's love, of deliberately choosing and living out the alternative values of the kingdom of God. . . .

I am profoundly disappointed by churches' failures to employ the very processes of Christian formation that our children and our neighbors need. . . . What does it mean to BE Church? . . . Studying the Scriptures is a way to begin to know the heart of God; . . . we must also consider deeply what kind of alternative/parallel community we must be to raise our children in the faith.

Prayer

O Lord, our Way and Truth and Life, direct our efforts as we seek to become a community of faith with an alternative lifestyle to offer our children and neighbors . . .   Amen.

Is It a Lost Cause? pp. 47-51.

Into your hands I commit my spirit;
  redeem me, O LORD, the God of truth.

Psalm 31:5

I have learned that the verb *to commit* involves more than an easy dependence arising out of desperation. . . . It suggests more profoundly to give attention to something. When we commit our spirit into YHWH's hand, our action is carefully intentional, seeking thoroughly to entrust our whole being into his care. It is not a superficial handing over — and we don't take it back!

The most graphic embodiment of the true nature of such thorough commitment is given us at the point when Jesus prayed this psalm. Just as he rested his head in death and completed all that had been prophesied about him, when he victoriously cried that everything was finished and all human debts had been paid, then triumphantly he could say, "Father, into your hands I commit my spirit" (Luke 23:46). If God is asking for our total relinquishment into his hand, then it means death to ourselves. . . .

The very next phrase in Psalm 31 . . . can be translated: "You have ransomed me, YHWH" (v. 5). Since Jesus perfectly entrusted everything into the Father's hand and fulfilled every dimension of the latter's plan, we can be confident that we are indeed redeemed. Jesus paid the price of forgiving us and submitting to us in mercy even when we killed him, and thus he released us from prisons of sin and death and pain and loneliness.

Most significant . . . is that the poet then calls YHWH the "God of truth." . . .

The truth of our relation to sin is that we are forgiven. The truth of our relation to death is that it has been overcome and we do not need to fear it. The truth of our relation to pain is that it will never be more than we can bear. And the truth of our loneliness is that when we feel totally cut off, we have in our panic forgotten the depth of God's thorough faithfulness. . . . He is the God of reliability and stability, and his gift to us in our loneliness is the whole truth about ourselves — especially the truth that we are beloved to him.

Prayer

  God of truth, we commit ourselves to you — knowing that in Jesus' death and
  resurrection you have redeemed us from sin, death, pain, and loneliness, to
  live as your beloved . . .   Amen.

I'm Lonely, LORD, pp. 16, 20-21.

Therefore, my dear brothers [and sisters], stand firm. Let nothing move you. Always give yourself fully to the work of the Lord, because you know that your labor in the Lord is not in vain.

1 Corinthians 15:58

Though we cannot escape the horrendous amount of evil in the world, the good news of the gospel is that God will not let us be defeated at the hands of sin and evil and death. Part of the meaning of the resurrection of Jesus Christ is that God has triumphed through Christ's suffering and is continuing to go about the business of restoring this world to its original design and purposes. Though we might have to undergo intense suffering in our present times of trouble, yet after the death comes the resurrection. As Paul so wonderfully claims in 1 Corinthians 15, since Christ is raised, we know that we too shall rise. Death and grave, sin and evil have all lost their sting.

Yet we remain in a meanwhile time beset with the problems of sin and the results of evil. We must face those ills realistically, truthfully. . . .

During my four years in graduate school in Indiana, . . . I rode the bus to the university. My visual handicaps necessitated this mode of transportation, but the daily bus trips were made easier by the frequent presence of a cheerful blind girl, who brought smiles and jokes wherever she went. What a lovely model she provided of a person who has seized the meanwhile. . . .

The value of our weakness is that it teaches us to wait for God's timing, to overcome evil with love, to respond with gentleness instead of violence. In our world people often try to overcome limitations with power, but power always causes resistance. . . .

One morning I awoke with stabbing pain in my eye. . . . All efforts to force whatever was causing the irritation to come out led to greater pain and more watering. I spent the entire day trying to avoid those movements that intensified the poke, and my eye chose to water all day long — while I gave the morning Bible study at camp, ate meals, and traveled by car from Iowa to Wisconsin. Finally, somehow, somewhere, at some time, the irritator was dislodged. All the tears had gently done their work.

Prayer
   Comforting God, may all our tears gently do their work in our "mean-whiles" . . . Amen.

Joy in Our Weakness, pp. 23-25.

Every valley shall be lifted up,
  and every mountain and hill be made low;
the uneven ground shall become level,
  and the rough places a plain.

Isaiah 40:4 (NRSV)

What can be the purpose of lifting up the valleys and bringing down the high places? Following the command to prepare the highway for our God in Isaiah 40:3, this verse asks for some tricky engineering. Why does faith have to move mountains anyway? . . .

What might be our task . . . in response to the voice that is heard making this proclamation? Perhaps we can find practical ways to lift up those engulfed in sorrow or those swallowed by poverty. Perhaps we can serve as prophets to warn those who have elevated themselves to positions on economic or academic mountains or those engaged in worship of various other idolatries in high places. Whether we serve as compassionate priests or as rebuking prophets, our goal is to prepare the way for God to come more deeply into our own life and the lives of others. . . .

The second set of two phrases in this verse speaks of openness and leveling, with the implication perhaps of productivity. . . .

Again, this has implications both for our ministries and for our own lives. Perhaps our role is to eliminate distorted understandings of God so that others' minds are made accessible to God's planting. Perhaps we have to help tear away the obstructions of overcrowded schedules or to remove the rocks of vocational ambitions that prohibit lush growth — in ourselves or in others. Our personal need might be to channel God's ever-flowing waters through devotional disciplines to water our thirsty souls. . . .

We each have a lot of earth to move — and so do our churches.

Prayer

> *Only true God, lead us down from the idolatrous high places in our lives and use us to lift up those caught in valleys of oppression. Through your Word, smooth the roughness of our characters and cultivate in us disciplines that will lead to growth and service . . .   Amen.*

To Walk and Not Faint, pp. 21-26.

"Bear in mind that the LORD has given you the Sabbath; that is why on the sixth day he gives you bread for two days. Everyone is to stay where he is on the seventh day; no one is to go out." So the people rested on the seventh day.

Exodus 16:29-30

One of the reasons that the Sabbath is so freeing is that when we cease working, we dispense with the need to create our own future. This was one of the most important lessons taught to the people of Israel during their wilderness experience. When the Sabbath was first becoming an important part of their regular life rhythm, God told them that they would not need to gather manna on the Sabbath day. . . .

The point of the whole story is that God will provide for his people; they don't have to struggle to work things out for themselves. Indeed, this is the message throughout the narrative of the Hebrew people — that their God will provide for them. That is the meaning of Holy War — "Stand by and watch the LORD fight for you." . . .

Sabbath keeping every week puts things back into perspective and stirs in us a great repentance for our failure to let God be God in every aspect of life. . . .

Letting God be God in our lives does not, of course, mean passivity. We do not simply sit back and say that God is in charge of our work. Rather, when we get our priorities straight and remember that God is God and that we are merely his servants, we are empowered to do all that we can do to be good stewards of the gifts and resources we have been given. I am convinced that I am freed up to work much better during the times when I am aware of God's direction and provision and empowerment in my daily tasks. Intentional Sabbath ceasing of my striving to be God also makes it more possible for me to think of all the work I do during the week as worship. . . .

What a relief it is not to have to try to be God, nor to create our future, nor to establish our security!

Prayer

    LORD *of the Sabbath, help us trust that our future and our security are in your hands and that you will provide for us . . .*   Amen.

Keeping the Sabbath Wholly, pp. 28-31.

At MTV we don't shoot for the 14-year olds, we own them.
MTV Chairman Bob Pittman

Believers in Jesus are called to live *in* the world. . . . From the *inside* we seek to understand it so that we can minister to its needs. Simultaneously, we struggle to be not *of* the world; we reject its values and stay *outside* its temptations and idolatries. To maintain this dialectical tension of being *in* but not *of,* the Church's worship must be *upside-down* — turning the culture's perspective on its head (thinking from God's revelation rather than human knowledge), teaching an opposite set of values (loving God and others instead of self), enabling believers to make authentic differences in the world. . . .

Without doubt this television age requires that we reflect more deeply on how we teach and what we are really learning, on whether what we now "know" has any effect on who we are and what we do.

Neil Postman, in his book *Amusing Ourselves to Death,* recognizing that even religion has to be cast in television terms, forces us to ask . . . if and how we can do that without dumbing down the substance of faith. . . . I am not convinced that worship must cater to television-age crowds craving entertainment, but our efforts to be faithful, deep, and truthful and yet accessible to society will be improved if we painstakingly analyze precisely how television affects us.

We live in a world loaded with "information" that is meaningless because it has no context, can lead to no response, and has no connection to everything else in our arsenal of "facts." A turn toward becoming a people consumed by entertainment was almost inevitable, for, as Postman asks, what do you do with all the information? . . .

The television age has enormous consequences for the Church. Will its attitudes and habits imperil the very work we do and prevent us from genuinely being the Church? Since television transforms the method by which people are persuaded of the "truth," how will we inculcate the truths of faith? What questions should we be asking to ponder the means we use to be in the world but not of it, as we seek to appeal to the culture surrounding us?

Prayer
> *Lord God, help us minister faithfully and effectively to people in our media-dominated culture . . .   Amen.*

Reaching Out, pp. 17, 20-24.

... but be [in the process of] being transformed by the renewing of your mind.

Romans 12:2b (my translation)

Through the encouragement and support of the Christian community and because of the transformation that the Spirit is working in us, we are enabled to live freely and creatively and genuinely the truth about ourselves. Of course, this is an ideal, and none of us in this world can be totally free to be ourselves, but our goal in working on this subject together is to strengthen our communities so that they will be more supportive of such freedom. . . .

We do not have to be conformed to the roles that might be assigned to us by our culture, ourselves, or our church. However, please notice that my comments do not advocate a "do your own thing" mentality that has no care for others. By espousing a freedom from the legalism of conformity, the Christian community does not at all condone libertinism (liberty without responsibility) or antinomianism (liberty without any rules). The key to the perfect balance between the extremes of legalism and false liberty is the way in which the transformation of Romans 12:2 takes place. Paul urges us to be continually in the process of being transformed by the "renewing of our minds."

The basic fact that we were made in God's image teaches us to find our truest self in accordance with his principles. . . .

The emphasis on the renewing of our *minds* challenges us to recognize the value of daily personal devotional habits and corporate Bible study. When we use our minds together with our hearts to investigate God's goals and principles as outlined in the Scriptures, we find ourselves and our communities changed. When our minds engage in fervent prayer and profound meditation upon the messages of the Bible and our daily experiences, we grow to know God and, thereby, the truth about ourselves. . . .

God is eminently reliable and infinitely loving. He will always prove to be true no matter how much we investigate. And his purposes for us will always be tender no matter how much they might change us. We don't ever have to be afraid of what might happen if we open our minds to learn the truth about ourselves. We might find ourselves dramatically . . . transformed.

Prayer

    Triune God, transform us through prayer, study, and meditation, so that we will live faithfully, as created in your image . . .   Amen.

Truly the Community, pp. 38, 42-45.

Church of God, elect and holy, be the people Christ intends,
strong in faith and swift to answer each command your master sends. . . .

James E. Seddon (1982)

Let me suggest a few questions to guide our thinking about what it means to be a congregation for the sake of our children. . . .

1. Does the pastor preach the whole counsel of God and not just what is politically correct? Do the congregational leaders urge you and your children to wrestle with the whole Bible and not just read the parts you like? . . .

2. Does the pastor preach sermons and do the leaders teach classes that rebuke and challenge you and your children? . . .

3. Do the congregation's small groups . . . hold you and your children accountable, support you in your times of weakness, and pray for you consistently? . . .

4. Are there some people in your congregation that you don't like? If not, where else (within such a protective covenant framework) will we learn, as God commands, to love our enemies? . . .

5. Are there people in the congregation from other ethnic and ability groups? . . .

6. Does the community's life demand a lot from you and your children and call forth your spiritual gifts? . . .

7. Does the whole congregation understand that everyone is responsible for helping to raise children in the faith? . . .

8. Does the congregation give young people meaningful jobs to do in the parish? . . . How else will they learn that being part of the Body of Christ involves us all in mission? . . .

9. Does the congregation encourage and enable your children to memorize the Scriptures, learn essential doctrines, delight in Christian symbols, value the noblest hymns and the best new songs, and cherish the heritage of the faith? . . . How else will they be nurtured to want to remain part of the Christian community? . . .

10. Does the congregation go beyond "evangelism programs" to help each member, young and old, become equipped to share his or her faith . . . ? How else will we fulfill the Great Commission?

Prayer

Lord of the Church, help us be a vibrant, committed community of faith, for the sake of our children, our neighbors, and each other . . .   Amen.

Is It a Lost Cause? pp. 48, 51-61.

To you, O Lord, I lift up my soul;
  in you I trust, O my God.
Do not let me be put to shame,
  nor let my enemies triumph over me.

Psalm 25:1-2

Consider this pastoral invitation from the Lutheran liturgy: "Lift up your hearts" . . . and the congregational refrain, "We lift them to the Lord." . . .

The Scriptures frequently invite us to lift up our heads or hearts or souls or eyes in order to observe the character of *YHWH* and to see his action on our behalf. . . .

The Hebrew text of this first verse of Psalm 25 begins with the address, "Unto you, *YHWH.*" Putting this first underscores the direction. Toward *YHWH* we want to be devoting our attention and desire in the course of everyday life. . . .

In the second phrase of the psalm, the poet lifts up to *YHWH* his soul . . . the essential part . . . , one's deepest self.

That sense of one's whole being or truest character seems most appropriate here in Psalm 25. We need to lift up to *YHWH* intentionally the true core of ourselves, our aspirations and desires. . . .

When we feel abandoned because God seems not to be there, we can still by an act of will lift up our inmost desires to him. We do not have to exert frantic intensity to secure God's attention or forgiveness, but we can focus on him with confident deliberation to receive more readily his comforting answers to our cries. . . .

To direct our passions to *YHWH* can't be done just once, decisively, for all time. Rather, the constant discipline of our daily lives must be to keep ourselves pointed toward *YHWH.* . . . No matter what is happening in our lives, the psalmist invites us to be lifting up our souls to *YHWH.* . . .

How can we develop such a habit? We are immensely assisted if we establish daily disciplines of prayer and Bible study and meditation. The more thoroughly we enfold ourselves in God's presence in our devotional times, the more readily he will be apparent to us in the other moments of the day.

Prayer
  O Lord, what a privilege it is to lift our souls to you . . .   *Amen.*

I'm Lonely, Lord, pp. 23-25.

To him who loves us and has freed us from our sins by his blood, and has made us to be a kingdom and priests to serve his God and Father — to him be glory and power for ever and ever! Amen.

Revelation 1:5b-6

In our post-Christian age we are very much like the believers for whom John wrote The Revelation. Christianity is not really in charge of our culture anymore, so it must be lived in the modern world from a minority position. We are all part of a society that forgets original sin, heaven and hell, the cross, and the absolute sovereignty of God. Consequently, we cannot simply assert what we believe and compel the rest of the world to believe it, too. However, the Christian community can gently continue to live as the people of God and offer a viable alternative to the rat race, smash-your-neighbor, violent society that surrounds us. We can live out the gospel in peaceful, caring ways that manifest the alternative lifestyle of those who follow Jesus Christ.

That model excites me because it genuinely follows Jesus, who brought healing to those who suffered and who demonstrated what it meant that the kingdom of God had come near. Then he sent out his disciples to bring the same healing message about the kingdom to the world in which they moved. Now The Revelation asserts in several places (such as 1:6 and 5:10) that he has made us a kingdom and priests, that our work in the world is to continue to model his alien values in a power-grabbing society.

Such a perspective acknowledges, too, that there is sin in our midst. We are not always going to be successful at modeling the alternative life in Christ. At those times we model other, core dimensions of our faith — the gift that we are forgiven, the care of the Christian community to restore those who have erred, and the opportunity to work together as a people to learn anew what it means to follow Jesus. Thus, we model in our failures what to do with the sinful weakness — forgive it, treat the sufferer with compassion, and work for restoration, reconciliation, and wholeness.

Prayer

Reconciling Lord, we have much to learn about modeling the Christian life. Help us show others what membership in your kingdom is all about by our caring, healing, forgiving, restoring behavior . . . Amen.

Joy in Our Weakness, p. 26.

"Then the glory of the Lord *will be revealed,*
and all flesh will see [it] together,
for the mouth of the Lord *has spoken."*

Isaiah 40:5 (NASV)

This verse anticipates the revealing of the glory of the Lord on the mount of transfiguration and at the empty tomb. It prophesies such revealing of the Lord's glory as took place on Pentecost when all the people in Jerusalem saw it together. But what might this verse say to our lives? . . .

The revealing of the glory of *YHWH* takes place when his importance is recognized, when his significant presence is made more fully known. Furthermore, that glorious revealing will be all the greater, verse 5 goes on to say, because all flesh shall see it together as one. . . .

The inevitability of that revelation is reinforced by the assertion, "For the mouth of the Lord has spoken." . . . *YHWH* himself has promised this revelation of his glory. And we know, for God has never failed yet, that his promise will be fulfilled. . . . Indeed, this verse asserts the sovereignty of God, his majestic omnipotence, his unalterable ability to fulfill that which he announces.

God especially wants to fulfill this verse through us. The apostle Paul highlights this idea in 2 Corinthians 3:18, where he declares that, as we behold the glory of the Lord, we shall be changed into his likeness, from one degree of glory to another. The glory of the Lord shall indeed be revealed *in our lives* in ways that are observable.

God's glory is so multifaceted (an image in 1 Pet. 4:10) that it requires all of us individuals to reveal all that God wants to say about himself. Consequently, Christians are to be neither nonentities nor carbon copies of each other, but unique vessels for God's self-revelation. We are each matchlessly created in God's image and have much to reveal to the world around us.

Prayer
> *Glorious Lord, we desire to be worthy of the honor of being vessels of your self-revelation. Help us live each day in awed awareness of this honor, privilege, and responsibility . . .   Amen.*

To Walk and Not Faint, *pp. 27-29.*

And the peace of God, which transcends all understanding, will guard your hearts and your minds in Christ Jesus.

Philippians 4:7

One of the greatest human needs is for security, and we do all kinds of crazy things to make sure that we successfully build it. . . . We assess various kinds of investments . . . ; our nation builds more and more missiles, bombs, and delivery systems in order to establish our national security. . . .

However, professional positions, finances, politics, technological solutions — all are part of the web of illusions that hide from us the fact that our security can be found only in our relationship with God. Professional positions will be eliminated; the stock market might crash; political parties will blunder; technological solutions often create more problems than they solve — but God is eternally the same in his love for us. We can count on his covenant faithfulness.

To face the truth that all our efforts to build security are illusions could lead us to brutal despair if we do not also study the character of God to see how he promises to be our security. Then to cease our striving will lead to the massive relief of totally giving up all our efforts to work things out by ourselves.

Similarly, to cease being in control of our own lives leads not to a servile dependence, but to a greater freedom. I would much rather experience the privilege of enjoying to the hilt who I am, seeking to be a faithful steward of my gifts and resources, than to try to manage everything by myself. Too many circumstances are out of my control. . . .

If I trust that there is a Lord over all of history — if I recognize that the white horse of Christ rides along with the red horse of war, the black horse of the economy, and the pale horse of affliction and death in controlling the course of history (Rev. 6:1-8) — I can cease to worry about the forces out of my grasp.

My responsibility in living is to be as faithful as I can to my own creation by loving my Creator and his will. That sets me free to enter into the adventure of a daily walk with him, of practicing his presence in all that I do and am becoming.

Prayer

Triune God, only your love is certain. Help us live in the freedom of that security . . .   Amen.

Keeping the Sabbath Wholly, pp. 31-32.

And hope does not disappoint us, because God has poured out his love into our hearts by the Holy Spirit. . . .

Romans 5:5

I believe that this is a critical time for the world and a momentous opportunity for the Christian community. Everyone around us is longing for a story that gives meaning to life. We have such a meta-narrative because of the God we know, . . . a story that can draw to the triune God the world he loves and longs to save. . . .

The Christian community, to be genuine gift to the postmodern world, must deliberately be an alternative society of trust and embodied faithfulness to our story and its God. Rather than becoming enculturated and entrapped by the world's values of materialistic consumerism, of narcissistic self-aggrandizement, of solitary superficiality, and of ephemeral satisfaction, members of Christ's Body must be Church by choosing his simple life of sharing, his willingness to suffer for the sake of others, his communal vulnerability, and his eternal purposes. Leaders in the Christian community must constantly equip parishioners for the mission and ministry of communicating the Christian meta-narrative, of enfolding the world around them in God's love, of deliberately choosing and living out the alternative values of the kingdom of God. . . .

The community gathers in worship to hear our story in the exhortations and challenges of our priests and prophets, in the retelling of the narratives of God's Word and works, in the singing of Christianity's new and old exalted hymns of faith, in the remembering of our great creeds and doctrines, and in the prayers for God's faithfulness and ours in response. The Christian community also listens together for the Holy Spirit's guidance. . . . Then we go out from our gatherings to bring the story we have learned to the world around us. In the Christian community, people left homeless by the postmodern ethos can find a home, . . . true roots, and a story that embraces them. Most of all, in the community and the community's meta-narrative, the godless can find the true God — . . . Jesus, the Truth, who brings healing, . . . the Way to the home for which they search, . . . and the Life who gives us hope for eternity.

Prayer

> *Holy Spirit, empower us to share with our neighbors and children the story of God's love for the sake of the world . . .   Amen.*

A Royal "Waste" of Time, pp. 55-57.

Then you will be able to test and approve what God's will is. . . .

Romans 12:2c

Probably one of the most frequently asked questions in Christian circles is the plea, "How do I know the will of God?" . . .

The issue . . . must be carefully linked to the focus of . . . becoming transformed by the renewing of our minds. . . . God teaches us about himself and his will through objective means. We don't discover it only subjectively, with our emotions, but also rationally, with our minds. . . .

In Romans 12:2 Paul . . . stresses that an outcome of the Spirit's transforming renewal of our minds is the consequent constant checking of God's will. . . . The action is a process. Paul urges us and our communities to be constantly approving the Lord's will, to be continually matching up our attitudes with the reality of God's purposes. . . .

For Paul's readers the Greek verb, *dokimazō,* signified, first of all, "to try to learn the genuineness of something by examination and testing, often through actual use." . . .

This word's whole field of meaning — to "test," to "regard as worthwhile," and "to judge as good" — seems to be implied when Paul chooses the verb for the process of Romans 12:2. He asserts that as we experience our transformation by the Holy Spirit's renewing of our minds, we will be enabled thereby to examine and accept for our own lives what the will of God is. The New International Version includes both of these options in its translation of the verb as "test and approve." . . .

To approve God's will implies living it out. When we test it thoroughly, we discover that to live in the center of God's gracious will is the only way to be truly satisfied. After all, because he created the shape into which we are being transformed, he must know what is best for us. . . .

By intelligent processes, in which the Holy Spirit is a powerful influence (but in which also our brains are actively at work and in which the whole community takes part), we discern what God would have us do in a particular situation.

Prayer

> *Good and gracious God, help us discover your will as we study and pray and live out your purposes — "testing and approving" how you have created us to live . . .   Amen.*

Truly the Community, pp. 46-51.

God has called you out of darkness into this most marvelous light;
bringing truth to live within you, turning blindness into sight;
let your light so shine around you that God's name is glorified;
and all find fresh hope and purpose in Christ Jesus crucified.

James E. Seddon (1982)

Ought we really to buy into the contemporary consumer notion that we *choose* a church and that we must *conform* our congregation to society's standards so that we can keep our children from leaving and attract enough new people to grow our parish? Don't the Scriptures constantly emphasize that *God has chosen us* and that *we are called to BE the Church?* . . .

Here are three questions that every congregation must constantly ask itself if we are serious about Church-being and about bringing up Christian children to share in Church-being. Does our congregational life keep *God* as the center, the focus, our source for truth and life? Do our parish activities and services form members with the *character* of God's people? Do our church events and worship times create us to be a *community* of faith according to biblical descriptions? . . .

I am worried that so many pastors and leaders in the churches . . . have fallen prey to the confusions of the "church marketers." Instead of faithfulness, the major goal of many congregations has become success. Instead of deepening the spiritual lives of members and training them for mission, the focus seems to be on parishes growing fatter by attracting consumers to their smorgasbord of ministry services. The results for our children are disastrous, for they are schooled by such congregational life to be narcissistic shoppers of religion instead of faithful followers of Christ.

It seems to me that if we and our offspring are a people formed by the scriptural narratives, an entirely different set of values will guide our thinking. We will want to know what God wants instead of insisting on our choices. We will want to be the persons God designed us to be instead of people like the rest of the world. We will want to be a community that passes on the faith in faithful ways.

Prayer
> *Christ Jesus, help our congregations keep you as the focus and guide in all we do, so that we will be formed as your faithful people, able to teach our children, by example, how to follow you . . .   Amen.*

Is It a Lost Cause? pp. 47, 51, 61-62.

To you, O LORD, I lift up my soul;
in you I trust, O my God.
Do not let me be put to shame,
nor let my enemies triumph over me.

Psalm 25:1-2

The second verse of this psalm doubly emphasizes our relationship with God. Not only does it contain the words *in you,* but also God is addressed as the object of trust and called "my God." . . .

This accentuates that we trust not in an unreachable God far away and only transcendent, but in One who can also be *"my* God," the One who personally cares for me and for you and has chosen us for himself. The constant message of the Scriptures is that God wants to relate to us. As a bumper sticker quips, "If we're not feeling close to God, guess who moved." . . .

Furthermore, in the Hebrew text, *trusted* . . . suggests that the act of trusting in God was a point of commitment that has been decisive. Now its results still stand. In realizing that unto *YHWH* we want to lift our souls, our direction in all circumstances has been established.

This intentionality has significant implications for the way in which we read the Scriptures. We choose to read them as law or as gospel — as our objectives for the day, which we *must* reach, or as our goal for the direction of our lives, the way in which we are *learning* to move.

If we read exhortations such as to "put on compassion" as law, we are crushed by our failure, for it is impossible for us to put on compassion perfectly. If we see those same promptings as gospel invitations, then to be compassionate is our goal; it orients the direction in which we move through our days, but it is not the day's objective, which we will have failed to meet if we don't get there by tonight. Our day's objectives might include doing *acts* of compassion, like caring for a sick neighbor or giving more money and more of ourselves away to help the poor, but these are simply movements toward the goal of being yielded to God, who forms us into compassionate people.

When we first believed in Christ and became a part of a Christian community, we became immersed in this goal in response to his love: to imitate his obedient life.

Prayer
> *Obedient Christ, we want to follow you, daily, faithfully . . .   Amen.*

I'm Lonely, LORD, pp. 23, 25-26.

"I tell you the truth, whatever you did not do for one of the least of these, you did not do for me."

Matthew 25:45

We who claim to be God's people must do some major rethinking about the place of the weak and the helpless in our society and in our churches. How much of a part do the handicapped, the retarded, the aged, the infants play in our Christian communities? . . . How much do we value the contributions of the old instead of wishing they wouldn't be so traditional? To our great loss, in such antagonism we lose track of the moral truths they are trying desperately to preserve. . . .

The Bible is always on the side of the oppressed. The prophets in the First Testament rage against those who sell the needy for a pair of sandals (Amos 8:6), those who add house to house and join field to field (Isa. 5:8), thereby robbing the poor. Throughout the Scriptures God's people are warned that their harmful actions toward the weak and helpless will be paralleled by God's wrath against them. Unless they repent of their lack of care, they will lose the kingdom of God. We must recognize this inextricable connection: the kingdom of God is made up of the poor, the humble, the weak, those who suffer.

This is made especially clear in the twelfth chapter of Luke. There it is recorded that Jesus said, "Sell your possessions and give mercifully," right after he said, "Do not fear, little flock, for your Father took delight to give you the kingdom" (vv. 33 and 32). In sharing the life of the poor we most richly experience the kingdom of God. . . .

However, this truth about God's care for the weak and helpless is frequently distorted in theologies that do not remain biblical and that often advocate resorting to violence to accomplish their purposes. The peaceable kingdom of God can never be brought in by violence. If we want others to know its meaning, we must introduce them to its ruler: the Lamb that was slain. If we want to follow Jesus, then we must take up our cross, which does not mean to suffer some minor inconvenience, but to shoulder the crosspiece on which we will die.

Prayer

> Gentle Jesus, forgive and transform our treatment of "the least of these" in
> our culture, our churches, and our lives . . .   Amen.

Joy in Our Weakness, p. 29.

For God, who said, "Let light shine out of darkness," made his light shine in our hearts to give us the light of the knowledge of the glory of God in the face of Christ. But we have this treasure in jars of clay to show that this all-surpassing power is from God and not from us.

2 Corinthians 4:6-7

Lest any of us get discouraged thinking we are failures because our lives don't reveal God's glory as they should, we must quickly be reminded that God is the one who does the revealing. . . . Not by our own abilities can we be the particular people God created us to be. . . . We are incapable of revealing God's glory — often because we strive instead to reveal our own glory and discover that there is nothing there. As Paul asserts in 2 Corinthians 4:7 and 12:9, . . . we are but clay vessels, yet our very weaknesses best reveal God's glory, for our weaknesses make it obvious that the transcendent power belongs to him. The possibility of revealing God's glory, then, is another gift of grace, which enters our lives to transform us into the image of God.

This promise is made real in our lives as we heed the voice crying out in Isaiah 40 for us to prepare in the wilderness the way of the LORD. As our lives become more and more attuned to the will of God, as we seek him, not just to know *about* him, but to *know him,* his glory shall be revealed in us. . . .

When we repentantly acknowledge our miserable failures, our arrogant assumptions, our mistaken efforts, and our subtle idolatries, then God's power at work *on* us can be brought to its finish. Then his glory can be revealed *through* us, and the world around us will see it. The mouth of *YHWH* has spoken, and he will do it. . . .

The challenge before Christians is not what we do for the LORD, but who we are by his fashioning. He wants to conform us to his image, to bring us down and lift us up, to straighten us out and remove our obstructions, so that his glory can be revealed in us and through us, from one degree to another.

Prayer
> *Triune God, we thank and praise you for using us, weak clay vessels that we are, to reveal your glory . . .   Amen.*

To Walk and Not Faint, pp. 30-31.

You will be made rich in every way so that you can be generous on every occasion, and through us your generosity will result in thanksgiving to God.

2 Corinthians 9:11

The relation of Sabbath keeping to possessions is an interesting paradox in Judaica. On the one hand, the Jews would choose gladly to live more frugally during the week in order to enjoy the special foods and candles of the Sabbath. On the other hand, the Torah commanded them to refrain from any buying and selling on that day. Thus, both a special appreciation of possessions and a desire not to be dominated by them are part of keeping the Sabbath day holy.

The key to keeping both sides of the paradox together lies in recognizing that the material objects the Jews used for celebrating the Sabbath were just that: not personal possessions, but vessels set apart for the holiness of the day. This is one example of the way in which, especially after the destruction of the Temple, the Jews emphasized the sanctuary of their own homes: they honored the vessels they used for celebrating the Sabbath as holy, even as the vessels used in the Temple services were holy, and the father of the household functioned as the priest for the worship of the home-temple.

This idea corresponds to the New Testament idea of stewardship — that we do not own our possessions, but are instead entrusted with them in order to serve God with them. . . .

I have chosen pink candles (since pink is the liturgical color for Joy) for my prayers that begin and end the Sabbath day. Those candles are holy — set apart — for that use only, and, whenever I light them, their gentle glow immediately ushers me into a sense of the Sabbath. . . .

In the same way, I experience a sense of the holy, the set apart, whenever I use my grandmother's china and silver for dinner parties (which I most often have on Sunday evenings). . . . To use my grandparents' treasures says to my guests that this dinner party is a very holy time, that their special presence in my home calls for the best and most beautiful I can offer, and that God is in the midst of our table fellowship.

Prayer
> *Giver of all good gifts, help us see that all our possessions are gifts, to be used in honoring you . . .   Amen.*

Keeping the Sabbath Wholly, pp. 36-37.

[Jesus said] "Love one another, even as I have loved you . . ."

John 13:34 (NRSV)

Advances in technology bring us many advantages, but the advantages are always coupled with profound losses — primarily the loss of community. . . .

For example, television fosters an easy — and mindless — subversion of familial intimacy. Instead of conversing, playing games, or baking cookies together, modern families often merely vegetate in front of the tube — and frequently in separate rooms with unshared program choices. . . .

Societal and familial loss of intimacy affects the Church, too, in many ways. Living far apart from each other, members of a congregation do not hold each other as their primary community. Consequently, churches do not experience the deep intimacy that could characterize our times together. We might know some facts about each other, but we do not actually know who a fellow congregant really is, so we talk about trivia when we gather. We do not know how to share what genuinely matters, how to deal with the real lives and deep hurts or doubts of honest people, or how to speak the truth. Lacking sincere intimacy in congregational fellowship, we often put false pressure on worship to produce feelings of intimacy. . . . Alienated by the lack of true "public" worship, many people, conditioned by our culture's sterility, prefer merely to attend, and not participate in, worship. They can get lost in a crowd of passive spectators or worship solely through televised services. . . .

Another factor in the mix of influences on contemporary religious life brought about by television coverage is . . . the propensity to question the trustworthiness of leaders and officials, . . . which is one factor causing the boomer generation to emphasize belief in themselves and their own inner strength. . . .

This (often excessive) search for self challenges enormously what we do in worship. Churches wanting to reach out to this generation must think carefully about forms and styles. . . .

How can the Church disarm the distrust? How can we pass on the objective beliefs of our faith that are true regardless of a person's experience? . . .

How can the Church respond to people who know that they need community and do not know how to create it authentically?

Prayer

O Lord, empower our churches to become welcoming, nurturing, trustworthy communities in your name . . .   Amen.

Reaching Out, pp. 17, 27-28, 32-33.

Then you will be able to test and approve what God's will is. . . .

Romans 12:2c

Much of our difficulty in finding the Lord's will arises from the panic that engulfs us as we search for it. We get desperate, thinking that we are going to fail and mess up our lives forever. . . .

We act as though our decisions will affect adversely the way God feels about us and how he will treat us, as if the failure to find his will might cut us off from him forever.

We must go back again and again to the Hilarious truth of who God is. He has already recorded his approval of us. . . . We are never condemned because Jesus Christ has secured for us our relationship with God. His cross also secures for us his loving presence and empowerment in our constant struggle to live out the implications of that relationship. . . .

God wants us to know his will. If we start with that fact, we will be set free from the panic of trying to find it. We will trust that in his time he will make his will known to us by both objective and subjective means. Perhaps we will discover it only at the time that we must know, but we can believe him for his revelation. It will not come a moment too late. . . . Then we can approve it for our own lives and live it out with confidence. . . .

One terribly overlooked aspect of testing and approving the will of God is that we do that within the framework of the Christian community and not alone. . . . Certainly God's will can be more clearly perceived when many hearts are attuned to the Holy Spirit. . . . It is my hope that Christian denominations will recover this gift of mutual decision making and mutual searching for God's will. . . .

Moreover, as we discover God's will within the community, we find greater motivation to pursue it. Ultimately, we do have a choice. God doesn't cram his will down our throats. But you know as well as I do that his will always turns out to be the best for us.

Prayer
> *Triune Teacher, help us trust that you will guide us to know your will . . .*
> *Amen.*

Truly the Community, pp. 46, 51-54.

The gifts [God] gave were that some would be apostles, some prophets, some evange-
lists, some pastors and teachers, to equip the saints for the work of ministry, for build-
ing up the body of Christ.

Ephesians 4:11-12 (NRSV)

The primary task of the pastoral leadership is to equip the saints for ministry. This works in more than one direction in terms of raising our children
to be Christian. Not only is our goal to equip all the adults in the congregation to care about all the children, but also we intend to equip the young
people for their ministries. . . .

What percentage of "church members," would you guess, belong to a
Christian community . . . for the ways in which it will equip them to serve
God's purposes in the world? Most of the pastors I know try valiantly to issue God's call into ministry, but a large proportion of the members are not
able to hear it because they have heard too well the siren call of . . . consumerism. Who knows how large a percentage of members belong for what they
can give? . . . I know how easy it is for me to start thinking about what I can
get out of a congregation instead of what I can give, and I'm even a full-time
"servant" of the Church! . . . I focus on my own feelings instead of on what I
know. It is easy for all of us to concentrate on how the community should
care for us, rather than growing ever more willing to spend the time it would
take to care for someone else. We are all too busy.

How, then, can pastors and youth leaders/teachers fulfill the picture of
the Church in Ephesians 4:7-16? Simply, by truly being pastors and teachers, . . . beginning with knowing that they are the beloved of God, presented
as God's treasure to the Body for its equipping, empowered by grace for life
and ministry. When the leaders understand themselves in that way, they will
more freely nurture in young people the same self-awareness.

It can hardly be said strongly enough: THE most important component
required for such a pastoral heart is daily immersion in the Word and
prayer.

Prayer

Empowering God, we pray for our pastors and youth leaders/teachers. Call
them to faithfulness in studying your Word, and give them an abiding sense of
your grace for their ministries . . .   Amen.

Is It a Lost Cause? pp. 89-92.

Remember, O Lord, your great mercy and love,
  for they are from of old.
Remember not the sins of my youth
  and my rebellious ways . . .

Psalm 25:6-7a

Plain old sin frequently causes our adult lonelinesses. Alienated from God and from the people around us because of our pride or temper or stupidities, we grapple with the sin and guilt that isolate us. . . .

The emphasis of "remember" and "do not remember" gives us hope in the face of sin. . . . God as *YHWH* . . . will *certainly* remember his compassions. This is the character asserted in the name "I AM." . . .

The psalmist is holding God to the character he has revealed over the ages. . . . David reminds *YHWH* that his loving-kindnesses . . . have existed from ancient times. . . . God's character could hardly change now. Knowing that *YHWH* will remember, the poet can turn with confidence from his sin and hope with assurance for forgiveness.

The poet further asks *YHWH* to turn away from remembering those sins. . . . The first word, which we translate "sin," comes from the verb meaning "to miss a goal or way, to go wrong," as when a person aims for the target but the arrow flies off into the field. Our lives are characterized by such missing of God's marks, because we often aim wrong and sometimes we slip; . . . sometimes our own selfishness causes us to miss the mark. . . .

The second word, which the New International Version translates "rebellious ways," is often rendered "transgressions." The term implies a deliberate defiance, the choice to step across the line into rebellious behaviors. . . .

The poet asks that *YHWH* not deal with him on the basis of these many sins of omission and commission, the slipping and the rebellions. If God were to relate to us on that basis, there would be no hope whatsoever.

The good news of the gospel, in contrast, is that God has chosen instead to act toward us according to his *chesedh*, his loving-kindness, as seen especially in redemption from sin. Not according to our character, but according to his character of steadfast love and faithfulness, God will remember us.

Prayer

> *O Lord, compassionate "I AM," we praise and thank you for remembering us, not according to our transgressions, but because of your steadfast loving-kindness . . .   Amen.*

I'm Lonely, Lord, pp. 30-33.

Blessed are the meek,
for they will inherit the earth. . . .
Blessed are the merciful,
for they will be shown mercy.

Matthew 5:5, 7

We can learn best about the redemptive power of suffering from those who can accept it even if it is imposed on them without their choice. We learn to value their gifts . . . instead of trying to change them, and we . . . learn better to welcome them into the community and encourage them to offer their gifts. . . .

My friend Linden, who is in a wheelchair, told me several years ago that he greatly longed for his pastor to stop praying in public worship for his healing. Such a practice enforced the attitude in the whole congregation that he was not acceptable in their midst until he was changed. He seemed to represent a failure on their part to claim God's power sufficiently, and so they could not tolerate this weakness that reminded them of their own. How much more helpful . . . if instead they could have learned how to pray for his life in the chair meanwhile. . . . If they could have prayed for his strength and ability to cope, then they would have learned how to be a community of support. . . . They could have begun to learn more readily from Linden all that he has to teach about the power of God in our suffering. . . . They might have learned from him what it means totally to depend on God and to learn the sufficiency of his grace. . . .

The nature of our times also makes it critically important to learn from the aged. As the values of our culture shift so much and so fast, our youth grope for something steady to hang on to. . . .

Every time I see announcements of anniversary parties for couples who are celebrating fifty years together, I weep with great Joy and great sadness. What a treasure to see in them the model of devoted steadfastness. . . . I rejoice that their relationships are indeed golden. And I weep for youth today and even for my generation, for very few people in our present society are willing to put up with the suffering enough to refine their relationships into gold.

Prayer
    O Lord, give us grace to value, serve, and follow those whose lives are truly
    models for us . . .   Amen.

Joy in Our Weakness, pp. 30-31.

A voice says, "Cry out!"
And I said, "What shall I cry?"
All [flesh is] grass,
their constancy is like the flower of the field.

Isaiah 40:6 (NRSV)

The Israelites experienced that impermanence when their pride was shattered and their glorious temple destroyed in their defeat by the Babylonians. They discovered that their power was fleeting, their place among the nations short-lived. This prophetic message pertained painfully to that particular moment in history.

It also applies particularly to our history. . . . But how often do we face the fact that it is applied directly to us? YOUR flesh is grass; MY constancy is like the flower of the field. . . .

Even our attempts to be good are incomplete and unstable. So the voice urges the prophet and us to proclaim this sorely needed message to our times: We are to remind our society, our churches, and ourselves that nothing lasts.

Too often in our personal lives we forget this truth and mindlessly invest all our time, all our energies, all our resources, and all our care in things that will only pass away. We spend our work gaining wealth, our effort building power, our talents achieving fame, our love comforting ourselves — only to discover in the end that these things, too, will fade and in the meanwhile will not satisfy our deepest longings. . . .

The good news of Jesus Christ is that he has overcome the ephemerality of grass and field flowers. In fact, he uses those same elements to illustrate the basis for our hope. In Matthew 6:28 Jesus says, "Consider the lilies of the field." . . . If our Father invested such care in clothing them in beauty, certainly we can trust him to take care of us, too.

The fact that our flesh is fleeting should do this one thing: It should drive us to total dependence upon the one who does not pass away. . . . If things of the world do not ultimately satisfy, if they do not push under our deepest longings, we can come to the realization that we are indeed made for another world — and that world has already entered our own and changed it eternally.

Prayer

Eternal LORD, *nothing is certain except your love for us — and that is more than enough! We thank you for caring for us eternally . . .   Amen.*

To Walk and Not Faint, pp. 33-37.

When the neighboring peoples bring merchandise or grain to sell on the Sabbath, we will not buy from them on the Sabbath or on any holy day.

Nehemiah 10:31

One of the reasons for refraining from buying or selling on Sabbath days is that to buy or sell puts the focus on all the wrong things. . . . We focus on what we will get out of a transaction instead . . . of how we can be generous toward others. . . .

I enjoy immensely the giving attitude of a dear Mennonite friend in Indiana; she usually puts extra meat in the pot on Sundays and invites any worshipers who don't have a place to go to come home with her family and share their dinner. Wouldn't it be wonderful if we could recover this custom in our culture — to be always prepared to welcome the stranger and the sojourner in our land? (Lev. 19:10, 33-34). . . .

On an even deeper level, to refrain from any buying or selling on the Sabbath relates to the day's whole meaning as holy time. . . . One of the most profound influences on my appreciation of the Sabbath has been Abraham Joshua Heschel's *The Sabbath*, which includes these thoughts:

> [R]eligions are frequently dominated by the notion that the deity resides in space, within particular localities like mountains, forests, trees or stones, which are, therefore, singled out as holy places. . . . There is much enthusiasm for the idea that God is present in the universe, but that idea is taken to mean His presence in space rather than in time, in nature rather than in history; as if He were a thing, not a spirit.
>
> . . . Judaism is a *religion of time* aiming at *the sanctification of time.* . . .
>
> Judaism teaches us to be attached to *holiness in time.* . . . The Sabbaths are our great Cathedrals. . . .
>
> One of the most distinguished words in the Bible is the word *qadosh,* holy. . . .
>
> It is, indeed, a unique occasion at which the distinguished word *qadosh* is used for the first time: in the book of Genesis at the end of the story of creation . . . [where] it is applied to time: "And God blessed the seventh *day* and made it *holy.*"

Prayer
> *Holy God, help us experience the holiness of time in our Sabbath keeping . . .*
> *Amen.*

Keeping the Sabbath Wholly, pp. 38-39.

[Jesus prayed:] "Sanctify them in the truth; your word is truth."

John 17:17

What we need in worship is the Truth. . . .

The Truth that the Church has to offer to people caught in the postmodern condition must be shared in all its wholeness. To those who criticize Christianity because it has been (and sometimes is now) violent and oppressive, we must respond with the repentant admission that they are right. Beyond accepting blame for Christians' failures in history, we must recognize the whole truth that we remain corrupt and fallible. The Scriptures teach us thoroughly that our nature is helplessly sinful, hopelessly lost. That truth forces us to see that we cannot know the truth entirely, that our eyes are blinded by sin, that our understanding of God is only partial. But that does not negate the Truth of God or our recognition of Christ who is himself the Truth, the Life, and the Way.

Against the postmodern rejection of meta-narrative — that is, of the possibility that there is any universal, overarching Truth that is true for all people in all places — I believe that Christians can humbly suggest the non-oppressive, all-inclusive story . . . of a triune God who creates, redeems, and unifies as manifestations of his perfect love for the whole world. The Christian meta-narrative is the account of a Promising God who always keeps his promises. . . .

This God of eternal mystery condescends to reveal himself to us — a process to which he invites us by drawing us to worship him. That is why our worship needs to be structured as richly and deeply as possible, so that we never lose sight of the fact that God is the One who enables us to come to worship and the Infinite Center who thus receives our praise.

Furthermore, our worship must contain nothing but the truth. Music, songs, Scripture lessons, sermons, liturgical forms, architecture, and other accoutrements of art and gesture and ambience are all means by which God invites, reveals, and forms us. . . .

Worship can never give us the whole truth, but worship must never give us untruth or less than truth. We cannot grasp all that there is to learn about God, but every time the community gathers we have the opportunity to add to our total store of truth.

Prayer

Promising God, Lord of mystery, may your Truth shape our worship and us . . . Amen.

A Royal "Waste" of Time, pp. 58, 66-68.

. . . his good, pleasing and perfect will.

Romans 12:2d

We recognize readily that certain things are good and other things are evil. . . .

We also recognize the fact that some things not necessarily bad in themselves are not good for a particular individual. Criteria must be carefully chosen to help us assess what is good for us and what is not.

Furthermore, we must remember that God is the Creator of all good. Things that are not good are not part of his design. . . . Pain, sickness, suffering, and death are not part of God's original plan for his creation. . . .

Yet believers know that God can take even those things that . . . are contrary to his perfect designs and turn them into good things in the midst of his purposes. . . . In Romans 8:28 the emphasis that God *causes* all things to work together for good solidly battles against the heresy that all things *are* good for the Christian. . . . God is able to take the things that are not good and work them together so that good might come out of them.

Now . . . we must consider our choices. Our freedom as persons . . . enables us constantly to choose between that which is God's good will for us and that which is not. When we choose to follow God's will for us, we know that it will be good. He who made us knows what is good for us.

However . . . we sometimes mischoose. Others sometimes do, too, and their choices affect us adversely. We live in a selfish world, and the result of that sickness is frequent mischoice. . . .

The greatness of God's love is that even when his best plans are spoiled, he can still bring much good. Though I grieve over the shattered state of my foot and leg, I can see now that God has used the times of discouragement to draw me closer to himself. Surely, he has also taught me many things about ministry to the physically challenged. . . .

That is why we can be sure, when we are God's, that even in the midst of turmoil we can experience good. Whatever is of God is good.

Prayer

Great and good God, we thank you for bringing good into our lives in and out of all circumstances . . .   Amen.

Truly the Community, pp. 56-60.

Come as a shepherd;
guard and keep your fold from all that fosters sin,
and nourish lambs, and feed the sheep,
the wounded heal, the lost bring in.

James Montgomery (1825), alt.

The Church needs leaders who are thoroughly engaged in studying and meditating on the Scriptures and constantly immersed in conversation with God to gain God's guidance and learn his purposes. Churches are not failing because their pastors are not savvy enough about business, but because they have so little to say if they are not immersed in the Word. They do not have the heart of God if their pastoral practice and care are not formed by that Word and undergirded with prayer for congregational members, for wisdom, for vision. . . .

Because the culture in which we live is not supportive of the Church's purposes in forming young people to be Christian, great prayer is required for wisdom to deal with the youth, for power to resist negative cultural influences ourselves, and for strength to abstain from taking the easy way out in planning our programs for the Christian community's children. . . .

Our Christian communities need pastors and youth workers whose absorption in the biblical narratives causes them to be open models of the kinds of choices we desire our children to make. How will our youth learn to care about the poor if their congregational leaders are as concerned about affluence and consumption as the rest of society? How will they learn to be peacemakers if those in authority in the community do not practice skills of stress reduction and conflict resolution?

Pastors', youth directors', and parents' . . . example in following the way of Christ is crucial. Young people will reject a Christianity that is hypocritical; they won't believe the lifestyle of Jesus is worth following if their elders do not care diligently about imitating it. . . . Youth in our society are desperate for examples of people who, in the ordinary situations of daily life, make courageous choices — and in this case, choices consistent with the biblical invitations. . . .

Faithfully formed by the Word and prayer, . . . contemplating God's Revelation and listening for God's voice, youth leaders and clergy will acquire God's heart for their children and young adults.

Prayer

> *O Lord, inspire us to study your Word diligently, pray faithfully, and live honestly as Jesus' followers for our children's sake . . .*   *Amen.*

Is It a Lost Cause? pp. 89, 93-95.

All the ways of the LORD are loving and faithful
for those who keep the demands of his covenant.

Psalm 25:10

In the psalm before us, the poet tells us . . . that all the ways of *YHWH* are characterized by steadfast love and fidelity. . . . *YHWH* always acts according to his attributes. His reliable faithfulness can always be trusted. . . .

The second part of verse 10 illustrates the importance of reading the Scriptures in their context; the addition of the phrase "for those who keep the demands of his covenant" seems to qualify God's faithfulness, as if it were available only to those who were perfectly obedient. Such a requirement might drive us to despair and intensify our loneliness.

Notice, instead, the placement of verse 10 in this context:

Verse 8: Good and upright is the LORD;
             therefore he instructs sinners in his ways.

(This verse stresses the connection between the character of *YHWH* and the availability of his instruction.)

Verse 9: He guides the humble in what is right
             and teaches them his way.

(Once again we are reminded that we learn to obey by *YHWH*'s gracious instruction.)

Verse 10: All the ways of the LORD are loving and faithful
             for those who keep the demands of his covenant.

Verse 11: For the sake of your name, O LORD,
             forgive my iniquity, though it is great.

After we have been reminded that our ability to "keep the demands of his covenant" has been taught us by *YHWH* himself, we are also immediately reminded that in our great failures we are forgiven. No matter how deliberate our trespassing . . . , we can know that *YHWH* will forgive us for the sake of his name — that is, that he will be true to his character. . . .

Because the ways of *YHWH* are loving and faithful, . . . we respond by gladly keeping the demands of his covenant.

Prayer
   Gracious LORD, because you are willing both to teach us and to forgive us
   when we fail, we can trust you to deal with us in loving-kindness and
   mercy . . .   Amen.

I'm Lonely, LORD, pp. 30, 33-35.

The revelation of Jesus Christ, which God gave him to show his servants what must soon take place. He made it known by sending his angel to his servant John. . . .

Revelation 1:1

The Christians suffering under the emperor's persecution in Asia Minor were in dire need of a vision of God's sovereignty to sustain them. The words of The Revelation, recording the vision of the seer John, offered them the hope they needed. The introduction to the book helps us to understand the nature of the vision that we must hold to give us Joy in our weakness.

In modern times the word *apocalypse* often denotes terrifying visions of bizarre battles; . . . sometimes there is also a picture of a radiantly beautiful new city, but usually those who write about the apocalypse focus more extensively on the lurid scenes.

The Greek text of The Revelation begins with the word *apocalypse*, which means "revelation" or "disclosure," and it occurs without the article *the*. That suggests either that this book is merely any old revelation or that it is so precisely *The* Revelation that no article is needed. Considering the subject matter of the text, we most accurately translate that opening phrase as *The* Revelation of Jesus Christ. . . . God gave Jesus this revelation to show the seer John what would happen so that God's people would be encouraged to trust his lordship in all their struggles.

The phrase "The revelation of Jesus Christ, which God gave him" reminds me of a concept expressed most clearly in the letter to the Ephesians. There the first chapter's glorious doxology exults in God's plan designed before the foundation of the world, purposed *in* Jesus Christ, the Beloved One, and made manifest to humankind *through* Jesus Christ. . . . How astounding to realize that God's best plan was to use the suffering and death of Christ and the weakness of his followers for the fulfillment of his purposes, which he manifested in Christ!

Ephesians 1 also uses the word *mystery*. . . . That word delightfully describes the plan of God. . . . Though we spend our lives studying the Scriptures and seeking to know his intentions, we can never thoroughly understand the deepest designs of God.

Prayer

> *God our Father, although we will never truly understand all you have designed for our world, we thank you for revealing to us your love and the way to redemption through Jesus Christ . . .   Amen.*

Joy in Our Weakness, pp. 35-36.

The grass withers, the flower fades,
when the breath of the LORD *blows upon it;*
surely the people are grass.

Isaiah 40:7 (NRSV)

This pronouncement ... concerns the glaring contrast between God's power and righteousness and the weakness of human beings. ...

We can hardly begin to know the amazing grace of God's love unless we first have known how much we deserve his righteous wrath. ... Otherwise, we assume that it's easy for God to forgive us. We think we are not too bad — that we can actually earn God's favor. We make grace cheap. ...

Isaiah 40:7 concludes, "Surely the people are grass." ... Surely we deserve the wrath of God because we are totally incapable of loving God perfectly. ... People are no more enduring than other flesh — beasts and plants. If we base our hopes upon our own ability to create our life, we are surely going to be crushingly disappointed. ... If we genuinely face ourselves, with the help of this verse, we have to admit that we are not able to change our fragile natures. It is not possible for us to make ourselves capable of avoiding the fate we deserve. ...

The biblical narratives make clear that death is God's gift to us — to keep us from having to live forever in this sin-broken and rebelliously corrupted world. Death is the door into meeting God face-to-face. ... To be biblically formed is to be prepared for that encounter in the present recognition of God's powerful breath and our withering nature. ...

In one of the Church's ancient prayers, used at funerals, this phrase suggests our response to the intent of verse 7: "Teach us all so to number our days that we may apply our hearts unto wisdom and finally be saved." We know the power of *YHWH;* he is LORD of life and death. We know the frailty of human beings; surely the people are grass. These two facts together call us to number our days. Realizing who we are and who God is, we can apply our hearts unto wisdom, not trust ourselves for any type of salvation, and rejoice in the one whose breath also creates life.

Prayer

O LORD, *teach us wisely to number our days and trust you for what lies beyond ...   Amen.*

To Walk and Not Faint, pp. 39-44.

71

Then the LORD said to Moses, "Say to the Israelites, 'You must observe my Sabbaths. This will be a sign between me and you for the generations to come, so you may know that I am the LORD, who makes you holy."

Exodus 31:12-13

Christianity is . . . composed of holy time and the events that took place in time — the Incarnation, the Crucifixion, the Resurrection, and the coming of the Holy Spirit at Pentecost. Nothing in Christianity supports our contemporary idolatry of space and things, for its God is the same God whose first declaration of *qadosh*, holy, applied to the Sabbath.

Consequently, our observation of the Sabbath is a special time of recognizing that, ideally, as members of the Christian community we are part of an alternative society, standing in contrast to the values of the world and able to offer to those outside the community the opportunity to choose another way. . . .

For the Jewish community, the keeping of the Sabbath day was one of the major marks that set them apart. . . . In fact, scholars credit their Sabbath observance with preserving their unique identity. . . .

The earliest Christians at first celebrated both the Sabbath on the seventh day (Saturday), in keeping with their Jewish heritage, and the Lord's Day on the first day of the week (Sunday), in keeping with their recognition that Christ's resurrection was the major turning point for their faith. . . .

It seems that Sunday became the exclusive day for worship only after persecution in Jerusalem dispersed the Christians and caused Christianity's great expansion among Gentiles. . . . In the process Christianity lost its sense of the importance of keeping the Sabbath day holy. Why is it that we pay great attention to the commandments not to murder or steal . . . but don't recognize the significance of our failure to obey the commandment to observe the Sabbath day?

It seems to me that to recover the command to keep the Sabbath might help our Christian communities to restore the other commandments. Certainly if we honor one day as a day set apart to concentrate on the holiness of God, our priorities will be restored, and we will again seek God's will concerning our relationships with parents, with sexual partners, and with possessions.

Prayer

Holy God, help us honor and obey your commandment to keep the Sabbath holy . . .   Amen.

Keeping the Sabbath Wholly, pp. 41-43.

Jesus calls us from the worship
Of the vain world's golden store,
From each idol that would keep us,
Saying, "Christian, love me more."

                                        Cecil F. Alexander, 1823-1895

The escalating disruption of intimacy and community in our culture is augmented by the technological society's idolatry of efficiency. . . .

When this technological mind-set invades the Church, it can be extremely destructive of true worship in multiple ways — especially if we "must" finish the worship service in an hour. The liturgy becomes clockwork, service elements are eliminated, free expression of praise is stifled, . . . the Eucharist becomes less communitarian, and there is no time for common prayer and sharing of concerns and thanksgivings. Worst of all, there is no time for silence or the surprising workings of the Holy Spirit.

Second, the bombardment of hyped media impressions creates the need for worship to be similarly "upbeat." There is no place for sorrowful hymns of repentance, mourning dirges for a crucified Savior, despairing cries for hope in the troubles of life, contemplative anthems that call for deeper thinking. . . . We lose the majesty of many hymns, the moving pathos of the laments of Lent, the profound significance of the Lord's Prayer and the Creed, the lessons that can be gained by close listening to a slow-paced reading of the Scriptures.

Third, a need for efficiency in the "fellowship time" between worship and Sunday school eliminates time for caring. Fellowship becomes a mere matter of coffee and cookies in the narthex between events. . . .

Above all, the technological society's push for efficiency has robbed most congregations of the Sabbath rhythm, . . . a whole day set apart for God and for each other, a day of delight and healing. Consequently, Christians mimic the frantic lifestyle of the world around them and have no understanding that God has designed a wonderful rhythm of rest and work, of refreshment and then response. In that rhythm, we don't have to rush out of the worship service at precisely noon, since there is no work to do on Sunday. The day is set apart for worship, for relationships, for growing in our sense of who God is and who we are as individuals desiring to become like Jesus and as a community of his people displaying his character to the world.

Prayer
   God of all time and times, save us from our idolatry of efficiency! . . .
   Amen.

                                        Reaching Out, pp. 41-43.

. . . his good, pleasing and perfect will.

Romans 12:2d

Whatever is good is pleasing to God. For example, when I am very deeply discouraged over the situation of my handicaps, the good is to choose to trust God to care for me. His will is for me to depend on him, and when I choose the good of faith, he is pleased. I don't always trust him, however, and when I don't, I have chosen to experience my own hopelessness and fears about the future. If I could trust him, then I would experience his peace and hope and love even in the midst of pain.

On the other side, I had to learn that grieving can be good. Mourning over what should not be is right and beneficial; grief brings the goodness of God's healing. Our sorrow over various mischoices in our milieu pleases God, for we share in his pain. That is why Jesus said, "Blessed are those who mourn, for they shall be comforted" (Matt. 5:4). Anguish is not good in itself, of course, but its effects on our spiritual growth are. . . .

One final point: . . . God's will is perfect. We are not. We will never be thoroughly successful at choosing and approving his perfect will. We are not able to discern his perfect will in all the murky choices that confront us. Our actions and choices will never be totally pleasing to him because we can never live out what is good. Yet the fact of his perfect will determines our direction. As we live towards the goal of his desires, we experience his good things, what is pleasing to him, and the perfection that he designed — though to a limited extent. Someday when we are made completely whole, we will know the perfection of his will. Meanwhile, our proving it does not make God's will good. Rather, in our testing it, we discover its goodness. We want to choose it, and that pleases him. We long for the final perfection of his will in our lives. . . .

God's will is that total perfection toward which we move, but at which we will never arrive in this life. However, his will always provides the goal, the direction in which to walk.

Prayer

Holy and loving Lord, guide and direct our choices and move us ever closer to your perfect will for us . . . Amen.

Truly the Community, pp. 59-61.

We bid you welcome in the name of Jesus,
our exalted Head.
Come as a servant; so he came,
and we receive you in his stead.

James Montgomery (1825), alt.

Pastors and youth directors should engage the congregation in conversations about the society that surrounds the Church so that the entire community is equipped to nurture our children in the midst of it. . . .

What the congregation does on Sunday mornings is key for "equipping the saints" in order that ministry to the youth takes place, for a parish cannot have worship that fosters easy listening and passive spectatorship if we want to encourage everyone to take time to care for the Church's children. Worship is the community's chief endeavor in which the saints participate in *leitourgia,* the work of the people. Their "work" to worship God trains them in habits of diligence for God's purposes to be done in the world — but this requires the constant comments of the pastoral leadership for them to understand it. Furthermore, if the sermons always ask how we live out these texts in daily life, if the hymns frequently invite active faithfulness, if the prayers issue calls to service, and if the spirit of the community highlights the Joy of involvement, worship will form the character of caring for our neighbors — and specific references to caring for our community's children will channel that disposition. . . .

The pastor's role is to share his or her heart with the whole congregation, so that everyone takes on the responsibility of caring in his or her own way for the children. Perhaps the clergyperson's role might also include rebuking those who are not shouldering their share of the discipling. . . .

Leaders of the congregation, especially the clergy and youth director, can train others to welcome the youth, speak to them, challenge them, be hospitable toward them, and invite them to participate. . . .

Recently a PBS documentary on the Amish revealed through the comments of the young people how much they loved being part of that community because they knew that everyone was working so hard to love them. Indeed, we need the input and outreach of the entire fellowship to raise our children, and the pastor can never be finished inviting such involvement and equipping the congregation for it.

Prayer

> *Our exalted Head, guide our pastors in equipping all of us in the congregation for nurturing your children . . .   Amen.*

Is It a Lost Cause? pp. 89, 100-102.

75

My eyes are ever on the LORD
  for only he will release my feet from the snare.
Turn to me and be gracious to me,
  for I am lonely and afflicted.

Psalm 25:15-16

These lines challenge us to deepen our devotional lives. When the poet says without a verb in Hebrew, "my eyes continually to *YHWH*," he invites us to develop habits of practicing God's presence in every situation. Such habits are best rooted in specific disciplined times of Bible study and meditation and prayer. . . .

The New International Version's translation, "for only he will release my feet from the snare," . . . urges us to observe more carefully how often we try to get our feet out of the net by our own strength or wisdom. . . .

What sort of snares have entrapped your feet? How can looking eagerly and consistently to *YHWH* bring you out of those traps? Whether others have spread the nets against us or we have tangled up ourselves, *YHWH* alone is the one who can bring us out successfully.

The overwhelming good news about God is that he really wants to release us. . . . When the poet goes on in Psalm 25 to say, "Turn to me and be gracious to me," the word *turn* strikes us with its royal reaching out. . . .

Considering all our mistakes and rebellions, what right do we have to expect that God would turn to look at us? Yet he always deigns to do so; our asking reminds us that he does. . . .

The poet continues with a lament about his loneliness. His time of adversity included a special need for the LORD to watch with graciousness. Don't you sometimes feel that what you crave more than anything is for someone to care about the little things in your life? . . .

The freedom with which the psalmist can say, "Turn to me and be gracious to me," comes from knowing that God, who has received him lovingly in the past, cannot be false to his character of covenant faithfulness. Therefore, we can with bold confidence — made more sure in the manifestation of God's love in the person of Jesus — go immediately to God and ask for his attention.

Prayer

  Gracious LORD, guide us, through Bible study, meditation, and prayer, to the untangling we need in our daily lives . . . Amen.

I'm Lonely, LORD, pp. 37-40.

Jesus Christ is the same yesterday and today and forever.

Hebrews 13:8

As we study the Scriptures, we will do the best we can to gain a clearer awareness of the meaning of the book of Revelation, but, ultimately, what God reveals to us will always remain mysterious. He is infinitely beyond us in his eternal majesty.

That is why we need Jesus Christ. He reveals the mysterious plan of God in ways accessible to human understanding. He makes things comprehensible to us because he was like us. . . . In relating intimately with us, he brought us into the possibility of relating intimately with God. . . .

Indeed, . . . The Revelation of Jesus Christ is the way he made known to the people of Asia Minor the mysterious purposes of God, the things that were about to take place as they struggled to understand the meaning of a persecution that nearly destroyed their faith. . . . And for us, the Jesus Christ who made God's purposes known in the first century is still the same, and still today he reveals the hidden things of God, so that we might have hope in the times of our tribulations.

Notice that once again in Revelation 1:2 the contents of this book are said to be the witness of the Word of God and the testimony of Jesus Christ. The seer John places his own name as bondservant between the two references to God and Jesus Christ in order to make doubly sure that we keep it straight. It is not his witness, his device, his artificial construction. The things that he is about to tell us are the very things of God, made available to us through the work of Jesus Christ on our behalf.

To make sure that we understand the importance of receiving this revelation as it comes to us from God himself, John continues by offering this guarantee: "Blessed the one reading and the ones hearing the words of the prophecy and heeding the things which are written in it" (v. 3, my translation). In other words, those who participated in the leading of worship by reading the seer's letter to the early Christians would find blessing in that action, and those who attended the worship celebration and who applied the word of prophecy to their lives in practical ways would also benefit.

Prayer

Jesus Christ, ever the same, bless us also as we attend to your Word and apply it to our lives . . .   Amen.

Joy in Our Weakness, pp. 36-38.

The grass withers, the flower fades;
but the word of our God will stand forever.

Isaiah 40:8 (NRSV)

There *is* something enduring, something to which we can cling. The Word of our God . . . will not evaporate over time. . . .

The fact of Easter enables us to know that God's Word does indeed abide forever. . . . What might this mean practically?

First, . . . we can't help but recognize the stability and security that the steadfastness of God's Word provides. "When every earthly prop gives way," the old hymn asserts, "He then is all my Hope and Stay./On Christ the solid rock I stand;/all other ground is sinking sand." God's Word to us in the person of Jesus Christ is a reference point, a source of equilibrium, a message of grace, the promise of forgiveness and healing that stands forever, in spite of our failures and sin and brokenness. God's Word to us is love, even though we are unlovable or unloved by the world around us. God's Word to us is Joy in the midst of sorrow and pain, Peace in the midst of tension and anxiety, Hope in the face of insurmountable obstacles and death. This is the basis of our faith: the realization that God's Word of victory over the powers of evil and of freedom from sin and death is true and eternal. . . .

Second, this assertion has powerful implications for the way we minister to other people. Why give them fading fantasies or withering words when instead we could communicate to them the sure hope and promises of an eternal Word?

Human words can't guarantee their fulfillment. When we offer our merely human words to comfort, we forget that all flesh is grass. Human words are often empty gifts, . . . and even persons who love us deeply can't always keep their promises . . . since the tragedies of life can preclude their best intentions.

In contrast, the eternal Word of God carries inherently within it the power to accomplish what it describes. If we say to someone, "Grace and peace to you from God . . ." those words carry within them the actual fact of grace and peace, already bequeathed in the Word of Christ, really to be received by our listener.

Prayer
Christ, our solid Rock, teach us to cling to, and to share, your eternal
Word . . .   Amen.

To Walk and Not Faint, pp. 45-48.

78

By the seventh day God had finished the work he had been doing; so on the seventh day he rested from all his work.

Genesis 2:2

One meaning of the Hebrew verb *shabbat* is "to rest." In the Hebrew Scriptures to desist from labor is associated with resting — for God, people, animals, even the land. . . .

Everything is turned around when we keep the Sabbath. If we don't observe it, Sunday just leads back into the humdrum of the regular workweek, . . . but keeping the Sabbath ushers us into the recognition that all days derive their meaning from the Sabbath. . . .

To deliberately set apart a whole day for rest makes "the choice to rest" easier, because the discipline of observing the Sabbath has reoriented our entire week's calendar. In fact, the Hebrew days of the week don't even have independent names but are named in relation to the Sabbath. . . . We spend three days getting ready (preparing for the bride) and three days afterward remembering it (the delight of the wedding).

In our . . . culture, in which every person is judged by his or her work and rest is determined by our labors, we desperately need this radical reorientation, made possible by the Jewish concept of time in which rest determines work. Such a concept reorients our entire way of thinking. . . .

In an age that has lost its soul, Sabbath keeping offers the possibility of gaining it back. In an age desperately searching for meaning, Sabbath keeping offers a new hope. In contrast to the technological society, in which the sole criterion of value is the measurement of efficiency, those who keep the Sabbath find their criteria in the character of God, in whose image they celebrate life.

The delight of Sabbath keeping and its resting, embracing, and feasting give new energy and meaning to life as its climax and focal point. . . .

The more persistently we practice the discipline of preparing for the Sabbath in the three days preceding it, and the more thoroughly we enjoy its benefits in the three days following it, the more delightfully restful the Sabbath itself will be for us in its actual practice — as well as in its anticipation and remembrance as these transform the entire week.

Prayer
> *Lord of Hope, may the rhythm of preparing for, celebrating, and remembering the Sabbath become our practice, to ground our life in your grace . . . Amen.*

Keeping the Sabbath Wholly, pp. 48-50, 53-54.

All Scripture is God-breathed and useful for teaching, rebuking, correcting and train-ing in righteousness, so that the [person] of God may be thoroughly equipped for every good work.

2 Timothy 3:16-17

If worship stays well focused on God as its Center, participants will become better equipped to be God's witnesses to their worlds. To introduce our families and neighbors and co-workers to the Trinity and to God's gifts for them, we need an ever-growing understanding of his promises, his charac-ter, his interventions in the world, his truth that underlies our realities. Out of a character formed by the biblical narratives, by their faithful interpreta-tion, and by resulting sound doctrine will flow love that responds to the love of God. Such a character will manifest forgiveness that recognizes the potency of the Father's grace, actions that follow the model of Jesus, en-couragement and compassion empowered by the Holy Spirit.

Of course, strong Christian character cannot be formed if the worship hour is the only time the Church has to nurture it, but worship's subtle in-fluence on character dare not be misdirected. . . .

Worship as Truth that is thereby formative of character must be a major issue for our churches because the immense needs of our world require per-sons nurtured by depth and faithfulness, rather than by what is flimsy, if not flippant. . . . It is essential that worship carefully equip the saints with the truths of the faith so that they can witness to, and serve, their neighbors. The Church needs both preachers and musicians with great faithfulness to give worship participants what they need instead of what they might think they need, to offer that which is needful instead of catering to neediness. . . .

Second Timothy 3:14-17 invites us to be trained in the Holy Scriptures — to *know* them and be formed by them and not just "believe" as if that were a leap in the dark, to have habits and not selfish preferences. . . . Yet many congregations these days present only sermons and music that lack theo-logical depth, biblical images, or motivation to be about God's purposes of witnessing, justice building, and peacemaking in the world. What kind of people are our worship services forming?

Prayer
> *Triune Center of our lives, keep us faithful in seeking your formative Word through study and worship . . . Amen.*

A Royal "Waste" of Time, pp. 68-69.

. . . his good, pleasing and perfect will.

Romans 12:2d

Understanding God's good, pleasing, and perfect will must be applied very practically to the nitty-gritty situations of our daily lives, and this is especially the arena in which the Christian community is immensely important. Because our world is so marred by sin and so many things run contrary to God's perfect designs, we need each other for encouragement and hope. . . .

For example, my former housemate Julie . . . had not been able to find permanent employment that used her artistic gifts. . . .

As Julie and I prayed about her situation, we had to keep reminding each other that the difficulty of her situation was not God's plan for good, but that he could bring good out of it. We had to cling to hope that those difficult times, too, could be valuable in making Julie the beautiful person God has designed her to be. Furthermore, Julie could choose to do that which is pleasing to God, to accept her present not-good situation with a peace that would reveal God's love to those around her. She could find many ways to minister to others through her own pain and frustration. Thus, what is not good can be lived out in dependence upon God, which is pleasing to him. Furthermore, as she chose attitudes from him, such as hope and confidence in his best purposes, she would experience the good Hilarity that such trust could bring into her life.

Someday God's more perfect will might be available to Julie. We continued to pray for, and to seek, a job requiring her gifts. In the meantime, her pain could be assuaged only by the comfort of knowing that God could bring good even out of this time and by the support of a caring Christian community.

Certainly we realize that God's bringing good out of evil does not mean that we continue forever putting up with that which is evil. However, it does give us the courage to endure suffering until things can be changed into good. In the Christian community we search for ways both to change things and to support one another in the trials of the meanwhile.

Prayer

Gracious Designer, in adverse circumstances, give us hope and courage to live with whatever good is available to us as we work and wait for your perfect will to be accomplished . . .   Amen.

Truly the Community, pp. 56, 61-63.

Grant us and all our children grace
in word and deed your name to praise,
and in each family, your will
and purpose to fulfill.

Frederick William Foster (1826), alt.

I believe it is impossible for parents to raise Christian children alone. The powers of evil are too dominant, the culture around us is too post-Christian, our children have too many options. Parents need the total support of the entire Christian community, of a vital Body of believers who contribute to the passing on of the faith. Because our congregations so often fail to be truly the Church, a really alternative society, parents are not equipped for their crucial role in the shaping of character in their children, nor are their efforts enhanced by the community's enfolding and training.

These are difficult days for raising children in the faith. . . . One particular problem is that our offspring are spending time in schools and activities with peers who have not been parented, . . . whose "parents" are expecting the schools to fulfill their job, or who are being raised by teenage mothers or by perpetual adolescents.

I must add a wake-up call. . . . I shudder when I see adults taking their children to . . . terribly destructive movies. . . . Parents, how can you expose your children to such banality, violence, greed, and narcissism? How can you let your children see such movies that distort their understanding of their sexuality and of its expression?

Parents, how can you let your children watch so much television when its destructive effects on your children's brains are documented? How can you not care what your children are learning in school, about who their friends are, about how they spend their leisure time? How can you not care about the disrespect your children breathe in from the culture, about how they spend their money, about who their heroes are? . . .

Perhaps you might have to be an agent of admonition with other Christian parents in order to build up a community of believers who work together to train their children in the habits of faith.

On the other hand, perhaps you, yourself, need a slight nudge.

Prayer
  Merciful Father of our Lord Jesus Christ, help us genuinely support parents
  in nurturing their children . . .   Amen.

Is It a Lost Cause? pp. 104-7.

Turn to me and be gracious to me,
*   for I am lonely and afflicted.*
The troubles of my heart have multiplied;
*   free me from my anguish.*
Look upon my affliction and my distress
*   and take away all my sins.*

Psalm 25:16-18

The poet has been reminding us, as we despair over the lack of human comfort, that God is present with steady faithfulness to look upon us with love. . . . It is true whether we feel it or not. However, sometimes in acknowledging it as a fact we might begin to feel *YHWH*'s presence as well. . . .

Furthermore, by asking God to take away all his sins, the poet implies that perhaps those same sins are the root cause of his troubles. If God will remove the source, then the poet can be freed from those symptoms of his sin.

We need to recognize the significant part sin plays in our distresses — but not in order to overwhelm us with guilt about our inability to be the persons we want to be. Rather, when we have a deep enough sense of our sinfulness, we will be more ready to receive the forgiveness that God freely offers. When we begin to have a more profound sense of that gracious forgiveness, we will become more able to accept ourselves. Finally, when we can accept ourselves more, we will be set free to think more clearly and to deal more decisively with our afflictions and distresses. Only when we are enfolded in *YHWH*'s love do we have the power to find hope.

The psalm ends with a plea for protection and a final declaration that the poet's hope is in *YHWH*. . . . Our covenant God is turning to us to be gracious, to release us from snares, to free us from anguish, to take away our sins. Our loneliness gets lost in the wonder of his comforting care.

Prayer

> *O LORD, when in our distress we feel no comfort at all, help us find in your faithful love the forgiveness and hope we need to be released from the snares of our anguish . . .   Amen.*

I'm Lonely, LORD, pp. 37, 40-42.

I, John, your brother and companion in the suffering and kingdom and patient endurance that are ours in Jesus, was on the island of Patmos because of the word of God and the testimony of Jesus.

Revelation 1:9

When the seer John identifies himself, he calls himself a brother and fellow participant in the tribulation. He does not write as one superior to his readers or distant from them. He understands their sufferings from the inside. He is participating in their anguish, too.

Moreover, John does not stop with the assurance that he shares in their suffering. He says that he also shares in the kingdom and in the patience in Christ, which they are all practicing. . . .

The word *kingdom* means, of course, the place or people over which a king reigns, but in the Bible the word emphasizes more the way in which God's kingdom affects the lives of all who engage in it. . . . Christ's kingdom, then, changes all those for whom his lordship is supreme, who acknowledge that he is the ruler over everything. . . . For those who believed in him, the reign of God continued to hold sway even in persecution. . . .

John's introduction reminds us that we are fellow participants in the reign of God. . . .

This is one of the most important parts of the vision necessary to sustain us: a recognition of the community in which the kingdom of God is experienced. We are not alone as we seek to bring the reign of Christ to bear on the situations of our times. . . .

Just as we are encouraged by the fact that we do not ever have to suffer tribulations alone, nor do we have to work alone as we carry out our particular calling in the kingdom, even so we also have each other to increase our patience.

When Jesus sent out the disciples to proclaim the kingdom, he sent them out with this message: "The kingdom of God has drawn near." . . .

What exciting things can happen when we join in the action of God's incursions into human history and life and become reoriented to God's future — when we recognize the precious commodity we carry with us, in us, through us, wherever we go.

Prayer
   Reigning God, thank you for the community of faith, through which we participate in your kingdom together . . .   Amen.

Joy in Our Weakness, pp. 38-41.

The grass withers, the flower fades;
   but the word of our God will stand forever.

Isaiah 40:8 (NRSV)

Why does God's Word prove to be genuine, meaningful, substantive, and eternal? It is all these things and more because Jesus the Word does not merely point to the truth; he IS the Truth. . . . He is there, incarnated in his Word to bring it about. The Word was made flesh to tabernacle among us, a historic fact absolutely too glorious to grasp with only our rational minds.

The tremendous applicability of these words to our increasingly postmodern and mixed-up times stirs us; we want zealously to follow the instructions of the voice that says, "Cry!" People are longing for some sort of Truth, some kind of reference point by which to sort out their lives and find meaning. Our postmodern society craves substance and confidence. How powerfully this message could benefit our searching neighbors. . . .

In Chaim Potok's novel *My Name Is Asher Lev,* a famous painter defines whether or not one is an artist by "whether or not there is a scream in him waiting to get out in a special way." His friend then immediately adds, "Or a laugh." . . . Christians have both. God's people know the scream, for it is painful to acknowledge that all flesh is grass and to live in its withered failures.

But Christians also can't help but laugh. We laugh with victory over despair. . . . We bubble with delight because we are God's children. We giggle in the freedom of divine approval. The promise stands forever that grace is the foundation of the world and undergirds our lives. God's eternal Word assures us of eternal life with him — already begun. . . .

How desperately our culture waits for us to respond to that voice which says, "Cry!" You and I can carry eternal truths away from our devotional time and into our world today. . . .

In every situation of life we confront grass and fading flowers. This eighth verse of Isaiah 40 promises, however, that we can also find this laugh: The Word of the Lord abides forever! Our laughter passes the gift to others who also need to hear an abiding Word.

Prayer

   Eternal Word, comfort our "scream" and fill us with holy laughter for the
   sake of our neighbor . . .   Amen.

To Walk and Not Faint, pp. 45, 49-50.

Grace to you and peace from God our Father and the Lord Jesus Christ.

Philemon 1:3

We can truly learn how to rest only when we are genuinely freed by God's grace. . . .

The progression from ceasing to resting underscores the basic movement from idolatry to faith. First we discover all the deception and falsehood of the securities offered by the world, and, with repentance, we *cease* to trust them. This includes . . . our efforts to make our own way or to save ourselves. Then we learn that God has done all the work of redemption for us and that he continues to work through us. We learn, by faith, to *rest* in his grace. . . .

The creation account in Genesis establishes the pattern for time by naming a day as evening followed by morning rather than morning followed by evening. According to Eugene Peterson, pastor and writer,

> [This] Hebrew evening/morning sequence conditions us to the rhythms of grace. We go to sleep, and God begins his work. As we sleep he develops his covenant. We wake and are called out to participate in God's creative action. We respond in faith, in work. But always grace is previous and primary.

The first creation account then concludes by setting apart the seventh day as a special day for rest. Thus, the rhythm of evening/morning grace and work is enfolded in the larger rhythm of a Sabbath set apart to focus on grace and six days of work within that grace. . . .

One of the necessary tools for spiritual resting is the Word of God. The Torah was the focus of the Sabbath for the Jews, who spent part of the day immersed in the study of it. For Christians, the entire canon of Hebrew and Christian Scriptures teaches us about God's covenant love — as we both privately read and meditate upon it in our personal Sabbath devotions and publicly hear it proclaimed and preached upon in our corporate worship.

Prayer

Covenant LORD, may we rest and work instructed by your Word and upheld by your grace . . .   Amen.

Keeping the Sabbath Wholly, pp. 55-58.

Jesus calls us from the worship
Of the vain world's golden store,
From each idol that would keep us,
Saying, "Christian, love me more."

Cecil F. Alexander, 1823-1895

Our society has lost its spiritual center. Too many children, teens, and adults don't have any purpose for their lives. They are bored because of a severe lack of meaning, and they are unable to see possibilities for finding it in chores and home activities and jobs and care for others. . . .

Few have mentors to guide them in discovering values that matter. Meanwhile, the media deluge us all with images of violence and sexual immorality and materialism, all of which draw us as easy alternatives to our boredom. . . .

Consequently, many people in our society live vicariously. They tune into Walkmans instead of learning to play the piano, escape into pulp literature instead of conversing. They don't experience art or nature, but simply take a photograph and walk on. . . .

We can observe the same patterns and habits in some congregations. Their services and fellowship times contain little silence, reflective waiting, or community sharing. There is not much sense of an objective God, whose majesty demands our awe-full adoration. Instead, overwhelming subjectivism focuses only on the individual's feelings and needs and not on God's attributes or character. . . .

To attract people from our culture, some Christian churches depend upon glitz and spectacle and technological toys, rather than on the strong, substantive declaration of the Word of God and its authoritative revelation for our lives. Our relationship with Christ is not superficial entertainment; rather, it is central to life. How can we be fulfilling the purposes of God when we ignore the need for congruence between means and ends? . . .

It is not too late. The meaning and purpose of the Church certainly aren't lost, and what has been destroyed can be recovered. But it will require diligence, careful theological reflection, new training for musicians and pastors, educating the masses, resetting priorities, and, most of all, building a Christian community strong enough to sustain the necessary efforts.

Prayer

Majestic Lord, what we have to offer the world in your name is not entertainment, but a way of life that is present and eternal! Strengthen us for the work that lies before us . . . Amen.

Reaching Out, pp. 41, 48-50, 55.

For by the grace which has been given to me, I say to each who is among you not to be thinking more highly [of yourself] than it is necessary to think, but rather to be thinking for the purpose of sane thinking, as God has assigned to each one a measure of faith.

Romans 12:3 (my translation)

Paul's message must certainly be a critical one since he took such great care to introduce it. Basically, the message is composed of these three parts: (1) that Christians should not be too proud, (2) that Christians need to have a healthy assessment of themselves, and (3) that the criterion by which such thinking can be accurately done is one's measure of faith. . . .

God's undeserved love reminds us that we are nothing except for what God does in and through and for us. . . . On the other hand, that same grace also chose us, each of us uniquely, for special ministries within the community. . . .

The solution to false thinking about ourselves is to think about the entire "ourselves," the community as a whole. . . . We need to think sanely about what it means to be the people of God. . . .

Understanding ourselves according to our particular place as a part of the whole Body, none of us would have any basis for pride. On the other hand, each would recognize his or her absolute necessity in the Body. . . . You are the only one who can fill your place in our community. . . .

Sanely estimating our gifts and potentials together would increase our eagerness to contribute our own unique functions to the wholeness of the Body — and the whole community would . . . celebrate together who we are as the people of God. . . .

We don't compare our different kinds of faith to see whose is greater or smaller; instead, . . . we think about our unique participation in the Body. The fact that all us of have our own particular measure of faith to offer connects us vitally to each other — with equal importance. . . .

The question is . . . whether or not we are being obedient with what we have.

Prayer

Creator of our particularity, we thank you for our unique places in your Church . . .   Amen.

Truly the Community, pp. 65-74.

[W]e and our house will serve you, Lord;
your word we will obey.

Frederick William Foster (1826), alt.

It is crucially important . . . to examine our fundamental perception of why parents in the Christian community have children. . . . Before conception became a matter of choice, children were more often received as a gift, and life was devoted to raising them; now, parents (or even individuals) decide whether having them is an inconvenience or of benefit to themselves. This . . . shift turns the focus away from how parents invest themselves in their children to a new stress on the advantages children will be to them. . . .

This shift in perspective is enormously significant. It changes the major question from "How shall we raise children?" to "Do I want children?" or even "How can I avoid having children? . . . Our society has lost the sense that the nurturing of our offspring is a full-time task for both parents. I especially appreciate the comment of an acquaintance who reported that when friends ask her if her husband is baby-sitting the kids . . . she responds, "No, he is parenting." The very fact that this remark takes most of us by surprise shows how little we honor the calling of parents as the major vocation of both mother and father. . . .

In his book *A Community of Character,* Stanley Hauerwas . . . laments that the prevailing cultural assumptions in present society leave parents bereft of any notion that being a parent is an office of the community and not a willful act. To them belongs the primary (but not sole) responsibility for passing on the values of God's people. . . .

As an alternative society, we who are members of the Christian community have behaviors, lifestyles, and beliefs worth passing on to our offspring. We know that what we proclaim is the One who is the Truth, who is worthy of our children's acceptance. Moreover, in spite of the state of our world, by bringing children into the world we declare that there is hope, that God is indeed sovereignly good, and that he is able to use us as agents in his care for all his children.

Prayer
Heavenly Father, help us regain a sense of the Christian calling of parenthood
and of the role we each play in raising our community's children . . .
Amen.

Is It a Lost Cause? pp. 104, 108-10.

I said, "Oh, that I had the wings of a dove!
  I would fly away and be at rest —
I would flee far away
  and stay in the desert;
I would hurry to my place of shelter,
  far from the tempest and storm." . . .

Psalm 55:6-8

We don't have to feel guilty about such yearnings to run away from everything or everyone. Psalm 55 shows us legitimate reasons for wanting to give up. What matters is how we deal with those longings; to be realistic about them is a constructive beginning.

Because he is surrounded by so much turmoil and tumult that is out of his control, the poet David cries out . . . "Oh, that I had wings to fly away." . . . The same is true for us. . . . At those times our longing for retreat is prompted by a holy disquietude.

In the Garden of Gethsemane Jesus, too, was overwhelmed by the battle against evil. . . .

We cannot even begin to comprehend the intense torment of Christ's becoming sin for us (2 Cor. 5:21). We know the guilt we feel when we do something wrong. How could one ever stand the enormous suffering of all the brokenness of our world, all the hardships human beings inflict on each other, all the groaning of the whole creation? . . .

Jesus was God, of course, but he had laid the powers of his God-nature aside in order to live and die as a man for us. Consequently, he faced all that physical pain and emotional anguish and spiritual separation with the fears and despair of a human being. Yet, the writer to the Hebrews insists, he did not sin (Heb. 4:15).

To be horrified by the immensity of the battles of suffering before us is not to sin. What matters is what we do with the burden or sorrow. . . . What separates us from God is our inability to add, "Yet not as I will, but as you will" (Matt. 26:36-44).

Are we willing to believe in the midst of everything that God is infinitely wise and gracious? . . . Do we know that, though the powers of evil rage and cause chaos in our lives and world, Christ has triumphed over them and will someday obliterate them forever?

Prayer
  Comforting LORD, *be our shelter and our hope in the face of overwhelming*
  evil and chaos . . .   Amen.

I'm Lonely, LORD, pp. 43-45.

Grace and peace to you from him who is, and who was, and who is to come . . . and from Jesus Christ, who is the faithful witness. . . .

Revelation 1:4b-5a

"Was Jonah really swallowed by a whale?" "And did God really create the whole world in just seven 24-hour days?" . . .

These are the kinds of questions often asked by those who . . . want to prove that most of the stories in the Bible are not believable and thereby to render not viable the claims of Christianity.

While we must readily acknowledge that these are good questions, it is important to stress instead that they are not the place *to start* if we want to discuss the relative merits of various faith claims. If we want to debate the authenticity of Christianity or its relevance in this century, then we must begin with this central question: What do you think of the Christ?

Right at the beginning of his introduction to the book of Revelation, the seer John proclaims to us his understanding of who the Christ is and his significance for our lives. . . .

Jesus is called "the faithful witness." The Greek word order placing the adjective *after* the noun makes the point even more emphatically since he is thereby called "the witness, the faithful one." Indeed, Jesus is faithful in presenting to us what God wants to reveal about himself. What he shows us about God is guaranteed to be true. What confidence it gives us to know that we can always trust all that Jesus has demonstrated to us in his life and teaching about God.

The seer John declares that Jesus is the faithful witness, and that is the challenge we can set before others who question the merits of Christianity. We can demonstrate from his life and death and resurrection, from his ascension and the sending of the Holy Spirit, that Jesus is who he claimed to be. We can survey the First Testament to sketch his fulfillment of God's promises for the Jewish Messiah. Jesus incarnates for us what God is like so that we can begin to grasp the infinity of his love.

Prayer

Lord Jesus, we are thankful for you and for all the faithful witnesses — in the Bible, throughout the history of your Church, and in our lives today — who have testified to your love for us . . .   Amen.

Joy in Our Weakness, pp. 43-44.

Get you up to a high mountain,
　O Zion, herald of good tidings;
lift up your voice with strength,
　O Jerusalem, herald of good tidings;
　lift it up, do not fear;
say to the cities of Judah,
　"Here is your God!"

Isaiah 40:9 (NRSV)

Love stories and sports pride and Isaiah 40:9 all illustrate the principles of heralding good news. "Get you up to a high mountain," Zion is told. "Lift up your voice with strength," Jerusalem is commanded. If you have good news to tell, make sure you are visible to all, and then say it again louder, to be sure it is heard. . . .

The prophet's words to Zion are especially urgent for us now. In this postmodern, post-Christian age, we all need this kind of pep-rally encouragement to stir us up. A mistaken view of pluralism makes us afraid to speak about our commitment, and we fail to realize the incredible hunger for the good news we have to proclaim. Look at this message we are trying to cry out: Our God is here! How can we be so unmoved by such good news? . . .

First we are told to declare the good news, not from the valleys or the churches, but boldly from the top of the mountains, out in the open. . . . We are to get ourselves up to those lofty peaks as pilgrims go up to the temple of *YHWH.* . . .

Next, we are to exalt, or lift up, our voices with great strength. . . .

Then the positive encouragement is suddenly interrupted. . . . "Is fear the problem behind your delay? Then cast it aside!" Immediately, then, this negative reprimand is swallowed up by the glorious content of our heralding, "Behold your God!" We are to introduce him to the cities of Judah, to the people nearby. . . . It is the first step in loving evangelism. We have the privilege of saying to our friends next door and down the block and in the next office, "Let me introduce you to God!" . . .

Our witness takes place within our daily lives, in ordinary interactions and loving relationships. . . . It comes from a spontaneous reaction to the Joy-full realization that God is here and from a genuine love for the neighbor.

Prayer

Ever-present Lord*, give our voices strength, urgency, and Joy as we witness to our neighbors . . .　Amen.*

To Walk and Not Faint, pp. 52-55.

The LORD is my shepherd, I shall not be in want.
    He makes me lie down in green pastures,
he leads me beside quiet waters,
    he restores my soul.

Psalm 23:1-3a

How much Psalm 23 is loved by believers of all ages, but how rarely we truly understand the depth of comfort that it offers! Our Shepherd LORD not only provides for our physical nourishment by taking us to green pastures, but also enfolds us in contentment and tranquility by leading us beside the waters of stillness. Those words promise us profound solace for our spirits. . . .

The Hebrew word *shalom*, which we translate "peace," means, most importantly, "peace with God." If we are not at peace with God, no other kind of true peace is possible. As Christians we know that reconciliation with God has been made possible by the atoning work of Jesus Christ. . . . The freedom we experience because our sins are not counted against us makes us eager to carry that message of forgiveness to the world.

When we celebrate the resting aspect of Sabbath keeping, we become immersed more deeply in this peace of God, this awareness that all the barriers have been broken down. As a result, we are empowered to work to break down the barriers that divide the world around us. . . .

The greatest result of Sabbath resting is the opportunity to know the presence of God, no matter what our present circumstances might be. We do not need to rely on our own strength to deal with the tragic. Rather, spiritual rest gives us the freedom to accept the fact that human happiness is fleeting and to trust that there will be enough grace to carry us through all tragedy. We might be experiencing a time of sadness and mourning, but our faith assures us that God is with us in our sorrow to bring us the Joy of his presence. . . .

We are given the ability to live with paradox, to have faith in what we cannot see, to deal constructively with the tensions of contradictions. In short, spiritual rest enables us to let God be God. When we cease from all our labors to control or to understand, there is time in our space for the eternal.

Prayer

    O LORD, our Shepherd, we thank you for the peace that we can know and
    share, because you have reconciled us to yourself . . .   Amen.
Keeping the Sabbath Wholly, pp. 59-62.

I call upon the LORD, *who is worthy to be praised.* . . .

Psalm 18:3 (NRSV)

Only those who believe in God can *worship* God! Since the term *worship* has to do with *worthiness* of the One who is worshiped, certainly only those who know and acknowledge that worth can genuinely ascribe it and proclaim it. . . .

The ultimate well-being of the church is gravely sabotaged by . . . pastors and other leaders asking such questions as "How can worship be made more exciting for people in these postmodern times?" or "What style of music should we use to make our worship appealing to the 'unchurched'?" . . . It is crucial for us to comprehend that arguments about appealing to unbelievers by means of a particular style of worship betray a serious confusion between worship and evangelism, to the severe detriment of both. . . .

Churches think they're a "community" because that is what the word *church* suggests, without realizing how much the technological milieu hinders us from really caring for each other with the gutsy, sacrificial love of genuine community. Moreover, when we find out how much effort it takes truly to be the kind of community the Bible describes, we are often not willing to involve ourselves in that much struggle and suffering. In our overly entertained and blatantly consumerism-oriented culture, with little concern for serving the common good, many "churches" have become, in George Hunsberger's masterful phrases, "vendors of religious services and goods," instead of "a body of people sent on a mission."

To be truly the Church instead of merely a collection of religious shoppers means, primarily, for every single member of a genuine community to realize that the triune God has loved us first and called us to be his own — and to be his instruments. . . .

This is extremely important, for only if we truly understand such Churchbeing . . . can we really rediscover again and again the profound Joy of being God's people . . . in the rhythm of being nurtured by worship and then sharing our faith and love with our neighbors.

Let us keep that rhythm in mind lest we confuse worship and evangelism. Put simply, we must remember that worship is *for God*, in contrast to evangelism, which is *for the unbeliever.*

Prayer

> Worthy LORD, *sending Love, help us to offer true worship and evangelism —*
> *to give you glory and to love our neighbors . . .*   Amen.

A Royal "Waste" of Time, pp. 120-22.

*For just as we have many members in one body, and all the members do not have the
same function, so we, who are many, are one body in Christ. . . .*

                                                    Romans 12:4-5a (NASV)

How rarely it is truly understood in the Church that we are really all together one Body in Christ, and each member has a different function! . . .
Seldom do we actually manifest true unity/diversity in the Body, and, therefore, rarely do we set one another free for functioning in our own unique
ways. . . .

One manifestation of the lack of understanding of true community is
the fact that some functions are thought to be more important than others. . . .

It is only "with our eyes wide open to the mercies of God" that we can
begin to learn to be a community together. Romans 12:4-5a stresses that we
are "one body *in Christ.*" Because of our vital union with him, we find our
places in the Body. . . .

Imagine what would happen if our congregations truly functioned by
means of each person offering his or her gifts to the working together of the
whole, if we all understood ourselves not so much as individual Christians
but as members within the framework of the unity of the Body. . . .

Consider the tremendous vitality . . . the Church would have if those capable of particular functions eagerly volunteered to offer their gifts so that
the whole community could be strengthened. We would never have to
scramble to find . . . Sunday school teachers, youth counselors, officers, ushers, baby-sitters, or anything else. . . .

To work and share together more closely as a community is beneficial
not merely for its own sake. . . . Beyond that, the results of such sharing
would increase the credibility of our message of Christianity. . . .

We would have new opportunities to tell others how the love of God
draws all our diversities into unity. . . .

The extent to which each of us can live with others as members in community will vary, but the challenge of being the Body of Christ to extend his
presence in the world is a vital one for all of us in these times.

Prayer
> *Triune God, help us recognize that the diversity of our gifts and the unity of
> our mission together allow wholeness and witness . . .   Amen.*

                                                    Truly the Community, pp. 76-82.

Hear, O Israel: The Lord is one God, the Lord alone.

Deuteronomy 6:4

The most important part of being a parent is to have a heart — that is, a will — formed by God. . . .

The book of Deuteronomy is filled with instructions to Israel for living out their relationship with the Lord, and chapter 6 gives the best guidelines for parenting, . . . especially the declaration in verse 2 that God's goal for our children and grandchildren is for them to "fear" the Lord all the days of their lives. . . . Genuine biblical fear gives rise to true worship and the reverence that accompanies it, for we will never take it for granted that God allows us to know him and dwell in his presence. . . .

The people of God remember that the Lord is the only true God, a covenant God who always keeps his promises — and therefore we can trust him as we seek to serve him by raising children in the faith. Keeping ourselves focused on God's reign in our lives is the most essential and most beneficial requirement for parenting. . . .

"You shall love the Lord your God with all your heart, and with all your soul, and with all your might" (Deut. 6:5). Loving God is not a feeling (though sometimes feelings follow), but it is an act of the will. . . . Parents will model for their children what it means to live in faith if they themselves keep God as the center of their attitudes and intentions and decisions (heart), of their use of their gifts and talents and personality (soul), of their very expenditure of energy and time and resources (might).

"Keep these words that I am commanding you today in your heart" (v. 6). Parents will be more able and more ready to communicate God's desires and purposes to their children if they themselves are formed by the narratives of the Scriptures, if they intentionally keep God's will as the ground and fulfillment of their own. Parents will be equipped more thoroughly for this "remembering" if they are faithful participants in regular worship, if they engage in Bible study both personally and corporately, if they have daily devotional times of study, meditation, and prayer.

Prayer

Holy Spirit, we pray for all parents. Strengthen their faith, guide their efforts . . . Amen.

Is It a Lost Cause? pp. 110-12.

If an enemy were insulting me,
    I could endure it;
if a foe were raising himself against me,
    I could hide from him.
But it is you, a man like myself,
    my companion, my close friend,
with whom I once enjoyed sweet fellowship
    as we walked with the throng at the house of God.

Psalm 55:12-14

The poet . . . announces what for many of us has also been the greatest grief of our aloneness: that it was a close friend who hurt us most deeply. . . .

How can we endure the pain of being betrayed? . . .

Many of us have searched in vain for an answer to that question. We'll never find an explanation for the evil that causes those we love to hurt us. Yet the reality of that pain is too overwhelmingly real. "It is you," the poet says graphically, . . . "my friend and my acquaintance." . . .

This friend is one to whom the poet has disclosed his hidden self, the most profound truths of his being. Yet this is the one who has attacked him, who has violated the covenant that knitted them together (see vv. 20-21 of the psalm). . . .

In fact, they had walked together with the throng of worshipers at the house of God. . . . How do we deal with the rending torment that our life has been broken apart by someone with whom we once worshiped?

Perhaps one of the deepest tragedies of sin in the world is that it hits us in the hardest places. We might expect that the last source of pain would be our churches, yet it is often there that we are most deeply injured. . . .

Sin is more rupturing when its perpetrators call themselves people of faith. I won't offer any superficial comfort here. . . . How can we bear these incomprehensible hurts?

That is the poet's agony. That is ours. And that was the burden of Jesus. Only in that last fact can we begin to find a way to deal with the immensity of the pain.

Jesus endured everything that we do, including betrayal by one of his best friends, so that he knows our suffering. Indeed, he can stand beside us in every aspect of our loneliness and understand.

Prayer
    Gentle Jesus, you know our pain in betrayal. Your understanding is our only
    comfort . . .   Amen.

I'm Lonely, LORD, pp. 43, 47-49.

97

. . . Jesus Christ, who is the faithful witness, the firstborn from the dead, and the ruler of the kings of the earth.

Revelation 1:5

The seer John calls Jesus "the firstborn of the dead." . . . Christ's resurrection from the dead positively assures us that his work of redemption has fulfilled God's purposes, and therefore we are set free from our sins. Furthermore, his resurrection comforts us with the hope that someday we, too, shall rise (1 Cor. 15:20-22). Consequently, as we struggle with the limitations of this body and life, we can look forward with Joy to the time when those limitations will be swallowed up in death and we will receive a new body and an incorruptible existence.

The seer also tells us that Jesus is the one ruling with power and dignity over all the kings of the earth. What a substantial security that must have given the early Christians being persecuted by the Roman powers! . . .

The amazing thing about the reign of Jesus Christ over all the kings of the earth is that it is coupled with love. . . . We would hardly ever think that any of this world's rulers love us. The idea is almost ludicrous. On the other hand, throughout the Scriptures God's reign over the world has been described uniquely as a lordship that combines his sovereignty with his infinite love.

The seer describes Christ as the one who both loves us and has released us from our sins by his blood. Not only does his love reign now in our lives, but also that love caused him to be willing to sacrifice himself to make possible our release from the demonic rule of sin. . . .

That is why the seer reminds us that all glory and power belong to him into the ages of the ages. . . .

John wrote to encourage Christians who were tempted to give up their faith because of the oppressive powers of the Roman state. Similarly, in our times, we are constantly tempted to give undue authority to the powers of this world. The Revelation calls us back to the priority of Christ. Our values and choices must be directed by Jesus alone.

Prayer

> *O Lord, King of Kings, keep us mindful of your power, authority, and love when we are discouraged or overwhelmed by events around us . . .   Amen.*

Joy in Our Weakness, pp. 44-46.

Get you up to a high mountain,
    O Zion, herald of good tidings;
lift up your voice with strength,
    O Jerusalem, herald of good tidings;
    lift it up, do not fear;
say to the cities of Judah,
    "Here is your God!"

                                                    Isaiah 40:9 (NRSV)

We can speak so easily about the good things that happen in our daily lives, yet . . . these very good things are only going to pass away. Now here we have a message that abides forever — our God is here! — and yet we are actually afraid to tell other people. We are afraid they might be offended. . . . One of the greatest needs of contemporary Christian churches is to recover the invitation of this verse for our times. We need the boldness of the Hebrew prophets, the exuberance of the early Christians, the contagion of brand-new Christians who cannot help but tell those around them that God is here. . . .

   We are encouraged, in our Joy over the presence of the LORD, to witness freely, openly, even if that might cause us to become a target for persecution (as long as we are persecuted for the sake of the gospel and not because we deserve it!). The nature of the good news about God's gracious care for us is such that we don't mind being seen; we find it a privilege to tell others about the One we see. . . .

   Besides its application to our evangelism, this verse prods the Christian community to greater care for each other in the Body of Christ. Isaiah 40:9 commands us to lift our voices and not to fear as we remind other members, who might be down in the valleys and having trouble seeing, that God is here. We can gently offer a different perspective and incarnate for them tangibly God's loving presence in our own hugs, listening ears, and tender, practical concern. The secret of building the Christian community is the privilege of taking others by the hand to reveal to them the presence of God. This is the center of the gospel. Without God we have nothing. If *YHWH* is here, behold: we have everything.

Prayer
   Faithful LORD, *help us to gently, reverently, fearlessly, and openly communicate to all around us that you are here! . . .   Amen.*
                                          To Walk and Not Faint, pp. 52, 55-56.

The Word became flesh and made his dwelling among us.

John 1:14a

Sabbath resting is a foretaste of eternal life. Someday we shall know this rest ... in its fullness. For that reason, part of our Sabbath celebration is a prayer that we might someday come to the fulfillment of the Sabbath. This grows especially strong for me during the Advent season. On the first Sunday of Advent I always put up my angel choir and manger scene (without the Christ Child in it yet) to remember again what it means that Jesus came the first time, to repent that I'm never ready for his coming and that I always lose track of his presence in my daily life, and to anticipate, and yearn for, his coming again.

Some of the yearning can blessedly be a part of all our Sabbath celebrations. The Jews bid good-bye to the Sabbath with final prayers that include a pang of longing for its next appearance seven days later. When we live for our Sabbaths, when they are the climax of our weeks, we know a healthy anticipation of the ultimate rest, the time when Jesus will come to take us home. . . .

Sabbath keeping is one way to anticipate our going home and, in part, to experience its Joys even now. . . . As Abraham Heschel teaches us, the Sabbath prayers are different from those of ordinary days in which we ask God to guard our going out and our coming in. On the Sabbath instead we ask God to embrace us with the tent of his peace. That image is extraordinarily powerful throughout the Scriptures because it connotes the presence of God in a very special way. When the earliest people of Israel wandered in the wilderness, their tent of God's presence was particularly visited with Yahweh's glory. . . . Furthermore, in the incarnation of Jesus, God "pitched his tent and dwelt among us, full of grace and truth" (a literal translation of John 1:14). Finally, at the end of the Scriptures, in the book of Revelation, we are promised that at the end of time "he who sits on the throne will spread his tent" over his people (Rev. 7:15b).

In our Sabbath prayers, then, we request the profound rest of God. We ask him to embrace us with the tent of his peace, the very dwelling of his presence.

Prayer

> O Lord, bless our Sabbaths with your tent of peace . . .   Amen.
> *Keeping the Sabbath Wholly,* pp. 62-64.

God's gift to his sorrowing creatures is to give them Joy worthy of their destiny.

                                        J. S. Bach, 1685-1750

If the Church's worship is faithful, it will eventually be subversive to the culture surrounding it, for God's truth transforms the lives of those nurtured by it. Worship will turn our values, habits, and ideas upside-down as it forms our character; only then will we be genuinely right-side up eternally. Only then will we know a Joy worthy of our destiny. . . .

God's revelation, conveyed in worship through hymns, sermons, and liturgies, unmasks our illusions about ourselves. It exposes our pride, our individualism, our self-centeredness — in short, our sin. But worship also offers forgiveness, healing, transformation, motivation, and courage to work in the world for God's justice and peace — in short, salvation in its largest sense.

Talking of sin and forgiveness certainly runs counter to the present culture, but the recognition of each and both together is the great gift of the Church's worship to our world's self-understanding. . . .

The Church cannot save the culture — but Christians could be the best thinkers in the world. Because our relationship with God frees us from having to justify our own existence, we do not have to prove our importance, fit in with our peers, mimic the politically correct, or think according to the current ideologies or idolatries. . . .

In attempting to enliven the Church's worship, many try to spice it up with new enthusiasm, engineered with the proper techniques. . . . Instead of techniques of revival, the Church needs genuine reformation. . . .

To utilize only new worship forms without connections to the past heritage is to isolate only a few years out of the 3,500-year history of the Judeo-Christian tradition. Reformation always returns to and deepens the gifts of the original. On the other hand, without reformation the tradition becomes distorted, stale, or dead — or an idolatry. . . .

By maintaining a vital, balanced dialectic of thought and feelings, the Church exposes the shallowness or emptiness of our culture's laughter and instead trains people in habits for thinking. Genuine worship does, indeed, teach people the depth of truth and enables them to laugh freely with a "Joy worthy of their destiny."

Prayer
> *Praiseworthy God, help us worship faithfully, experiencing true Joy in response to your message of salvation, rather than just fun according to our culturally induced desires . . .   Amen.*

                                        Reaching Out, pp. 57-60, 69-72.

. . . and each member belongs to all the others.

Romans 12:5b

How little the Church truly understands that we actually belong to one another! How much power is short-circuited . . . because we have not learned, or are not free, or do not want to belong to each other? . . .

Certainly, our separation from God is the root cause. . . . We get greedy because we do not believe that God truly will provide for all our material needs. We become anxious because we do not trust God for the future. We resort to violence because we think that we have to create our own way. We are selfish and possessive because we fear that we will not be able to satisfy our emotional desires. When our devotional and worship lives suffer, we lack the relationship with God that enables us to find harmony with others and with ourselves. Lacking peace with God, we cannot be at peace with anybody else. The root of our failures to share in community, then, lies in our unbelief.

Fundamentally, part of what it means to be made in God's image is that we are all created with an intense longing for God. If we cannot meet that need, we desperately try to fill the gap with all sorts of other gods.

As long as we look for our needs to be met by persons, we will always be disappointed. . . . No person is perfect; no one can take the place of God in our lives. Rather, in . . . true community we learn together that we will find our needs thoroughly met only in our relationship with God. Our alienation from him prevents us from discerning ways in which other persons can minister to our needs. . . .

Above all, we must continually recognize that the only source of ultimate contentment is God. All other gifts just point to his adequacy. Only his grace carries the promise of sufficiency for all our needs (2 Cor. 12:9).

If our relationship with God is sound, then we are set free to work to dismantle the barriers that alienate us from one another.

Prayer

Enfolding God, forgive us and draw us close, so that as we belong to you, your intention for us to belong to each other will also be fulfilled . . .   Amen.

Truly the Community, pp. 84-88.

Keep these words that I am commanding you today in your heart. Recite them to your children and talk about them when you are at home and when you are away, when you lie down and when you rise. Bind them as a sign on your hand, fix them as an emblem on your forehead, and write them on the doorposts of your house and on your gates.

Deuteronomy 6:6-9 (NRSV)

What a delightful command these verses are — urging parents to talk about the Word of God continually with their children. The New Revised Standard Version's translation "recite" sounds a bit too formal for the intention of verse 7. The Hebrew root actually means to whet or sharpen, so the recitation is meant to teach, to repeat so that our children understand and appreciate. The New International Version captures the spirit of the Hebrew phrase better by rendering it "impress them on your children." By talking of God's purposes and instructions both when we are at home and when we are away (in other words, all the time), we will really imprint our children with these formative influences. By talking of biblical guidelines and desires when we lie down and when we rise . . . we will begin and end and continue our days in light of God's direction. . . .

Metaphorically, Hebrew literature uses the word *hand* to signify our actions, and still today the image of the forehead portrays our thinking. Thus verse 8 urges parents to keep God in all of their conduct and thoughts. . . . While symbols might help to keep us focused, the chief emphasis of this verse is that the values of God's kingdom should be firmly inscribed and established in our minds and wills, our behaviors and deeds. Just as verse 7 gives us four times (encompassing all times) in which we speak to our children about God, verses 8 and 9 give us four places (thus every place) that we can put symbols to help ourselves remember God's instructions in all of life. . . . Do the symbols on our walls, the magazines on our coffee tables, the books on our shelves, our habits and behaviors demonstrate God's presence? Our children are formed by the milieu in which they live, both visibly and experientially.

Prayer

> *Ever-present Lord, help us talk about your Word with our children and live it before them — everywhere and always . . .   Amen.*

Is It a Lost Cause? pp. 112-14.

But I call to God,
  and the LORD saves me.
Evening, morning and noon
  I cry out in distress,
  and he hears my voice. . . .
Cast your cares on the LORD
  and he will sustain you;
  he will never let the righteous fall.

Psalm 55:16-17, 22

As in many other lament psalms, the composer David moves in Psalm 55 from stating his difficulties to asserting, "But I call to God." This is the response to adversity by the person of faith. . . .

In verse 17 . . . the poet says graphically, "In the evening and in the morning and at midday I will complain and groan." This is the picture of a soul in dire distress and prayer, and it underscores the deep compassion and sympathy with which *YHWH* responds. . . .

A student once asked me how often to pray for a particular request. As long as our mind is not settled about an issue, we might as well be honest with God and with ourselves by pouring out our feelings about it. Why compound our struggles by being phony with God? . . .

That freedom to be real is especially comforting because, as the poet continues, *YHWH* "hears my voice." When we complain continually to those around us, they get tired of listening and sometimes close their ears to our pleas. In contrast, *YHWH* will always listen to our cries. . . .

We can be sure when God sustains us that he does not merely prop us up. His nourishment enables us to endure. When we cast our burdens upon the LORD, they might not go away, but we will be able to stand them. . . .

The pain is there. We cannot chase it away; we cannot deny its existence; we cannot even cope with it successfully. But we can cry out to *YHWH,* and he will hear. When we fling the burden of that pain upon him, he will grant the relief that enables us to bear the scar constructively. We will learn in truth to love the scar as a sign of how deeply we are loved and of the suffering involved in bearing the cost of loving. It is a sign that links us to Jesus, who paid the ultimate price of costly loving.

Prayer

  O Lord Jesus, you paid the price to listen in love, to bear our pain with us, to sustain us. Thank you . . .   Amen.

I'm Lonely, LORD, pp. 50-55.

Look, he is coming with the clouds
  and every eye will see him,
even those who pierced him:
  and all the peoples of the earth will mourn because of him
    So shall it be! Amen.
"I am the Alpha and the Omega," says the Lord God, "who is, and who was, and
who is to come, the Almighty."

Revelation 1:7-8

We cannot know the times or seasons for the purposes of God. Jesus declared that even he didn't know. . . . All that we can know about Christ's second coming . . . is that when he comes in the clouds no one will miss him. That is all we need to know. And because we do know that, we don't have to fear about the end, but we can be busy until it happens doing the work of the kingdom and being faithful to our priesthood. . . .

"So shall it be! Amen" doubly emphasizes that this shall indeed come true, and reminds us that the coming of Jesus will introduce a dramatic division of the world into those who have responded to his love and accepted his ruling lordship and those who continue to pierce him. Then, extra affirmation is added by the potent reminder in verse 8 of who this God is who declares these things, for the Lord God himself is the Alpha and the Omega, the beginning and the end. . . . Surely here, as nowhere else in the New Testament, the image of God as the powerful one, able to do whatever fits his purposes, is especially reinforced. . . . As surely as God has always been and always will be and truly is now — as surely as he is the Almighty One, totally capable of accomplishing whatever he purposes — so surely can we know that when Christ comes the whole world will know it, and everyone in it will be compelled to acknowledge his lordship.

All sorts of principalities and powers do battle against that lordship . . . and many times the circumstances in which we find ourselves seem to indicate anything but his lordship. That is why we need the book of Revelation — to keep reminding us . . . that when he comes again the whole world shall recognize the truth of his claims.

Prayer
  Alpha and Omega, we praise you as the Almighty One, able to accomplish all
  that you purpose . . .   Amen.

Joy in Our Weakness, pp. 47-48.

*Behold, the Lord G*OD *comes with might,*
with His arm ruling for Him.
Behold, His reward is with Him
and His recompense before Him.

Isaiah 40:10 (NASV)

Two strong uses of the Hebrew word for "Behold" begin the two sets of parallel lines to urge us to sit up and take notice of the way God comes. . . .

It is the "Lord GOD" who comes with might. The Hebrew words are *Adonai YHWH,* sovereign ruler and covenant God. He comes with all the fullness of his paramount lordship, but also as the faithful, promising "I AM." His might is directed toward the fulfilling of his covenant vows, the perfecting of his relationship with his people. . . .

How frightful it would be if God exerted his might without the covenant relationship! How terrible God would appear to us if we did not know that his power has its dominion for our benefit! His arm upraised to rule for him would terrify us if we did not know the graciousness of his lordly rule. . . .

Isaiah 40:10 also presents the picture of the Lord GOD bringing gifts with him, though the nature of the reward that is with him is not specified. The Hebrew word means "wages." . . . The term implies the fulfillment of God's promises to those who serve him. He has promised to his people rewards of present freedom, constant security, ultimate victory, and eternal rest. How different this is from the world's rewards, which depend upon human circumstances right now and eventually pass away. . . .

These are fruitful images for showing God to a hopeless world. The great overarching narrative of the Hebrew and Christian Scriptures reveals the Lord GOD as one who always keeps his promises. That invites us to understand our own life story as it is placed into the larger story and to claim God's promises and fulfillments for our own lives. The promise in Isaiah 40 of his coming with might is only partially fulfilled now for us, too, but the resurrection of Jesus and his sending of the Holy Spirit convinces us that God's promises can be trusted for time and eternity.

Prayer
*O Lord G*OD, *we praise and thank you for coming to us mightily and faithfully and for blessing us so richly as we live in a covenant relationship with you . . . Amen.*

To Walk and Not Faint, pp. 58-61.

*Observe the Sabbath day by keeping it holy, as the Lord your God has commanded
you. Six days you shall labor and do all your work, but the seventh day is a Sabbath to
the Lord your God. On it you shall not do any work, neither you, nor your son or
daughter, nor your manservant or maidservant, nor your ox, your donkey or any of
your animals, nor the alien within your gates, so that your manservant and maidservant may rest, as you do.*

Deuteronomy 5:12-14

When we know the spiritual rest of Sabbath keeping, we are thoroughly set
free to rest physically. My Sabbath days often include sleeping later in the
morning or taking naps or going to bed earlier at night. . . .

The emphasis upon physical rest as the meaning of the Sabbath is especially strong in the account of the commandment recorded in Deuteronomy 5, in contrast to the account in Exodus 20, which celebrates the Sabbath as an imitation of God's ceasing from his creative activity on the
seventh day. . . . The commandment is quite clear: each person is to cease
from work — not only the masters, but also all the servants and the foreigners and the animals. . . .

We might have trouble putting this idea into modern terms. . . . However, we can look for a similar contrast between our weekday and Sabbath
activity. If we are primarily engaged in physical exertion during the week,
the Sabbath offers a physical respite. For those of us involved in the opposite rhythm of sedentary labor, the Sabbath offers us a contrasting change
of gentle physical enjoyment. . . .

We must often take extra care to make it possible to rest from our labors on the Sabbath. Sometimes it means doing extra work the day before
or spreading our work out throughout the week a bit better so that the Sabbath can truly be restful. If I'm going to teach on Monday, I need to do the
final review of my plans on Saturday — which usually means double duty,
since I'm generally teaching on Sunday, too. . . . But in the freedom I experience throughout the complete day of Sabbath rest I continually find that
the extra effort to get everything done before Sunday is worth it.

Prayer
    *O Lord our God, we thank you for the blessedness of Sabbath rest . . .
    Amen.*

Keeping the Sabbath Wholly, pp. 66-68.

I will praise you, O LORD, with all my heart;
I will tell of all your wonders.

Psalm 9:1

Many pastors, lay leaders, and national church officers seem to be thoroughly disdaining God's own instructions when they accept the false advice of marketing gurus to "throw out the traditions" of their churches in order to "appeal" to the world around them and thereby "grow." . . .

The result of this hard sell is often a push for a worship style that lacks theological substance, invites passivity, and fosters an easy-listening consumerism that provides neither music nor words that will help worship participants remember deep truths. One dire consequence of adopting this quick-fix technique is that *the real problems* — namely, *failure to educate* concerning the meaning and practice of worship, *failure to understand* the real idolatries that keep people from participating in the Church, and *failure to equip* the priesthood of all believers for outreach to the world — *remain unaddressed.* . . .

The worship service is part of the entire educational process of the Christian community by which God's people are equipped to introduce others to his worthiness. Evangelism or sharing is done by all of us who realize that everyone around us needs God's grace. Out of our love for God and our love for those neighbors, we are eager to serve them and pass on the witness of faith. Evangelism happens in our daily lives, our regular encounters, our simple conversations and caring — or at evangelistic events, which have a focus different from that of worship — in order that we can bring others with us to worship God. . . . Evangelism is the means; worship is the end.

Worship is the language of love and growth between believers and God; evangelism is the language of introduction between those who believe and those who don't. To confuse the two and put on worship the burden of evangelism robs the people of God of their responsibility to care about the neighbor, defrauds the believers of transforming depth, and steals from God the profound praise of which he is worthy. . . .

Prayer
> *O LORD, forgive us for thinking we can use the time we have set aside to worship you to cop out of our work of evangelism. Empower us both to worship you and to witness to others in ways that honor you and meet our neighbors' needs . . .   Amen.*

A Royal "Waste" of Time, pp. 122-24.

But having grace-gifts according to the grace which has been given us — different. . . .
Romans 12:6a (my translation)

Most of the English translations of Romans 12:6 miss the utter simplicity of the text as it describes God's grace-gifts. They are not worked for, cannot be created by us, and could never be bought or sold or acquired in any way by human effort. They simply are there. Given. . . .

We simply continue to have the grace-gifts that have been given to us. They are an immense power inherently there, waiting to be used and exercised for the benefit of the whole Body of Christ. Since we are members one of another, we are called to a great responsibility in that having.

Now what exactly do we have? . . . The Greek word for grace is *charis,* and so the word *charismata* signifies gifts that come from, and reveal, God's grace, God's unlimited and undeserved love. . . .

The very idea of grace implies lavishness. . . . How could God be stingy about his gifts which distribute grace? . . .

Paul gives us a list of seven gifts in Romans 12. . . . The very fact that seven are itemized here confirms that the list offers samples. Throughout the Scriptures the number seven is used symbolically to indicate perfection. . . . Paul used sevens in a similar way simply to offer a symbolic representation of all of the grace-gifts. . . .

God's grace is all of one kind: totally undeserved, never to be repaid, never to be earned, always fully flowing, . . . never arbitrary, nor anything but holy and perfect. . . .

Such a concept eliminates any possibility for jealousy in the Body of Christ. There is no such thing as being more or less gifted than another. All persons are gifted with a fullness of grace, though that grace takes different manifestations in particular individuals. Still the grace is the same. . . .

We can never figure out how the Giver of grace-gifts does the dispensing. His work is never the same.

He gives to each of us different combinations of gifts. Furthermore, he gives us each different gifts for different times. . . . appropriate to the circumstances. . . . Grace has already been given; we are privileged to serve as channels for its flowing.

Prayer
Generous God, we thank and praise you for the grace-gifts we are privileged to receive and share . . .   Amen.

Truly the Community, pp. 92-99.

The LORD your God you shall fear; him you shall serve, and by his name alone you shall swear. Do not follow other gods, any of the gods of the peoples who are all around you, because the LORD your God, who is present with you, is a jealous God. . . . Then the LORD commanded us to observe all these statutes, to fear the LORD our God, for our lasting good, so as to keep us alive, as is now the case.

Deuteronomy 6:13-14, 24 (NRSV)

Do we take seriously enough the righteous jealousy of God? To recognize that God has a *right* to our obedience . . . is properly to fear the LORD. Though many psalms and proverbs repeatedly tell us that "the fear of the LORD is the beginning of wisdom," the language of fear is hardly used in our day. We want to turn God into a nice cozy buddy, with whom anything goes. But God's righteous jealousy is directed toward our benefit. . . .

The Israelites continually rebelled against God's Lordship in their lives — and paid the price in human terms. They deserved and got oppression, destruction, bondage, exile. God certainly doesn't want such things to happen to his people, but our sin carries within it the potential and impetus for consequences. Our enemies are totally different these days — heart attacks and other stress diseases, family breakdown and dissolution, public exposure and legal recriminations, the principalities and powers of our society — but the logic is the same. We wreak our own havoc when we turn to other gods and away from the covenant LORD who is, and promises to be, present with us. . . .

The truth is that life simply works better when we live in tune with the designs of its Creator. God's commands are not hammers over our heads to get us to shape up. Rather, they are his loving instructions for how to do what is right and good, so that life may go well. . . . God's instructions are not onerous burdens; they are for our good, "so that it may go well" with us. It is critical that we help our children learn that about God. The LORD never gives commands to spoil our fun; rather, his rules are intended to deepen it.

Prayer

O LORD our God, help us to trust and follow your commands, and teach us to fear and honor you . . .   Amen.

Is It a Lost Cause? pp. 114-16.

When I am afraid
  I will trust in you.
In God, whose word I praise,
  in God I trust; I will not be afraid.
  What can [flesh] do to me?

Psalm 56:3-4

To be Christians does not necessarily mean that we are not afraid. . . .

The words of Psalm 56 speak great comfort to us — especially because . . . the great hero David admits honestly that at times even he is afraid. It is in those times that his trust in *YHWH* is particularly developed. . . .

He says "When I am afraid" as a preface to the declaration "I will trust in you."

More than our English translations, the original Hebrew construction emphasizes that trust can characterize those times when we are afraid. . . . In other words, at the very time when we are afraid, that is the time for trust. . . .

We can react to fear in this way because we have complete assurance that *YHWH* will take care of us. His covenant relationship with us has provided us with promises that are foundations for our trust. That is why the psalmist continues by proclaiming, "in God, whose word I praise." His word is to be praised because it reveals to us the character of our faithful God. Scriptural accounts give us more than enough evidence that he is eminently worthy of our trust. . . .

Furthermore, the discipline of memorizing the Scriptures can put the Word in our thoughts, readily available for us to be reminded of the character of our God. Then we have something tangible to lean on — specific promises addressed to us to cling to when we are afraid. . . .

In the final phrase of verse 4, the poet adds this extra reason why we no longer have to be afraid: "What can flesh do to me?" . . .

Psalm 56:3-4 shows us what to do with our fears. If we begin by looking at the character of the God on whom we rely and concentrate on trusting him even though we fear, then we will be able to move to thanksgiving for the truth of his Word, which will set us free to trust without being afraid.

Prayer
  Comforting God, when we are afraid, help us follow King David's example
  in trusting and praising you . . .   Amen.

I'm Lonely, LORD, pp. 58-64.

I turned around to see the voice that was speaking to me. And when I turned I saw seven golden lampstands, and among the lampstands was someone "like a son of man" . . .

Revelation 1:12-13a

We need to take the Scriptures seriously, to believe that what they say is indeed the vital Word of God, authoritative to guide our lives in truth. To interpret the Scriptures literalistically, on the other hand, is to forget that the Word of God is magnificent literature, making inspired use of symbols and metaphors and other artistic devices to underscore its message. The book of Revelation offers many pictures that are not to be understood as "visual reality," but as true symbols signifying various dimensions of the character of God. Thus, from the picture of Christ in Revelation 1:12-20, we learn much about his character, but certainly cannot draw a portrait of him. . . .

The truth is that we cannot use the Scriptures to describe anything other than the character Jesus reveals to us. All these images are designed to usher us into his presence, but once there we realize that he is too glorious in his lordship for us to do anything but describe him inadequately and recognize our limitations in perceiving him. . . .

This does not at all discount the fact of inspiration. Rather, it underscores the wonder that God condescended to inspire the biblical writers to convey the truth of his character in words that bring his presence to readers unable in their human and finite abilities to comprehend his transcendence.

Thus, the seer describes the Son of Man with many expressions of majesty, each of which brings to mind images and attributes revealed in the Hebrew Scriptures. The first of these is the very title "Son of Man." Occurring over fifty times in the book of Ezekiel and at a strategic spot in the book of Daniel, the term was well known in Israelite circles, to the extent that when Jesus called himself by that name, he was greeted immediately with charges of blasphemy. . . . In Daniel 7:13-14 the Son of Man goes to the Ancient of Days and receives from him dominion and glory and a kingdom that shall not be destroyed.

Prayer
    Ancient of Days, thank you for revealing your character through Jesus' life, death, and resurrection and through the words of Scripture . . .   Amen.

Joy in Our Weakness, pp. 49-50.

Like a shepherd He will tend his flock,
In His arm He will gather the lambs,
and carry [them] in His bosom,
He will gently lead the nursing [ewes].

Isaiah 40:11 (NASV)

"Like one shepherding," the original Hebrew literally begins. . . .

What a gently loving contrast this verse forms with the preceding one. The same Hebrew word for arm occurs in both, but the arm that ruled and declared God's might in Isaiah 40:10 now fondly gathers the lambs whom he shepherds. This is a picture to be cherished. . . . We need to know that God exerts his power and strength on our behalf — but we also need to know that in his dealings with us he comes faithfully like a shepherd. . . .

"Like one pasturing, his flock he tends." . . . God carefully provides for our feeding in all situations. A strong hope lies in this promise that wherever we go or whatever we do, as we make use of the means of grace that God provides in his Word and his people, *YHWH* will sustain us and address our deepest needs. . . .

With what variety and thoroughness the LORD provides so that his people are fed! He nurtures us through the disciplines of our own devotional times and meditations. He propels us by means of preachers and teachers and practitioners of his Word. He sustains us through the vitality of Christian communities and assemblies of believers. He nourishes us through music. He uplifts us with breathtaking sunsets and the myriad hues of flowers. . . .

The last two phrases of verse 11 amplify the picture. . . .

When we are young and not able to walk, *YHWH* lifts us up and furnishes the transportation. When we are older and don't know which direction to go, he shows us the way. We don't know how to walk in the freedom of the Christian life unless we have first been carried by grace. We must begin by resting in the LORD and allowing him to do everything on our behalf (that is, forgiving us, giving us new life, transforming us). With that essential foundation of grace, we then learn to live out the freedom of our faith.

Prayer

> *Loving Shepherd, we thank you for your tender care. Truly, we shall not want . . . Amen.*

To Walk and Not Faint, pp. 64-71.

Elijah was afraid and ran for his life. . . . He came to a broom tree, sat down under it and prayed that he might die. . . . Then he lay down under the tree and fell asleep.

1 Kings 19:3-5

In our lives we experience the same kind of emotions that overwhelmed Elijah in his encounter with the priests of Baal on the top of Mount Carmel. No doubt he felt fear, exhilaration, terror, confidence, panic, delight, and doubt all mixed together. No wonder he wanted to die. Yet the first thing Yahweh does for him is put him to sleep.

This makes perfect sense. We cannot deal very well with our emotional needs unless we are first physically rejuvenated. The Sabbath offers us physical rest — the ceasing of labors and sleep to restore us — and then it offers us emotional rest, especially by giving us a new perspective.

I remember viewing a series of eight Impressionist paintings in a special exhibit and discovering that, when I stood in a new place, the painting that I liked least danced out of the corner with a new beauty. In the same way, the Sabbath gives us emotional rest by offering us a different place to stand in our relationship with God, with ourselves, and with the world.

After Elijah has been strengthened physically, God deals with his emotions by meeting him in a new way — in the quiet, gentle whisper of his tender love. God doesn't criticize Elijah for his doubts and fears, but meets him graciously, asks him why he is so upset, listens to his repeated complaint, and gives him new instructions for what to do next. . . .

The Sabbath is a day set apart for deepening our relationship with God, and that necessarily leads to emotional healing. God meets us graciously in the reading of Scripture and the sermon, in the hymns and the liturgy, and in the prayers of our corporate worship services. He reveals himself to us in tender and compassionate ways. Moreover, God meets us in our personal prayers, which give us the opportunity to pour out our feelings — knowing that God will listen. In our quiet devotional times, too, God often gives us specific instructions for proceeding with whatever is happening in our lives.

Prayer

Loving God, help us discover in Sabbath rest the perspective you would give us to deal with our emotional upheavals . . . Amen.

Keeping the Sabbath Wholly, pp. 73-74.

I have tasted You, and I hunger and thirst for you.
You have touched me, and I ardently desire Your peace.

Augustine of Hippo, 354-430

In genuine worship God is the subject — and we are not. . . . Augustine's poem makes clear this most crucial criterion for assessing our worship: True worship arises because God calls us. As an echo, our worship directed to God is a gift in response to his gifts. . . .

It is absolutely essential that the Church keep God as the subject of worship since to be Christian means to believe that the God revealed in Jesus Christ is everything to us — Creator, Provider, and Sustainer; Deliverer, Redeemer, and Lord; Sanctifier, Inspirer, and Empowerer. Friendship, instruction, and other aspects of the gathered community are important, but we lose our reason for being if we do not constantly remember that God has called us to be his people and that our ability to respond to that call in worship and in life is totally the gift of God's grace.

We who live by the name *Christian* are those rescued from ourselves by the salvation wrought by Jesus. Since salvation is entirely God's gift and not deserved or earned, Christian worship above all makes clear who is the giver of that and every other gift and challenges the world to respond to who he is.

The word *worship* comes from the Old English roots *weorth,* meaning "honor" and "worthiness," and *scipe,* signifying "to create." Of course, we cannot "create" God's honor because it is inherently God's, but we do devise ways to honor God that bespeak his worthiness, all the while recognizing that our attempts are inadequate, that we will never duly laud the Trinity until we join the saints and angels in perfectly glorifying God forever.

Prayer
O Lord, our Creator, Deliverer, and Empowerer, may our worship ever be our gift of gratitude in response to your call — that we may focus on who you are and all that you have given, in love, to us . . .   Amen.

Reaching Out, pp. 75-77.

. . . whether prophecy — according to the agreement of the faith!

Romans 12:6b (my translation)

Why would anyone undertake being a prophet? Simply, one must be faithful to God in the "having" of the prophetic gift. . . .

The dramatic terseness of Paul's style intensely underscores his point. Whatever our gifts might be, the only response is to use them. . . . Indeed, we can only discover the truth of our lives when we explore it full tilt. . . .

Paul first advocates full tiltedness in using the gift of prophecy — a good one to begin a study of the charisms (grace-gifts) since it is the one most frequently misunderstood. Too often the word *prophecy* is associated with slightly odd persons who predict such things as the collapse of the field-house roof at the University of Georgia, a "prophecy" given but not fulfilled the year my brother went there. . . .

Discussions about the "end times" especially distort biblical truth. Spiritual power for the work to which God calls us is lost through worrying about signs that count down the calendar to "prove" that Jesus is coming again soon. . . .

The Church desperately needs a new emphasis on the prophetic gift because true prophecy equips us for being God's people in the present.

Genuine prophecy entails applying the message of God, usually from the Scriptures, to the situations of our times. Rather than merely foretelling, it can be better defined as "forthtelling." The latter might give rise to the former if a person observes circumstances thoughtfully enough to recognize what events might follow. Especially if a person carefully reads the Scriptures, he or she will know that particular styles of life lead to inevitable consequences. The function of a prophet, then, is to speak out against these destructive elements in order to warn participants of their dangers. . . .

We must especially keep in mind . . . that grace-gifts are given to the *Church,* for the strengthening of the community. . . . If prophets among us exercise their desperately needed gifts, the Church will be changed. . . . Only as we become a Christian community with a truly biblical lifestyle can our prophetic words carry the credibility of a demonstrated alternative to the society around us.

Prayer

Lord of the present and future, give courage to the prophets among us to speak your truth. Give us courage to listen . . .   Amen.

Truly the Community, pp. 101-7.

When your children ask you in time to come, "What is the meaning of the decrees and the statutes and the ordinances that the LORD our God has commanded you?" then you shall say to your children, ". . . If we diligently observe this entire commandment before the LORD our God, as he has commanded us, we will be in the right."

Deuteronomy 6:20, 21a, 25 (NRSV)

Verse 20 presupposes several things — that our children will be acquainted with the decrees and statutes and ordinances, that they will know the LORD, that they will want to know the meaning of what he has commanded. These assumptions provide clear guidelines for parenting that are being ignored these days. For example, too many youth that I encounter have never heard from their parents anything about God's commands for their sexuality. Too many young people don't ask their parents about the meaning of the latter's faith because they don't see that it makes much difference in their elders' lives. . . .

The faith the people of Israel recounted to their children was a communal one — not so much the testimony common today of one's personal relationship with God, but rather a witness to the way in which God has led and dealt with the community. Many of the phrases in these verses are customary creedal lines by which the Hebrew people reported their faith. In the same way, it is essential that we immerse our children in the *Christian* faith, the belief of a community that goes back to Abraham and Sarah, Mary and John, and that stretches throughout the globe. We don't so much seek to develop in them their own faith as to make them an active part of the faith that already exists in a people.

The original Hebrew sentence of verse 25 begins with the end of this English rendering: it will be *righteousness* to us. It will be fitting, good, for our well-being. Oh, how blessed our families will be if we live according to God's design! How blessed are the children who grow up in a home devoted to God's purposes, with mothers and fathers who fulfill their parenting role first of all by loving the LORD their God with all their heart and soul and might, and then by passing that love on to their offspring!

Prayer

O LORD our God, help us as parents, teachers, and friends to share with our young your guidelines for a righteous life . . .   Amen.

Is It a Lost Cause? pp. 116-17.

You have kept count of my tossings;
 put my tears in your bottle.
 Are they not in your record?
Then my enemies will retreat
 in the day when I call.
 This I know, that God is for me.

Psalm 56:8-9 (NRSV)

Differences in translations reveal the Hebrew text's ambiguity. . . . The New Revised Standard Version reports that *YHWH* has "kept count of my tossings." The New International Version renders the Hebrew noun as a "lament" to be recorded. The Jerusalem Bible uses the translation "agitation," whereas the New American Standard Version employs the idea of "wanderings." The point in all these versions is that God cares about us. In the midst of our confusions, aimless wanderings, agitations, tossings, and lamentations, he is keeping a careful record. . . .

The command to God to "put my tears in your bottle" (NRSV) is an arresting image. The child who cries in our presence wants us to share in her sadness. Similarly, our tears are usually easier to bear if someone knows about them. If there could only be someone significant to consider that we have cried ourselves to sleep! The poet asks God to keep all those tears in his wineskin, lest they will have been cried in vain. . . .

Ultimately, tears cannot overwhelm us because God has recorded them. That is why the poet can continue, "Then my enemies will be turned back in the day when I call." . . .

The stronger Hebrew expression of confidence insists, "Then shall the ones hating me turn back [in fear and shame] in the day when I cry out for help." Because God is on our side to record our tears and fears, the foes will be either ashamed or terrified of the power he uses on our behalf.

The concluding belief of verse 9 proclaims even more assurance. "This I know, that God is for me" (NRSV). We might not know any other comfort in the troubles of our lives, but this is not an empty promise: Our God is for us. . . .

Therefore, we respond with thank offerings. The poet promises to fulfill his vows, and we turn with praise to use our lives in gratitude and Joyfull acclamation. After all, this is what we know: Our God is for us!

Prayer

God who records our tears and tossings, how comforting is your care. We thank you that we can say with the psalmist: Our God is for us! . . . Amen.

I'm Lonely, LORD, pp. 65-70.

. . . When I turned I saw seven golden lampstands, and among the lampstands was someone "like a son of man," dressed in a robe reaching down to his feet and with a golden sash around his chest. His head and hair were white like wool, as white as snow, and his eyes were like blazing fire. He feet were like bronze glowing in a furnace, and his voice was like the sound of rushing waters.

Revelation 1:12-15

This Son of Man is . . . dressed in the golden belt that might be expected of one so royal. His long, flowing robe reaching to his feet, however, differs from the usual short tunic worn by warriors and lords of power. His head and hair are unusual also in their brilliant whiteness — as wool and as snow. In the context of this picture, such an image . . . signifies his purity and victoriousness and, undoubtedly, the wisdom and spiritual maturity that are associated with white hair in the Hebrew Scriptures. The whiteness of the wool and snow reminds us of Isaiah 1:18 and comforts us with the assurance that this Son of Man is the one who forgives our scarlet sins. . . .

We can understand the images of fire also because they come from Daniel 7:9-10; 10:6; and Ezekiel 1:26-27. Eyes that are flames of fire and feet that glow as bronze having been set on fire in a furnace emphasize the penetration of his vision, the strength of his power, the radiance of his majesty.

From the book of Ezekiel comes also the description of the voice like the sound of many waters. . . . Listeners to John's word of encouragement in The Revelation . . . probably remembered the Hebrew context of that picture at the beginning of the prophecy about the departure of the glory of the LORD from the temple and its return when the people of Israel were restored after the Babylonian captivity. In the same way, then, first-century Christians could draw hope for their eventual deliverance from the present captivity under the Roman emperor. Similarly, Christians today can look for the final restoration of the people of God, though now our world is captive to the materialism and self-centered egoism of our age. The voice of the waterfalls still flows.

Prayer

Restoring Lord, we trust in your power to forgive our sins and deliver us from any captivity . . .   Amen.

Joy in Our Weakness, pp. 50-51.

119

Who has measured the waters in the hollow of his hand
    and marked off the heavens with a span,
enclosed the dust of the earth in a measure,
    and weighed the mountains in scales
    and the hills in a balance?

Isaiah 40:12 (NRSV)

In this verse we catch a glimpse of God's astonishing transcendence. . . . Images such as these of weighing and measuring enable us . . . to notice the infinity of God's greatness. . . .

The entire verse is set up as a rhetorical question. . . . Of course, there is only one answer. The Lord GOD is the only one capable of such feats. Each phrase is valuable, however, for stirring up a deeper wonder, for filling us with astonishment at the inconceivable dominion of God.

"Who has measured the waters in the hollow of his hand?" Even if we limited our picture to just one ocean, . . . to imagine the Lord GOD holding that in the palm of a single hand is superlatively staggering. . . .

The second picture in this verse makes us laugh. The measure of a span is the distance between the end of one's little finger and of one's thumb when . . . spread apart. Imagine God . . . establishing whole galaxies by the spanful! . . .

The third phrase of this verse . . . says literally, "and all in the third part the dust of the earth." . . . The unit of measurement is thought by most scholars to mean the third part of an ephah, or about a quart. . . . All the soil of the earth God can hold, or measure, in his strawberry bucket.

And then, as if that weren't demonstration enough, he weighs all the mountains in a single scale and all the hills in a double balance. . . .

I'm sure that at this point you are realizing . . . that we can't even begin to imagine what God is like. . . . Why are we such blind fools . . . that we do not trust this God who exercises his might on our behalf? "Who can do these things?" Isaiah 40 asks, and the galaxies sing out the answer. . . . How, then, shall we respond?

Prayer
    God of the galaxies, we praise you for your greatness, which is far beyond our
    knowing . . .   Amen.

To Walk and Not Faint, pp. 72-75.

Drop thy still dews of quietness,
Till all our strivings cease;
Take from our souls the strain and stress,
And let our ordered lives confess
The beauty of thy peace.

John G. Whittier, 1807-1892

In our modern world emotional strains often continue to build in our lives because so many things lie outside of our power and understanding. . . .

As an alternative to the world's methods, Sabbath spirituality offers us several means to combat the "out-of-control-ness" of modern society. First of all, its very order and rhythm bring about emotional rest. When so much of life is unsure and dependent upon circumstances beyond our control, the sureness of one day in every seven to set everything aside gives us emotional stability.

Moreover, on the Sabbath day we deliberately remember that we have ceased trying to be God and instead have put our lives back into his control. Concentrating on God's Lordship in our lives enables us to return to his sovereign hands all the things that are beyond our control and terrifying us. . . .

Our times of worship and of sharing with others in the fellowship of the Christian community enfold us so that we can rest in the belief that God's provision for all our needs will always also include the emotional as well as the physical and spiritual.

We can also find great rest in realizing that our emotions are not the foremost determiner of our lives. Our culture tells us, "If it feels good, do it." . . . Sabbath keeping reminds us that our wills are stronger than our emotions, that we can resist the temptations that our emotions put us to, that we can even deliberately change our emotions by an act of will. Do not get me wrong: I'm not advocating that we repress our emotions — which can lead to great scarring. Instead I'm advocating that we put emotions back into their proper place as the caboose of our train of living. Our will or deliberate thinking is the engine, and our emotions properly just come along for the ride. . . .

Letting God be God in our lives gives us the freedom to deal constructively with our emotions, to accept them and listen to them, but not to be controlled by them.

Prayer

O God of grace, when we are emotionally out of control, help us regain peace
and order in Sabbath rest . . .   Amen.

Keeping the Sabbath Wholly, pp. 75-77.

"For we cannot help speaking about what we have seen and heard."

Acts 4:20

When and how will our congregations begin to equip the people for both worship and witness? . . . Many congregations and denominations have failed for decades or perhaps even centuries to teach people what worship is and to educate members to be witnesses, to care for their neighbors, and to minister to the world around them as active parts of the Body of Christ.

Why don't Christians talk about their faith with their neighbors? . . . Here are some of the most common excuses . . . and some beginning responses:

"I don't know enough." . . . "I'm not skilled enough." . . . "I'm not sure enough." . . . "I am a very timid and shy person." . . . To tell others how God has changed your life does not require skill. . . . What is most required is genuine love for your neighbor. . . . Let your Churchbeing affect your daily conversations.

"I don't have enough time." . . . Giving witness to your faith is not an added-on job. The original Greek version of Matthew 28:19 literally says, "While you are going, be making disciples."

"I don't have any non-Christian friends or neighbors." . . . "I don't have a friendly Church." . . . "TV preachers have given evangelism a bad name." . . . "We can't talk about faith anymore in our culture. This is a pluralistic society." . . . Others need to see in you a Christian who is . . . trustworthy and faithful, a Christian who speaks of God with integrity and gentleness.

Perhaps we don't talk about our faith because it hasn't really grabbed hold of all of our lives. Perhaps we are merely religious consumers ourselves. Then may God evangelize us! . . .

Part of our congregation's training for Churchbeing must be to nurture in all the members a spirit of hospitality. May the infinitely welcoming triune God teach us all to embrace our neighbors with the fullness of his love through our care and witness. Then, if they are drawn to worship the Trinity, may we each greet them warmly with graceful assistance and gentle mentoring and kindred ardor for all the ways in which God will teach us about himself through our corporate praise.

Prayer

Triune God, teach us, and empower us, to share our faith with Joy . . .
Amen.

A Royal "Waste" of Time, pp. 127-31, 134.

. . . whether prophecy — according to the agreement of the faith!
Romans 12:6b (my translation)

Manifestations of prophetic gifts usually flow from a deep knowledge of the Scriptures. As Jesus promises in the Gospel of John, the Holy Spirit brings to our remembrance what we have already learned from him (14:26). In order for the Spirit to do that work, however, the Scriptures must already be in our minds. Therefore, Paul's words about prophecy are a strong stimulation for daily personal devotional habits and corporate study of the Bible.

One practical aspect of the Church's life that needs immensely the gift of prophecy is the stewardship of possessions. Indeed, in many ways churches have succumbed severely to the temptations of money and power. God's Word, however, is very clear; both Testaments constantly emphasize God's special concern for the poor. . . . To choose the values of God we can do no less than rethink our priorities.

Tragically, very few Christian communities are doing a thorough job of caring seriously for the poor in their budgetary allotments. Therefore, we need prophets among us to call Christians back to more obedient discipleship in their concern for the hungry and malnourished and jobless and homeless. . . .

If the gift of prophecy is exercised according to the faith, then we realize that we are often called to proclaim the Word precisely when we don't feel like it or when a situation seems to be absolutely a lost cause. The Greek noun for *faith* in this case specifically has the article *the* with it, so Paul's emphasis seems to be on the specific content of the Christian faith. One who is a prophet proclaims the truths of the Christian faith. . . .

A lifetime task of studying the Scriptures is necessary to learn what God would say to the Christian community in our world. By studying the prophets we learn God's values. By studying the world we learn how to apply God's truth to the reality of contemporary life situations. Our prophetic work requires a careful balance of intense study of the Bible and a deep relationship with the Lord, with ourselves, with the Church, and with our world in order to forthtell accurately God's messages for the situations of our times.

Prayer
> *Holy Spirit, call us to faithful study of your Word, and give us courage to proclaim it . . .   Amen.*

Truly the Community, pp. 101, 107-9.

Fathers, do not provoke your children to anger, but bring them up in the discipline and instruction of the Lord.

Ephesians 6:4 (NRSV)

Surely it is devastating to children to leave them without boundaries, without trained habits that eventuate in their own self-control, without behavior patterns that build relationships and lead to service. . . .

In our many tasks as parents we do the best we can to image God. The picture in Genesis 1 of our roles to image God as male and female puts such instructions as Ephesians 6:4 above into perspective. We are not expected to be God for our children; rather, we do whatever we can in God's stead. This perception sets us free to put ourselves under the same grace that we want to characterize our nurturing of our children.

We don't have to pretend we are perfect or expect ourselves to be, for fathers and mothers are fallible human beings. None of us could ever parent as well as we would like to. But we can humbly admit to our children that we are doing the best we can to serve as representatives of God's fathering and mothering. In our failings, we can model for our children repentance and humility; we train them in common mutuality by asking them for forgiveness. Furthermore, we specifically teach them always to know that their totally successful Parent is unceasingly there for them. Meanwhile, our methods of parenting are guided and our courage for the task is heightened by the way in which God reveals himself in his care for us.

Finally, the Christian community's perspective on raising children helps us recognize it as God's art, the Lord's craftsmanship in which we participate and which then encourages our offspring to make of their life the best art. We get this insight from such texts as Ephesians 2:8-10, which emphasizes that we are saved by grace and not by works and then concludes, "For we are his workmanship, created in Christ Jesus for good works, which God prepared beforehand, that we should walk in them" (RSV). . . .

Will our work of raising children be artificial — that is, without heart — or will we in the Christian community engage in the highest art of parenting?

Prayer
> *O Lord of the community, help us raise our church's children with your heart,*
> *by your grace . . .   Amen.*

Is It a Lost Cause? pp. 118-19.

Know that the LORD has set apart the godly for himself;
  the LORD will hear when I call to him.

Psalm 4:3

We are commanded to know this truth: "The LORD has set apart the godly for himself." ... One of the consequences is in the next line: we can trust the LORD to hear when we call him. ...

If *YHWH* has set apart the godly for himself, we must ask if the godliness comes first and causes him to set apart those who exhibit it — or if God's setting them apart creates the godliness. In the context of the rest of the Scriptures, we can interpret this text to mean that God is the actor in the setting apart. ... Godliness is a gift first and then a response, not a characteristic that itself causes *YHWH*'s choice.

To be set apart means to be made distinct, to be separated out. Sacred vessels were thus consecrated for use in the temple sacrifices. Different from other vessels because of their designation and service as sacred, they were used only for the purposes of worship. ...

Some of us might be saying, "But I don't want to be separated. I'm already lonely; I don't want to be cut off any more." Blessedly, we are not separated to be alone, but to be part of a community, the people of God. Furthermore, we are separated not only *from* the world but also *to* the LORD and therefore *to* the world in his service. *YHWH* has called us apart for himself to make available to us all the gifts of his work in our lives. Our loneliness is eased by the care of the community into which he places us and by his caring gifts to us.

The first of those gifts, the assurance in this verse that he will hear us when we call to him, is much like the choosing of a beloved. One whose attention is fixed upon someone special will listen more eagerly to that person's requests than to those of others.

It is our delight that God chooses each of us that way. When a person selects a beloved, everyone else is eliminated. But the special position and relationship with himself that the LORD creates guarantees that he will hear each one of us when we call him.

Prayer

Sanctifying LORD, we delight in all that it means to be "chosen"...   Amen.

I'm Lonely, LORD, pp. 71-74.

In his right hand he held seven stars, and out of his mouth came a sharp double-edged sword. His face was like the sun shining in all its brilliance. When I saw him, I fell at his feet as though dead.

Revelation 1:16-17a

The image of the Word of God as a sword seems to have been "in the air" in the first century — that is, in the environment of the early pacifist Christians, the figure of the Scriptures as their sword was used in contrast to the various weapons of the Roman military.

This concept of figures of speech "in the air" is very important for our historical perspective on The Revelation. Many images used in the book are no longer accessible.... Certainly the images were clearly understood by the seer's readers, for he employed those that were used in the worship and conversation of early Christians so that his letter might lucidly convey the hope he intended.

Because twenty centuries have intervened, however, it is dangerous to suppose that we can know for sure to what the images refer. Our guesses must always be tentative. We certainly can't pin down various elements of these visions and assert that they are particular signs being fulfilled in our age to help us calculate the chronology of Christ's return.... The only way we will know for sure when Christ will return is when we actually see him coming in the clouds — and, since clouds always represent in the Scriptures the presence of God ... that image, too, is more important as a symbol than as an actual description of how Jesus will physically come.

Once again, the Son of Man's power is underscored in the description of his face as shining like the light of the sun in its strength. This image is easy for us to grasp.... No wonder the seer, upon seeing him, immediately fell at his feet as though dead. Throughout the Scriptures we read of those who, confronted by the holiness and majesty of God, fall down in worship and dread. No one can face the holy God and stand unashamed....

The majesty of God turns us upside down, and we fall on our face in unworthiness. It throws us to our knees in adoration and utmost humility.

Prayer
> *O majestic God, as we study the Scriptures, may we ever show adoration and*
> *humility ...   Amen.*

Joy in Our Weakness, pp. 51-53.

Who has directed the spirit of the LORD,
    or as his counselor has instructed him?

                                                    Isaiah 40:13 (NRSV)

Down through the ages, these words from Isaiah have mocked the folly of those who presume to instruct the Spirit of the LORD. . . .

    How little we understand the purposes of God for our lives and, through us, for others. . . . How often don't we try to instruct the LORD instead of waiting for his direction, instead of submitting to his perfect will. . . .

    We might ask, then, about the value of prayer. Why should we spend time putting into words our feelings and concerns or our needs and cares? . . . Does this verse indirectly negate the value of prayer?

    Certainly not — especially since prayer is decidedly more a matter of relationship than of words. One of the gifts of prayer for me arises from this very fact that the LORD does not need anyone to counsel him. In our words of praise, we remember his power and sovereignty. We are reminded of his infinite wisdom and care, and consequently we are assured that he is watching over everything that concerns us (1 Pet. 5:7) and that he will work all things together for our good (Rom. 8:28).

    Furthermore, as we unfold to him our perceptions of ourselves and others, we find them deepened and clarified. He has promised to give wisdom to those who ask (James 1:5-8). . . .

    What better picture of grace is there than this: No one directs the Spirit of the LORD and no one can be his instructor, yet he deigns to use us and to make us valuable members of his Body to effect his will on the earth. In his perfection he hears our cry and comes to comfort us, to give us guidance, and to instruct us in ways we can serve his purposes. . . .

    The irony of the prophet's questions pinpoints our major problem — that we are not as directed by the Spirit as we could be because too often we are trying too hard to direct him. When we insist upon our own perceptions and mastery, we cannot be open enough to see and hear and feel the insights, commands, and nudges the Spirit is trying to give us.

Prayer
    Holy Spirit, use our prayers to guide us into paths of service . . .   *Amen.*
                                        To Walk and Not Faint, pp. 77-80.

And God raised us up with Christ and seated us with him in the heavenly realms in Christ Jesus.

Ephesians 2:6

One of the stultifying effects of our culture is that it doesn't give us much time for creative and reflective thinking. We need all of our thinking time just to keep in touch with what is going on, to cope with what is happening to us, in us, and because of us. However, the fragmented nature of our experience prevents us from grasping a coherent view of the whole. . . .

In Jacques Ellul's *Humiliation of the Word,* he laments the fact that our view of reality is so distorted by the "news," which comes to us in small, disjointed pieces that change every day and that usually focus on the catastrophic. The result is that we develop an inadequate perspective on world events and a consequent dwindling of our sense of hope and meaning. We don't have much time to think about any of the headlines except when they impinge on us directly, and then our view is usually an isolated one that does not take into consideration the relationship of that one dimension to the whole of our situation.

Sabbath keeping offers us the time to gain a perspective, to view our fragmented existence in light of a larger whole. . . . Our concentration on who God is, as part of our Sabbath keeping, gives us a new framework in which to refocus our thinking in the days to come.

Related to this is the fact that Sabbath keeping enables us to understand the larger purposes of God. . . . When by faith we take our position in the heavenly places (Eph. 2:6), we can become detached enough from the world's notions of success to understand more clearly what God intends to do in the world and thereby to find more carefully our place within his purposes. . . .

Moreover, since to keep the Sabbath means to rest thoroughly, on that day we can rest from our usual kinds of intellectual labors. We don't have to think about the things that occupy our minds during our workdays. Such a temporary setting aside of those problems refreshes us so that we can return to our usual subjects of thought with new eagerness.

Prayer
> *O Lord, bless our Sabbath keeping as we center our thought in you and see our world and our lives from this perspective . . .   Amen.*
> > *Keeping the Sabbath Wholly,* pp. 78-80.

I have tasted You, and I hunger and thirst for you.
You have touched me, and I ardently desire Your peace.

Augustine of Hippo, 354-430

It seems unnecessary to spend time emphasizing that God calls and enables us to worship — yet how difficult it is to keep God as the subject of worship in the present narcissistic and subjectivized culture. . . .

However, by myriad means we *can* keep God as the subject of our worship. The Church's historic liturgy models God-centeredness powerfully — starting with a prelude to offer worshipers opportunity to move away from the distractions of their workaday or family-life worlds and into the presence of God. . . .

The liturgical invocation beginning worship (often after an opening hymn) again makes God the subject. The proclamation that we are here "in the name of the Father, and of the Son, and of the Holy Spirit" reminds us that the triune God now calls us together to worship him. Only in God's name — that is, in God's character of constant grace — is any worship possible.

Some congregations are replacing the invocation with a casual greeting by the pastor or priest in a false attempt to create "community" and make worshipers feel comfortable. . . .

It is surely important for the clergy to be friendly with the parish, rather than austere and distant as many pastors once were — but the pendulum has now swung so far in the opposite direction that many congregations seem to have become the private cult of a charismatic leader. I'm stating the extreme case here, but it is because I fear the subtle replacement of the mystery of the Trinity with the pastor's personality in initiating worship. It is almost as if the priest invites us into his living room instead of God welcoming us into his presence. I suggest that a pastoral greeting and the necessary announcements be made first to establish the community and that then the turn into actual worship be decisively made by urging the congregation to let the prelude lead them into God's presence or by a statement like, "Now we give all our attention to the God who has called us here. In the name of. . . ."

Prayer

God the Father, Son, and Holy Spirit, when we gather for worship at your invitation, help us center all our thoughts and feelings on your grace-filled presence, which alone makes worship possible . . .   Amen.

Reaching Out, pp. 75, 77-78.

. . . whether service — in that service!

Romans 12:7a (my translation)

The *charismata* are the grace-gifts, given to us by grace and serving as vehicles through which God's grace is poured out to others. . . .

To use any gift is absolutely impossible without the power of the Holy Spirit, upon whose grace we utterly depend, but under the Spirit's inspiration and guidance and empowerment every grace-gift is a source of freedom and delight . . . and of being who we were created to be. . . .

If we are faithfully listening to the Lord with the help of the community and trying to discern his will, he will constantly be showing us who we are and how he can best use us. That gives us the freedom, then, to decline tasks that take us too far out of the spheres of our gifts. . . .

Consider the importance of balance in accepting roles in the Christian community for which we are gifted and in refusing those that take us away from our primary tasks. We can only discover that balance for our individual lives in a moment-by-moment testing and by a continual process within the Christian community. We want to be open constantly to God's revelation of how we can best serve him in a particular situation at a given moment.

All of these phrases in Romans 12 describing the grace-gifts, phrases that have no verb in the Greek, are translated in Today's English Version with the verb *must* or *should*. . . . Verse 7, for example, is rendered, "If it is to serve, we must serve. If it is to teach, we must teach." This legalism . . . destroys our freedom. We do not use gifts because we have to; we rejoice in the task. . . .

What, then, is the gift of serving? . . . The phrase seems to concentrate on those who perform necessary functions in order to enable others to use their gifts. . . .

Without the unnoticed ministry of those who serve, the "people behind the church," . . . we cannot function as a community that is whole. . . .

Perhaps the question we should ask is not whether we have the gift of service, but whether we are letting grace empower each of us in our opportunities to serve.

Prayer

Grace-full Lord, help us to discern faithfully how best we can serve, and free us to use our gifts for serving . . .   Amen.

Truly the Community, pp. 111-15.

Train a child in the way he should go, and when he is old he will not turn from it.
Proverbs 22:6

If we want our children's character . . . to be different from that of the world around them, then we cannot suddenly begin to teach them when they are teenagers about holding alternative values. It is important that we begin when they are tiny to invite them into the delight of being different. . . .

Take, for example, the celebration of holidays like Christmas or Easter. What can we do to help our children to learn that we have different understandings about those holy days and also to help them enjoy being different in our celebration of them? My parents followed many old German Lutheran customs to make the days different for us so that we both knew what the celebration was all about and didn't feel deprived not to have all the material accoutrements other children had. . . . Instead of Santa Claus, we focused on the Christ Child coming to our home.

When doing workshops on alternative Christmas celebrations, I am often asked, "What's wrong with Santa Claus?" Basically what is wrong with Santa Claus as he is portrayed today is that the theology is backwards. Santa Claus teaches children that if they are good, then they will be rewarded. The Christ Child comes instead to tell us that, even though we cannot be good, God gives us the greatest gift of all anyway. . . .

It is possible to talk about Santa Claus in a Christian way, emphasizing the goodness and social concern of the original St. Nicholas and how he exemplified the gifting of God. The crucial point is that we help our children to know what we believe — namely, not only that salvation is an enormously wonderful and totally essential gift but also that it is the entire reason for the season — and that what we believe influences the way we celebrate.

Similarly, what we believe affects how we spend our money, what we wear, how we allocate our time, whether we watch this violent or immoral television program, what we do with our Sundays, how we relate to our neighbors, for whom and what we vote, what occupations we choose, and how we behave sexually.

Prayer

Loving Father, guide our everyday choices as we teach our children, by example, what we believe . . . Amen.

Sexual Character, pp. 137-39.

Tremble and do not sin;
  Meditate in your heart upon your bed,
  and be still.
Offer the sacrifices of righteousness,
  and trust in the LORD.

Psalm 4:4-5 (NASV)

In his writings Martin Luther . . . kept stressing that the Law cannot make us good; rather, it is a mirror to show us how bad we are and how much we're in need of a Savior. By its standard we can see that we utterly fail to act like the saints that we are by virtue of God's gracious declaration and atoning work. Though the LORD has set us apart as godly, our human nature keeps us from ever living like that. . . .

To stress this dialectical balance, Martin Luther begins all of his explanations of the Ten Commandments with the declaration, "We should so fear and love God that we . . ." When we hold fear and love in proper tension, our recognition of the wrath of God . . . is overpowered by gratitude and wonder at the mercy that has borne that wrath for us. . . .

"Fear [or tremble] and do not sin" is reinforced further by the next phrase of Psalm 4. The poet continues with the invitations to "offer the sacrifices of righteousness, and trust in *YHWH*." . . .

However, we cannot be righteous by ourselves. Righteousness before God, as with holiness, is granted to us when the LORD sets us apart for himself. . . . Therefore, the exhortation to present offerings of righteousness is for us a constant invitation to respond to Christ's sacrifice of himself with lives that seek what is right and just. . . .

Because *YHWH* has set us apart for himself, we want to respond by choosing righteous ways to fulfill God's will. For those of us who are lonely, this is a call to morality, an invitation to servanthood, an exhortation to give ourselves fully to whatever God might call us to do as we care for those around us.

In our trusting, we realize that our sacrifices are perfectly acceptable to him. . . . Moreover, in offering ourselves first to God and then to others, we often find to our delight that we are set free from loneliness to find new purpose and fulfillment and wholeness.

Prayer

  O LORD, empower us to live the set-apart, godly lives that you offer us through
  Jesus' atoning love . . .   Amen.

I'm Lonely, LORD, pp. 71, 74-77.

When I saw him, I fell at his feet as though dead. Then he placed his right hand on me and said: "Do not be afraid. I am the First and the Last. I am the Living One. . . . And I hold the keys of death and Hades."

Revelation 1:17-18

Though we deserve to be slain, though we cannot bear to face the holiness that cannot tolerate our sinfulness, yet we are invited by the pure and holy one to enjoy his presence without fear. What amazing grace! What a wonder to be welcomed in this way!

When the Son of Man continues by naming himself "the First and the Last" (v. 17), his words carry tremendous import. . . . In claiming to be the first and last he uses images from the Hebrew Scriptures and thereby asserts unequivocally his deity. He takes for himself the titles of Yahweh, the covenant God of Israel.

The Son of Man fills the name, First and Last, with new meaning, for he received the dominion and glory from the Ancient of Days not by any huge manifestation of power, but by dying and then being raised to life. Thus, we can know that he holds the keys of death and of Hades, for surely he has passed through their clutches and come out on the other side as victor over their purposes. Into the aeons of the aeons, therefore, he reigns as Lord over death and life. . . .

This identification raises again the most important issue in all of life, this question that we can ask the world around us: What do you think of the Christ? Is he God himself — more than simply a good teacher, more than a prophet, and more than someone whom God adopted to fulfill his purposes? Is he actually both God himself incarnated in human flesh to dwell among us and yet also God who was and is and eternally is to come? Do we believe that this Word was always God, though now he takes a human form? The seer John and all the rest of the Scriptures answer yes; the early church and its persecuted believers answer yes; we boldly answer yes and invite the world around us to answer yes, too.

Prayer

Lord Jesus, we join all the saints before us in declaring yes! You are the eternal Word, reigning over death and life, the Word of love for us . . .   Amen.

Joy in Our Weakness, pp. 53-54.

133

With whom did He consult and [who] gave Him understanding?
and [who] taught Him in the path of justice and taught Him knowledge,
and informed Him in the way of understanding?

Isaiah 40:14 (NASV)

With all verse 14's queries, the answer is obvious: Only God possesses perfect understanding. . . .

Truly he understands us infinitely better than we can ourselves. . . .

How could we ever be understood more deeply than by the One whose very character is to understand, to be just, to have all skill?

The immensity of God's wisdom and understanding and insight is a tremendous source of comfort for us. Most of us struggle continuously with the terrible tension of trying to keep all the dimensions of our lives in balance. . . . Often we feel misunderstood by caring friends who try to give advice, but who don't know all the factors that affect our decisions about how best to be good stewards of our time and abilities.

Meanwhile, the slogans that human beings devise deceive us. The lifestyles promoted by the culture that encroaches upon us betray us. Following the gurus of the times, we travel dead-end streets. And presumptuous rejections of God's answers prove disastrous for us.

Does God really guide us with his Spirit? Can we learn to listen to his wisdom? . . .

What peace it gives us to realize all the ways in which the LORD communicates to us his wisdom and understanding. His Word offers the clearest picture of genuine justice. The Christian community together hears the Spirit of the true Counselor to give us insight for our decisions. Our personal prayer and devotional lives enable us to perceive directions for better balance and greater wholeness in our lives. The discovery of new skills that God fashioned in us often ushers us into fresh avenues of interest and service.

I long to be more attentive to the Counselor, and I pray that . . . you, too, have a desire to trust more fully God's perfect understanding. The One who needs no one to teach him or to give him counsel longs to be gracious to us (Isa. 30:18). How blessed we are if we reject the world's empty philosophies (Col. 2:8) and learn from him (Matt. 11:29)!

Prayer

Holy Counselor, you know us, and you desire to lead us. Help us to seek and
follow your perfect wisdom for our lives . . .   Amen.

To Walk and Not Faint, pp. 83, 86-88.

. . . be transformed by the renewing of your mind. . . .

Romans 12:2b

Sabbath keeping . . . directly affects our attitudes. When we are rested, we can think more objectively. Oftentimes our great frustrations in thinking arise because our perspectives are so clouded by the immediate impact of problems or pressures or pains. After setting everything aside for a day and ceasing to stew about it during Sabbath celebration, we can think more clearly.

Furthermore, the delight we experience in keeping the Sabbath frees us to be more realistic. We can face the negative dimensions of the world and of our more immediate worlds with a realism born out of our knowledge that God is still Lord over everything that seems so crazy, that the invisible Truth of his love is larger than the visible reality of this world's pain.

Holy time also creates calm. Not only will that calmness last into the rest of the week and enable us to think things through more thoroughly, but also it will free us to be more creative. . . .

One of the reasons that the intellectual rest of Sabbath keeping is so important stems from the fact that the Holy Spirit works primarily through the renewal of our minds — as the Scriptures continually remind us. The following exhortation . . . is especially descriptive:

> Therefore, I urge you, brothers and sisters, with eyes wide open to the mercies of God, as an act of intelligent worship, to offer your bodies as living sacrifices, holy and pleasing to God. Do not conform any longer to the pattern of this world, but be transformed by the renewing of your mind, so that you may prove in practice that the plan of God for you is good, acceptable, and moves toward the goal of true maturity. (Rom. 12:1-2, composite translation)

Intelligent worship is the way to avoid the pressures of the world around us to conform to its values and goals. . . . As J. B. Phillips phrases it, we don't have to let the world around us squeeze us into its mold. Instead, we can be remolded from the inside — and God's means for doing that is the renewing of our minds. The Greek world *anakainosis*, which we translate "renewing," suggests a major renovation in our thinking.

Prayer

Holy Spirit, come into our Sabbath thinking with your renewing power; transform our understanding, our attitudes, and our lives . . .   Amen.

Keeping the Sabbath Wholly, pp. 80-83.

You have radiated forth, and have shined out brightly,
   and You have dispelled my blindness.
You have sent forth Your fragrance, and I have breathed it in,
   and I long for You.

                               Augustine of Hippo, 354-430

Many pieces of a worship service can work to keep God the subject. I espe-cially love the set of liturgical lines, "Glory to you, O Lord" and "Praise to you, O Christ," before and after the Gospel reading. The first line prepares our hearts and minds for the first climax of the service, the words and deeds of Jesus himself. While we sing this line with great gusto, we leap to our feet to exalt Christ and say, "You are honored, Lord! Come to us now and teach us. Tell us again what you have done for us. What a great gift that you come to us this way!" The second line recognizes that what we have just heard is life-changing because Christ, the Word, has met us in the Scripture that tes-tifies of him. "You are worthy of praise, Christ, for you are indeed God in the flesh, and you have come to us in this revelation of truth for our lives." When such lines in the liturgy are well taught, the refrain opens our minds to receive the Gospel as the presence of Jesus Christ. He is there to draw us to worship and thoroughly to change our lives by his Word.

If parishes do not use these responses, what other appropriate liturgical rituals might be employed to highlight God's presence in the Word? What symbols convey, and thus heighten, worship participants' anticipation of the encounter with God in the Scriptures? . . .

The accumulation of all such liturgical lines and rituals creates a power-ful environment of God-centeredness. Also, even pre-reading children learn to recognize God's presence in symbolic actions and can participate if weekly repetition allows them to memorize liturgical responses. Moreover, this aura is amplified by other elements of the worship milieu, such as the majesty of an organ, symbols on banners and chancel furniture, stained-glass windows, bread and wine, statues and crosses. All of these work to-gether to create the sense that God, who is the subject of what we do, is in this place in special ways. His grace enables us to respond to him with daily lives of total worship.

Prayer

   Honored Lord, may we always welcome your presence with Joy and rever-ence . . .   Amen.

                                 Reaching Out, pp. 75, 79-80.

. . . whether the one exhorting — in the exhortation!

Romans 12:8a (my translation)

Paul is modeling the very thing that he urges, for this whole section of his letter demonstrates exhortation, and here specifically he urges those who have that gift to exercise it in encouraging others.

The word Paul chooses here to describe the action of this grace-gift comes from the verb with which he began this section of Romans when he "urged" his readers to present their bodies as living and holy sacrifices pleasing to God (12:1). . . . The word possesses an enormous field of meanings, including to encourage, comfort, urge, entreat, warn, admonish, or exhort. . . . Paul probably chose it specifically to express the range of activities that are involved when members of the Christian community use their spiritual gifts to uphold one another. The concept gives us a striking picture of what our relationships with others in the Body of Christ can be and how much more effective our encouragement of one another in the community is when it is empowered by the Holy Spirit. . . .

We want to avoid any definitions of this gift that smack of pushiness or adamant goading. Rather, throughout the Scriptures the gift seems to be characterized by gentleness. Its proper functioning within the community might involve admonition or rebuking, but these are done with tenderness in order to build up the one who needs to be criticized and to enable that individual to change. Perhaps the most needful kind of exhortation in contemporary congregations is that which criticizes constructively, reproves, calls back from error, or disciplines. . . .

The terms *encouragement* and *exhortation* stress well the profound need in our communities for lifting up one another, for motivational prodding. How we do such stimulation is critically important because both discouragement and lack of personal discipline are problems in the Church. We don't want our prodding to cause the other to feel guilty. . . . On the other hand, fellow believers who are betraying the values of the community need to be challenged to repent and change.

An enormous amount of grace is required to be an encouraging person. One who is exhorting well, however, will be tenderly and fruitfully passing on the love of God as the motivation for someone else's life and ministry.

Prayer

Gentle Lord, teach us to exhort and encourage — tenderly . . .   Amen.

Truly the Community, pp. 121-25.

[I]f anyone is in Christ, there is a new creation.

2 Corinthians 5:17a (NRSV)

It is not just we who are different if we are in Christ. *Everything* is new. We live in an entirely different milieu if we are in Christ. . . .

One example is the use of our time in parenting. Probably you have seen the sociologists' statistics on the extremely small average number of quality minutes (or seconds) spent by our society's parents with their children. . . . In the Christian community we want to be decisively different, for we know that formation of alternative character takes a great investment of prime time to counteract all the influences of the dominant culture. . . .

We must pay attention to customs and habits, practices and attitudes that will counteract the social influences that pull our children away from God. . . .

One great gift of time that Jews and Christians carry together to the world is God's design for Sabbath keeping. . . . I cannot emphasize enough the positive changes it brings to our hectic lives when we faithfully reserve an entire Sabbath day set apart to deepen our relationship with God and family and to learn more thoroughly who God is and the kind of character he wants to develop in us and in our children.

One key use of time for raising our children to be part of the parallel society is conversation. . . . Can our families institute . . . a regular habit of daily conversations and devotional moments? . . . In contrast to our society's "ships passing in the night" living arrangements, can our families specifically set aside time for devotions, meals together, intimate conversations, and shared hobbies and chores so that the children can easily question their parents when issues, such as sexuality, come up? . . .

One element of family conversation that is rapidly getting lost in our culture but is needed for the sake of preserving our history and values is the telling and retelling of stories — from the family tree, from the local community, from the community of faith.

Prayer

Faithful Lord, help us commit our prime time to nurturing our children through conversation, storytelling, Sabbath keeping . . .   Amen.

Is It a Lost Cause? pp. 120-24.

Many are asking, "Who can show us any good?"
  Let the light of your face shine upon us, O LORD.
You have filled my heart with greater joy
  than when their grain and new wine abound.
I will lie down and sleep in peace,
  for you alone, O LORD
  make me dwell in safety.

Psalm 4:6-8

The verb rendered "are asking" in verse 6 is, in Hebrew, a participle indicating a state of being or continuous action. People keep on searching for good somewhere, somehow, because they are constantly becoming dissatisfied with what they find. . . .

The poet's request for *YHWH* to lift up the light of his face upon us uses human terms we can understand. . . . When the LORD's face shines upon us, we know that we will receive all the fullness of his gifts. Inevitably will come a genuine Joy that is available only to God's people. . . .

This Joy is not merely an abstract concept; the poet praises God for filling his heart/will with a genuine actuality . . . a Joy that permeates grief and changes it into good, not only for ourselves, but also for others.

Meanwhile, we do not have to . . . pretend that all is well when it is not. Happiness is temporal, dependent upon the circumstances that create it. . . . I don't think that to be Christian necessarily means that we will be happy. For those of us struggling with loneliness, there are many times when we cannot be happy.

Joy, on the other hand, is eternal, dependent upon the accomplished fact that Christ has risen from the dead and made reconciliation with God an established, eternal truth.

We *can* "rejoice in the Lord always," . . . because the command to rejoice is plural and reminds us that we are glad in the midst of the Christian community that carries the Joy for us even when we can't find or feel it ourselves. . . .

Furthermore, a biblical peace goes hand in hand with Joy. As our relationship with God keeps enabling us to deal with the sorrows of our lives, we will have enough tranquility, the poet anticipates, to both lie down and to sleep. . . . Not only can we be awake with him in Joy unspeakable, but we can also sleep in him with peace illimitable.

Prayer
  Blessing LORD, *may the good we seek be your unfailing, eternal Joy . . .*
  Amen.

I'm Lonely, LORD, pp. 79-85.

". . . The seven stars are the angels of the seven churches, and the seven lampstands are the seven churches."

Revelation 1:20b

The fact that the images in The Revelation stand for practical realities of the first-century church is made clear by the last verse of Revelation 1. After the seer receives explicit instructions to write the things he is learning, he is told overtly what the stars and the seven golden lampstands represent. Yet their definition is shrouded in mystery, because we do not know what the angels of the seven churches are. Does that name refer to angelic beings . . . "a messenger" . . . the local pastor in each situation? That last possibility seems very likely since each of the seven letters that immediately follow this description of the Son of Man begins with . . . specific messages to the angel at each particular place. It would be tremendously comforting to the leaders of these churches to receive the letters that assert that the Son of Man holds them in his right hand, the symbol always in the Scriptures for fellowship and personal relationship.

Finally, we are told that the seven golden lampstands stand for the seven churches themselves. . . . Various scholars recognize that these seven cities to which these letters are addressed form a circle in the order in which they are given, that they were also the postal centers for the seven regions of Asia Minor, and that they were primary centers for emperor worship. For whatever reason they were chosen, the churches in these particular cities are assured that the Son of Man stands in their midst, that he is present, right there in the area of persecution, with all the power and glory that has been described.

Just as the Christians of the first century struggled, . . . so in our time we face the conflicts of being Christians in a post-Christian age and need to hear again the encouraging word that the Son of Man walks in the midst of the lampstands. While we are called to be light givers in a sin-darkened world, the Son is walking among us to trim the wicks, to stir up the flames, to make our lamps more effective in transmitting his light.

Prayer
> *Son of Man, we too are encouraged by your presence among us, helping us be your faithful lampstands today . . .   Amen.*

Joy in Our Weakness, pp. 54-55.

Lebanon would not provide fuel enough,
  nor are its animals enough for a burnt offering.

Isaiah 40:16 (NRSV)

This is such a tangible picture of the insufficiency of any sacrifices. Consider the ancient country of Lebanon. . . . All the wood of that entire nation in antiquity . . . would not suffice for fuel for the offering God deserves. . . . Furthermore, all the living creatures inhabiting those vast forests are utterly paltry as a burnt offering, altogether unfit to honor *YHWH*. . . .

What is the true worship of God? Does God ask us to make sacrifices? Certainly we know that our feeble oblations cannot earn his favor — yet how often do we deceive ourselves, subconsciously assuming that we gain God's grace with our pious efforts? . . .

How hard it is for us truly to receive God's grace as freely as it is given! It hurts our egos to admit that all we are and all we do is made possible by God's action within us and that we can never do anything out of our own abilities to please him. . . .

How and when will we learn this truth that instead of burnt offerings God looks for contrite and diligent hearts? . . .

Elsewhere the book of Isaiah describes the sacrifices God desires: sacrifices of praise and rejoicing, the heart's gifts of commitment and trust, offerings of justice and compassion. God longs for our very selves, our willingness, devotion, humble submissiveness, faithful obedience, confident dependence, eager witness. He wishes that we would love him with all our heart and soul and mind and strength.

The outcome of that kind of love, of course, is that all the rest of our being is directed properly as well. Then we make the right sacrifices. We do indeed burn up our Lebanons (our very lives) and offer all the animals therein (our gifts and labors). However, the motive is exactly opposite. It is not an attempt to be sufficient; rather, it is the realization that there is no better use of Lebanon or her animals than to offer up our complete selves and service in praise of God.

Prayer
  Holy God, we thank you for the very gift of life. We offer our obedience, our
  commitment, our service, and our witness, in grateful praise for your gifts
  and your love . . .   Amen.

To Walk and Not Faint, pp. 96-99.

Whatever God ordains is right;
his will is just and holy.
He holds us in his perfect might;
in him, our lives are godly.

Samuel Rodgiast, 1649-1708

I have never heard the phrase "social rest." Instead, we usually hear a lot about *social unrest*. An exciting aspect of Sabbath keeping is the fact that it leads to very practical consequences both in our immediate communities and in our confused, war-torn world. . . .

I believe we have never really paid attention to any of the commandments, beginning with our refusal to honor Yahweh, our God, and to serve him only. We may not steal by robbing a bank or kill by murdering our spouses, but Christians are involved in the stealing from the poor that present economic policies foster, as well as in the killing that is done in the name of "preserving democracy." . . .

Our refusals to worship only Yahweh and to worship him especially on a day set apart for that purpose are inextricably intertwined with our refusal to love the poor, the hungry, and the enemy. All of our refusals reject the wisdom of God's instructions for truly enjoying life: to be devoted to the One who creates life; to live in a rhythm of six days of work and one day of Sabbath ceasing, resting, embracing, and feasting; to live out our sexuality in healthy relationships according to God's design; and to love our neighbors and our enemies by seeking to build both economic stability and political peace.

On the positive side, if we devote a special day to the worship of God, we will be changed so much by that Sabbath keeping — spiritually, physically, emotionally, intellectually, and socially — that our service to God and to others will fall more in line with the rest of the commandments. To choose to keep the Sabbath will irrevocably transform how we relate to the rest of the world. . . . It will enable us to behave differently in the midst of the world's tensions. I am utterly convinced that if all the Christians in the world could thoroughly practice Sabbath keeping, we could also learn that we don't need to kill each other.

Prayer
> *Holy Spirit, inspire us to keep the Sabbath faithfully, for the sake of our neighbors and the world . . .   Amen.*

Keeping the Sabbath Wholly, pp. 88-90.

O Lord, open my lips,
      and my mouth will declare your praise.

Psalm 51:15

These lines from Psalm 51 emphasize the interrelation of God as both subject and object of our worship, for his presence opens our lips to proclaim
his glory. We cannot respond to God as the object of our praise unless we
first see him, know him, let him be God in our lives. . . .

   Some worship planners and participants think that to praise God is
simply to sing upbeat music; consequently, many songs that are called
"praise" actually describe the feelings of the believer rather than the character of God. In the extreme, a focus on good feelings distorts the truth of the
gospel into a "health, wealth, and victory" therapy. We must recognize this
for the idolatry it is. Centering on happiness makes us forget that the world
gains redemption not through the Church's glory but through Christ's sacrifice and the suffering of God's people.

   As Leander Keck powerfully reminds us in *The Church Confident*, genuine
praise of God depends upon truth. It is not just an attitude of appreciation
or an emotion of well-being or delight; instead, it acknowledges a superla-
tive quality or deed. Praise does not express our own yearnings or wishes; it
responds to something given to us. . . . Genuine praise challenges our
secularity and idolatries and narcissism by concentrating not on our feelings of happiness, but on qualities in God that are truly there, not just there
for me.

   An emphasis on what we "get out" of a worship service — above all that
we feel good about ourselves — displaces the theocentric praise of God with
anthropocentric utilitarianism. Since the worship of God is an end in itself,
Keck explains, "making worship useful destroys it, because this introduces
an ulterior motive for praise. And ulterior motives mean manipulation, taking charge of the relationship, thereby turning the relation between Creator
and creature upside down."

   Instead of trying to force happiness or making the music more upbeat,
the Church best renews its praise by gaining a fresh apprehension of God.

Prayer
      O Lord, purify our motives in worshiping you. May we always do so to honor
      you, not to gain something for ourselves . . .   Amen.

Reaching Out, pp. 87-88.

. . . the one imparting — in simplicity!

Romans 12:8b (my translation)

The gift of imparting that Paul mentions in his list of grace-gifts in Romans 12 is probably the most often overlooked. We superficially assume that his injunction to be generous is meant only for those who have lots of money to give away. . . .

To understand the concept correctly we must stress again that grace is the basis for these gifts. One who is gifted with liberality gives generously not because he or she has much to give, but because that individual has a freer understanding of possessions and their importance.

Because the Greek word *metadidomi* is perhaps best translated "to share with someone else what one has" or "to impart," its object is not limited simply to financial resources. . . . God's people have the privilege of sharing whatever we have that someone else might need.

Especially this matters in connection with the Christian community's care for the needs of the poor and oppressed. Often our money is not the best thing we could give them. More urgently they might need your farming skills, your medical expertise, or your time to help refugees resettle in a strange land. What is called for here is not necessarily financial generosity, but — vastly more important — an attitude of heart that says, "Whatever is mine is yours." . . .

An open heart produces open purse strings and open refrigerators and open clocks. . . .

The Greek word translated "generously" here in Romans 12:8 also conveys the notion of "sincerity as an expression of singleness of purpose" or "purity of motive." . . . With singleness of purpose (namely, to serve God!), we are invited to live with as little as we need in order to share as much as we can with others. . . .

This grace-gift makes us realize again how important the Christian community is. I have heard it said that "Individuals can resist injustice, but only in community can we do justice." Individuals might take a stand against various ills in our society, but only as a group can we change them. The tasks of justice-building are too large for us alone. Only as we join together in giving generously can God's people generate enough resources to tackle the tasks.

Prayer

> *Giving God, open our hearts to share generously all that we have . . .*
> *Amen.*

Truly the Community, pp. 126-28.

Lord, who lived secure and settled,
safe within the Father's plan,
and in wisdom, stature, favor
growing up from boy to man —
with your grace and mercy bless
all who strive for holiness.

Timothy Dudley-Smith (1965)

As we contemplate the wanderings, the rumors, and the derisions of Jesus' earthly life, we are nudged to deeper reflection when we discover his security and safety at the center of his Father's will. In the midst of a world besieged by troubles of all sorts, what a wonder it is to discover the sanctuary available to us in seeking holiness. It is a great gift — and a sure one in the face of the impossibility of true ease in this world — that we can promise our children the safety of God's eternal care and the security of the resurrection.

Furthermore, God has promised, and Jesus reiterated this promise, that we *shall* be holy as his Father is holy. By Christ's work of grace, we are counted as saints — and our genuine safety lies in living out that sainthood. . . .

In the midst of the world's anguish because no one can find permanent happiness or ease, those who suffer sometimes look to the Church — and what shall we give them? Do they see in our lives a better goal? Do our children see that to aim for holiness is much more fulfilling than to be ceaselessly chasing after an elusive happiness?

We cannot respond to the yearnings of our children and neighbors with easy answers or the guarantee of ease. God and his people do not promise an end to suffering in this life, but instead the Scriptures and the Church train us in the truths of faith, which enable us to recognize sorrow's source in sinfulness and its meaning in the grace of God. . . . What our children need is not the illusion that they can escape from suffering, but purpose to endure it. Rather than pursuing an exhaustively fleeting comfort, we all need to be immersed in a faithful community that supports us in our adversity, that works to alleviate what can be eased, that embodies the presence of the God who genuinely comforts the afflicted and also afflicts the comfortable, that enables us to cultivate holiness in the midst of, and in spite of, our struggles and sorrows.

Prayer

Safekeeping God, may our life's goal be holiness; may we share your blessings with everyone . . .   Amen.

Is It a Lost Cause? pp. 139-40.

I will extol the LORD at all times;
  his praise will always be on my lips.
My soul will boast in the LORD;
  let the afflicted hear and rejoice.

Psalm 34:1-2

As David looks back, he recognizes that *YHWH* was in ultimate control of his life, and therefore he responds to God's love with these words of praise. His words urge us to choose the discipline of remembering the character of God who cares about us. Even when we don't feel like praising, there is comfort in the very habit.

David begins with a verb that has its roots in the word meaning "to kneel or to adore with bended knee." . . . It suggests that extolling the LORD at all times is based on humility, our own kneeling recognition that, despite surface evidences to the contrary, *YHWH* is always worthy of our praise. . . . Though the normal nastiness of everyday life will tempt us away from extolling the LORD "at all times," the choice to praise is made easier not only by *YHWH*'s supreme worthiness but also by our surprise at the benefits of praising him. . . .

Because I get discouraged about the peridontal problems that have caused my jaws to deteriorate, I kid my Christian dentist that I have named my partial bridges His Praise, since they are continually in my mouth. That joke has turned out to be a good reminder when, after hours and days of teaching, they cause painful irritation. . . . The discomfort nudges me to keep my words constant in reflecting worship. . . .

The Hebrew word *nephesh* or "soul" means the whole being, the true essence of a person. In other words, with his deepest self the poet David recognizes that his boasting should be about *YHWH*'s character rather than his own. . . . To boast properly is to recognize humbly where credit is due. Thus, to boast in *YHWH* means to point out to others what he has done and how we have seen him at work in our lives and, more important, in the world. . . .

The purpose of our boasting is made clear by David's next line, which promises, "The afflicted ones will hear and be joyful." We need more genuine witness in the Church so that those who are weak or humbled or oppressed can be glad with us.

Prayer
  Praiseworthy LORD, may our boasting in your goodness bring gladness to us
  all . . .   Amen.

I'm Lonely, LORD, pp. 86-88.

"He who has an ear, let him hear what the Spirit says to the churches."

Revelation 2:7a

When two things seem to contradict each other, yet both are necessary to keep the proper balance in the middle, they form a dialectical tension. . . .

The seven letters to the churches in Revelation 2 and 3 show us several dialectical tensions, such as the poles of truth and love. These must be kept in balance in order for our congregations to become the kind of churches that Christ wants them to be — lovingly truthful and truthfully loving. . . .

Even though most of the letters contain stern rebukes, they are intimately tied to the person of Christ, who holds their leaders in his hand and walks among them to comfort, to admonish, to praise. That would indeed be a great source of consolation for the struggling Christians of the first century. In the same way, we can find it vastly comforting that Christ is present in all his glory even when we deserve rebuke. . . .

We need the comfort of these seven letters. . . . In our doubts, or lack of trust, or attempts to know today all the answers for tomorrow, Jesus is with us — as the First and Last, as the One who holds the seven stars in his hand, as the One who says, "Do not be afraid." . . .

Five of the seven letters contain a call to repentance for immorality, false teaching, and losing the first love. In all these instances we recognize ourselves. When we glibly rely on ourselves — our own wisdom to figure out doctrine, our false pride as we gauge our morality, our own enthusiasm to be the focus of our love — then we need to repent.

The good news is that our failure to be the people that God would have us be does not remove us from the sphere of his care. His call to repentance is a sign of his continuing grace and the constant opportunity to come back into relationship with him. Furthermore, all the calls to repentance in these letters are followed by this summons: "Let the one having an ear listen to what the Spirit is saying to the churches." The Spirit keeps talking with us and inviting us to hear him.

Prayer

Lord Jesus, comfort and rebuke us. Call us to repentance and invite us to listen to your Spirit's guidance . . .   Amen.

Joy in Our Weakness, pp. 57-60.

Lebanon would not provide fuel enough,
  nor are its animals enough for a burnt offering.

Isaiah 40:16 (NRSV)

The realization that there is no better sacrifice than to offer up our complete selves and service in praise to God gives rise to difficult questions regarding stewardship — of our talents and treasures, our time and trust. How do we use our abilities? Do we devote all our skills to making money and a name for ourselves, or do we spend them to fight famine, to secure justice in the world, to support our spouse, to raise godly children, and quietly and reverently to give a defense to those who ask us to account for the hope that lies within us (1 Pet. 3:15-16)?

What about our treasures? Do our offerings to our congregations buy only organs and stained-glass windows and new shrubs for the landscaping, or are our financial resources being used for the spreading of the kingdom of God, to offer the narratives of faith to those without a story into which they can place their lives, to feed the hungry, to comfort those without hope? There is nothing wrong with pipe organs; they enhance our worship and lift us to God in incomparable ways. Beautiful furniture, vestments, and other signs and symbols of our adoration are good worship aids, useful assistants for fixing our minds on God. But do our luxurious buildings with all their gorgeous accoutrements become places of pride instead of houses of worship?

Do we realize that *any* percentage of our income is not enough for our offering? . . . Is our lifestyle in keeping with the One who called us to sell our possessions and give to the poor?

Perhaps all our stewardship can be summed up in the word *trust*. God's desire is for us to surrender all to him and trust his guidance for our way and his provision for our needs. We cannot ever really understand the Atonement, but we know that Jesus' sacrifice of his life and suffering, work and death, was sufficient to reconcile us to God because it was based on a simple trust in the Father's plan for human salvation. Our offerings are a response to Christ's gift of himself when we follow his model of dependent submission.

Prayer
  Generous God, may the stewardship of our lives honor your gifts of grace . . .
  Amen.

To Walk and Not Faint, pp. 96, 99-100.

This is what the Sovereign LORD, the Holy One of Israel says:
  "In repentance and rest is your salvation;
  in quietness and trust is your strength. . . ."

Isaiah 30:15

On the interpersonal level, keeping the Sabbath is a good way to be held accountable to God for our relationships. I can't enjoy a day set apart for fellowship with him if my relationships with others whom he has also created are out of whack. To receive his grace and to experience his restoration of my broken and sinful life stirs me to want restoration for everyone. To discover ourselves enfolded by grace in the holiness of God causes us to desire that same celebration for each person.

Furthermore, Sabbath keeping exposes our political illusions. To think about God and the lifestyle to which he calls us forces us to see that our political power plays do not accomplish God's purposes. Just as the Israelites needed to heed Isaiah's warning that their efforts to secure military alliances and to trust in weapons were futile, so we need to recognize the truth of Yahweh's warning that "in repentance and rest is your salvation; in quietness and trust is your strength." Instead of scrambling for security in national victory and domination, in preparations for war and military aggression, we must relearn the values of cooperation and sharing, of nonviolence and support.

The New Testament letter to the Ephesians exclaims that Christ has broken down the barriers that sin has created between people. . . .

We live in such a harsh society. The technology that brings us all kinds of benefits also brings impersonalization and a loss of control over our own circumstances. . . . Frenzy about time, possessions, sex, and status leads to violence, rage, rape, technological aggression, exploitation, and manipulation. The humility and serenity engendered by Sabbath keeping empower us to be agents of healing both near and far. Our prayers at Sabbath dinner might include the petition that our own privilege of celebrating would remind us of the needs of others and deepen our activity in caring for the hungry. Similarly, the prayers for Sabbath peace in our own lives will inevitably lead us to prayers and action for the peace of the world.

Prayer
  Prince of Peace, we pray that our Sabbath keeping will lead us to greater efforts in bringing peace and justice to all our world . . .   Amen.
Keeping the Sabbath Wholly, pp. 92-93.

You shall not make for yourself an idol, whether in the form of anything that is in heaven above, or that is on the earth beneath, or that is in the water under the earth. You shall not bow down to them or worship them; for I the LORD your God am a jealous God. . . .

Exodus 20:4-5a (NRSV)

God is the Subject of our worship, for he is the one who makes it possible for us to enter into his presence; God is the one who gives us himself in the Word, the water, the supper. How we conduct worship must teach all the participants that and enfold them in that reality. Worship is not the pastor inviting us into his or her living room, but God welcoming us into a holy place set apart to honor him.

Keeping God the Center does not narrow our options, though it gives us our primary criterion for sorting through them. That sentence might seem like a contradiction, except that God is infinitely beyond our imagining. Therefore, we need all kinds of sounds, spirits, styles, and shapes to evoke the Trinity's splendor. They must all be consistent, however, with what God has revealed about himself.

This truth leads to many questions that we who plan worship and the worship space must ask. Does the order of worship clearly reflect that God is the Subject? Is there too much focus on the pastor or musicians that would detract from participants' awareness that God is the inviter? Does the worship space reveal God's special presence? Do the participants' attitudes, the leaders' demeanors and gestures, the worship ambience keep God as the Subject?

Is the God portrayed by our worship the biblical God of Abraham and Sarah, Jesus and Mary? Does our worship focus one-sidedly on comfortable aspects of God's character, such as his mercy and love, without the dialectical balancing of his holiness and wrath? Is Jesus reduced to an immanent "buddy" or "brother" without the accompanying transcendence of God's infinite majesty? Is the Trinity diminished to merely rigid doctrines without the unsettling winds of the Spirit? . . . All these questions ask whether our worship really keeps the God of the Bible as its Subject. . . .

Nothing that we do should ever let us forget that worship is for God.

Prayer

Triune God, protect us from any form of idolatry in our worship. It is our desire to worship you . . .   *Amen.*

A Royal "Waste" of Time, pp. 152-53.

. . . the one presiding — in diligence!

Romans 12:8c (my translation)

This sixth function on Paul's list of grace-gifts has a broad field of meaning as it is used in the New Testament. The Greek verb *prohistemi* . . . is defined as so to "influence others as to cause them to follow a recommended course of action" — "to guide, to direct, to lead." This leads to a secondary meaning, "to be engaged in helping or aiding." Furthermore, in some instances in the New Testament the verb stresses engaging "in something with intense devotion." . . .

It seems here that Paul is intending to encourage those who bear within themselves an inherent authority that gives them legitimacy as leaders in the community. . . .

Paul says that a person's gift of administration or leadership should be used "to work hard," to govern "with intense effort and motivation," "to do one's best." The Greek noun carries a field of meaning best associated with words like "eagerness" or "readiness to expend energy and effort." Because Paul focuses in Romans 12 on members of the community learning that they all are necessary to one another and belong to one another, it seems that here he chooses the term to combine care with eagerness, a special urgency and intensity about the leadership tasks. The attitude necessary for such leadership involves the idea of readiness of heart to seek the community's well-being. . . .

The more single-minded we become, the more thoroughly committed to God all our efforts will be, the more his purposes can be accomplished in them. . . .

The need for diligence is critical in this age of extremes. A caring zeal enables us to find a balance in leadership between the over-productivity that characterizes workaholics and the mediocrity of those who limit their work to just enough to get by. Members of the community of God's people can offer to the world an alternative of excellence in leadership that calls forth the gifts of all the members of the Body. This highlights one of the unique problems of the grace-gift of administration. Those who govern must be especially sensitive to the fact that their diligence in leadership serves as a model for the zeal of the whole community.

Prayer

Holy Spirit, empower our leaders with a desire for excellence and a zeal for service that will be a faithful witness to us and all the world . . .   Amen.

Truly the Community, pp. 130-33.

Lord, who leaving home and kindred, followed still as duty led.
sky the roof and earth the pillow for the Prince of glory's head —
with your grace and mercy bless sacrifice for righteousness.

Timothy Dudley-Smith (1965)

Jesus was, of course, the perfect Sacrifice so that we might be covered over with a righteousness that is alien to our sinful nature, but perfectly conformed to the kingdom of God. Can we ever grasp these truths: that God has declared us holy, that Christ has made us righteous, and that the Holy Spirit empowers us actually to live out that holiness and righteousness?

The stanza of the hymn quoted above invites us and our children to follow, as Jesus did, where duty leads in order that we, too, might sacrifice for the sake of righteousness in the world. It is an amazing answer to give children who are screaming for candy or toys to suggest that we choose not to indulge ourselves, that we sometimes sacrifice pleasures for the sake of justice for others. . . . We don't give up certain things to be more holy, but out of our holy calling we gladly renounce some pleasures in order to contribute to the goodness of the world.

All of family life is a sacrificing for the sake of righteousness. We each give up some of our leisure time to do the chores that have to be done to keep the house clean, to feed ourselves nutritiously, to care for each other's physical and emotional, intellectual and spiritual needs. We must help our children to see that their contributions to these processes are as important as anyone else's. Fathers and mothers need their hugs as much as children require strong affection and enfolding. Both parents require the spiritual lessons that come "from the mouth of babes," and our offspring need careful nurturing in the faith.

The next verse of the hymn quoted above especially encourages us to think of others in the midst of our own sufferings. Let these words . . . remind us of the work of Christ:

Lord, who in your cross and passion hung beneath a darkened sky,
yet whose thoughts were for your mother, and a thief condemned to die —
may your grace and mercy rest on the helpless and distressed.

Prayer

Holy Spirit, help us model for our children a willingness to live righteously
and sacrificially, turning always toward the needs of others . . .   Amen.

Is It a Lost Cause? pp. 130, 140-41.

Glorify the LORD with me;
   let us exalt his name together.

Psalm 34:3

David's words urgently call us to apply them actively in our Christian circles. If we only appreciated the immense value for others that comes from speaking about what the LORD is doing in our lives, we would do it more often and thus be further strengthened. . . .

The prevalence of support groups in our society indicates the great need for finding strength in the positive experiences of others who have gone through what we are encountering. The Church could more often be a safe haven where the afflicted could be nurtured in hope. . . .

This underscores the importance of the fellowship of those who boast in the LORD. The poet first calls his listeners to magnify the LORD with him. . . .

We gladly magnify *YHWH* because we know that those who are introduced to his presence and purposes and compassions will greatly profit. We have no doubts that God will faithfully prove himself worthy of praise to anyone who accepts the challenge to get to know him. Evangelism becomes a delightful privilege and a natural reaction. We don't raise *YHWH* up; we simply enable others to see how great he already is.

The poetic parallel, "Let us exalt his name together," makes the invitation more intimate. Since the term *name* designates a person's character, to exalt *YHWH*'s name emphasizes recognizing his *chesedh,* or loving-kindness, and all the other attributes we have been discovering. . . . The invitation is for us to do that together as a community in action. Since each of us has our own unique perspective on God's character, we need each other to see more of what God is like.

The best part is that such glorifying together in a bond of praise eases our loneliness. . . .

In the rough moments, when we can't crank ourselves up to get going, we don't have to manufacture our own Joy or pretend our energy. Renewal is readily available to us in the habit of praise. As we bless *YHWH*, we are blessed. As we boast in his love, the recounting fills us with his presence. And when we do that together, we are doubly encouraged.

Prayer
   Exalted LORD, we thank you for the many ways we are blessed even as we together offer our praise to you . . .   Amen.

I'm Lonely, LORD, pp. 86, 89-91.

"To him who overcomes, I will give the right to eat from the tree of life, which is in the paradise of God."

Revelation 2:7b

The combination of differences and similarities in the letters to the seven churches in Revelation 2–3 tells us something else about being churches in the present century. All of the churches are given a challenge, and all of them receive a promise — even those most strongly rebuked, and even Laodicea, which receives no praise at all. No matter how desperate we think a situation might be in a particular congregation, God still gives his promises to that church. Grace is always present for any group of Christians, no matter how much they might be struggling.

Furthermore, even those churches that are not rebuked . . . are still given a challenge. . . . There are always certain ways in which we still must grow. . . .

The fact that each church receives a challenge and a word of promise is especially relevant. . . . Each church of the seven has something to offer the other churches and things to learn from the others. . . .

No Christian community can stand alone, nor can any individual within the community think that he or she does not have to be in relationship with the rest of the body. . . .

God's Word to the churches applies in any age. . . . The letters are part of the whole biblical narrative that nurtures the character of the people of God. Each letter gives important warnings, and at specific times our particular churches might need them directly. At other times, to hear what the Spirit is saying helps us to know how weighty each matter is — that we regain our first love as well as maintain pure doctrine, that we persevere as well as repent.

What a shame that the book of Revelation is so often ignored or so often used for bizarre purposes! It must be understood as a book of prophecy, but to prophesy is to speak the Word of God to a particular situation (with or without implications for the future). This book of prophecy applies God's truth to each of us and to all of us together.

Prayer
> *Lord of your Church, help us be open to praise and rebuke, promise and challenge, so that as your Church we will continue to grow in faith and service . . .*
> *Amen.*

Joy in Our Weakness, pp. 61-62.

All the nations are as nothing before him;
*   they are accounted by him as less than nothing and emptiness.*

Isaiah 40:17 (NRSV)

Christians who recognize that this world is not our real home must also wrestle with questions of citizenship. When we love *YHWH* and seek above all to be devoted to him and his purposes in the world, what does it mean to sing "I Love America"? What is a biblical perspective on patriotism? . . .

These are the implications of verse 17: . . . that nations are nothing before the LORD except as they are with the LORD and that they become meaningless when they contradict our deepest purposes and heritage elsewhere. Both points really are the same. . . .

We forget that our national heritage is not our primary birthright. We are above all, as the Scriptures tell us, strangers and aliens. We are sojourners and ambassadors here. It is good to be grateful for the land that is our home. It is good to recognize our nation's strong points and to be thankful for her resources, but it is dangerous to live entirely for the sake of our country. . . .

Though I am grateful for my country, I cannot give it undivided loyalty. Loving it forces me to be critical of its business tactics and governmental policies, its selling of weapons to feed the world's atrocities, its flagrant practice and exportation of immorality, its exploitation of poorer countries, its consumerism and waste. These certainly cannot be my practices if I am a loving citizen of God's kingdom.

Augustine fully understood the meaning of verse 17 . . . when he wrote . . . *The City of God.* That important work contrasts earthly kingdoms with the heavenly Kingdom and recognizes that Christians are citizens of both at the same time. . . . God told Israel . . . to "seek the welfare of the city where I have sent you into exile, and pray to the LORD on its behalf, for in its welfare you will find your welfare" (Jer. 29:7). What enables us to be the best possible citizens, however, is our awareness that our primary heritage is our citizenship in a greater Kingdom.

Prayer

Our true King, help us to serve our nation best through our greater commitment to you . . .   Amen.

To Walk and Not Faint, pp. 102-7.

The spiritual rest which God especially intends in this commandment [to keep the Sabbath holy] is that we not only cease from our labor and trade but much more — that we let God alone work in us and that in all our powers do we do nothing of our own.

Martin Luther

The more intentional we are about our choices, the more God's Spirit can work in us to develop a certain character, a certain set of virtues, a lifestyle of godliness. . . .

Our ethics are founded upon the grace of God. . . . We do not make moral choices because we *have to* live in a certain way; we don't discipline ourselves to behave in certain ways because we have to carve out our lifestyle by our own efforts. Ours is an ethic of freedom, of loving response because God loved us first.

The emotional and intellectual rest of the Sabbath day keeps us from blocking God as the Spirit works to transform our minds and personalities from the inside. He sets us free and empowers us to become more fully the people he has designed us to be. Moreover, this is true on a worldwide scale, . . . connecting Sabbath keeping with peace-building. If we become people of peace through the intentionality of our Sabbath keeping, then we will, out of that character of peacemaking, live in a way that promotes peace.

All of this means that the Sabbath rhythm leads to an ethics of *becoming* (how our character is being developed) and not of *doing* (how we react in specific situations). By the latter I refer to ethical systems that concentrate on making moral decisions in particular circumstances on the basis of what rules to follow or what results will be gained by a certain action. An ethics of character concentrates instead on what kind of people we are becoming. If the Holy Spirit has developed certain virtues in us, then in any particular case our behavior will issue from that character. . . .

The more we worship Yahweh, our God, and desire to serve him only, the more we will want to be like him and to follow his instructions against idolatry, killing, stealing, adultery, and coveting, and his commands to honor parents and keep the Sabbath.

Prayer
> *Holy Spirit, use our Sabbath time of rest to mold our characters in God's image . . .   Amen.*

Keeping the Sabbath Wholly, pp. 52, 95-97.

You were within me but I was outside myself, and I sought You there!
In my weakness I ran after the beauty of the things You have made . . .
   the things which would have no being unless they existed in You!

Augustine of Hippo, 354-430

When we agree that God must be the subject and object of our worship, we discover that the bitter war between "traditional" and "contemporary" styles misses the real issue. Both can easily become idolatrous. Many defenders of traditional worship pridefully insist that the historic liturgy of the Church is the only way to do it right, while their counterparts advocating contemporary worship styles often try to control God and convert people by their own efforts. Neither pride nor presumption can inhabit praise; both prevent God from being the subject and object of our worship.

Enthusiasts for contemporary worship are right in seeking to reach out to persons in the culture. . . . Those who value the Church's worship heritage are right to . . . seek a noticeable difference in worship that underscores the Church's countercultural emphasis. . . .

Debates about worship style usually arise because, in their desire to reach out to the culture surrounding us, parishes are striving to make worship meaningful to that society. C. Welton Gaddy, in *The Gift of Worship*, insists that this approach asks the wrong questions:

> To explore meaningful worship is to examine worship. . . . Authentic worship is always meaningful worship.
>
> Quests for meaning in worship are best served by discovering how to worship with integrity. Determining the nature of true worship is much more important than exploring the ways humans can bring novelty to worship.

Gaddy insists that a concern for meaning will be well served if we start with a study of these principles: Worship must center on God, glorify Christ, involve people, express praise, communicate the truth of the Bible, encourage faith, promise redemption, reflect the incarnation, build up the Church, instill vision, make an offering, nurture communion, and evoke an "Amen."

Prayer
   Triune God, lead us to authentic worship, for your sake, our sake, and the
   world's . . .   Amen.

Reaching Out, pp. 75, 93-94.

. . . the one extending mercy — in Hilarity!

Romans 12:8d (my translation)

Paul lists as the seventh grace-gift in Romans 12 the charism of mercy or kindness to those sorrowing or in need. Again, the position of the phrases in Paul's entire discourse is significant, because the very next admonition — to keep love from being hypocritical (v. 9) — is an essential qualifier for the way in which concern is dispensed. We don't offer gifts of mercy only when we feel like being helpful to those in distress, but we must also remember that acts of mercy done without appropriate compassion are empty and hypo-critical. . . .

No one really does anything well unless she or he enjoys the process of doing it. To be persons of Hilarity is all the more appealing because we live in such an age of pain and overwhelming confusion. Human beings live in fear of nuclear war, terminal illness, and economic chaos. We do not super-ficially ignore those problems when we live Hilariously, but we reveal the uniqueness of the Christian life, which is founded upon a wholly different basis for existence.

Hilarity in its biblical sense connotes profound gladness arising from a deep sense of the rich treasure of God's grace for us, from an awareness that God's love sets us free to enjoy being truly ourselves, and from trusting the Grace-Giver to work through his gifts to us. Hilarity in the Christian com-munity comes from being transformed rather than conformed. It expresses itself in eager and generous love for others. . . . It depends upon the renewal of the mind, though that doesn't hamper its spontaneity. As such it is the focus of everything we desire in the community. . . .

At various times and in various ways appropriate to our personal situa-tions and arising out of our particular relationship with the Lord, we are unique bearers of that grace. Each time, the power and freedom of doing what God has called us to do fills us with Hilarity, an immense cheer and ex-ultant gladness for the privilege of serving him in whatever way he chooses and out of our truest selves.

Prayer

   O Source of our Hilarity, empower us in showing mercy . . .   Amen.

Truly the Community, pp. 130, 135-37.

Lord, who rose to life triumphant
with our whole salvation won,
risen, glorified, ascended,
all the Father's purpose done —
may your grace, all conflict past,
bring your children home at last.

Timothy Dudley-Smith (1965)

It grieves me that churches these days rarely teach much about heaven. Many pastors and congregational leaders seem to me to be embarrassed by the whole idea. . . . The modernist world of scientific rationalism has stolen heaven from Christians.

It is true that heaven was used falsely as a recompense by oppressors in days past. . . . However, these serious errors in the application of the biblical basis for awaiting God's heaven are no reason to reject what the Scriptures say. . . .

Heaven is not an *escape* to help us ignore our suffering now. It is not a *reward* for getting through these present pains. Rather, it is a *gift*, already received, that enables us to know the truth of God's love and presence underlying our present realities. . . . We can *know* that the Lord will bring his children home at last because Christ rose, ascended, fulfilled the Father's purposes entirely, triumphed over the principalities and powers, and completed our salvation. That we will someday experience God's presence face-to-face makes us not less involved with this world now, but more so, for salvation invites us to be agents of God's purposes, too. Furthermore, living in the light of eternity gives us a freedom for that service that the world cannot give. We don't have to justify our existence, prove our worth, make a name for ourselves, or accumulate wealth. With our spiritual longing genuinely stilled by our present possession of eternity, we can expend our energies for others instead of chasing after our own happiness. Heaven and its holiness, sacrifice and its righteousness, are the perfect antidote to our society's fruitless pursuit of comfort and ease.

What greater gift can we give to our children than knowledge of heaven, assurance of the promise that the Lord will "bring [his] children home at last"? What greater life can we nurture in them than that of the kingdom of God? What greater purpose can we imbue them with than making heaven known to the world by the way we live now?

Prayer
  Eternal Lord, we praise and thank you for the gift of heaven . . .   *Amen.*
Is It a Lost Cause? pp. 130, 142-43.

Those who look to him are radiant;
  their faces are never covered with shame.
This poor [one] called, and the LORD heard him;
  he saved him out of all his troubles.

Psalm 34:5-6

When the people of God look to him, they are made radiant by the wonder of his embracing love.

Immediately we think of Moses, who had to wear a veil over his face after he came down from being with *YHWH* on Mount Sinai for forty days and forty nights. The people could not look on him because he was so luminous, according to Exodus 34:29-35 and 2 Corinthians 3:7-13. In the latter passage, Moses' secret is let out of the bag. After he had been down for a while, his face began to lose its illumination because he was no longer in the presence of God himself.

Moses' need to wear the veil to hide his fading radiance urges us to stay continually in the presence of *YHWH*. The brightness of which David speaks is not a once-given gift that lasts for all time, but a reflection of what we are observing. The more we look to *YHWH*, the more we will continue to be changed into his likeness, from one degree to another, as Paul stresses in 2 Corinthians 3:18. . . .

The faithfulness of *YHWH* . . . is underscored by the fact that here again he has heard and delivered the afflicted one from all distresses. . . .

We must read that carefully lest we complain that God hasn't set us free from all our struggles. The verb says that in those challenges, *YHWH* creates for us range and scope so that we have enough space to stand firm. The particular adversities in which we find ourselves might not be taken away, but . . . God saves us out of all our troubles by giving us strength to hold on and friends to stand with us and by creating enough space and peace so that we can more sanely handle our problems. . . .

If our eyes and heart are open, God has all sorts of surprises, . . . and his Word is always there for us, with surprises of its own.

Prayer
  Surprising LORD, we praise you for the privilege of staying in your presence, radiantly reflecting your loving care, which strengthens us in the face of all our troubles . . .   Amen.

I'm Lonely, LORD, pp. 92-95.

"To the angel of the church in Ephesus write: . . . I know your deeds, your hard work and your perseverance. . . . Yet I hold this against you: You have forsaken your first love."

Revelation 2:1a, 2a, 4

The Christians at Ephesus are commended for their deeds, their work, and their patience. . . . Nevertheless, they had lost their first love. . . .

The lesson is especially essential for us because our personal and corporate faith lives can so easily fall into the same trap. Too often, particularly if we have been believers for quite a while, there is great danger that we will do the acts of faith without any love underneath. . . .

We all run into this danger when we use our spiritual gifts. At first, in response to God's grace, we love doing what our gifts enable us to do. . . .

The hazard, however, is that we might start loving our ministries for the wrong reason, envisioning the tasks as the end rather than the means. . . . Then our service becomes self-centered instead of God-centered, people-pleasing rather than God-pleasing. . . .

The Ephesians' ability to have patience in hard times was a powerful strength, but if its end result was patting themselves on the back for their courage, then God was not glorified. . . .

The secret of retaining love is the discipline of nurturing it. . . .

The desire to retain our first love invites us to have a daily devotional period for reading the Scriptures, meditating on them, and spending time in prayer. We need such disciplines to focus our attention on who God is and how he loves us, how he has gifted us, and how his grace sustains us. As we ponder those blessings, truly our love is quickened and nourished and sustained.

If we are not passionately in love with God, it is not because he has stopped blessing us. . . . God is always at work in our circumstances to bring the best for us. The letter to the Ephesians invites us, when we have moved away, to repent of that movement and to receive again God's immense love for us.

Prayer

Loving Lord, we recommit ourselves to practices that will nurture our first love and, thereby, our loving service . . .   Amen.

Joy in Our Weakness, pp. 63-67.

161

To whom then will you liken God,
  or what likeness compare with him?

Isaiah 40:18 (NRSV)

This verse serves as a center, a focus in the midst of the fortieth chapter of Isaiah. It helps us to understand all the chapter's rhetorical questions about the magnificence and dominion and immeasurability of God. All the main themes of the chapter evolve from this basic point: Nothing — not flesh, nor idols, nor nations — can compare with *YHWH*.

This verse's significant questions ought also to be the focus of our existence: How can we describe God? By what means shall we come to a greater understanding of *YHWH?* The prophet . . . forces us to realize that the ways we describe God and the false deities that we array against him indicate our miniscule comprehension of his character. . . .

This verse urges us to increase our appreciation for all that God is by enlarging our vocabulary about him. The way we perceive *YHWH* affects how we come to him. If we perceive that the name *Father* reduces God to the kind of oppressive, abusing men that many have experienced in their dysfunctional families, we certainly won't turn to him as trusting children. But if we search the Scriptures and discover the totally loving Father that he is — if we picture his gracious sustaining, tender enfolding, and gentle care — we will recognize in him the perfect Father that every human being needs. It is a crucial question, then, "To whom will you liken God?"

Obviously, we cannot compare anyone or anything to God. Nothing comes close to corresponding to him. All our language is inadequate. Even our composite pictures of many attributes grouped together only scratch the surface of all God is.

The lifelong challenge before us as believers is continually to explore the nature of God as deeply as we can in order to love and proclaim that nature more accurately. As much as possible we want to grasp the characteristics by which *YHWH* has made himself known. Certainly we gather for worship and spend time in Bible study and devotional meditation so that we can add and add and add some more to our understanding of what God is like.

Prayer
  O God beyond our full knowing, keep us ever searching to know you better
  and eager to share all that we learn . . .   Amen.

To Walk and Not Faint, pp. 108-11.

All who keep the Sabbath without desecrating it . . .
these I will bring to my holy mountain. . . .

Isaiah 56:6c, 7a

One of the most important aspects of Sabbath keeping is that we embrace intentionality. . . .

Sabbath keeping says clearly that we are not going to do what everybody else does. We are going to be deliberate about our choices in order to live truly as we want to live in response to the grace of God. We are committed to certain values and, therefore, live in accordance with them as fully as we can. Everybody else catches up on yard work on Sundays, but we have chosen to rest from work on our Sabbath day. Everyone else goes window-shopping at the mall on that day, but we have chosen to cease the American hankering after possessions. . . .

One of the treasures of learning about Sabbath keeping for me has been coming to understand better the Jewish emphasis on acting intentionally. . . . Of course, the carefulness of Jewish practices can easily become empty formalism or legalistic duty. On the other hand, we must respect their insistence on practices that set them apart from the culture . . . in a way that attempts to prevent their biblical faith and its particular values from being swallowed up by the surrounding culture. . . .

We offer to the world the beauty of our lifestyles when we choose to be careful about each aspect of them. Such intentionality is not legalistic; on the contrary, it frees us to see and make manifest to others in new ways all that is special about life. . . .

The paradox is that we are removed from our bond with the material by making the material objects that surround us sacred. By focusing on how we treat our food and our dishes — even on where we put our napkin — we concentrate on holy time. . . .

Christians would do well to follow that kind of intentionality. If we were more deliberate about our lifestyles, we might be more conscious ourselves of God's grace, of who we are as God's people, and of how discipleship involves careful choices. Paying such close attention to living a truly Christian lifestyle would give better witness to the world.

Prayer

God whose intentions never fail, help us witness to others by living what we say we believe . . .   Amen.

Keeping the Sabbath Wholly, pp. 100, 103-9.

And they, continuing daily with one accord in the temple, . . . did eat their meat with gladness and singleness of heart, praising God, and having favor with all the people. . . .
Acts 2:46-47a (King James Version)

In our fragmented and alienated, individualistic, and competitive society, many people wonder if the Christian Church is any different. . . .

We would do well to reflect upon the question of how to build genuine and welcoming community in our congregations. . . . What elements in the corporate service can contribute to the nurturing of our common life together? How can a sense of the Christian community be established and reinforced while we are meeting together to praise God and grow in faith? How can we display in our gatherings in the "Temple" the "one accord" of the early Christians, whose "singleness of heart" led to having great favor with their neighbors? . . .

In *Christian Ethics Today* (June 1996), Molly T. Marshall wrote about the dangers of thinking about the church as a family — for that can inhibit our ability to welcome strangers or cause us to squeeze out people with whom we cannot attain intimacy. . . .

Community in the biblical sense is more open to the realities of differences, more openly gracious to all, more deliberate, an act of will. It does not depend upon feelings of affection. In fact, sometimes (perhaps always?) God seems to put us in a community together with people whom we don't like so that we learn the real meaning of *agapē* — that intelligent, purposeful love directed toward another's need, which comes first from God and then flows through us to our neighbor. To develop a community . . . takes a lot of work and time, sacrifice and commitment. . . .

We must note this obvious, but often overlooked, truth: the triune God wants our churches to be genuine communities. . . .

Since we know that God is at work to make us all one, we are set free to enjoy the process — knowing that it does not depend upon us. What we do to build community is a response to the grace of a unifying God; who we are as the *people* of God is an image of the relationship within the Godhead.

Prayer
> *Unifying Trinity, direct us in community-building behaviors that welcome everyone in your name . . .   Amen.*

A Royal "Waste" of Time, pp. 178-80.

. . . the one extending mercy — in Hilarity!

Romans 12:8d (my translation)

Focusing particularly on the grace-gift of showing mercy, we recognize that God's people often do not link doing deeds of mercy with gladness. Somehow the cheer gets lost between our study of the Scriptures and the practical application. Or maybe we don't study the Scriptures deeply enough and consequently don't experience the constant Hilarity that could mark our lives. . . .

When we are thoroughly involved in the passing on of God's great love to others, we will become more and more aware of the immense privilege that we have to serve the Lord as we do with his power and direction and freedom. Then our acts of love and mercy, as well as our exercising of whatever gifts God bestows, will all be characterized by this grand Hilarity, the Joy of being what God intended us to be — uniquely gifted and immeasurably important as participants in the Body of Christ.

As Paul says later in his letter to the Romans, the kingdom of God is "righteousness and peace and joy in the Holy Spirit" (14:17). The word *righteousness* defines our right standing with God by means of our faith and trust in him. Peace marks our relationships with others. . . . And joy marks our relationship with ourselves, as we live out the reality of God's purposes in our lives and the extension of his grace to others through the use of our gifts. . . .

Moreover, our joyful Hilarity is heightened because we celebrate it together with other members of the Christian community. Our sense of belonging to one another sets us free to be truly ourselves, each one characterized by grace-gifts valuable to the community and not burdened by responsibilities for which others possess the gifts. Our togetherness sets us all free to use our gifts with more Hilarity.

Life is not all roses if we are Christians. We still mourn and struggle. However, underneath all the responsibility and grief will always be the deep sense of wholeness, the Hilarity of being in a community of caring, the profound knowledge of the truth that God is God — and a grace-giving God at that.

Prayer

God of grace and mercy, free us to delight in living as a community of grace-gifted people, each uniquely serving for the sake of others . . .   Amen.

Truly the Community, pp. 130, 137-38.

God, whose giving knows no ending,
from your rich and endless store . . .
Now direct our daily labor,
lest we strive for self alone.

Robert Edwards (1961)

I especially worry about teenagers in our society. Since so many young people are growing up in homes that do not provide them with a family story and a web of reality by which to understand themselves, they constantly remake themselves according to the latest fads or heroes of rebellion. . . .

These ongoing refabrications of self arise because there is no core of character by which the young people can set their priorities and guide their life's choices. Constant consumerism . . . makes the person's character increasingly pinched, more "inward-turned" as Martin Luther would say. . . .

I am also especially concerned about parents and churches because, as J. Christoph Arnold of the Bruderhof writes, in our society "all too often what sways our decisions is not really our children, nor even their futures, but money." Arnold continues,

> What does it really mean to give a child love? Many parents, especially those of us who are away from home for days or even weeks at a time, try to deal with our feelings of guilt by bringing home gifts for our children. But we forget that what our children really want, and need, is time and attentiveness, a listening ear and an encouraging word, which are far more valuable than any material thing we can give them.
>
> We cannot deny that, as a whole, our society is driven not by love but by the spirit of materialism, which the Bible calls Mammon. Mammon is more than money — it is greed, selfishness, and personal ambition; violence, hatred, and ruthless competition. And it is diametrically opposed to the spirit of child-likeness and of God.

Are we, as parents and congregations, willing to bear a heavy cross for the sake of nurturing our children in genuine Christian faith? . . . Are we willing to wage war against the principality of Mammon for the sake of genuine spiritual growth in our children and ourselves?

Prayer
Merciful Father, forgive our idolatry of things; empower us to choose eternal
values and pass them on to our children . . .   Amen.

Is It a Lost Cause? pp. 145, 148-49.

The angel of the Lord encamps around those who fear him,
   and he delivers them.

Psalm 34:7

Sometimes the words *angel of the Lord* in the Scriptures seem to suggest *YHWH* himself. At other times the word *angel* appears to signify a human being who functions as a messenger of God. We each know "encamping" persons who have been ministering angels to protect us and speak God's words to us. . . .

The Scriptures also speak of literal angelic beings, invisible warriors who guard us and fight for us. . . . Angels have become too much a New Age fad these days — and the tendency is to believe that they exist only for our personal benefit. In contrast, the Bible does name angels, archangels, seraphim, and cherubim as part of the heavenly hosts and invites us to be grateful for their ministering work, including their constant war with the "spiritual forces of evil in the heavenly realms" (Eph. 6:12). . . .

One favorite story summarizes all we need to know about angels anyway. When Elisha is in danger of losing his life, his awed servant panics because he can see only the horses and chariots of the Aramean army surrounding the city of Dothan (2 Kings 6:8-23). When he cries to Elisha, the prophet calmly answers, "Those who are with us are more than those who are with them" (v. 16), and then prays for *YHWH* to open the servant's eyes. Immediately the latter is amazed to see "the hills full of horses and chariots of fire all around Elisha" (v. 17). . . .

Our problem is that we don't usually see them either. We need the Lord to open our eyes to recognize his messengers. . . . They encamp around us to bring us the truth of God's presence. When we are afraid because we are alone, we need to take angels seriously as the forces that God constantly provides to protect us and take care of us.

Prayer

   Enfolding Lord, we thank you for the ways you provide comfort, protection,
   and the encouragement of your Word . . .   Amen.

I'm Lonely, Lord, pp. 92, 95-97.

"To the angel of the church in Smyrna write: . . . Be faithful, even to the point of death, and I will give you the crown of life."

Revelation 2:8a, 10c

The letter to Smyrna . . . does not have any warnings or negative criticism of the church. Because of their sufferings the Spirit has only words of encouragement for the members of this community. . . .

The first is that in their tribulations and poverty they are actually rich . . . , in their relationship with the Lord and in the gifts he showers on them, . . . in their relationship with the community of his people, and in the support for their tribulations that the community provides. Moreover, their wealth is founded on the assurance that these tribulations are not God's last word to them. . . .

Second, the Spirit assures the people of Smyrna that he knows about the slander they are receiving . . . and comforts the Smyrna church by declaring that God understands. . . .

Next, the people at Smyrna are urged not to fear what they are about to suffer . . . because the suffering is limited . . . to only that which is necessary to accomplish the purposes of God. . . .

This is a substantial hope for our times of trials. Those around us who wonder about God might observe our response to suffering and judge accordingly. Our attitudes in suffering can be powerful vehicles for evangelism. . . .

The next reason that we need not be fearful in times of suffering is that we have this promise: if we continue to be faithful unto death, the Lord will graciously give us the crown of life. . . . Knowing, then, that the gift is ours — not by virtue of *our* success in remaining faithful, but because of *God's* — gives us the assurance to keep carrying on, . . . to keep trying to be faithful in all the tribulations of our lives, . . . until only one obstacle remains. . . . When we pass that last door of death, we are set free from all the limitations that keep us from seeing God face-to-face.

Prayer

Faithful God, thank you for your promises of support and ultimate victory, which give us courage to face our tribulations in the meantime . . .   Amen.

Joy in Our Weakness, pp. 68-73.

To whom then will you liken God,
   or what likeness compare with him?

Isaiah 40:18 (NRSV)

The entire quest of theology can be summarized in these two words: "Know God!" Our primary source for doing that is the Bible with all its narratives of God's work in the world and its names for God and descriptions of God's character. The biblical illiteracy in contemporary U.S. culture has resulted in a terribly narrow picture of God. Some of the biblical pictures we would rather not face — and some of them we overemphasize.... For example, our culture likes the coziness of a loving God, but skips over his wrath. We want to feel comfortable with God, but we bypass "the fear of the LORD," which is "the beginning of wisdom." We need all of the Scriptures to reveal to us all that God wants to tell us about himself....

Furthermore, no matter how many times we study particular sections of the Scriptures, these same passages will continually unlock new truths for us about the nature of God....

One of the essential reasons for the Body of Christ is that it takes all of God's people to show us everything that God wants to tell us about himself. Consequently, 1 Peter urges us to be good stewards of that which has been given to us, employing our gifts for one another and revealing, by our stewardship, some of the facets of God's many-sided grace (4:11)....

Each day, in all the "ordinaries" of life, we append dimensions of perception to our appreciation for the character of God — always knowing that our cognition is still inadequate....

Many things, people, and incidents give us bits and pieces to add to our growing knowledge of the character of God. It's not that they ARE God, but rather that his creatures reveal their Creator. Above all, *YHWH* is to be found in his Word.

When we try to compare him or draw an image of him, we find that nothing will do. God cannot be contained.... Now we merely catch glimpses through his gifts to us. Some day we shall know him face-to-face.

Prayer

Incomparable LORD, we praise you for revealing yourself to us in your Word and through all of creation ...   Amen.

To Walk and Not Faint, pp. 108, 111-13.

Grant, O heavenly Father, that the spiritual refreshment I have this day enjoyed may not be left behind and forgotten as tomorrow I return to the cycle of common tasks.

John Baillie

One of the main reasons for being deliberate about how we do what we do is so that we can recover more firmly in our lives the different set of values that we hold because we are God's people. Not only do we need to cease the enculturation that so easily entraps us, but also we must positively — and deliberately — choose the values of the kingdom of God. In order to accomplish God's purposes, we recognize a different ordering of priorities. . . .

One of those priorities in the Christian community is worship. We choose to spend our time, especially on Sabbath days, in company with others committed to God, remembering our identity as his people together, celebrating our oneness in his grace. During our worship times we praise God and adore him, focus on who he is and try to learn more fully what he is like so that we can imitate him. We hear his Word, his instructions for living as his people, and we rejoice in the delight of his covenant designs. We spend time in prayer, searching for his will and resting in his presence. We choose to meditate on his Word more deeply in Bible classes and in our personal devotional lives, immersing ourselves in his truth so that we might enjoy its freedom. . . .

The grace of Sabbath refreshment and the consequent deliberateness of Sabbath contemplation and prayer can thus be carried over into the week in the ways in which we act on the values of the Christian community in every aspect of our lives. . . .

Our choosing of God's values is possible only because God's grace enlightens and guides and leads us to a deliberate rejection of the values of the culture around us. For example, in a society that chooses promiscuity, we intentionally pursue faithfulness and chastity. In an age that chooses materialism, we deliberately seek to share with those in need. In a world that chooses violence, we take care to build peace and to be agents of reconciliation whenever possible.

Prayer

Gracious and empowering Lord, may our Sabbath worship and study empower us in living our Christian values every day . . . Amen.

Keeping the Sabbath Wholly, pp. 111-15.

Too late have I loved You, O Beauty so ancient, O Beauty so new. . . .
                                        Augustine of Hippo, 354-430

What kind of God do our worship practices portray? Is God shown chiefly in judgment or in grace, in power or in mercy? Does our God come to us primarily in law or gospel, in rules or in compassion? Are the humility and servanthood of Jesus portrayed faithfully so that worshipers strive to become like him, willingly offering themselves in service to God and others in all of life? . . .

Most weaknesses of worship arise when we forget the constant dialectics of God's character. Holiness without love incites terror; love without holiness invites libertinism. Worship that focuses on God's transcendence without God's immanence becomes austere and inaccessible; worship that stresses God's immanence without God's transcendence leads to irreverent coziness.

As C. Welton Gaddy emphasizes, "Every word and act in worship constitutes a witness about God as well as an offering to God. The manner in which God is worshiped is a message about how God is perceived, about how God's holiness is to be reverenced and approached." We want, therefore, to give God not only "what is best, what God deserves, what is consistent with God's nature," but also "that which most accurately reveals the nature of God to others. People will have difficulty understanding that God's being requires reverence if they know worship services that are not reverent." . . .

One of the best aids to creating worship that portrays the dialectical attributes of God, that praises the totality of God's being, is the liturgical year. Beginning in Advent's season of repentance, which confronts us with our desperate need for a Messiah, God comes to us in mercy, in sovereignty over time, and with the promise that Christ will come again. The Christmas and Epiphany seasons convey God's grace, tenderness, and splendor. Lent reveals the faithfulness of God's suffering on our behalf through the immensity of Christ's sacrifice. Easter demonstrates God's power and victory over the principalities and powers. Pentecost brings us the mystery and wonder of God at work in us. The nonfestival half of the Church year then celebrates many other attributes and actions of God in its focus on segments of Christ's teaching and life.

Prayer
   Infinite God, we want our worship to reflect all that we have come to know
   about your love for us . . .   Amen.
                                        Reaching Out, pp. 75, 95-96.

The love — not hypocritical!

Romans 12:9a (my translation)

The Living Bible paraphrases this verse: "Don't just pretend that you love others; really love them." To do that is absolutely impossible without supernatural empowering. On the other hand, to do so is also absolutely necessary for our Christian witness and vital for our own realization of the power of God at work through us. . . .

Paul helps us to understand that the exercising of gifts in response to God's grace ("therefore") will be characterized by attitudes and actions of genuine love. . . .

Always we must be aware of the hollowness of using gifts without love, so that our service for Christ is continuously lived out in the context of our relationship with him. . . .

However . . . we must also remember that a great diversity of manifestations of these virtues characterizes the unity of the Christian community. . . .

By God's gifting some persons are more outgoing and affectionate; others demonstrate his love in quiet ways that are just as genuine. Some persons are more suited to hospitality (Rom. 12:13) or are more able to pursue peace (v. 18). Others are able to be deeply compassionate in sharing the emotions of others (v. 15) or are empowered for fervent prayer (v. 12). . . . We dare not become legalistic in expecting all these traits to take the same forms or to be equally manifested in each of us.

This is why we must be careful to notice that Paul's description of the fruit of the Spirit in Galatians 5:22-23 is decisively singular. The fruit of the Spirit is manifested in nine different ways, including love, patience, and peace, but that one fruit is the life of Christ within us. Some persons are more loving as Christ lives through them; others are more self-controlled, and still others, more gentle. Our proportions of the nine manifestations are uniquely different, though we all want more and more to reflect each of the qualities. Furthermore, together the Christian community manifests them all.

Prayer

> *God of all mercy and compassion, give us grace to recognize and use our unique gifts of love . . .   Amen.*

Truly the Community, pp. 139-42.

Save us from weak resignation
to the evils we deplore;
let the gift of your salvation
be our glory evermore.

Harry Emerson Fosdick (1930), alt.

How is it that our celebration of Christ's Incarnation has come to be . . . the major supplier of retail stores' profits? . . .

What might we do in our families to celebrate Christmas as a holy day? . . . What can we do to help our children not only learn that we have different understandings about this holy time but also to enjoy being different in our celebration of it?

My parents followed many old and lovely German Lutheran customs to make the days different for us so that we both knew what the celebration was all about and didn't feel deprived not to have all the material possessions other children had. One of my favorite traditions was the daily lighting of candles on the Advent wreath. . . .

Another occurred on Christmas Eve, when my folks would open the doors of Dad's study to reveal the lighted Christmas tree. What a surprising, luminous, beautiful sight it always was to teach us that Jesus is the Light of the world, that Christmas celebrates his coming to our world — and to our house. . . .

Now my husband and I try to keep presents out of Christmas entirely by opening them instead on Epiphany (January 6th) in honor of the gifts of the Magi. Families whose children couldn't wait that long could open gifts on the Festival of Saint Nicholas (December 6th), as long as the parents help their children to see that the original saint devoted his life to serving the poor with his gifts. Emphasizing the goodness and social concern of the original Saint Nicholas invites our offspring to imitate him in the ways he exemplified the gifting of God. . . .

The crucial point in all this is that we help our children know that what we believe influences the way we celebrate Christmas — namely, that salvation is not only an enormously wonderful and totally essential gift, but also the entire reason for the season. . . . Jesus said that we cannot serve both God and Mammon; that choice needs to be made more apparent especially at times like Christmas.

Prayer

Incarnate Word of God, may our desire to serve and honor you be evident in the way we celebrate your birth . . .   Amen.

Is It a Lost Cause? pp. 146, 151-55, 165.

Taste and see that the LORD *is good. . . .*

Psalm 34:8a

The eighth verse of Psalm 34 seems to be meant especially for those who learn best in tangible ways. The poet doesn't merely say, "Check out the goodness of *YHWH*." He encourages us to "taste and see that the LORD is good." The verb *to taste* urges us to examine by experience, to jump right into God's goodness. How can we know *YHWH* is noble unless we give him a try?

That statement is a strong motivation for our witness to others. Many people have not entered into a relationship with God because they have never tasted of his mercy, his truth, his generosity, his excellence . . . . or had the opportunity to examine the biblical claims in tangible ways. . . .

Several years ago a Christian journal carried the story of a young woman who had become a believer because someone had challenged her to test whether the Scriptures "worked." In practicing a principle that she had read concerning not retaliating against enemies, she discovered the truth of the Christian life. . . .

The Lord's Supper provides Christians with an opportunity to taste God's goodness in three tenses — past, present, and future. In that tangible partaking, believers look back at what Christ actually did for us in the breaking of his body and the pouring out of his blood in death. While sharing the bread and wine, we also experience Christ's presence in our eating and in the present community of those gathered around the table. Finally, we look forward at that table to the fulfillment of Jesus' promises that someday we will feast with him and all the saints at the great banquet of heaven.

Throughout my adulthood, one of my best ways to ease loneliness has been to invite others to share God's presence with me in a meal. Conversation, the delight of being together, the aromas, the textures of foods from God's creativity, and holding hands in prayer enable us to taste and feel the goodness of *YHWH*.

Prayer

> *God of all creation, we praise you for your goodness. Teach us to share our life-changing experiences with those who have not yet been invited to the feast . . .   Amen.*

I'm Lonely, LORD, pp. 98-100.

"To the angel of the church in Pergamum write: . . . I know where you live — where Satan has his throne. Yet you remain true to my name."

Revelation 2:12a, 13a-b

This letter praises the saints at Pergamum because they have remained true and have not denied their faith in Christ, even though they have been threatened by the death of one of their greatest witnesses. . . . He was killed right in their own city — therefore, the letter repeats that, indeed, this is the place where Satan lives. . . .

Where does Satan live? What gives him a throne? Pergamum provided a throne because it was the center of emperor worship in Asia Minor in the first century. . . .

And what about you? Perhaps you work in a place where everybody curses or cheats or is involved in sexual immorality. Or maybe the demonic influence is much more subtle — perhaps in the power plays co-workers use to manipulate each other. It is difficult to maintain one's Christian witness in a demonic atmosphere.

Similarly, those challenged physically or mentally often encounter difficulty as they try to keep clinging to Christ in the constant discouragement of worsening handicaps. Illness and disability are certainly not God's intention, so we might say that in our afflictions we can also recognize Satan's dominion.

Yet the people of Pergamum are praised. They have remained true in their circumstances. They have clung to the name of Christ, by whose power the thrones of Satan have already been cast down. Their faithfulness provides a model of the ability to continue in circumstances largely overwhelmed by the powers of evil. The name of Christ enables his people to be true. . . .

God's people can keep living righteously right where Satan has his throne only by continual participation in the Word . . . which, in his grace, God has made . . . readily available to us.

Living intentionally requires great deliberation, choosing our actions carefully so that they do not contribute to the various idolatries of power and wealth in our culture. . . . Therefore, we must ask ourselves these searching questions: Of what idolatries do I need to repent? In what areas of my life do I need the cleansing/pruning Word of God?

Prayer

> *Merciful Lord, Satan's throne is near. Forgive our idolatries, and empower us by your Word to live faithfully and courageously . . .   Amen.*

Joy in Our Weakness, pp. 76-79.

To whom then will you liken God,
   or what likeness compare with him?
An idol? — A workman casts it,
   and a goldsmith overlays it with gold,
   and casts for it silver chains.

Isaiah 40:18-19 (NRSV)

Notice how verse 19 accentuates the beautiful and thorough work of the idol makers. . . . What idolatries do we spend great effort constructing, hiding the emptiness of our images under an overlay of gold?

When my doctoral dissertation got snagged . . . in committee problems, I sought a counselor's help for the ensuing depression. He asked me why I needed the degree, and . . . his next question exposed how I had turned it into an idol. "Why is it always 'Jesus and . . .'?" . . .

How often we decorate our idols with a gold overlay of service to God. "I would serve God much more effectively if I just had more money," ". . . a better congregation to work with," ". . . more time." What are the "Jesus ands" in your life?

So much of what we construct with our own hands — our position or reputation, our books and lectures, our homes and other possessions — is covered with some beautiful veneer to create the illusion of true worth in the service of God. How often does our religious piety mask an idolatry of our own accomplishments or attributes?

When we mistake our character and work for ends in themselves . . . and not merely tools for God's service, we add another chain to the idol. . . .

The key is remembering the difference between means and ends. . . . Sometimes our very church buildings are turned into ends. . . . Do our churches or professions or accomplishments entice us to worship them, or do they aid us in serving and focusing our attention on God? . . .

When everything we use and have and do is understood as a gift on loan from God, we break the silver chains by which our idols are hung.

Prayer
   Holy Trinity, only true God, forgive us for making idols of your gifts — and
   even of our churches and service to you. Help us to worship only you . . .
   Amen.

To Walk and Not Faint, pp. 108, 114-19.

We gather together to ask the Lord's blessing. . . .

                              Netherlands folk hymn, trans. by Theodore Baker

One of the special meanings of Sabbath keeping for me has been the notion that the Christian community *gathers* on that day. If our Sabbath days become set aside for spiritual purposes and set apart from work and productivity, we can afford to spend more time together with our fellow believers so that we can be more thoroughly strengthened in the values of the community. One of the reasons that teenagers find it so hard to be Christians today is that they experience so little support from the Christian community and have to contend with so many worldly values — concerning faith, materialism, their sexuality, and drugs and alcohol. . . . If we could more fully enfold our youth in our communities so that they felt profoundly loved and thoroughly supported, they might find it much less difficult to choose the values of the Christian community as their own, despite the pressures of their peers.

We can gather together for all sorts of things when we observe Sabbath keeping. Not only will we meet for worship and Bible classes, but perhaps we can have meals together. Breaking bread together might also give us an opportunity to serve the larger community. One congregation with which I worshiped during graduate school hosts family dinners for the neighborhood after worship on Sunday. . . . The most delightful aspect of the whole program was that many of the neighborhood children also participated in the worship and Sunday school that preceded our meal together. . . .

Perhaps our Christian communities can gather together for special extra times of worship such as Sunday-evening Advent services. . . .

Perhaps we can gather together in small fellowship clusters as part of our Sabbath keeping. Some congregations have such fellowship groups that extend the Christian community into the week. These caring groups offer further opportunities for Bible study, sharing, encouragement, and prayer. . . .

My whole point is that to be a Christian community together we need time together. Observing the Sabbath gives us the intentional time for deepening the bonds of our community and enfolding each of us more foundationally in the values that we share.

Prayer

  Lord of the Sabbath, strengthen our community as we gather for worship, study, and fellowship . . .   Amen.

                              Keeping the Sabbath Wholly, pp. 117-18.

Like good stewards of the manifold grace of God, serve one another with whatever gift each of you has received.

1 Peter 4:10 (NRSV)

Genuine community in worship is made more possible by some of the mechanical things that we do before the service begins. In order for the worship to be open to everyone, we must remove any barriers to public, common life. . . . Overhead projections are often difficult to see — impossible for elderly persons who have cataracts. We want to be sure that there are plenty of songbooks and bulletins or whatever else we use, large-print worship materials for the visually impaired or partially sighted, perhaps interpreters or earphones for the hearing impaired, no impediments to wheelchairs.

The alternative Christian community must be an inclusive one. Are our churches being formed to be inclusive of the great mix of ages, social classes, races, and gifts among God's people? I belong to a black, inner-city congregation that gives me, a white person, the opportunity to learn from my African-American sisters and brothers; it is a congregation devoted to its neighborhood, offering room in its building for Scouts, African dance classes, economic development groups, and local black history month celebrations. These services provide enormous opportunities for genuine hospitality to our neighbors. . . .

Members of the congregation need to be trained specifically to be hospitable to strangers (and to each other). Do our worship practices form us to welcome outsiders, to invite newcomers, to tell others about our faith? We can each welcome those who sit beside us, make sure they know how to follow our order of service, point them to pages or instructions. . . .

Any kind of music or style of worship, including both new and old, can be hospitable if the persons who participate in it welcome strangers, if the customary rituals do not become empty performance, if the leaders give gentle and invitational explanations of what we do and why, if melodies for singing are clearly played or perhaps led by a cantor, if the printed music is available to everyone, if *corporate* worship is kept as a "public space" into which every person can enter.

Prayer

> *Gracious Lord, help us as a community and as individuals to do everything we can to be welcoming and hospitable — so that we truly share your love in our community and in our corporate worship . . .   Amen.*

A Royal "Waste" of Time, pp. 180-81.

The love — not hypocritical!

Romans 12:9a (my translation)

So how can we avoid a phony love? The secret lies in understanding the true meaning of the Greek term *agapē*. . . .

Christians use it to describe God's unique love, . . . his being able to give love wisely, thoroughly, without any demand of return, freely. Such love allows what is truly best for us, and what is completely appropriate for God's perfect purposes. Thus, when we pass that love on to others, it is the intelligent, purposeful love which God creates in us and which flows through us to minister to the needs of the person loved. Let us heavily accentuate the intelligence of this love, its specific direction toward the needs of the other, and its source in the Hilarity of knowing how thoroughly God has loved us first. . . .

Agapē is also intensely practical. . . . Integral to Paul's whole message is that love is the core of all the gifts in the Body, all the living sacrifices, all the offerings of our lives. . . .

Consequently, this verse convicts us with its challenge: we are ashamed of the hypocrisy of our love. Indeed, we would be destroyed by grief at our failure if it were not for the fact that this phrase, too, like everything else in Romans 12, is hinged on that great word *therefore*. Our understanding of giftedness, of "body-ness," of being holy sacrifices, of being transformed, and now of love is based all on the same grace. "With eyes wide open to the mercies of God," we recognize that he wants to fill us with his perfect love. . . .

Only when we are set free from the demands of the law can we discover the Hilarity of living in love through faith. Indeed, this is not of ourselves, but a gift of grace. . . .

If a person is not loving, John says (1 John 4:7-8), he or she does not know God. . . . The solution, John implies, is to know God better. . . . Then, as Paul asserts in 2 Corinthians 3:18, we will become more like him as we reflect his character from one degree of glory to another.

Prayer

> *Loving Lord, forgive our hypocrisy, and teach us to know you better and to love more genuinely, in your name . . .   Amen.*

Truly the Community, pp. 139, 143-46.

Now direct our daily labor,
lest we strive for self alone,
born with talents, make us servants
fit to answer at your throne.

Robert Edwards (1961)

In our acquisitive and covetous world, God's people must deliberately nurture their children in an entire community of generous and self-sacrificing Christians if they want them to choose the alternative culture of the kingdom of God and to resist society's materialism and greed. . . .

Let me emphasize . . . that my remarks about money are particularly concerned for the deep attitudes that channel our expenditure of it. . . . Our money should be directed not only to address immediate needs but also, more deeply, to counteract the systemic roots of poverty and oppression. Calls to our congressional representatives and senators and president to support economic development throughout the world, protests against excessive military spending and other governmental policies that hurt the poor, activities that organize our neighborhoods to fight prejudice and racism and unfair business practices — these are a few of the ways in which our money can be paired with actions of true love for those in need. However, since our society is so distorted in its expenditures of money, it is critical that we begin with new assessments of our family's stewardship and think carefully about how we are training our children to understand the purposes of money. . . .

So many children seem to have no idea of the value of things, no ability to delay gratification, no sense of the meaning of life and work. . . . Nothing is special because they can have everything. . . .

In order to raise children who can withstand the allures of materialistic consumerism, we need the support of the whole community. If Christian parents band together, they will be more able to help their children resist the peer pressure and . . . the bombardment of media advertising that fosters greed. . . .

Also, our family's orientation toward community gives us the best reason for refusing certain purchases. When our children whine for extra treats, when they scream for instant gratification, we can remind them that it is our godly *choice* not to indulge ourselves, that we sometimes sacrifice pleasure for the sake of justice for others.

Prayer

Holy Spirit, guide our efforts to live and teach an alternative to materialistic consumerism . . .   Amen.

Is It a Lost Cause? pp. 145, 149-51, 160-61.

. . . blessed is the [strong] man who takes refuge in him.
Fear the Lord, you his saints,
  for those who fear him lack nothing.

Psalm 34:8b-9

David urges us to fear *YHWH.* . . . Twice in verse 9, he selects the verb that means "to reverence or to honor" him. Because of the context — the previous words about the blessedness of those who take refuge and the next statement that those who fear lack no good thing — we can hear in this word *fear* an invitation to thankfulness and praise. When we honor God, we learn to recognize his goodness in all that is around us, and in that reverent awareness we are more likely to respond with gratitude.

The ones who are to fear him are his saints. That name reminds us that God has chosen us to be set apart as his people. In doing so, he has given us that very quality of sanctity that is his. The scriptural pictures of God's holiness, such as the scene in Isaiah 6, are breathtaking visions. The prophet was filled with fear and horror and shame at his own sinfulness when he observed the holiness of God in his majestic enthronement and heard about it in the calling of the angels. . . . Like the prophet, we also are persons of unclean lips, and we dwell among people who are the same.

Yet the Joy of our faith is that God has made us holy by covering us over with his righteousness, through our incorporation into the body of the perfect Christ. Like the prophet in Isaiah 6, we have been cleansed with the burning coal of grace. That is why Paul addresses his letters to the "saints" of the various New Testament churches. . . .

The Joy of our relationship with God, furthermore, is that he continues to enable us to act like the saints we are by his forgiveness and affirmation and gracious empowerment. Nevertheless, the fact of our sainthood remains, whether or not we are living it out.

Therefore, we who are rejoicing in that sainthood want, of course, to fear the Lord. We want to give God the proper honor and to receive the holiness he is creating in our lives.

Prayer

Holy Lord, we want to honor you with lives of gratitude for the forgiveness, acceptance, and holiness you bestow on us because of Christ's righteousness on our behalf . . .   Amen.

I'm Lonely, Lord, pp. 98, 100-101.

"To the angel of the church in Thyatira write: . . . To him who overcomes and does my will to the end, I will . . . give him the morning star."

Revelation 2:18a, 26, 28

Jesus is the bright Morning Star. Only this letter to Thyatira offers to a church such a particular promise of the presence of Christ. However, also only this particular letter attaches the additional words "and does my will unto the end" to the constant phrase in all seven letters, "To the one overcoming. . . ." The presence of Jesus is integrally connected with the doing of his will.

We must clear up one false notion right away. The connection does *not* turn faith into an effort of works to create our own righteousness. We are not warned by this letter that we earn the presence of Jesus by being good.

Rather, the combination reminds us again that Christ's constant presence is missed by us if our faith does not change the practical dimensions of life. We do not know his Spirit at work in us if we reject his lifestyle. We fail to appreciate his loving presence if we are controlled by other gods.

Every time we turn to other gods, we move away from his presence. . . . On the other hand, when we are doing God's will, we experience the intimate connection that is possible with Jesus. . . .

The praise given to Thyatira is noteworthy: they are commended for their deeds, their love and faith, their service and perseverance, and for the fact that they are now doing more than they did at first. What a wonderful list! However, those extraordinary accomplishments do not matter if the grand successes are marred by idolatries and immoralities.

That contrast is crucially important for us. We excuse various sins if a person is faithful in attendance at worship. We let ourselves succumb to various idolatries and excuse them because we are pretty decent Christians, doing nice things and being very loving toward our neighbors.

We dare not misinterpret this letter. . . . It is intended to draw its recipients back to grace, to call them to repentance — and forgiveness.

Prayer
> *Bright Morning Star, forgive our excuses. We want to live in ways that keep us close to you until the very end . . .   Amen.*

Joy in Our Weakness, pp. 82-84.

An idol? — A workman casts it,
   and a goldsmith overlays it with gold,
   and casts for it silver chains.

Isaiah 40:19 (NRSV)

The writer of Isaiah 40 was justly sarcastic with the Israelites. To be swept into the worship of the false deities of their neighbors was sheer folly on their part. God had warned them that they must destroy the pagan influences that surrounded them, and he had proved himself time and again to be faithful to his promises and powerful to care for his people. . . .

Lest we condemn them heedlessly, however, let's remember that we all do the same thing. God has warned us, and he has proved himself faithful time and again — and yet, in blatant rejection or whimpering complaint, we turn away from him to all sorts of false gods. We array against him material pleasures, power and prestige, or the ambitions of the surrounding culture . . . and never realize how ludicrous is the comparison. . . .

How do we reduce God and miss what he wants to be for us and to give to us? When I choose the ease of temptation instead of the struggle of obedience, I miss the ecstasy of victory. When I choose the pleasure of sin instead of the pain of faithfulness, I miss the multifaceted *Shalom* of well-being with God and with myself and with my neighbor. When I crave affirmation from the world to boost my ego, I get hollow accolades that prevent me from hearing the true sense of worth that God allows.

We make so many things into idols without pausing to realize that they are the products of our own hands. We commit our lives to them and invest all our wealth in them. We spend our time crafting them and all our resources decorating them. . . .

The understanding of idolatries does not mean the elimination of possessions or the ending of pleasures. We must remember, however, that such things are never ends in themselves. Our pleasures and possessions, our positions and professions are means to the end of loving God and glorifying him forever.

Prayer
   Giver of all good things, teach us to value your gifts of time, talents, and possessions for their true purposes — to love and serve only you . . .   Amen.
                                       To Walk and Not Faint, pp. 114-18.

On a Sabbath Jesus was teaching in one of the synagogues, and a woman was there who had been crippled by a spirit for eighteen years. . . . When Jesus saw her, he called her forward and said to her, "Woman, you are set free from your infirmity."

Luke 13:10-12

One of the specific choices among the values of the Christian community is the embracing of time instead of space. . . . Surrounded as we are by the rapid pace of too much change, we think we cannot set aside time to spend a whole day in Sabbath keeping. . . . However, when we take the day to assess our use of time, we learn what is important in all those changes and how to prioritize our tasks and desires so that we aren't overcome by the tyranny of the urgent. . . . This perspective has many aspects, but one of the foremost is the deliberate decision to focus on events in time with persons rather than using time to accomplish things. . . .

Ceasing our work and concentrating on spiritual resting creates the possibility for deeper caring about the persons whom God brings into our day. There is no need to hurry — for there is nothing that we *have to do.* There are no tasks that demand our time. Time is a gift to us, and we can in turn pass that gift on to others. . . .

In our society it is difficult to embrace people instead of things, to cherish time rather than space. So much of our technologically efficient and materially exploitative culture militates against these values. Accordingly, we must, by deliberate effort, consciously establish our intentions. Moreover, if we keep the Sabbath by embracing persons, that practice invites us to carry those same values into the other six days of the week. Our Sabbath remembering strengthens us to . . . pursue the intimacy of Christian community and Christ-like caring. . . .

When we experience being enveloped by Sabbath time, we become people who are not enslaved to time. As we embrace time, then, we squander less and less of it for the things of space. We get in touch with eternity and bring eternal values into all the days of our week.

Prayer

Jesus, Sabbath Healer, help us learn, in Sabbath keeping, to value time spent in worship and with others above anything we could have or accomplish . . . Amen.

Keeping the Sabbath Wholly, pp. 119-23.

O God, teach me to see You, and reveal Yourself to me when I seek You. . . .
Let me seek You in longing, and long for You in seeking.
Let me find You in love, and love You in finding.

Ambrose of Milan, 339-397

Ambrose's poem invites us to keep God as the subject of our worship and reminds us that to do so will change our lives. When God comes to us in all
the fullness of who God is, our character will be transformed. Consequently,
if our worship practices accord God the proper place and scope, who we are
and what we are becoming as Christians will be rightly developed.

However, notice that I phrased the paragraph above in terms of "we."
Who you are as an individual believer depends greatly upon the character of
the community of believers in which you are nurtured. . . .

Morality is best formed not by dwelling on rules . . . or by considering
our actions' outcome . . . but by making use of all the means in the Christian
community to nurture a godly character, out of which moral choices will be
well made. Christian character is nurtured by all the scriptural narratives
and rules, our images for God, specific worship practices, prayerful consideration of means and ends, tiny choices in daily life, the values of the community, and our interactions with its members. All these things together
contribute to who we are, how we live. . . .

How are our worship and educational practices failing that they do not
form Christians who follow Jesus in his willingness to suffer for the sake of
God's kingdom? How can we crave money and possessions and still follow
the One who had nowhere to lay his head?

What great gifts the Church offers the world if it nurtures persons of
godly character who devote their financial resources and time to God's purposes of caring justice. . . .

We who are God's people *know* how to find life's real meaning — which
is not merely morality, but the fullness of relationship with God. Worship is
meant to usher us into God's presence so that we can delight in that relationship and consequently be formed to live according to God's best purposes.

Prayer

God whom we seek, use our worship and educational endeavors to form and
transform us into ever more Christ-like followers of you . . .   Amen.

Reaching Out, pp. 105-7, 115-16.

Abhorring the wicked thing! Glued to the good thing!

Romans 12:9b (my translation)

The connection of this injunction with the previous exhortation to let love be without hypocrisy is important. We strengthen our unhypocritical love by not letting it be spoiled by any involvement in evil. If we compromise our principles in any way, our love is made impure. We are to stand firm against even the appearance of evil and not let love be weakened by any contamination.

Imperatively we detest whatever is evil in ourselves and in a brother or sister's lifestyle or attitudes. The phrase "loving the sinner and hating the sin" expresses excellently this sequence in Paul's exhortations. Our love for the person committing wrong should be genuine, not pretended in any way; but in true love we will abhor the evil that can only harm him or her.

God's love is like that. The freedom we have because we are loved by God is wonderfully summarized in this sentence: "God loves us so much that he accepts us just as we are, but he also loves us too much to let us stay that way." He certainly loves us without any phoniness and with total acceptance, but he cannot stand anything in us contrary to his purposes. God is working constantly to purge that from us and to transform our lives. . . .

Consequently, this is the nature of the love that we are to have for each other in the Christian community. We will exhibit compassion toward the one suffering from guilt, but we will not condone the errors that cause it. Furthermore, we can learn to deal with ourselves that way also. By faith we are learning to love ourselves with a genuine and proper love, but the more our faith matures the more we grow to hate everything in us that is evil. . . .

Daily that with which we are associated will change us. Each moment the choice is ours how we will be changed. Will we conform to the influences of evil or will we abhor it? Will we cling to the good and learn to cherish it? Will we let our love be marred by evil or will it be increased by good?

Prayer

Jesus, our Perfect Model, help us follow your example of love — cherishing good, hating evil . . .   Amen.

Truly the Community, pp. 149-50, 157.

Open wide our hands in sharing,
as we heed Christ's ageless call,
healing, teaching, and reclaiming,
serving you by loving all.

Robert Edwards (1961)

Two key biblical ideas help us teach our children resistance to our society's materialistic consumerism. These concepts are not old-fashioned or quaint, but are vital and stunning. Imagine with me the adventure of enabling our children to choose to be different from the gluttony that surrounds them.

The first biblical notion is that of stewardship. This idea gives children dignity because it emphasizes that God, to whom all things belong, has entrusted them with material things, personal talents, and all the years of their life for the good of everyone and the praise of God. Recognizing that our possessions really belong to God encourages us all to be careful of our things, to use them well, to offer them freely for the needs of others. It also trains us not to be performers, because our skills are not our own, but are God-given gifts. . . .

The other scriptural notion that really assists our children in gaining a new attitude about consumerism is that of tithing. . . . Tithing is a good symbol for teaching that all 100 percent belongs to God (and therefore we are stewards of it). Tithing is not a law for us New Testament people; it is a grace. . . . It is also a gracious reminder that God cares about what I do with the rest of my money. . . . And tithing is a great reminder that God provides for our needs. . . .

Tithing is a wonderful way for families to experience the provision of God. I urge you to think how far beyond the tithe your family could go in giving to your local congregation, to associations that feed the poor and shelter the homeless, to advocacy agencies like Bread for the World, to coalitions working for peace and justice. When the children suggest and participate in deciding each month who should be the recipients of the family's gifts, they will gain and maintain a vision for mission, for, as Jesus said, "Where your treasure is, there your heart will be also" (Matt. 6:21).

Prayer

> *Generous Lord, knowing that all we have comes from you, inspire us to use*
> *and share it faithfully, as a witness to our children and all the world . . .*
> *Amen.*

Is It a Lost Cause? pp. 146, 155-58.

Fear the Lord, you his saints,
   for those who fear him lack nothing.
The lions may grow weak and hungry,
   but those who seek the Lord lack no good thing.

Psalm 34:9-10

Why does God sometimes seem to deny us what we need most deeply? Is David just speaking about food-and-shelter kinds of things? . . .

Once again we are thrown back on the character of God. Is he good or isn't he? Sometimes we don't see that goodness, but we are invited to try it out — to search for it, in fact — because it is there. . . .

David's assertion is very carefully constructed to remind us that only by honoring *YHWH* do we not lack any good thing. We might miss certain elements that we think are good, but if we are seeking *YHWH*'s purposes, we will not fall short of anything that *is* good for us. . . .

Nevertheless, some things we will never understand. . . . Sometimes it is imperative simply to rest in what is happening today and not worry about the future — or about comprehending the reasons for the way things are. . . .

Blessedness is indeed promised to those who seek the Lord, but the key lies in the seeking. That means to study and pray, to search and wait, to worship and serve — even to be tested, to struggle and suffer. Such disciplines of mind and spirit are often hard. . . . In those times especially we are invited to cling to this promise: "Those who seek the Lord lack no good thing." In believing that statement to be true we find the contentment to accept whatever blessings are or are not in our lives. . . .

Sometimes we will be able to taste and see how good God is, but true maturity of faith will recognize his love even though from a human perspective we might lack good things. That kind of maturity grows as we continue to seek him. Not in the power of a lion, but in the waiting of a saint we know the fullness of blessedness.

Prayer

   God of all provision, when we feel something is lacking, encourage us with your Spirit to seek you, and we will surely know your goodness in the blessings you faithfully provide for our salvation . . .   Amen.

I'm Lonely, Lord, pp. 98, 101-5.

"To the angel of the church in Thyatira write: . . . Then all the churches will know that I am he who searches hearts and minds. . . . Only hold on to what you have until I come."
Revelation 2:18a, 23b, 25

The Son of God says he will cause affliction in order that the churches might know that he is the one who searches minds and hearts. In the Bible the word *heart* never refers merely to feelings. Rather, the word conveys the idea of deliberate will, or careful intentions. God does not accept the excuse that we were led into sexual temptation by our feelings. Instead, he searches for the will that would project itself over feelings and act on the basis of what the mind knows about the commands of God. . . .

Though God warns those who refuse to repent, he has a precise word of encouragement for those steadfastly trying to remain pure. He urges them simply to keep holding on to what they have — their faith and love, their perseverance, their good deeds and service, their deliberate will and mind to stay away from the idolatry and immorality of their brothers and sisters. . . .

A strong way to resist temptation is to keep reminding ourselves that Jesus is coming.

He is coming some day to end temptation and evil forever. We certainly want to be among his people when he comes.

Furthermore, he is coming now to aid us with his power in the fight against temptation. Perhaps he is coming in the person of a friend who will stand by us with strength for the fight. He is coming perhaps now in music or beauty to uplift us and sustain us. . . .

How does he come to you? How remarkable that he comes to each of us in ways appropriate to our particular loves! . . .

Our Christian lives are a matter of holding on until he comes. . . .

Christ wants to be present in us and to impart his authority to us — our church communities, our country. . . . He calls us away from sexual immorality and sacrifices to other gods, and empowers us instead to live in the center of his will.

Prayer
  Sustaining Lord, keep us safely in the center of your will — holding on until your final coming . . .   Amen.

Joy in Our Weakness, pp. 86-88.

The one too impoverished for [such] an offering
   selects a tree that does not rot,
then seeks out a skilled artisan
   to establish an idol that will not totter.

                         Isaiah 40:20 (composite)

In verse 20 the prophet intends to force the Israelites to confront the irrationality of their dependence on idols. . . . They want to construct the idol securely enough so that it won't topple. But making it that secure reinforces the realization that this god can't move at all to help you. What is the value of a non-tottering image? . . .

   The accent here is on the things or events or circumstances we trust for protection. No matter how carefully we choose and establish what will keep us safe, our gods lead only to futility and meaninglessness. . . .

   Sometimes . . . out of our impoverishment, we clutch frantically at anything that seems dependable. We grasp for some sort of god to sustain us in the crises of our lives, to withstand the rapid changes in our culture, to keep us safe until we die. How much money is enough to last us, how much power will keep us important, how many business contacts will assure us that we can maintain our lifestyle?

   What god can weather the stock market crashes . . . ? What god can make sure that people we love will survive with us into old age? What god can keep our homes from fire or theft? What god will ease the longing . . . deep within us? Sometimes we even make false gods out of the securities of our worship. . . .

   We recognize our rebellions against God as we crave other securities and purposes in life.

   Into that failure . . . comes the grace of Jesus Christ. . . . We don't need chains to keep our god erect. Instead, we believe that *YHWH, the* Skillful Craftsman, has given us the uncreated image of himself, the One begotten but not made, the Christ, in whom alone we rest.

Prayer
   Lord Jesus, forgive our idolatry as we attempt to create for ourselves something upon which we can depend. In faith may we learn to live securely by placing our trust in you . . .   Amen.

                  To Walk and Not Faint, pp. 120-23.

Remember this: Whoever sows sparingly will also reap sparingly, and whoever sows generously will also reap generously. Each [person] should give what he has decided in his heart to give, not reluctantly or under compulsion. . . .

2 Corinthians 9:6-7a

Our acquisitive society has . . . turned our major holy days into commercialized holidays, days of "gimme" instead of special times of adoration and worship. . . .

Perhaps the Christian community could repel this invasion with a weekly counteroffensive — the Sabbath practice of giving rather than accumulating, of caring for the needs of others instead of requiring for oneself. . . . Especially for the sake of our children, we want to model the importance of embracing a lifestyle of giving; for our own sake, we adults need the freedom that inevitably results from choosing to be stewards rather than possessors. . . .

Paul urged the Corinthians to make their gifts to the poor as a fulfillment of their own goals — not according to any prescribed regulations. . . . Unfortunately, such freedom in the church often degenerates into the notion that we can give skimpily because we are not required to pay a certain amount. But Paul's exhortation follows his reminder of the example of the Macedonians, who were undergoing the "most severe trial," and yet "their overflowing joy and their extreme poverty welled up in rich generosity" (2 Cor. 8:2). This is the most unusual equation in the history of humanity:

most severe trial + overflowing Joy + extreme poverty = rich generosity!

Good stewardship in the biblical sense lies in recognizing that God gives us all that we need to abound in good works and in trusting him to provide what is needed for the ministries to which he has called us. . . .

To keep the Sabbath is to focus on the immensity of God's gifts to us, especially the priceless gift of salvation. We can respond in no other way than to want to give in similar fashion. "Christ's love compels us . . ." (2 Cor. 5:14a).

Prayer

Treasured God, empower us with a spirit of generous stewardship . . .
Amen.

Keeping the Sabbath Wholly, pp. 124-27, 130.

Consequently, you are no longer foreigners and aliens, but fellow citizens with God's people and members of God's household . . .

Ephesians 2:19

The Christian community, as the New Testament emphasizes repeatedly, is a unity of diversity. We capture that best musically when we learn to sing each other's songs, . . . when different persons in the community contribute their gifts of playing musical instruments or singing, arranging and composing, . . . and when we make it possible for each person to join in the singing of the worship service. . . .

Our worship also needs the offerings of those who make banners, grow flowers, write or perform chancel dramas, choreograph or present liturgical dances, weave vestments or altar cloths, carve furniture, make pottery vessels, or bake bread for the Lord's Supper. Other members of the Body devote their energies and skills to ushering, designing worship folders, serving at the Lord's Table, reading Scripture lessons, or leading prayers. . . .

It is especially important that we highlight the gifts of the children and teenagers in the community. In one church in upstate New York, the elementary school children play their bells and chant to lead the congregation every Sunday in singing a psalm. In another congregation, entire families do the ushering for the week, so that young children participate with their parents in passing out bulletins and taking the offering. Other churches feature their children's artwork as bulletin covers or use their prayers in the worship service. In my home congregation, the young people serve as greeters, Scripture readers, drama participants, acolytes, ushers, and providers of refreshments for the fellowship hour following worship.

Another particularly important aspect of worship for building community is the corporate prayers. . . .

All of these are ways in which our particular worship services can build community. . . . We do not manipulate community; it is God's initiative to make us one. But we can foster community, work to prevent anything from hindering or disrupting it, and celebrate it.

Prayer
> *Unifying Lord, may we each offer our best gifts within the community, so that together we can be formed as your household of faith, where each is valued and all serve . . .   Amen.*

A Royal "Waste" of Time, pp. 182-85.

Abhorring the wicked thing! Glued to the good thing!

Romans 12:9b (my translation)

Throughout the centuries theologians have wrestled with this terrible question: If God is all powerful and God is good, why is there evil in the world? No one can thoroughly explain why evil exists, though we know that loving God out of freedom necessitates the possibility to choose not to love him. Furthermore, human choices that reject God's will throughout history have resulted in that which is apart from him — namely, evil.

Our response to evil, then, is to hate it — to abhor or detest it — and to flee from it (see 2 Tim. 2:22). The Amplified Bible expands Romans 12:9b with "loathe all ungodliness, turn in horror from wickedness." That addition captures the deep sense of Paul's exhortation: we are to shrink from everything that is evil (in us and in others whom we love). . . .

We must realize that whenever we dabble with evil in the slightest way, our love is spoiled. If we fudge truth just a little in talking to a friend, the relationship is marred. The community is made unclean by the slightest bit of gossip. The smallest trace of games, pretensions, or manipulations in our care for others makes our love less than whole or holy. . . .

We need the encouragement and support of our fellow believers to have the courage to abhor the evil of our world. Certainly for each of us a greater shrinking from evil is . . . a disciplined possibility and an urgent necessity. . . .

God is at work in us to renew us. One of the ways in which we cooperate in that renewal is by a growing refusal to let our minds and lives be polluted by the garbage that surrounds us. . . .

Meanwhile, all sorts of enrichments, all kinds of positive values, all healthy disciplines of body and mind and spirit are the good to which we are invited to cling. . . .

When we learn to cherish the good, we gain appreciation for the treasure that all things from God are.

Prayer
> *God of all good, help us choose daily that which is whole and holy . . .*
> *Amen.*

Truly the Community, pp. 149-57.

Lo! The hosts of evil round us
scorn the Christ, assail his ways! . . .
Grant us wisdom, grant us courage
for the living of these days.

Harry Emerson Fosdick (1930), alt.

We and our churches must understand the stakes of our technological times and what Christians must do in the present media revolution to raise children of faith. . . .

Let me introduce . . . for your further consideration six dangers of media consumption:

1. The most obvious problem with the proliferation of media options, most clearly demonstrated by television consumption, is that involvement with them *wastes so much time. . . .*

2. Watching television or scanning web pages *stifles the imagination. . . .*

3. Much more critical, research by Jane Healy has demonstrated that children who watch a lot of television develop *smaller brains. . . .* Only in conversation and by manipulating things — toys, a musical instrument, one's legs in running — does the brain build new pathways and the information received actually get learned. Thus the media's bombardment not only causes our children to be unable to think, it also prevents them from actually having the brain space in which to think and learn. . . .

4. Neil Postman's *Amusing Ourselves to Death* accentuates also that children are *less motivated to think* because television lulls them into passivity — and this is true even of the supposedly "good" programs. . . .

5. No one can doubt that television and all the developing computer shopping possibilities promote and foster *greed. . . .*

6. The greed fostered by media is just one aspect of the larger problem of *muddling our perception of reality. . . .*

I believe this is a key time for congregations and Christian parents to be at the forefront in setting limits to media consumption, in deepening family bonds and faith roots for children so that they have moral values by which to weigh the media they observe, and in offering to the world both prophetic wisdom and workable solutions to the problems that the media inherently engender.

Prayer

Creator of our minds and imaginations, give us courage and wisdom as we deal with these issues of media consumption . . . Amen.

Is It a Lost Cause? pp. 164-72.

Come, my children, listen to me;
  I will teach you the fear of the LORD. . . .
The righteous cry out, and the LORD hears them;
  he delivers them from all their troubles.
The LORD is close to the brokenhearted
  and saves those who are crushed in spirit.

Psalm 34:11, 17-18

The nearness of the LORD to the brokenhearted implies . . . tenderness. No matter how dirty our face, how dark our shame, how troubled our spirit because we have spoiled our relationship with the Shepherd or have mistrusted his goodness because of the immensity of our sorrow, yet he still chooses to be beside us in our grief.

Much of the sorrow of the brokenhearted takes the form of those disabling questions, "Why?" or "What could I have done?" Our brokenheartedness is often multiplied by the intense guilt we feel. . . .

David declares that *YHWH* saves or delivers those who are crushed in spirit. The verb is from the root *Yashah,* from which we get *Yeshua,* the Hebrew word for our English name Jesus. This meaning of the name is noted when the angel Gabriel commands Joseph, "You are to give him the name Jesus, because he will save his people from their sins" (Matt. 1:21).

Looking back from our perspective in time, we New Testament people know *how* the LORD saves those who are crushed in spirit. No matter how shattered we are by our experiences, the Trinity has accomplished our deliverance through Yeshua, the Saving One.

"Crushed in spirit" may be interpreted in several ways. It is often understood as contriteness for flaws in moral character. In that case, the salvation promised in this psalm is the gift of forgiveness and reconciliation for those who are repentant. In addition, we could construe the phrase more in the sense of being shattered or crushed emotionally — or, as in the Good News Bible's version, to have lost all hope. In our most despairing times we identify with this reading.

Whatever the nuances, this message is the same: *YHWH* is near, and *YHWH* rescues. . . . In the midst of the blackness of despair, we need to keep hearing the word of comfort that *YHWH* is near, until we can believe it and see its true light.

Prayer

  Listening LORD, when we are "crushed," help us find in repentance your saving, comforting presence . . .   Amen.

I'm Lonely, LORD, pp. 106-9.

"To the angel of the church in Sardis write: . . . Remember, therefore, what you have received and heard; obey it, and repent."

Revelation 3:1a, 3a

The letter to the Christian community at Sardis is urgently valuable for us. The problem in that church has been repeated in the lives of God's people throughout their histories, for all kinds of forces draw us consistently away from a Christ-like lifestyle. . . .

Right away, the Christ . . . berates the people of Sardis for their false front; he knows, though they appear to the rest of the world to be alive, that they are really spiritually dead. He does not criticize them for any particular sin, but simply for the fact that their deeds are not complete — and the only thing to do about that is to wake up!

The command is like an alarm clock that rings every few minutes: wake up! Strengthen the things that remain but are about to die! Remember what you have received and heard! Obey! Repent!

The ordering of those phrases is essential. We cannot strengthen what remains by ourselves. What we have received and heard — the gospel! — revitalizes us. Our deeds, like those of the people of Sardis, are not complete in the sight of God, but God constantly calls us with the gospel to new life, new hope, new response. This letter wakes us up to hear his call. . . .

When we would flounder in regrets or confusion, God wants to enable us instead to strengthen what remains. His grace empowers us for the disciplines that strengthen us; we respond to his immense love by spiritual exercise. For the people of Sardis the situation was critical — the things that remained were about to die. Our spiritual lives, too, shrink and get flabby without training. When we neglect the means God has provided for us to receive his grace — God's Word and prayer, the sacraments and forgiveness, his love incarnated in the Christian community — our spiritual lives get weak. Those gifts are given to strengthen what remains. . . .

Consequently, when Christ says that he holds the church in Sardis in his hand, he reemphasizes this glorious truth of grace: that Christ always continues to hold his people in his care, no matter how desperately they need renewal.

Prayer

Calling God, wake us up! Renew us through your Word, sacraments, and Church . . . Amen.

Joy in Our Weakness, pp. 89-91.

Friday

Have you not known? Have you not heard?
  Has it not been told you from the beginning?
  Have you not understood from the foundations of the earth?

Isaiah 40:21

The four questions of this verse are not mere rhetoric. They are terribly indicting. Are we so ignorant? Why are we so deaf to the words of God? Why can't we comprehend God's speech? Can't we grasp what has been going on for a long time? It has been declared for us; why haven't we perceived it? . . .

If we as God's people have not known, perhaps we have never been taught. If we have not heard, maybe it is because we have not taken advantage of opportunities to hear the Word of God being spoken. Above all, God desires to reveal himself to all people. We fail to trust him for his revelation because we do not yet understand that he is such a God of grace.

We can hear this Word as a message of gracious invitation, . . . a Word of hope. . . . We have failed to hear and understand and know, but God's Word to us is forgiveness and not condemnation. He does not come to us with wrathful judgment against our ignorance and neglect. He comes to us through the reconciling work of Jesus and invites us to change that situation, beginning now. These words can serve as an inspiration to us to accept his forgiveness and grace and to let them free us to begin to know better, to pay more attention, to listen, to see.

God does indeed want to reveal himself to us more deeply. . . . If we fail to perceive his grace and learn of his character, it is because we have passed over spending time with him. . . . What better motivation can there be for us to establish habits of quiet time and study and worship?

It IS possible for us to know. We CAN hear. Good news HAS been declared to us from the beginning. We WILL be able to understand — by the grace of God. It's a matter of opening our eyes, ears, hearts, and minds — and Bibles.

Prayer
  Revealing Lord, thank you for desiring to be known by us. Thank you for
  your Word, your Spirit, and your Church, which make this possible . . .
  Amen.

To Walk and Not Faint, pp. 125-30.

It is good to praise the LORD
  and make music to your name, O Most High. . . .

Psalm 92:1

After a day of genuine Sabbath keeping . . . I always am reduced to repentance for my complaining spirit. Inevitably the day impresses me with the goodness of God, and invariably it increases my longing to be more faithful in serving God according to the gifts and resources he has given and the calling he has issued. The time spent in worship and with other members of the Christian community, the time devoted to solitude and prayer . . . — however my day is spent, its components contribute together to fill me with gratitude for God's immeasurable gifts. . . .

Sabbath keeping also gives us holy time for actually discovering as well as embracing more thoroughly our calling in life. This is implied in Psalm 92, which . . . reveals some of the practices in the worship of the Hebrew people. . . .

All the practices mentioned in the first stanza of this Sabbath psalm invite our Sunday imitation — praising Yahweh, making music, proclaiming God's love and faithfulness. . . .

In the second stanza the poet rejoices in Yahweh's deeds. . . .

His own participation in God's purposes is implied more strongly in the third stanza, when the poet declares that Yahweh has exalted his horn (which means strength) and that fine oils have been poured upon him, signifying a commissioning for the special purposes of God. . . .

Finally, the poet declares in the last stanza that the righteous flourish like palm trees and the cedars of Lebanon. Even in old age, the people of God will bear fruit and stay "fresh and green" because of Yahweh's continued presence in their lives.

Prayer
  Lord of all ages, empower us to establish Sabbath practices that reflect the lessons of this psalm . . .   Amen.

Keeping the Sabbath Wholly, pp. 132-34.

O God, teach me to see You, and reveal Yourself to me when I seek You.
For I cannot seek You unless You first teach me,
nor find You unless You first reveal Yourself to me.

Ambrose of Milan, 339-397

God's best purposes for us involve the highest self-identity — not to be satisfactorily found by endlessly pursuing self-improvement, but received as a gift of grace. . . . The culture *of* worship thus offers an alternative to the culture *in* which the Church seeks to serve.

It is crucial to stress character formation because believers do not enter into the life of Christ through a system of rules. . . . We are formed by Christ's presence in the Word and in the community. We experience God's life in the narratives of the Church and seek to follow God's designs. Our motivation for obedience is never rules or laws but the positive invitation of God's grace at work through us by God's power.

To form character, the means must match the ends. If we want deep faith, we must be nurtured by deep experiences of its reality. That is why it is so essential to plan worship well, for we must be concerned with how every action in the process of the faith journey affects the development of our character. . . .

Against the toxicities of our milieu the Church creates an alternative society. Each believer needs to be enfolded in a caring community of faithful people who offer guidance, wisdom, the perspectives of the Scriptures, and love to nurture character growth. . . .

Our primary source for character formation is the Word of God. As God's people, the Christian community will continually ask how that Word guides us in seeking the truth about our humanity and God's design for it. What is revealed by the biblical accounts of God's people in their ethical choices, in their instructions to each other? What virtues are displayed? What commands are issued that we ignore to our peril? How does the Bible give us courage to stand against false values and idolatries in our society because it announces to us the defeat of the principalities and powers? How can the worship of the community especially pass on the narratives and the hope that form us in faith? How does worship invite us to respond to the Word in faithfulness?

Prayer
> *Triune God, form our community and our character by your Word . . .*
> *Amen.*

Reaching Out, pp. 105, 116-17.

In friendship love — tenderly affectionate toward each other!

Romans 12:10a (my translation)

Many lonely persons simply drop out of our congregations. . . . How can the Church more directly address the problems and needs of this group of persons? . . .

One way to begin is to listen carefully to the words of Paul in Romans 12:10 . . . where Paul exhorts us to "be devoted to one another" in the family of Christ. The phrase — literally to be "tenderly affectionate" — means to have a heartfelt love and gentle care toward each other. . . . We need to learn to express community concern in wholesome, pure ways that will enfold lonely persons in genuine love so that they do not try to get their needs met in cheap affection or one-night stands. . . .

How imperative it is for the Church to realize that hurting and lonely persons need affectionate friends to be committed to them. . . . How can we learn to express tenderhearted affection in the Christian community? . . .

Why can't we concentrate in our churches on caring for individuals, on helping persons to become more committed to each other so that no one ever has to go through trials alone? Why don't we form small, caring groups in our churches to pray and study together to grow in family affection? Why don't we pray for one another more deeply? Why can't we be more real about expressing our care in ways that bring warmth and glad Hilarity to those who are hurting? . . .

Jesus' love . . . needs to be incarnated. When persons are lonely, they can't easily remember that Jesus cares. . . . In our friendship love for one another, we can incarnate the love of Christ with all the tender affection that he displayed toward the people around him. The apostle Paul told his close friends, the Philippians, "God can testify how I long for all of you with the affection of Christ Jesus" (Phil. 1:8). . . .

I long for the Christian community to discover such intimate affection and to practice it. Then we would draw the lonely back into the Hilarity of the community and make real for them the steadfast love and tender faithfulness of our God.

Prayer

Compassionate and tender Christ, empower us to offer tender affection in our churches, enfolding everyone . . .   Amen.

Truly the Community, pp. 158, 161-67.

Grant us wisdom, grant us courage,
lest we miss your kingdom's goal. . . .

Harry Emerson Fosdick (1930), alt.

As Christian communities and Christian families we *can* and *must set limits* on media consumption. Unless we do so . . . we will reverse the worldwide, ageless custom of parents teaching their children the wisdom of their faith and heritage, as children instead tutor their parents in media-savvy and themselves float aimlessly — without a sense of who they are or what life is really for. . . .

It seems many children more often listen to instruments on their Walkmans than play them, more often watch sports than engage in them, more often observe activities than discover their pleasures directly. It seems a sadly vicarious life — with not much proliferation of brain dendrites, not much outlet for responsibility and creativity, not much of the deep delights of learning many skills. . . . It really is a choice, and here we are back to the basic issue: Do parents realize that one of their primary callings in life is to invest time in the training of their children for life? The television set cannot accomplish that, but projects and games and chores together as a family can. Moreover, think what security and esteem children savor when they recognize (even subconsciously) that their parents choose to engage in leisure time activities together with them. . . .

Besides setting limits on the amount of time children spend with media consumption, I want to urge parents to work deliberately as their children grow to strengthen family ties, to develop the children's faith foundations, and thereby to give them constructive guidance as a basis for their own intelligent evaluation of the media. We certainly cannot separate our children entirely from media influence, even if we make certain choices about limits. Therefore we *can* and *must root children in the Christian worldview, its morals and values,* so that they never explore media without consciously assessing it, . . . choosing wisely, with deepened conscience for rejecting what is ungodly, and with Christian insights into the meaning of life and the purposes for which they were created and given time.

Prayer

Father of us all, unite us in helping parents raise their children with the values and abilities needed to deal with the influences of the media on their lives in faithful and productive ways . . .   Amen.

Is It a Lost Cause? pp. 164, 172-76.

A righteous [one] may have many troubles,
  but the LORD *delivers him from them all.*

Psalm 34:19

According to C. S. Lewis, there are two mistakes we can make about Satan and all the powers of evil (in whatever material or spiritual form they take). One error is to not take them seriously enough. . . . The other mistake is to take them too seriously and fail to remember that in his death Christ defeated the principalities and powers by exposing them and disarming them (see Col. 2:13-15). The Easter empty tomb is the seal of that victory. Therefore, we can assert with the poet of Psalm 34 that, though there are many troubles for the righteous, "The LORD delivers [us] from them all." . . .

The verb *to deliver* comes from a Hebrew root that emphasizes "snatching away," so it produces an image of God rescuing us from the midst of those troubles. That verb choice is important, because sometimes our circumstances cannot be changed. . . . We must be patient with the long process of healing, yet we can be confident that ultimately the LORD does deliver us from our straits and distresses. . . .

I think the text further invites us to learn from all those whose greater years with the LORD have given them deeper wisdom. We gain hope by listening to those who have suffered the same griefs we bear. We can glean from them how they survived their sorrows, how they have grown from them, and how *YHWH* was near in the midst of them. That is the great value of support groups and prayer partners, of biographies and testimonies of faith. . . .

Psalm 34 reminds us that we need to listen to instruction that will help us learn to fear the LORD. That truth will enable us to deal with our brokenheartedness, because in honoring *YHWH* we will discover that he is near. In fact, he is nearest in our broken repentance. When we are crushed — by our sin or by our circumstances — then we know most deeply that he comes to love.

Prayer
  O LORD *of infinite compassion, in our brokenheartedness help us listen to David and to all your saints, who can point us to repentance, trust in your nearness, and salvation . . .   Amen.*

I'm Lonely, LORD, pp. 106, 110-12.

"To the angel of the church in Sardis write: . . . Wake up! Strengthen what remains and is about to die. . . ."

                                                                    Revelation 3:1a, 2a

A friend, Connie, who is blind, demonstrated long ago the important lesson of rejoicing in what remains. She admitted to me that for a while she had been envious of my vision. As she was praying about her attitude, she heard God's comfort to her so powerfully that it seemed almost audible. The voice assured her, "That's OK, Connie. For what I've called Marva to do, she needs her vision. For what I've called you to do, you don't necessarily need your eyes." (Connie is program director for Vision Northwest and helps 34 support groups and over 500 people in Oregon cope with the difficulties of living with visual impairment in a seeing world.)

Connie's words rang in my ears the next day when an orthopedic specialist informed me that I faced possible amputation of my foot. "It's OK," God says. "For what I've called you to do, you don't really need your feet." Connie's insight motivates me to write books as well as I can for as long as eyes and brain and finger functions still remain. By myself I can't accept my crippled leg and diminished eyesight, but coping with the loss is made easier by the challenge to focus instead on God's gifts to strengthen what still remains.

The Christians at Sardis are commanded to remember — a common scriptural theme — what they have received and heard. Constantly God urges us to remember what he has taught, how he has intervened in history, what we have learned from the traditions of faith. The gospel in our memories, then, leads to these results: obedience and repentance. As we hear again God's exhortations, we want to respond with eager acceptance of his commands and desires and will, and we are sorry for the many times we have failed to respond positively. Our repentance . . . is a genuine turning around of both thought and behavior.

All the warnings of the letter to Sardis summarize excellently the elements needed for true renewal. Growing spiritually requires a steady repetition of the truths of faith, which will lead to repentance for our failures, a turning around of mind and deed, a desire to strengthen what remains, and an eagerness to obey in the future.

Prayer

Holy Spirit, use our memories of all God has done to promote repentance and renewal . . .   Amen.

                                                        Joy in Our Weakness, pp. 92-93.

It is he who sits above the circle of the earth,
*   and its inhabitants are like grasshoppers;*
who stretches out the heavens like a curtain,
*   and spreads them like a tent to live in.*

Isaiah 40:22 (NRSV)

This verse revolves around the theme of dwelling. . . . God's sovereignty is imagined by his dwelling above the dome of the earth's sky — his reigning majestically from the throne of the heavens. In stark contrast, those dwelling under the dome are as grasshoppers — small, insignificant, noisy, perhaps even pesky. . . .

The presence of God "tabernacling" himself among us forms a thread throughout the history of God's people. This theme begins in the book of Exodus, when God gives specific instructions for his people to construct the tabernacle in which he will dwell. After several chapters of instructions, several more chapters detail the completion of the tabernacle's fabrication. Finally, in Exodus 40, the most glorious event occurs: God comes to dwell in that tabernacle. . . .

The image of dwelling is also found in John 1:14. . . . The beloved evangelist writes that the Word became flesh and "tabernacled" himself among us. Jesus actually pitched his tent among human beings to dwell with them to reveal the grace and truth of God.

The book of Revelation anticipates God's final tabernacling. God declares that he, the Alpha and the Omega, the Beginning and the End, will make his dwelling with human beings. . . .

Most important, in 2 Corinthians 12:9 Paul proclaims why he can glory in his suffering. . . . He declares, literally, "I shall all the more glory in my weakness that the power of God may tabernacle in me." When God tabernacles himself in us, his grace is all we need. . . .

Isaiah 40:22 presents wonderful images of God's transcendent preeminence. God is not only a great God beside whom we are less than grasshoppers but also a God who establishes the endless galaxies to dwell in. Yet that same infinitely unfathomed God comes into space and time to dwell with us in all the grace and truth of Christ. Someday *YHWH* will pitch his tent with us forever, and then all his transcendence and immanence will be one.

Prayer

> *Triune God, we praise your transcendent glory and rejoice in your immanence — dwelling with us as Creator, Savior, Comforter, and our eternal Hope . . .   Amen.*

To Walk and Not Faint, pp. 131-36.

My gracious Master and my God,
Assist me to proclaim,
To spread through all the earth abroad
The honors of your name.

Charles Wesley, 1707-1788

Reflecting upon God's character during Sabbath days always incites me to renewed zeal for his purposes, a holy restlessness in my desire to serve him more effectively.... For example, when thinking about Jesus as the Prince of Peace ... I become more discontent with the violent nature of our society and more eager to serve as an agent of reconciliation in the local — and even the global — community. The more I contemplate his character of love and healing, the more I want to be like him. Thus, to keep the Sabbath always deepens my understanding of, and enthusiasm for, his call in my life.

Various Sabbath activities contribute to this end. In worship the Scripture lessons and sermons and prayers often give us clear instructions for ways to fulfill our calling. For example, a prayer for a congregational member who is ill might spark insight into how we can serve as care-givers — visiting, bringing flowers, preparing food, sending cards. Similarly, the Holy Spirit uses our personal Bible study, meditation, and prayer to reveal to us and develop in us the character of God.

In addition, quality time spent with others in conversation and prayer often strengthens our own notion of who we are and what we are to do with our lives ... and that helps us know the resources with which God created us in order that his purposes could be uniquely fulfilled in our lives....

Above all, we realize in our Sabbath keeping that God's love is to be proclaimed in the world. Each of us has certain gifts and personality traits that contribute uniquely to that proclamation.... All of those gifts and all of our personalities are needed to tell the world all that God wants to say about himself. The strengthening that we experience on the Sabbath day empowers us to use those particular resources during the week to communicate God's love in our specific fashion to those around us.

Prayer

Prince of Peace and Joy, may Sabbath blessings equip us for proclaiming the
message of your love wherever we are throughout the week ...   Amen.

Keeping the Sabbath Wholly, pp. 134-35.

[L]ead a life worthy of the calling to which you have been called, with all humility and gentleness, with patience, bearing with one another in love, making every effort to maintain the unity of the Spirit in the bond of peace.

Ephesians 4:1b-3

I have heard it said that every congregation must have at least two styles of worship, two points of entry into the congregation. Wrong! . . . Worship is not the entry point; *you are!* I want 490 points of entry into the congregation if there are 490 members. . . .

According to a 1995 study in the Evangelical Lutheran Church in America dealing with effective ministry and membership growth, a mere 1 percent joined a congregation because of its musical style. The largest proportion, 28 percent, joined because of faith and beliefs, 22 percent because of family and friends, 5 percent because of the hospitality ("atmosphere"), and 19 percent because of the location of the facilities.

Many churches have bought into the notion that they must have at least two "styles" of worship services in order to attract new members. The major reason for the popularity of this notion is that it gives a quick-fix answer to the problem of declining numbers in churches. . . . It is much easier to change the kind of music offered than to change the hearts of members to make them more hospitable in worship and daily life, more willing to witness, more loving toward their neighbors.

Certainly the desperation of churches to get the society interested in them also arises because Christianity is not supported by the culture as it once was. Biblical images are no longer taught in literature studies, and the faith roots of our nation's history are overlooked in history courses. Sunday sports interfere with the possibility of worship for our youth. Even the churches' own rites (the chief example of which is weddings) have been taken over by cultural values of consumerism and glamour, competition and glitter. So much is desacralized that there no longer seems to be a need in our society for churches. . . .

Nevertheless, those who advocate more than one style of worship as good for a congregation are deceiving us, for in truth such a development is injurious (often fatally) to genuine community.

Prayer

> *Lord of your Church, may each of us be genuine entry points for others into our faith households . . .   Amen.*

A Royal "Waste" of Time, pp. 187-89.

In the honor — leading each other!

Romans 12:10b (my translation)

The idea of "honor" was much stronger in Roman society than it is in contemporary cultures. Paul chose in Romans 12:10 to use the Greek word *timē*, which signified the concrete worth or merit of something and thus, secondarily, its price. As a result, the noun's meaning grew to include the reverence, status, and respect we accord to that object or person of value. The term here acknowledges the worth of all members of the Body of Christ and underscores the honor and respect with which the Christian community cares.

To hold others in honor prevents us from doing anything to hurt them or our relationship with them. . . . Furthermore, this verse invites us to be urgent about it. . . .

Obviously, that is not our normal human reaction (at least, I know it is not mine). Such a characteristic must be imparted by faith, created by God's love flowing through us. Our tender heavenly Father loved us first and showed us the greatest honor of all by giving up his Son to reconcile us to himself. . . .

Not by our worthiness but by his choice God values us so profoundly. This, then, is the honor we are to have for one another in the Christian community: a deep awareness of how valuable each individual is to God and therefore of how valuable we can be to each other in his family.

Such an honor especially creates a proper kind of affectionate love among those who show godly respect. . . . How much more effectively we would show to those around us the love of God if we more carefully nurtured each other. . . .

To put this exhortation into practice will demand sacrifice. To live this principle requires careful choices. But that is the whole point: what and whom do we value? . . .

What does honoring others above ourselves mean in light of our possessions and comfort and the needs of the world for our care? . . .

What can we do to show honor, not only for our brothers and sisters who worship together with us, but for our neighbors in our communities, and for the Church at large, and for a suffering world?

Prayer

Tender Father, help us honor others as you honor us . . .   Amen.

Truly the Community, pp. 169-75.

Add to your believing deeds that prove it true —
knowing Christ as Savior, make him Master too;
follow in his footsteps, go where he has trod,
in the world's great trouble risk yourself for God.

Bryan Jeffery Leech (1975)

One critically dangerous effect of too much media consumption is that frequent use of the media and of the rapidly proliferating technological toys and tools leads to inactivity or merely experiential consumption. . . . For example, television offers its viewers tons of data about which they cannot do a thing; consequently, it trains them to receive and discard it without acting on it. This response produces what Neil Postman calls a "Low Information-Action Ratio." Think what such training does to sermons, Christian education, and schools! Have you wondered why your children or your parishioners do not seem to be able to respond to information with appropriate action? . . .

Nothing is wrong with information, of course; we all need all kinds of it to survive. To be sure, our Christian communities pass on specific details about God, but those facts are anchored in an enduring faith that puts into action what it knows. . . . Our society, however, is glutted with fruitless or contextless data. . . .

Our children can hardly escape being plunged into this morass of chasing after information primarily for the sake of entertainment. . . . They may not know how to put limits on their use of technological toys and tools or how to distinguish between mastery of tools and domination by them. . . .

The most important gift we can give to our children in such an age is the ability to ask why and the reasons to say no. As parents and Christian communities, let us nurture in our offspring a profound awareness of the meaning of life that teaches them to be selective about everything, including the information they investigate and how they spend their time. Let us give them reasons for living that enable them to say no to destructive or delimiting technology, to the media's demeaning trivialization, to addictive behaviors, to knowledge without wisdom, to powers that would control them, to any immersion that would tear them away from the Joy of serving God.

Prayer

Gracious Master, help us teach our children the Joys of living for you — and the desire to evaluate all experiences and opportunities in terms of their contribution to a faithful life . . .   Amen.

Is It a Lost Cause? pp. 181-86.

Who will rise up for me against the wicked?
  Who will take a stand for me against evildoers?
Unless the LORD *had given me help,*
  I would soon have dwelt in the silence of death.
When I said, "My foot is slipping,"
  Your love, O LORD, *supported me.*
When anxiety was great within me,
  your consolation brought joy to my soul.

Psalm 94:16-19

When we look at this psalm through contemporary eyes, we must imagine the different sorts of enemies that our culture produces. . . .

We cry out with the poet, "Who will rise up for me against the wicked? Who will take a stand for me against the evildoers?" . . . No one seems to be on our side. . . .

The poet in Psalm 94 records how deep his fears and anxiety were. Unless the LORD had given him help, he "would soon have dwelt in the silence of death." . . . Though the word *death* does not appear in the Hebrew text, it seems to be implied, and that matches our experience. In times of despair we think we are almost going to die — or wish we would. . . .

The psalmist has recorded his anxiety to encourage us. . . . The horror of evil rising up against us is very real, and a person being overwhelmed does indeed feel starkly alone and defenseless.

However, the poet goes on to describe how mistaken he was. "If I said, 'My foot has slipped,' your *chesedh, YHWH,* will support me." . . . *Chesedh* connotes a depth of loving-kindness unmatched in the world's various kinds of love. When we feel we are slipping over the edge, *YHWH*'s steadfast care will support our deepest being. . . .

This is what supports us best in our moments of pain and panic: the assurance that we are loved. . . . Then we can discover that the sense of falling is a false one, for we are really being sustained tenderly by our LORD.

The last verse of our text contains the surprise. Not only does the *chesedh* of *YHWH* support us, but furthermore it actually brings us past the point of panic into a sense of well-being that can even issue in delight.

Prayer
  Sustaining LORD, *help us trust that you are indeed holding us in your loving hands when we feel we are falling . . .   Amen.*

I'm Lonely, LORD, pp. 114-18.

"To the angel of the church in Philadelphia write: . . . I have placed before you an open door that no one can shut. I know that you have little strength, yet you have kept my word and have not denied my name."

Revelation 3:7a, 8b-c

What a glorious promise we receive when Christ declares in the letter to the saints at Philadelphia that the ones with little strength will become pillars. They have kept Christ's word and have not denied his name. They have endured patiently and so will be spared the hour of trial that will test the whole world. . . .

The letter begins with a picture of Christ as the holy and true one, the one who holds the key of David, the one whose opening and shutting no one can oppose. It is amazing that in his holiness he can look at our weakness and commend it. How different the values of Christ are from those of the world, which praises the ones who are beautiful, successful, rich, ambitious, skillful, powerful. We humans praise such things because we are not holy, and in our lack of perfection we fumble for the "best," which is epitomized by those who seem to have it all.

In contrast, the holy/set apart One sets apart those . . . who speak the truth about their inadequacies and do not claim any false superiorities.

He holds the power to open and close all that pertains to the true Israel, for he holds the key of David. Therefore, he can open a door before those who are humble. He knows them truly — that they are not falsely pretending to be greater than they are — and so he gives them unrestricted entrance. . . .

Sadly, if we get too caught up in the world's success syndrome, we might try to close the door. Sometimes in our churches we shut out the weak and prevent them from offering their gifts to the community. Actually, we cannot ultimately shut the door, for no one can shut what Christ has opened. The weak who depend on him will serve him and become what he has in store for them with or without our approval and care, but in the process we lose the gifts they could bring to the Body.

Prayer

> *Holy and true Lord, help us see the weak with your eyes, valuing their gifts and the example of their patient endurance . . .   Amen.*

Joy in Our Weakness, pp. 95-96.

[He it is] who reduces rulers to nothing,
  who makes the judges of the earth meaningless.

Isaiah 40:23 (NASV)

Prestige and fame, influence and glory are brought to naught by the LORD. . . .

These words had a double significance for those first hearing this verse. They rebuked any rulers of Israel who were unduly proud or falsely confident in their divine chosenness. And this verse also spoke about the rulers of the nations that threatened Israel. . . .

Still today — though we hardly realize it — God brings princes to naught, for the LORD and his justice will ultimately prevail. This message has international, national, and personal consequences. . . .

Nationally, this verse carries a painful reminder and a warning. . . . For example, in U.S. politics in recent years there have been too many examples of government officials who have sought power with deceptive and immoral means. . . . This verse warns our present governmental leaders to remember the importance of morality, to realize constantly that the power of earthly authority is vanity.

It speaks directly to our political illusions. Jacques Ellul's book *The Political Illusion* rebukes Christians for forgetting the lordship of Christ and thinking that if we just elect the right governmental leaders all our problems will be solved. All earthly officers are sinful human beings. They will fail; some will fall. We cannot place our hopes on a particular political party or program. Human problems are greater than that.

Moreover, verse 23 speaks to the issue of the lordship of our own lives. Does God reign in how we spend our money and time? Do we live out of power or servanthood? If God is really going to be LORD in our lives, WE can't be. If Jesus is really King, we cannot be antagonistic princes or princesses trying to usurp the throne.

Prayer
  O LORD, our only true Ruler, forgive our sinful love of power. Help us to keep
  you on the throne in our hearts and your purposes foremost in our thinking
  and behavior . . .   Amen.

To Walk and Not Faint, pp. 137-40.

The important point in all our imitation [of God] is its deliberate intentionality. We don't just think God's values are good. We embrace them wholly. . . . To embrace is to accept with gusto, to live to the hilt, to choose with extra intentionality and tenacity.

from *Keeping the Sabbath Wholly*

Sabbath keeping is not just negative ceasing . . . but also the positive embracing of Sabbath values. . . . Intentionality and deliberateness characterize the lifestyle of those who keep the Sabbath. . . . In making this choice we embrace time instead of space and giving instead of requiring. In response to the grace of God we gladly embrace our calling in life, and in the fullness of healing brought by our relationship with God we can embrace the wholeness of God's *shalom*. Finally, all these Sabbath gifts set us free to embrace the world. . . .

Part of the weakness of our Christian witness stems from the fact that often it is so lackadaisical, so lackluster. The early Christians set their world on fire with the exuberance of their Joy. We might not necessarily be happy in the particular circumstances of the moment, but we can always know Joy because the Resurrection is an accomplished fact. We can be sure "that our present sufferings are not worth comparing with the glory that will be revealed in us" and "that in all things God works for the good of those who love him, who have been called according to his purpose" (Rom. 8:18, 28). Furthermore, we can be confident that nothing will ever be able to separate us from the love of God in Christ Jesus (Rom. 8:38-39). These unfailing assurances lead us to profound Joy. Everyone in the world is looking for such confidence and hope, and each of us is particularly suited for sharing it with those whom we encounter in our daily worlds.

We can embrace our calling to share God's love with the exhilaration of knowing that God has uniquely equipped each of us for our particular roles and that he has called us. Immersing ourselves in his love in the Sabbath overwhelms us with his grace, clarifies our perceptions of our role, and empowers us for the tasks that he makes clear.

Prayer

Resurrected Lord, forgive our lackluster witness and inspire our efforts, so that the grace we know will be Joyfully, faithfully, and uniquely offered to everyone we encounter . . . Amen.

Keeping the Sabbath Wholly, pp. 100-101, 136.

"I was a stranger and you invited me in. . . ."

Matthew 25:35c

Worship leaders and participants alike sometimes base their expectations for worship on a false perception . . . which causes us to think that participants in a worship service must feel cozy and close to each other. This fallacy prevents worship from being truly *public* and open to those who are not part of the community.

The Christian community does develop warm and caring relationships that are nurtured in times of fellowship. However, worship is for God and should not depend on cozy feelings either toward each other or toward God — although the result of good worship will be a deepening of both. In fellowship times, we welcome strangers best by conversation and actions that focus on them. In worship, contrarily, we welcome them best by worshiping God in a public way.

Genuine worship that "welcomes the stranger" can only happen by means of objective proclamation — for no one can enter into the feelings of others, nor will newcomers feel they belong to an already established group. . . . For this reason, our theologizing must search for the best means to keep worship public. My emphasis on God as subject underscores the same point. How can worship convey God's self-giving presence to a stranger in our midst?

The Christian heritage of liturgical rites and responses has functioned in such a way throughout the ages. That heritage also serves to widen our concept of community.

A crucial part of making the worshiping people a community is acknowledging our unity with the entire Church, the Body of Christ, throughout time and space. Though we thoughtfully put the wine in fresh wineskins by using new forms, new melodies, new instruments, new instructions about the meanings of the old, we always preserve faith's heritage, the fundamental core of the historic Church. . . .

The heritage of the Church is crucially necessary to preserve genuine "community" worship — worship that is not the property of its leaders, worship that crosses lines of time and space, worship that involves us in each other and not in our own private mullings, selfishness, or falsely cozy "personal relationship with Jesus."

Prayer
Welcoming Lord, guide us in devising worship that is truly public — so that every stranger is welcomed . . .   Amen.

Reaching Out, pp. 140-43.

In the diligence — not poky! In the spirit — boiling! In the Lord — slaving!
                                                          Romans 12:11 (my translation)

With regard to service, Paul urges *all* the members of the Christian community to keep an eager and attentive steadiness up, with no waning of its exuberance or power, . . . an awfully large order when the going gets tough. . . .

The secret lies in always remembering our goal. We are not diligent for
merely human reasons. Our enthusiasm is not empty because we are not
serving that which will soon wither and fade. . . .

The next pair of key words in verse 11 — literally, "in spirit boiling" — is
one of the most vivid pictures in Scriptures. . . . To have "a heart full of devotion" (TEV) . . . "great earnestness" (JB) or "ardor of spirit" (NEB) is our
goal; we are to "be aglow" (RSV). . . .

Only when our spirits are taken over by the Holy Spirit can they remain
on fire. Thus we see that these exhortations cannot be fulfilled by our striving, but rather by our yielding. Our efforts cannot sustain a spiritual glow,
but the presence of Christ's Spirit at work within us will. . . .

Now the last phrase of verse 11 reminds us to what end we want to have
a non-poky diligence and a boiling spirit. Our purpose is always to be slaving "in the Lord." . . . This phrase is not an "ought to" over our heads, but
rather the good news of how God's love does indeed work through us. . . .

Who is our Lord? How have we decided? If our Lord is Jesus, then our
service of others will be empowered and inspired and directed by him. . . .

One of the most important goals for our spiritual growth is to become
more and more aware of the constancy of that choice so that we will learn in
every situation to practice the presence of God.

Prayer
   Ever-present Lord, may all our serving be "in you," so that it is sustained,
   empowered, and directed by your love, for your glory . . .   Amen.
                                          Truly the Community, pp. 177, 180-85.

Here on earth applying principles of love —
visible expression God still rules above. . . .

Bryan Jeffery Leech (1975)

The Christian community is called to be different from a world that makes idols out of informational or experiential consumption. Both the Word of God and the needs of the world that surround us call the Church to be an alternative society. . . .

Karl Barth said that Christians should be people with the Bible in one hand and the newspaper in the other — that is, the situation of the world creates the ways in which we apply the biblical instructions and, conversely, the biblical perspective teaches us how to read the world. . . .

Rather than having a low information-action ratio, we model for our children and invite them into an active application "here on earth" of the "principles of love" so that we all become a "visible expression" of God's rule. . . .

For example, in the Christian understanding of work, artists don't only paint, dance, compose, perform. They use their gifts to express the wonder of God's creation, to make us aware of the brokenness of our world, to stir up compassion, to bring God's Joy to observers, to lift the audience's souls to the other world for which we were begotten. . . . Farmers don't simply grow crops or raise animals; they labor to feed the world as agents of God's provision. . . .

What a difference it makes if we understand our employment as a means by which to glorify God and love our neighbors — just as it makes an enormous difference if parents understand their role as stewardship of their children for the sake of helping them to love and serve God. And when we understand our labor in such a way, our children learn from that modeling that whatever work they do, they perform it as a sacrifice of praise.

Such a theology of work counteracts the low information-action ratio syndrome. We don't gather information for its own sake; it, too, becomes a vehicle for God's purposes.

Prayer
> *Loving and merciful God, help us to apply your Word to the world's needs in*
> *all that we do for your glory . . .   Amen.*

Is It a Lost Cause? pp. 181, 188-91.

Surely God is good to Israel,
  to those who are pure in heart.
But as for me, my feet had almost slipped;
  I had nearly lost my foothold.
For I envied the arrogant
  when I saw the prosperity of the wicked. . . .
When I tried to understand all this,
  it was oppressive to me
till I entered the sanctuary of God;
  then I understood their final destiny.

Psalm 73:1-3, 16-17

Like the psalmist, we rant and rail against the injustices of life. . . . Because we get ourselves into such a state of mind, the poet begins with a statement of faith. . . . Later he will question whether or not it is worth the effort to keep one's heart pure, so he begins by asserting that it is and then wrestles through to belief in the truth of that statement. . . .

The psalm itself begins with the word *surely*. . . . Purity is worthwhile after all, he claims, but then he continues as if to say, "But let me tell you how I almost forgot." . . .

The poet summarizes his immense frustration: Some people have it all! . . . Things were onerous as long as the poet was trying to interpret them with his own mind; the bitterness could be changed only by his going to the sanctuary of God. . . .

We will never be able to explain satisfactorily such problems as the breaking of covenant marriage relationships, the limitations of physical handicaps, . . . or accidents. . . . Nevertheless, in the sanctuaries there are answers of another sort. . . .

Always life seems unfair until it is put into the whole picture of forever. We who believe in Jesus Christ already possess eternal life. . . . Having an eternal perspective means that we learn to recognize that the reality of pains in this life is not all that there is to truth. . . .

Where there is sin there will also be guilt and sorrow and emptiness. Cruelty works its own rewards, and evil bears its consequences. Therefore, seeking revenge does us no good. Rather, our frustrations can enable us to grow in compassion and in our eternal perspective.

Prayer

  God of the ages, help us view life with an eternal perspective! . . .   Amen.

I'm Lonely, LORD, pp. 121-27.

"To the angel of the church in Philadelphia write: . . . I am coming soon. Hold on to what you have, so that no one will take your crown."

Revelation 3:7a, 11

This letter challenges each of us to look at our attitudes and actions toward the weak. Christ says that he will make all those who lie to come and fall down at the feet of the weak and acknowledge that he has loved them. In modern society we often lie about God's love for the weak by our own refusal truly to welcome them into our fellowships. Maybe we lie about God's love for them by not helping to care for their physical needs. Sometimes our lies are more subtle — inward attitudes that we don't reveal, hidden animosities that we hide, repressed impatience that we don't vent.

Three times this section uses the word *Behold!* to call our attention to what we usually fail to notice. God shows very clearly that those who have little strength — in whatever form that might take in history — are the special objects of his concern. The mentally deficient are often very sure about his love and clearly capable of loving others. Those whose handicaps make them utterly reliant on God's strength are often profoundly taught by their situation to forego the world's methods of power. If we are caught up in our own capabilities, we won't notice such things now, but we will someday. . . .

Christ commands those with little strength in Philadelphia to hold fast to what they have so that no one will take their crown. Perhaps they have been persecuted for so long that they wonder if they can hold out any longer. God's gift of the crown of life enables them to continue persevering. Even so, the anticipation of Christ's coming soon, the experience of his gracious coming now into our lives, and the process of holding fast to faith meanwhile enable us to enjoy that crown to some extent even now. We have already been crowned with the Joy promised in the messianic age (Isa. 35:10), which makes us look forward all the more to the perfection of Joy we will experience someday when all the present tears and pain, the sorrow and sighing, will flee away.

Prayer

God of patience and hope, we have so much to learn about trusting and enduring from those who exhibit those virtues daily. Open our eyes — and hearts! . . . Amen.

Joy in Our Weakness, pp. 96-97.

217

[He it is] who reduces rulers to nothing,
  who makes the judges of the earth meaningless.

Isaiah 40:23 (NASV)

If we thoroughly learn that the LORD brings princes to naught, we will be more willing to forego our attempts to assert power over others. Instead, we will want to ask Christ to reign in our lives wherever that might take us, whatever that might cause us to do, however that might lead us to suffering. . . .

Do we want to make that kind of commitment? Are we seriously willing to serve no matter what the cost? Are we able to give up our rights?

Clamoring for rights is the national pastime these days, it seems, . . . but we can't clamor for rights and still obey Christ's model and instruction to be servants of all (Mark 10:42-45). . . . Christ is the supreme model of humility and submission, of giving up rights for the sake of God's purposes.

Our leadership is never based on power that withers or fame that fades. As servants, instead, we will grow more and more willing for God to bring our power to naught so that he might be glorified through us. What really matters in life are the eternal things, and eternal values have little or nothing to do with earthly accomplishments. This certainly does not mean that we accept mediocrity from ourselves in leadership. Choosing to be servants who glorify God causes us to strive after excellence, to serve with the best of our abilities. But if we are willing to let the LORD be our God, he creates our worth and value — eternally. Then our importance does not fade with the passing of time. . . .

It is God's grace that the LORD brings our attempts at importance to naught. Then he can confer upon us the greatest significance of all, his rule in our lives.

Prayer
  Humble Jesus, help us renounce our desire for power and discover eternal Joy
  in servanthood . . .   Amen.

To Walk and Not Faint, pp. 137, 140-42.

I will grant peace in the land, . . . I will put my dwelling place among you. . . . I broke the bars of your yoke and enabled you to walk with heads held high.

Leviticus 26:6a, 11a, 13b

Sometimes when we are really tired, we long desperately just for some "peace and quiet" — by which we mean the absence of hassle and conflict. . . .

God wants much more for us. . . . The Hebrew word for peace, *shalom,* begins in reconciliation with God and continues in reconciliation with our sisters and brothers — even our enemies. Moreover, *shalom* designates being at peace with ourselves, health, wealth, fulfillment, satisfaction, content-ment, tranquility, and — to sum it all up — wholeness. . . .

We find integrity in each dimension of our being — physical, spiritual, emotional, and intellectual — through a day of rest. Our spirits become more unified when our relationship with God is the center and focus of our lives and all other aspects find their proper priorities in the worship of the Lord. Our bodies are more sound when we enjoy a rhythm of fasting and feasting, when we truly rest by giving up the burden of possessions, when we have time for naps. . . . Our minds become more robust when the narratives of our heritage as God's people remind us of our redemption and when, as a result, our attitudes are more wholesome and our freedom leads to the gen-erating of new ideas. . . .

As we become more intentional both about being a gathered Christian community and about enjoying our special times of solitude with God, the two work together to create a greater sense of both individual and corporate wholeness. . . .

Perhaps the most important aspect of Sabbath keeping that contrib-utes immensely to wholeness in our human existence is the prevalence of or-der. We crave order to give us a sense that things are under control, that we can cope with whatever might be happening because it fits into a larger plan. That is why the keeping of the Sabbath rhythm is so important: the or-derly cycle of six days of work and one day of resting and embracing God's values matches the rhythm of our creation, which God has revealed to us in the Scriptures.

Prayer

   Creator of our life and its rhythms, we thank you for the shalom that we expe-rience in Sabbath keeping . . .   Amen.

Keeping the Sabbath Wholly, pp. 137-39.

"My prayer is not for them alone. I pray also for those will believe in me through their message, that all of them may be one."

John 17:20-21a

If the leadership of a church decides to split worship into two services with different "styles" for the sake of attracting the neighbors . . . several very harmful effects of such splitting may occur. . . .

If we set up different kinds of worship at different times, this fosters the "vendors/consumers" disposition and promotes the notion of marketing religion. . . .

The division into a "traditional" and "contemporary" service . . . causes narrowing of the community's appreciation. . . . Older music, written in eras that were more objective in orientation, most often stresses doctrinal content, whereas new music is frequently more directed to loving God. Both are needed, so they ought not to be separated.

Furthermore, of all the various tastes in music that there are, why should we limit ourselves to traditional and contemporary? How will a community decide which taste to follow? Research shows that people in the United States are quite evenly divided among those who prefer hard rock, soft rock, classical, jazz, blues, country and western, contemporary easy listening, and several other kinds. . . .

Having a "traditional" and a "contemporary" service . . . often separates the old from the young according to their preference for what they know. The result is that young families no longer worship next to those more experienced in the faith who could be mentors to them — and the old are bereft of the vitality of the young. . . . It also deprives the "traditionalists" of new expressions of faith . . . and robs "contemporaryists" of continuity with the Church throughout time. . . .

If the words are theologically sound, then . . . Christians should be willing to sing a song they might not like for the sake of brothers and sisters for whom it might be especially useful spiritually. . . .

The worst result of turning worship into a matter of taste is that to do so is to lose sight of the fact that it is *God* we are worshiping — not ourselves. And God, I hear, has widely eclectic tastes!

Prayer

Creator of music, forgive our selfishness in destroying the community's wholeness for the sake of our tastes! . . .   Amen.

A Royal "Waste" of Time, pp. 189-92.

In the hope — rejoicing! In the tribulation — remaining under!

Romans 12:12a-b (my translation)

Some things are serious, but not hopeless . . . because in everything that is serious, God will be there to accomplish his purposes and to be our God. . . .

Our hope will not disappoint us. It cannot, for it is founded on a deeper reality than hope — the very fact of God himself. . . . Paul names God with the title "God of hope" and says that God is able to "fill you with all joy and peace as you trust in him, so that you may overflow with hope by the power of the Holy Spirit" (Rom. 15:13). . . .

Obviously, the biblical concept of Joy is much different from the idea of happiness. Happiness is dependent to a great extent on one's external circumstances. . . . But many things in life also make us sad. We grieve when we lose a loved one. We feel the pain of illness or difficult circumstances. . . . We cry out at the world's evil.

Yet Joy remains Joy throughout. No matter whether our circumstances are conducive to happiness or sadness, darkness or light, our Joy remains firm because it is based in our hope and in the One who is deeper than hope. . . .

"Joy is the flag that is flown o'er the castle of our hearts when the King is in residence there." His presence makes possible our hope — hope for how he can create good from even the negative elements in our lives (Rom. 8:28) and hope for how we will discover that the sufferings of this present time are not worth comparing to the fulfillment of God's promises as they will be revealed to us (8:18).

Moreover, this hope does not disappoint. God has proven his love to us time and again, through the subjective witness of our own hearts and through the objective fact of the death of Christ on our behalf. Can there be any doubt? We might encounter serious circumstances, but they are not hopeless. The King is still in residence here.

Prayer

> *O risen King, reside in our hearts, so that hope may abound, no matter what the circumstances of life . . . Amen.*

Truly the Community, pp. 186, 192-93.

Let your heart be tender and your vision clear —
rouse yourself to action, serve God far and near.

Bryan Jeffery Leech (1975)

At least four dimensions of prayer equip us to counteract the dulling passivity that the media induce and to oppose the mindless entertainment in which so many escape active participation in the purposes of God. . . .

First of all, prayer is the means by which we share God's burdens for the world. . . . Jesus teaches us, as do all the great persons of prayer in the Bible, that prayer is focused on God, not on us. To ask for God's will to be done and his kingdom to come is a means of placing ourselves into God's hands for insights into that will and an envisioning of that kingdom. When we teach our children to pray, we instruct them in "having the mind of Christ"; this is the true meaning of praise — to acknowledge God's character and interventions in the world, to honor his burdens and concerns. We cannot truly develop this mind of Christ without wanting to act on it.

Second, prayer helps us comprehend what God wants us to be. . . . When we ourselves pray and teach our children to pray, we practice dwelling in God's presence, so that we can become more like him. Consequently prayer is often combat against our worst selves.

Third, prayer is waiting to hear what God would have us do and how to do it. . . . When we teach our children to pray, we are inviting them into waiting — for God's way and timing, clearer insight, firmer wisdom, giving up our own control in order that God's purposes can really be done. . . . When we teach our children to pray with openness to God's wisdom and understanding, truth and freedom, we are giving them the critical weapon they need to withstand the powers of the world around them that would draw them away from faith and service.

Finally, prayer *is* action, for if we have asked for God's will to be done in our lives, our every action is prayer. . . . To pray truly is not simply to say words or even to sit in silence, but to be available to God for the effecting of his will through us.

Prayer

Listening and answering Lord, in prayer we seek your heart for the world . . .
Amen.

Is It a Lost Cause? pp. 182, 196-98.

When my heart was grieved
  and my spirit embittered,
I was senseless and ignorant;
  I was a brute beast before you.
Yet I am always with you.

Psalm 73:21-23a

The poet's graphic picture of his previous ingratitude and poor attitude is something with which we can all identify. . . .

Truly, much suffering comes to us from the outside, when others hurt or reject us; however, we multiply it many times by our envy and our untrusting spirits. . . .

The poet also realizes that his attitudes affect his outward behavior. The word *brutish* (or "senseless" in the NIV) . . . describes one whose spiritual sensitivities are too dull to perceive truth. . . .

To see ourselves this way is a necessary part of our spiritual growth . . . so that we can see, with Joy-full wonder, the infinite surprise that God would love us anyway, in spite of our ignorance and brutishness. . . .

It is not an on-again, off-again deal. "I am with you *continually.*" . . . The always-ness of our relationship with the LORD takes us away from our brutishness into the freedom of acceptance. Too easily we might . . . think that we justly deserve God's love. A good hard look at the beastliness of our ignorance is a necessary dose of strong medicine.

To say that we are with *YHWH* emphasizes that we are in his thoughts and care. . . . But in verse 23 an unusual fact surfaces. The pronoun that is attached to the preposition *with* in the Hebrew is the feminine singular *you.* . . .

Thus the wonder and surprise multiply, for when we have been beastly and senseless, the LORD still directs maternal care toward us. God still holds us as special children in relationship.

Prayer
  God who holds us in grace, thank you for loving us in spite of ourselves! . . .
  Amen.

I'm Lonely, LORD, pp. 128-32.

"To the angel of the church in Philadelphia write: . . . Since you have kept my command to endure patiently, I will also keep you from the hour of trial that is going to come upon the whole world to test those who live on the earth."

Revelation 3:7a, 10

We must be very careful when we discuss the tribulation from which the Philadelphians will be spared. It grieves me that Revelation 3:10 is often taken out of context, improperly joined together with Luke 17:34-36 and 1 Thessalonians 4:17 (which speak of entirely different things in their original contexts) and made into "the rapture." This procedure constructs a major doctrine on the basis of a misreading of the texts.

Instead, a major rule for reading Scripture accurately is that each verse must be read in its own context. In the context of the words of Christ in Luke 17, the verses about "one taken and the other left" mean that Christ will come suddenly and that we won't know who is part of his kingdom. Chapter 4 of 1 Thessalonians was originally intended to comfort people who had already lost loved ones before the expected return of Christ. The apostle Paul offers this hope to them: they will all be together when Christ comes. . . . These verses in Revelation 3 about being spared the tribulation cannot be disassociated from the words to the people of Smyrna that they would suffer in the coming peril. Not all Christians will be spared the suffering. . . .

Furthermore, some groups who read these verses out of their historical and literary context also spend much of their time debating the "when" of the rapture, even though Jesus specifically told his followers in several places (such as Luke 17:23 and 21:8) that they should not chase after the people who claim to know about the time of the end. . . . We would do much better . . . to concentrate on these messages that Christ gave us for the meanwhile: repent, watch, tell others, do justice and mercy, walk humbly with God.

Prayer

Alpha and Omega, First and Last, help us trust that the end of time is in your hands, and empower us to commit ourselves to living faithfully as your disciples in the meantime . . .　Amen.

Joy in Our Weakness, p. 98.

Scarcely are they planted, scarcely sown,
    scarcely has their stem taken root in the earth,
when he blows upon them, and they wither,
    and the tempest carries them off like stubble.

Isaiah 40:24 (NRSV)

This verse attaches several significant dimensions to the emphasis on im-permanence in Isaiah 40. The stress is placed on the relationship between the temporality of the planting and the finality of the carrying away. . . . The domination of flesh cannot be firmly rooted. . . .

In contrast, those who depend on the power of God and not their flesh can be firmly planted, as many images of the New Testament show. . . .

For example, the epistle to the Colossians encourages the people that, just as they trusted Christ for salvation, so they might also trust him for each day's problems, that rooted and grounded in him they might grow up to know the fullness of his provision for their needs (2:6-7). These prayers remind us that there is no danger of being blown away when we are rooted in Christ. . . .

The rooting and grounding of the Church depends on careful nurtur-ing. . . . In our essentially superficial and entertainment-centered culture, the Christian community needs to be an alternative society offering the nar-ratives of faith clearly and profoundly to root people in the ongoing belief-formed life of God's people.

The last phrase of Isaiah 40:24 . . . is analogous to both the seed planted in the path and the seed that fell among thorns in Jesus' parable (Matt. 13:4, 7). In these cases we are either carried away by the powers of evil or choked out by the cares and temptations of the world. Both have the effect of a whirlwind on strawlike faith.

The conclusion of Jesus' parable gives us the positive hope for this verse from Isaiah 40. Rather than being carried away or dried up because we have not been adequately planted, the people of God provide the milieu in which the seed — the Word of God, Jesus says — falls on good soil and bears fruit (Matt. 13:8). The Christian community prepares the earth so that its mem-bers can be rooted and grounded in Christ.

Prayer
    Grounding God, help us to become so firmly rooted by our faith in you that
    nothing can blow us away . . .   Amen.

To Walk and Not Faint, pp. 143-46.

Do not be anxious about anything, but in everything, by prayer and petition, with thanksgiving, present your requests to God. And the peace of God, which transcends all understanding, will guard your hearts and your minds in Christ Jesus. . . . And the God of peace will be with you.

Philippians 4:6-7

The most important ordering takes place in our lives when we observe the Sabbath focus of placing God at the center and then prioritize everything else in proper relation to that focus. . . .

This ordering . . . gives us the ability to weave together all the bits and pieces of our lives, which often become severely fragmented because of the strains of our surrounding culture. . . .

Observing the Sabbath each week enables us to establish a deeper sense of family unity. We can establish customs that hold us together and build a special bond of meaningful and Joy-full memories from happy, celebrative times together.

Even those who are single can discover such Sabbath wholeness with friends and extended families. . . .

And in times of darkness and sadness, keeping the Sabbath gives us a means for finding wholeness in the midst of our pain. . . . Of course, the pain does not automatically go away. But when the habit of observing the Sabbath is a constant one, the very order of that remembrance enables us to grasp a sense of the presence of Yahweh. . . .

Even as we cease working although our work is not done and spend the Sabbath as if we have no work to do, just so we embrace wholeness on that day even when we are not experiencing wholeness in our present circumstances. . . .

We move from the negative action of trying to cease being anxious into the positive hope of wholeness. As Paul says to the Philippians, not only will "the *peace of God*, which transcends all understanding, guard your hearts and minds in Christ Jesus," but also "the *God of peace* will be with you" (Phil. 4:7 and 9b, my emphasis). Sabbath keeping ushers us into the wholeness of God's order, the *shalom* of his love.

Prayer

> God of Peace, may we find in Sabbath keeping an order and wholeness for our lives . . .   Amen.

Keeping the Sabbath Wholly, pp. 141-44.

I love to tell the story, for those who know it best
  seem hungering and thirsting, to hear it like the rest.
And when, in scenes of glory, I sing the new, new song,
  I'll sing the old, old story that I have loved so long.

Katherine Hankey, 1834-1911

Many think that newness or creativity requires dispensing with old traditions. This arises from such factors as movement away from the classic understanding of worship as a community's praise of God to a new individualized expression; rejection of doctrines as a means for finding our way in favor of emancipation from connections with institutions; the boomers' search for a church to meet their needs instead of commitment to the Church through which to serve. . . .

We must ask if church effectiveness and preserved traditions are mutually exclusive and whether traditions prevent genuine creativity. What is lost in the process if we throw away traditions for the sake of success and novelty?

One of the great myths of contemporary marketing analysis is the idea that churches fail because of their ties to traditional belief and practice. On the contrary, sociologists with hard data about why churches decline reveal a different picture. . . . To create long-term loyalty, churches need to offer orthodox substance, a system of belief that is strong enough to be empowering. . . .

Those who spurn tradition itself, instead of the atrophy of tradition, forget that real creativity is impossible without the grounding in truth that tradition conveys.

So much is lost if churches arbitrarily throw out all tradition in response to marketing myths, yet . . . it is extremely difficult to fight the modern trivialization that is happening in churches for the sake of newness. . . .

Sometimes in their attempt to make worship "exciting" parishes lose the very members who can best teach them about true worship. Even more important, those congregations lose their source of stability — the continuity, durability, and fruitfulness of the Church's heritage.

Prayer
  Eternal Trinity, grant us wisdom as we struggle to make the "old story" of
  our heritage also our "new song" in worship today . . .   Amen.

Reaching Out, pp. 144-48.

In the hope — rejoicing! In the tribulation — remaining under!

Romans 12:12a-b (my translation)

Some things are hopeless, but not serious. In such tribulations, Paul exhorts us to remain patient. . . .

The afflictions spoken of here are tribulations that come from the outside. . . . Such trouble involves direct suffering. That very accurately describes the struggles that we experience as circumstances press us into tight places, confinements from which we cannot escape. . . .

We all suffer from various kinds of tribulations from the outside. Pressures come from our peers, . . . in our work or at home, or, sad to say, even in our churches. Afflictions arise from accidents or hazards of nature or other forces over which we have no control. . . .

What can we do when something is hopeless? The second phrase from Romans 12:12 reminds us that such situations are not serious. We are invited by Paul to keep remaining under them because we will not be destroyed by them. . . .

The idea is to remain steadfast instead of fleeing, to hold out, standing one's ground, enduring in the face of all sorts of trouble. . . . With a clear perspective on what gives us hope, we remain under the things that are hopeless. Not resigned to those situations, we bear them confidently because we firmly know their value as less than ultimate. . . .

In 2 Corinthians 1:3-7 Paul especially demonstrates the importance of the community in our learning to endure tribulations. Not only are we helped by the comfort that we can share with one another, but also the desire to let our sufferings benefit others gives us a purpose in enduring them. . . .

Also, Paul declares that it is possible to exult in one's tribulations because they teach us the hope of the sufficiency of grace. . . .

Some situations are hopeless in human terms, but we can remain under and endure them because our hope lies elsewhere. . . . This is a victory of a different sort. We don't overcome the situations, but we overcome ourselves and learn to rest in God's grace, which is sufficient to carry us through the tribulations that don't *ultimately* matter. In the things that do, our hope is sure to give us Joy.

Prayer

God of Joy and endurance, when our earthly situation is hopeless, keep us steadfast in faith, grace-filled with eternal hope . . .   Amen.

Truly the Community, pp. 186, 193-97.

For the joy of human love,
brother, sister, parent, child,
friends on earth, and friends above,
pleasures pure and undefiled. . . .

Folliott Sandford Pierpoint (1864), alt.

That profound yearning for love was planted in each of us by God. . . . Beginning with Abraham, God has called a people to incarnate his love for the world through the many kinds of love that the community is called to practice responsibly and joyfully for the sake of the neighbor. . . . Let us examine the various Greek terms for love to emphasize all the ways in which true love can be expressed by the Christian community. . . .

Most important is *agapē* — that intelligent, purposeful love directed to the needs of the other — which only God can bestow perfectly, but which his people can learn from God and pass on to others. If our Christian communities are truly characterized by *agapē*, we will enfold our children in constant caring that helps them know that they are the beloved both of God and of the entire congregation in which they are a cherished part. . . .

Philia, or friendship love, . . . is based on mutual concerns, interests, and goals. Friends are drawn together by common hobbies, pursuits, and passions. . . . Friendship in the Lord knits us in lifelong — in fact, eternal — companionship, in relationships that are deeper because we share the highest goal of serving God together. . . .

Two other Greek words for love are *philostorgē,* . . . which means family love, especially the kind of connection between a mother and her children, . . . and *philadelphia* . . . which combines *philia* with *adelphos* or "brother," and so connotes brotherly or sisterly companionship. . . .

As the Christian community imparts to our children and nourishes in them purposely directed love that does not require return *(agapē),* brotherly/sisterly love *(philadelphia),* and friendship-family love *(philostorgē),* we empower them to reach out to the world with the true intimacy that so many long for. Because the Church dwells in the love of God, our children can be agents of love and care in a desperate world.

Prayer

Loving Lord, empower us to love our families, friends, and those in need in ways that reflect your purposes and grace . . . Amen.

Is It a Lost Cause? pp. 217, 227-29.

Sacrifice and offering you did not desire,
   but my ears you have pierced; . . .
"I desire to do your will, O my God;
   your law is within my heart." . . .

Psalm 40:6a, 8

The poet of Psalm 40 . . . reminds himself and us that *YHWH* does not really desire sacrifices and burnt offerings. . . .

What he wants is still the same today as in the First Testament times. God longs for us to desire to do his will. He wants his instruction to be so important to us that we eagerly hold it within our hearts. . . .

YHWH doesn't want our burnt offerings. He wants us. Therefore, Paul urges us to "offer [our] bodies as living sacrifices, holy and pleasing to God — which is your spiritual worship" (Rom. 12:1).

David announces in the middle of the sixth verse of Psalm 40, "but my ears you have pierced." When slaves were set free, yet chose to stay with their masters and serve them, their ears were pierced with an awl to signify their devotion. God would have us choose to serve him gladly, even though his love has set us free. The apostle Paul uses this image in the many places in his letters where he calls himself the slave of Christ. . . .

Once we grasp the immensity of the righteousness and steadfast love and faithfulness and salvation and truth of our God, it is impossible for us to keep silent about those things. We can't hide them. They must spring forth and become apparent to those around us.

If we all get started now telling others about his wonderful works on our behalf, we won't be finished by the time we get to heaven. And there we will perfectly praise him, even as there we will perfectly know his comfort and hope and peace. . . . There in Joy we will never be lonely again, and the LORD himself will wipe away all the tears from our eyes.

Prayer

   Faithful LORD, we know that what you desire most is the offering of ourselves. May our witness to your salvation be a part of that offering, pleasing and acceptable . . .   Amen.

I'm Lonely, LORD, pp. 220, 226-28.

"To the angel of the church in Philadelphia write: . . . Him who overcomes I will make a pillar in the temple of my God. Never again will he leave it. I will write on him the name of my God and the name of the city of my God; . . . and I will also write on him my new name."

Revelation 3:7a, 12

What Jesus promises to the Philadelphians is delightful. Not only will they not have to leave the temple of God, but they will be pillars. . . . The kingdom of God is carried not by strength according to the world's idea, but by the weakness that lets God's grace shine through. Those who suffer or grow faint already wear the crowns that cannot be taken. Their mettle will someday be proved, to the astonishment of those who served Satan's purposes by buying into the world's stratagems for power. Those who scorned the weak will discover that faithful people with little strength are the beloved of God.

The other promises of the letter to Philadelphia are equally encouraging. The ones overcoming by holding on in their weakness and consequent humility will be inscribed with several names. Remember that the idea of "name" in the Scriptures always refers to the character of the one named. . . .

Thus, to receive God's name means that someday those who lack strength will become totally fashioned after the likeness of God. Furthermore, they will receive the name of the city of God, the New Jerusalem. . . . Then in John's vision we shall observe all the glory and splendor and purity that will be manifested at the end of time through those who depended on God. Finally, Christ promises that he will even write on them *his* new name. . . .

Only as we all become totally dependent on God and his grace will we find ourselves part of this great company that will receive the very name of God at the end of time.

Prayer

God our King, make us weak enough to live by your grace and strong enough to trust in your glorious promise to share your very name at the end of time . . .   Amen.

Joy in Our Weakness, pp. 99-100.

Scarcely are they planted, scarcely sown,
    scarcely has their stem taken root in the earth,
when he blows upon them, and they wither,
    and the tempest carries them off like stubble.

Isaiah 40:24 (NRSV)

The image of fruit being produced raises an issue inherent in Isaiah 40:24. When the world's rulers and lawmakers are brought to naught, their works are revealed for their true value. This image is reinforced in the New Testament when the apostle Paul writes about our works being tested by fire so that what we are and what we have done with our lives are manifested (1 Cor. 3:12-13). . . .

Do we live in the light of eternity? Are we spending our time and abilities to do what withers, things that are mere straw and will be blown away, things that indicate our own lack of rooting? Or are we grounded in the faith of the community and in the community of faith so that what we do has permanent value, so that when our work is tested by fire it will be revealed as truly eternal? . . .

If all of us are only grass, our time is best spent proclaiming what stands forever and rooting people deeply in that Word. . . .

One of the major failures of many contemporary churches is that we are not "[equipping] the saints for the work of ministry" (Eph. 4:12). Christians might have many occupations, but the *vocation* of all of us is to be agents of the kingdom of God — offering to all our neighbors the good news of God's mercy in Jesus Christ, of God's forgiveness and healing and direction, of moral truth and living hope. Let us pray that we will be open to the possibilities God presents us to bring his love and grace to our needy world by being actively engaged in feeding the hungry, sheltering the homeless, caring for the ill and for those in prison. In an increasingly calloused and violent world, may we who are God's people be speakers of truth, builders of justice and peace. . . . May the church and all its members be a beacon of light and trust, a community of caring and God's salvation.

Prayer
    May our faith order our priorities, O Lord, so that serving you is always foremost . . .   Amen.

To Walk and Not Faint, pp. 143, 146-47.

God's Word is our great heritage . . .
Lord, grant while time shall last
Your Church may hold it fast
Throughout all generations.

Nikolai F. S. Grundvig, 1783-1872

Sabbath keeping teaches the dialectical truth that Christian feasting is both temporal and eternal. Our weekly celebrations help us to be more aware that God is eternally present, but the fact that Sunday moves on into Monday keeps reminding us that our short-lived Sabbath celebrations are but a fore-taste of the eternal feast that we will someday enjoy in God's presence. . . .

We go back week after week for the effect of the Sabbath in order to paint into our spirits the eternal, the presence of God. We do this primarily through our personal and corporate study of the Scriptures, in moments of silence, and through our personal and corporate worship. Furthermore, the continual repetition of the very habits of Sabbath keeping paints the light of the eternal into our souls and stirs up eager longing for the Sabbath consummation. . . .

A major Sabbath activity for both Jews and Christians is our reading and study of the Scriptures — both with others and by ourselves — by which we come to know their diverse portraits of God. Many eternal aspects of his character are revealed by the inspired words of the apostles and the prophets. Although the language and the images are transient, they capture the essence of God and reveal it to those minds and spirits that are open to the continued inspiration of the Holy Spirit. In Karl Barth's terms, the Word of God becomes Revelation to us when we receive it as God's Word addressed personally to each of us.

Since God is eternally the same, we can receive his revelation of himself in this century even though it was first recorded in the language of the seventh century B.C.E. or the first century C.E. Just as God revealed himself to be compassionate and gracious to the Hebrew people, and just as he revealed himself in a manger and on a cross and by an empty tomb, so he makes himself known to us every time we bow before his Word. . . . Only with humility and gratitude can we approach the table of God's Word to feast there on his eternal love.

Prayer

Revealing Lord, thank you for meeting us in the Scriptures and preparing us
for the eternal feast . . .   Amen.

Keeping the Sabbath Wholly, pp. 153-57.

Now to each one the manifestation of the Spirit is given for the common good.

1 Corinthians 12:7

This seems to me to be a critical time for the Church to be very clear about our identity and not to be ashamed of offering our gifts of genuine authority, unfailing stability, trustworthy security, and true freedom. Perhaps worship is the most important realm in which the Church is significantly countercultural, for worship is under authority — first that of God and then that of the *charismacracy* (my coined word to signify leadership by those exercising Spirit-endowed gifts, *charisma* in Greek). . . .

This is not authoritarianism. . . . It is never a unilateral authority, but always that of a grace-filled community. . . .

It is the authority of the pastor who has daily devotions and a regular Sabbath to keep his or her spiritual life strong, who diligently explores and submits to God's Revelation in the Scriptures and to the Word himself, who has studied the meaning of worship and its practices throughout the Church, who works together with the congregation's musicians and worship committee to plan the best, most cohesive way to immerse the congregation in the splendor of God revealed in the texts for the day.

It is the authority of the musicians, who have studied church music . . . and work . . . to understand the scriptural foundation for each worship service, who attend training seminars and research new resources. . . .

It is the authority of the worship committee composed of a diversity of people . . . who are all spiritually diligent people, engaging regularly in Bible study and worship practices, attending worship conferences or other educational possibilities, who are committed to working together as a team with the pastor and musicians, open to comments and suggestions from the rest of the congregation. . . .

In other words, this is the authority of the gifted community, under the Holy Spirit's directions, talking together to create worship services that keep the focus on God, unite the members of the congregation into a genuine community, and form the believers to be faithful followers of Christ.

Prayer

Triune God, give us the wisdom to seek out spiritual, faithful leaders for the designing of our community's worship services, so that what we do in worship will honor you, build the community, and deepen our faith . . .   Amen.

A Royal "Waste" of Time, pp. 195-99.

In the prayer — continuing steadfast!

Romans 12:12c (my translation)

Prayer is the basis for our service, our zeal and commitment, our love, our use of gifts, and our offering of ourselves together as a holy, living sacrifice.

Prayer is critically central to all that we are and do as God's people. We should be bothered, therefore, if it is not having much of an effect in our lives and if it is not a mainstay of our community's life together. If this is the case, we don't understand its nature, its practice, and its power.

One of the main ideas in all of Paul's writings about prayer is his recognition that it is wrought in us by the Holy Spirit. . . . Just like faith itself, prayer is a gift from God and is not dependent upon our efforts or any work on our part that could earn God's love — though the disciplines of prayer are a vital part of our active involvement in the process. . . .

Two specific sections in Romans 8 give background on Paul's sense of prayer. . . . Our vital intimacy with the Father as sons and daughters . . . issues in expression to him of our needs and concerns (8:15-16). Furthermore, when we are not able to pray because of our weaknesses, the Holy Spirit is at work within us to intercede for us (8:26-27).

Keeping these things in mind, therefore, we realize that when Paul calls us to a steadfastness in prayer in this verse he is calling us again to a deeper reliance upon God's actions. The perseverance in prayer that carries all the rest of Romans 12 with it into deeper spirituality is possible only as a gift. . . .

If prayer is a gift, how can we do anything? And if we can't do anything about it, why does Paul exhort us to remain faithful in it? This paradox is part of the larger dialectic of faith. Our response to God is, indeed, entirely a gift from him. . . . Yet we are active in the process; God cannot respond for us. . . .

We are invited to spend much time in prayer, . . . to give it priority in our daily choices about time.

Prayer

Interceding Spirit, may we devote enough time to receive and use faithfully
your gift of prayer . . .   Amen.

Truly the Community, pp. 199-202.

May the God of hope go with us ev'ry day,
filling all our lives with love and joy and peace. . . .
Working for a world that's new,
faithful when we hear God's call.

Alvin Schutmaat (1984)

Is it really possible . . . at this time in history to raise children who love God and choose to live according to the beliefs and ethics of the kingdom of God? . . . Can we work "for a world that is new," especially for the sake of our children? Unequivocally, I believe that we can because Jesus Christ is Lord of his Church and of the cosmos. He has promised that he will always be with us and that no one can snatch us out of the Father's hand. The God of hope is present in our world to prepare us for his kingdom.

But I believe that it takes great effort and deliberate action . . . to equip our children to counteract the many societal forces that would pull them away from the One who is, both for them and for us, the Way, the Truth, and the Life. I believe that it takes an entire community, faithful to God's Word, for our children to be immersed in, to welcome, and to respond to the life of discipleship. . . .

Raising genuinely Christian children in a culture that chooses many idolatries to try to assuage or repress its restless hunger is NOT a lost cause IF the Church stands as an alternative community, incarnating — though imperfectly now — the kingdom of God for which everyone most deeply yearns. We must help our children to understand that the materialistic consumerism, desire for ease, craving for entertainment, passivity, violence, and sexual immorality of the society around us all arise out of vain attempts to quench life's deepest thirst. We must equip them with skills to resist the deceptions, to remember the truth that God alone will satisfy their deepest longings, and to reach out with love to neighbors searching for the Living Water of eternal life.

Prayer

O Lord and God, we desperately long to raise our children to BE the Church,
with us, in your world . . .   Amen.

Is It a Lost Cause? pp. 243-44.

Whom have I in heaven but you?
  And being with you, I desire nothing on earth.
My flesh and my heart may fail,
  but God is the strength of my heart
  and my portion forever.

Psalm 73:25-26

Having the LORD of all lords to be our God, would we ever again settle for anything less? . . .

To choose discipleship necessitates some hard wrestling, however, because many times we do settle for less. The verses from Psalm 73 bring us back to a balanced (and godly) outlook on the things of this world. Sometimes we think we can't get along without a certain possession or a certain person or a certain kind of comfort. To insist on these is to make idols out of whatever we desire. . . .

What ambitions become gods for us and distort our visions? . . . What do we substitute for total dependence on God?

What keeps us from trusting God — our need for love, our insecurities, our fears or sufferings or sorrows or doubts about God's character? What prevents us from following Jesus, from relinquishing our control to the Holy Spirit, from relying on the Father?

Do we know who we are primarily because we are the beloved of God? . . .

Though my heart might fail, the poet insists, the rock of my heart will endure. Moreover, God is also my "portion." This is the word that is used in Psalm 16:5-6 to emphasize that *YHWH* has given his people "a delightful inheritance." . . .

Here in Psalm 73 *YHWH* himself is the portion. Even more than the gifts that he pours out upon his people, the LORD himself is actually the best possession of his servants. . . .

The very God who alone resides in the heavens . . . gives himself to those who believe in him and desire him above all else.

We can't possess him if we don't desire him. If we make anything on earth a god in his place, then we neglect and deprive ourselves of his gifts, which are available to us both now and in the future.

Prayer

Jesus, Father, Spirit, we desire many things and make idols of our desires. Open our eyes and hearts to desire only you and thereby to receive the best gift of all . . . Amen.

I'm Lonely, LORD, pp. 135, 137-40.

"To the angel of the church in Laodicea write: . . . I know your deeds, that you are nei-
ther cold nor hot. I wish you were either one or the other!"

Revelation 3:14a, 15

The letter to the church at Laodicea fits in very well with the actual geo-
graphic circumstances of that city. Its message poignantly rebukes the
Christians there because its water image is true to their experience and
thereby underscores the point more forcibly.

Laodicea was an extremely difficult city to defend because it lacked its
own water supply. Water was brought by aqueducts. . . . Colossae, ten miles
away, was known for its cold, pure waters. By the time water got to Laodicea
from the cold springs, however, it was tepid — not very refreshing.

On the other hand, six miles to the north of Laodicea were the hot min-
eral springs of Hierapolis. However, by the time the healing and restorative
waters flowed across a wide plateau and over a broad escarpment opposite
Laodicea, they were naturally lukewarm — not soothing.

Thus, the Holy Spirit's message to the church at Laodicea is very clear:
don't be like your water — lukewarm from the journey, neither invigorating
nor healing, but merely to be spewed out. The message projects a clarion call
to decisive commitment, as well as the recognition that our commitment
functions in different ways according to the needs. At certain times our dedication will be manifested in soothing warmth — comforting words, gentle
caressing of weary spiritual muscles. Sometimes we serve as a Jacuzzi in our
ministry to others. On the other hand, at times we must serve as an ice water
drink, to refresh, motivate, resuscitate. We serve as prophets, stirring up
people and alerting them to the dangers of sloth and greed.

Just as the first-century people chose the waters of Hieropolis or
Colossae according to their health concern, so in our century we must become more discerning and learn whether to minister to others with a cold
plunge or a hot sauna. Paul instructs the church at Thessalonica to "admonish the unruly, encourage the fainthearted, help the weak, and be patient with all" (1 Thess. 5:14). Our care for one another must match the
need.

Prayer
    Holy Spirit, empower us to be prophets or healers, as needed, to serve in your
    name . . .   Amen.

Joy in Our Weakness, pp. 101-2.

"To whom then will you compare me,
   that I should be equal?" says the Holy One.

Isaiah 40:25 (composite translation)

Of course, *YHWH* is unparalleled, unrivaled, unequaled. . . . The question is so backward that it is ludicrous. The LORD is infinitely more than a mere countervailing equal. Indeed, God does not just equal, but is incalculably beyond everything and everyone put all together all at once.

For the first time in this fortieth chapter, *YHWH* calls himself the Holy One, a name frequently used elsewhere in the book of Isaiah. The Hebrew term, *kadosh,* means that God is separated, set apart in his purity. Vessels that were *kadosh* were isolated for use in the temple because they had been particularly consecrated by the Israelite priests. *YHWH,* on the other hand, is separated because holiness is his very character. No one or nothing can be compared to *YHWH.* . . .

When we are confronted with the holiness of God, we cannot help but acknowledge the total absence of holiness in our lives, our complete lack of worth in the presence of *YHWH.* . . .

Critical to the background of the Reformation was Martin Luther's unique terror and trepidation because he did not know how to please the Holy One. He tried everything — doing every conceivable sort of penance, beating his own body mercilessly, confessing the smallest of sins and even some he had not committed — and yet he was utterly aware that he could never please a holy God.

When we put that sense of *YHWH*'s holiness into the context of this verse, we are aghast at human audacity. What presumption that we should think that we could compare anything to God! What arrogance to think that we can worship God glibly, turning him into a buddy, with no sense of the infinite distance between us mere creatures and our sovereign Creator — not to mention the chasm dredged by our sinfulness. . . .

How can we compare the LORD to anything else? We must ask that question again in light of God's holiness. When we realize afresh that *YHWH* alone is holy, it is a shattering discovery. We couldn't survive if we didn't also know the perfection of his grace and the fullness of our holy calling.

Prayer
   O Holy One, we thank and praise you for your grace, which alone allows us
   near you . . .   Amen.

To Walk and Not Faint, pp. 149-53.

Come and see what God has done,
  how awesome his works in [humankind's] behalf!

Psalm 66:5

Sabbath keeping helps us by offering a day in which we recognize that we are incapable of providing for ourselves — either physically or spiritually. If we are to feast spiritually, God must provide the manna of his Word. Only by his grace has he chosen to reveal himself to us; only by his grace can we understand and believe what his revelation declares. . . .

Many times we cannot hear God's voice because we want him to speak our language. Only when we love him so much that we prefer his ways to ours will we be open to receive his gracious revelation of himself. . . .

The great gift of Sabbath keeping is that we set aside a whole day to focus on seeing God, to choose his holy ways in order to experience his presence. . . .

The corporate worship in which we engage on the Sabbath day is the main event that puts us in touch with the eternal presence of God. . . .

Worship enables us to experience the inward and outward movement of coming together to feast in the presence of God and then going out to carry his presence into the rest of the world. In order to function as such a bridge, our worship includes prayers for the members of the community and for the needs of the world, Scripture lessons that provide the narrative which nurtures the formation of our character for daily living, sermons that instruct us in the ways of God's kingdom so that we can extend that kingdom every day, offerings that are gathered to support the Church's ministry in the world, relationships that support us in our personal ministries throughout the week, and liturgy and hymns that remind us of the power of God at work in our daily vocations. . . .

The presence of God in our worship, in his Word, and in our customs for keeping the day transforms us for the entire week into persons whose values are not transient, into Sabbath people who carry the kingdom of God within them wherever they go.

Prayer
  Eternally reigning LORD, *bless our Sabbath worship. May it transform us into Sabbath people equipped to carry your kingdom into the world . . . Amen.*

Keeping the Sabbath Wholly, pp. 158-59, 163-64.

Therefore, since we are surrounded by such a great cloud of witnesses, let us throw off everything that hinders and the sin that so easily entangles, and let us run with perseverance the race marked out for us. Let us fix our eyes on Jesus . . .

Hebrews 12:1-2a

Faith is not worth passing on if God is not its subject and object. We can only pass on the faith if it has nurtured our character to be its carriers and if we are part of a community, the Church, that has carried the faith down through the ages. Worship is a crucial key, for in worship we experience the presence of the self-giving God to create and nurture our faith. Worship forms us; all the elements of the service develop the character of believer in us. And worship forms the community if it unites us in common beliefs, traditions, renewal, and goals. Worship schools us in the language of faith as we listen and sing and participate in its rites.

The major reason why tradition often grows stale is that we have failed to educate worshipers to know why we do what we do and who we are as a community carrying the faith together. Moreover, we have not taught the vibrancy of renewed worship rooted in the heritage of faith and expressed in new forms. We must constantly be teaching people what is happening and why. . . .

Who does such teaching? We might think it is the job of the congregation's clergy and musicians and education leaders, but it is really the responsibility of the entire community to hand on the faith to the next generation. I once surveyed a confirmation class of seventh and eighth graders. Their responses matched exactly — every kid who loved the liturgy was the child of parents who sang it. . . .

To appreciate genuine worship, no matter what style or form, requires training, sensitivity, and patience with the mysteries of God that are beyond our ken. . . .

The whole community must always be in a process of growth to become more grounded in the faith it seeks to pass on and to practice its proclamation.

Prayer

Lord, heart of your Church, kindle in each of us the desire to proclaim and to pass on the faith that past generations preserved and nurtured in us . . . Amen.

Reaching Out, pp. 149-50.

In the prayer — continuing steadfast!

> Romans 12:12c (my translation)

No mere continuing in prayer is advocated here. Rather, we are invited to spend much time in prayer. . . . God is the one who prays through us, who stirs up our prayer, who makes it effective, but the choice is ours whether or not we will participate in it. Our response to this exhortation, then, can be a careful decision regarding the importance of prayer in our personal and corporate allocation of time.

Martin Luther commented on the translation of Paul's phrase "instant in prayer" as follows:

> [T]he word "instant" is a call to order and vigilance that everyone . . . must hear and fear. For it means that praying must be a constant effort . . . a labor that is harder than every other labor . . . for it requires a subdued and broken mind and a high and triumphant spirit. . . . Christians must practice prayer frequently and with diligence. For "to be instant" does not only mean "to be constantly engaged in something" but it means also "to press on," "to quicken one's pace," "to demand earnestly." So then, as there is nothing that Christians must do more frequently than praying, so there is also nothing that requires more labor and effort and, for this reason, is more effective and more fruitful. . . .

Martin Luther also said, "I have so much to do that if I didn't spend at least three hours a day in prayer I would never get it all done." . . .

If we believe that prayer is so important, why don't we value prayer enough to deepen its operation in our lives? . . .

We need structured times of prayer to give focus and direction and depth to the "flash" prayers and the actions of prayer. The Scriptures consistently urge us to pray, to lift up holy hands, or to gather for prayer in our assemblies. . . . The Gospel of Luke particularly shows the significance of structured prayer times in Jesus' life. . . . We can't escape the need for a quality discipline, a habit of spending time in prayer.

Prayer

Interceding Lord, fill us with a desire to pray and a spirit to do so constantly . . . Amen.

> *Truly the Community,* pp. 201-3.

If anyone is in Christ, there is a new creation.

2 Corinthians 5:17a (NRSV)

As an alternative society, the Christian community nurtures its children differently. All of us in the community are responsible for helping youth to see that the values we hold as God's people provide for much better choices for how we live. We encourage our children to delight in non-conformity, to rejoice in the Spirit's transforming work in our lives. Thus, the sex education for our children begins when they are very tiny, for we want them from the very start to recognize the goodness of God's design, the truth of God's instructions, and the Joy of following them — not as a duty, but as glad response to God's gracious revelation and invitation.

The world is desperate for better models. A few years ago I was invited to address seven "Family Living" classes at a public high school in Omaha. After I had presented the basic design of God (without using any religious terminology), the first question asked in each class was, "How do you *know* your husband is going to be faithful?" In this and the students' many other questions could be heard a great yearning for stability, for the assurance that relationships really could be permanent, for deep bonds. The next day I received thank-you notes from the kids, and they resoundingly affirmed what I had said and reported that they had passed it on to their boyfriends and girlfriends, their parents — even to a mother's boyfriend! One of the black leaders among the seniors insisted that the whole high school needed to hear this presentation and promised to work on making an assembly possible. These students liked the idea — the old-fashioned, biblical idea — that marriage could be permanent, that sexual union could be a special sign of a unique relationship. I had been saying for years that the world around us really wants what we as God's people know about sexuality. This experience and many others similar to it confirmed my belief. The Church has a great gift to offer our society, and many in our world long to hear it.

Why isn't the Church telling the world about God's design for sexuality? Why aren't we even telling our own members?

Prayer

Gracious Creator, give us courage to share what we know to be true about your design for our sexuality . . .   Amen.

Sexual Character, pp. 25-27.

The cords of death entangled me,
  the anguish of the grave came upon me;
  I was overcome by trouble and sorrow. . . .
The LORD is gracious and righteous;
  our God is full of compassion.
The LORD protects the simplehearted;
  when I was in great need he saved me.

Psalm 116:3, 5-6

No one else can do our dying with us or carry the ache of our cruel loss. No one can really comprehend the fears and doubts that go through our minds and spirit. But others can be with us, hold our hand, pray with and for us, sing to us, remind us that God is near.

Notice that the poet of Psalm 116 responds to his dying anguish of soul and body by calling on the name of the LORD. . . .

"The LORD is gracious and righteous; our God is full of compassion." . . . Because of that intense love and the unique fullness of his graciousness, we can trust that what contradicts God's righteousness (the death of his saints) he will turn to ultimate good (their resurrection). . . .

The next verse is even more comforting. The poet declares that "the LORD protects the simplehearted." The Hebrew verb is one that emphasizes watching over in order to preserve or keep safe. . . . God doesn't just protect once in a while, but constantly, indefatigably, he guards his saints. . . .

Surely to believe that *YHWH* still saves requires a simplicity of faith when one is suffering excruciating pain, battling against overwhelming odds, agonizing in suffocating loneliness, or mourning a tragic loss. Sometimes the LORD saves by delivering unto death, but then his salvation is experienced most fully. The important point is to recognize his saving action in whatever takes place in one's life — or death.

When a person who is dying can wrestle through to that kind of assurance, then that person can truthfully make the next statement with the poet, "Be at rest once more, O my soul, for the LORD has been good to you."

Prayer

  Resurrected Lord, as we face death — ours or another's — be there beside us to comfort and protect . . .   Amen.

I'm Lonely, LORD, pp. 141-45.

"To the angel of the church in Laodicea write: . . . You say, 'I am rich; I have acquired wealth and do not need a thing.' But you do not realize that you are wretched, pitiful, poor, blind and naked."

Revelation 3:14a, 17

The problem with the folks in Laodicea was that they had too many things going for them. Because the city was so prosperous, they weren't aware of their desperate need for grace. . . .

Laodicea was renowned for its financial institutions. . . . Consequently, it makes sense that the message of the Spirit should remind the believers there not to trust in human gold. . . .

We must always remember that human wealth does not in and of itself accomplish God's purposes. This message is urgently needed in our times, when so many churches seem to think that prosperity is essential to serve God . . . or when reliance on human gold creeps into our lives. . . .

We worry about not having enough money; we hoard it; we use it carefully, and in our "responsible stewardship" lose the generosity of grace. . . .

Once when a royalty check arrived (in the days before I had arranged with the publishers to send royalties directly to specific ministries), I was tempted to question my previous decision about such monies. I was in graduate school in the Midwest and yearned to visit my friends on the West Coast. Perhaps I could keep for myself just enough to buy one plane ticket.

However, it became apparent immediately how hard it would be for me to draw the line! If I kept some for myself to buy a plane ticket to the West, then why not more? . . .

The situation forced me to confront my own tendency to multiply my "needs," in contrast to an earlier careful determination to follow Jesus' command to share wealth. . . .

So easily our churches and our personal Christian lives become enculturated! We think we *need* all the things that make for a pleasant life. As our income increases, our needs and desires grow to match it. Unless we choose deliberately to live more simply and to care more intentionally for others, we can easily spend all that we have.

Prayer

> Giver of all good gifts, help us to see the true needs of others and ourselves and to share our wealth accordingly . . .   Amen.

Joy in Our Weakness, pp. 103-5.

"To whom then will you compare me,
that I should be equal?" says the Holy One.

Isaiah 40:25 (composite translation)

Any time people confronted the holiness of the LORD in the Bible — even when it was glimpsed through the appearance of his angels — they reacted with fear, even falling on their faces. How can we recover that deep awareness of God's infinite separateness in our irreverent culture, without losing the dialectical balance of God's equally infinite compassion for us broken people? I am not asking for terror. Genuine, healthy fear of God is counterbalanced with an equally deep sense of God's gracious love — but we don't understand that mercy well if we make grace cheap by neglecting God's holiness.

Other attributes of God are intertwined with his holiness. *YHWH*'s perfect holiness also, of necessity, embodies perfect Truth. We can confidently trust that our relationship with God is the ultimate reality. We can believe that God will be totally faithful to his character. . . . The holiness of God's love means constancy.

For that reason . . . we can come boldly into the presence of the Holy One. We know that the constancy of his grace and the perfection of his love are fully incarnated in his Son, who came to secure holiness for us. . . .

What Joy can fill our Christian lives because God has set us apart already by grace. When Leviticus 20:26 records *YHWH* saying, "You shall be holy to me; for I the LORD am holy, and have separated you from the peoples, that you should be mine" (RSV), that should not be interpreted to mean that we'd better shape up and become holy as God is. . . . We do not become holy by extended effort, but because the Holy One has already made us so. . . .

The First Letter of John emphasizes that "if we confess our sins, he who is faithful and just will forgive us our sins and cleanse us from all unrighteousness" (1:9, NRSV). That the LORD provided for our cleansing is part of his character as the Holy One. In his holiness, he desires fellowship with a holy people. He has planned for his people to be set apart, separate from the world, in order to offer it an alternative.

Prayer
   O holy Lord, help us to understand our calling as your holy people . . .
   Amen.

To Walk and Not Faint, pp. 149, 152-53.

For the beauty of the earth . . .
For the wonder of each hour . . .
Christ our Lord, to you we raise
This our sacrifice of praise.

Folliott S. Pierpoint, 1835-1917

One of the reasons that I am so attracted to the Jewish observation of the Sabbath day is that throughout the history of Judaica there has been an emphasis on the beauty of the day. . . . In a society such as ours, scarred by hatred and violence, there is a tremendous need for great intentionality concerning beauty. . . .

Observing the Sabbath gives us the opportunity to be as careful as we can to fill our lives with beauty and to share beauty with the world around us. When we observe a day especially set apart for beauty, all the rest of life is made more beautiful. . . .

Some dimensions of beauty specifically relate to our worship life, including the beauty of our sanctuaries and the beauty of our homes as temples. . . . We want to design our places of worship to be congruent with what we are doing in them and to continue to instruct us as we gather there.

In the sanctuary of . . . my hometown congregation, the front of the nave is dominated by two large stained-glass windows depicting the hand of blessing of the Father, a figure of Christ, and a dove representing the Holy Spirit. Each Sunday as we confessed our faith in the words of the Apostles' or the Nicene Creed, I contemplated the images of the three persons of the Trinity in that pair of windows and affirmed my belief in God. . . . The windows were very useful tools for nurturing my faith. Their beauty lifted me in awe to contemplate the mystery of the Trinity.

Whatever our liturgical traditions — or absence of them — it is important that our places of worship be places of beauty, and it is especially wonderful if the beauty can be produced by members of the worshiping body. . . . If the labor of another member's workweek adds to the delight of worship on the Sabbath day, the rest of us learn more thoroughly to consecrate all our weekday labor to the glory of God.

Prayer

Creator of all Joys, thank you for the blessings of beauty. Teach us to create it
and share it . . .   Amen.

Keeping the Sabbath Wholly, pp. 173-75.

My soul thirsts for God,
  for the living God.
When shall I come and behold
  the face of God?

Psalm 42:2 (NRSV)

One of the ringing cries of contemporary U.S. culture is for ease, comfort, the total absence of any kind of suffering. Consequently, many of our major social controversies . . . are argued on the basis of a false compassion that "eases suffering" in the short run, but causes long-term consequences that are only beginning to be recognized. . . .

In the midst of anguish, those who suffer often look to the Church — and what shall we give them? We ought not to respond to their yearning with easy answers or the guarantees of ease. We certainly do not want to respond to this searching with worship services that avoid the problems of evil and suffering or merely attempt to cover them up with an "upbeat" happiness. The Christian community does not promise an end to all suffering in this life; rather, it trains its members in the truths of faith, which enable us to recognize suffering's source in sinfulness and its meaning in the grace of God. . . . What people need is not the illusion that they can escape from suffering, but purpose to endure it and hope that it can be redeemed. Rather than chasing after an endlessly elusive comfort, we all need to be immersed in a faithful community that supports us in our suffering, that works to alleviate what can be eased, that embodies the presence of God who genuinely comforts the afflicted and also afflicts the comfortable.

Some of the suffering experienced in our culture is brought on by the perpetual pursuit of material possessions — even as those treasures are sought as an escape from suffering. . . .

In such a world, the generosity and self-sacrifice of the people of God must be deliberately nurtured in a community that understands itself as an alternative culture and that resists society's materialism and greed. If Christian churches truly manifested the gracious self-giving of Jesus, that love would draw into the community many . . . searchers who could be helped to discover that their deepest yearnings are gratified as God fashions them to be selfless and truly themselves in relationship with him.

Prayer

Generous God, help us offer to those seeking meaning in suffering, or search-
ing for a purpose beyond acquiring, the reality of a faith that nurtures ser-
vice, giving, compassion, and support . . .   Amen.

A Royal "Waste" of Time, pp. 242-44.

In the prayer — continuing steadfast!

Romans 12:12c (my translation)

Various structures give tools to discipline our corporate prayer life. Denominational assemblies specialize in planned prayers printed in liturgical books or spontaneous prayers offered by members of the Body. We need both in our community life — for planned prayers widen our horizons beyond the narrow interests of our group and spontaneous prayers make us more receptive to the immediate work of the Spirit and the immediate needs of our fellow saints. . . .

Our specific structures of prayer enable us to notice more God's definite answers to our intercessions and petitions. Also, we will increasingly discover how much God is changing us in those hours. As we employ various disciplines God will faithfully show us concrete courses of action for our lives and particular insights into the needs of our friends and enemies. Finally, the whole process will deepen our commitment to one another in the community. . . .

One particular tool helpful for both personal and corporate prayer is to group lists of persons into categories. A specific time of prayer begins with the plea that God will bring to mind all the individuals for whom we should be praying in the various categories. . . . A few of the many categories I use are:

Praise

Confession

Thanksgiving and intercession for:

- persons I was with today, persons that I will be with tomorrow, persons with whom I live
- my extended family, my godchildren, members of my congregation
- friends involved in difficult ministries, persons in ministries we support financially
- the hungry, homeless, ill, handicapped, peacemakers, teachers, pastors.

Petitions about personal attitudes, allocation of my time, aspects of my work.

It is crucial to remember in structured times that prayer is two-way communication. We must allow uncluttered time for God to speak to us. Often he brings new Hilarity to our lives and community when he changes our attitudes, deepens our insights, gives us specific guidance, or sets us free to adore him.

Prayer

Holy Spirit, strengthen our commitment to faithful times of prayer, when we can listen and be directed . . .   Amen.

Truly the Community, pp. 199, 203-8.

For he chose us in him before the creation of the world to be holy and blameless in his sight.

Ephesians 1:4

I have one "glittering image" leg and one crippled one. The latter requires a leg brace, which is quite awkward and ugly, but keeps me from breaking that leg again and thereby requiring amputation. . . . When I want to wear dress shoes, I need a very clumsy orthopedic shoe with a wedge on it to keep me from falling over since the leg is quite bent. On my good foot I like to wear a more attractive sandal that is the same color rather than the ponderous matching orthopedic shoe, but the problem is that the sandal is not very stable for walking.

Isn't the same often true for us in our pastoral roles? (I use the word *pastoral* for all of us, . . . whether we serve in a professional/ordained capacity or whether we minister for the sake of the gospel in other ways.) We are tempted to hide behind our glittering images and hope that thereby others will approve of us. We would rather not acknowledge our broken selves, our selves with problems, with secret faults we would very much prefer everybody not to know.

How much easier it is — and more beneficial for the whole Church — if we can manifest our true selves. Such honesty alone can lead to genuine growth and stability. . . .

Let me encourage each of you at some point to spend time in quiet reflection considering the ways in which your glittering image surfaces and the reasons why it might exist. Do we sometimes pretend to be other than what we are? . . .

The only way we can have the courage to live without a glittering image is if we thoroughly recognize that everything we do well as a servant of the Church is entirely empowered by grace. Then we won't need a glittering image, for it will be the authority of God and God's mercy that works through us.

Prayer

God of all Truth, empower us to serve you without hiding behind a "glittering image" . . .   Amen.

The Unnecessary Pastor, pp. 24-25.

Precious in the sight of the LORD
  is the death of his saints.

Psalm 116:15

More than anything, people in our confused and tumultuous society long for security. We who are Christians can look forward to our death, for when we leave this life of sorrow and pain and go home to our Father . . . we will know a perfect security. Furthermore, in looking forward to that unmarred rest we are able to rest securely now. "I know where I'm going, and I know who's going with me," a Christian song from the '80s said. In the LORD's company we have assurance for the meantime.

Probably the most comforting message of all is the fifteenth verse of Psalm 116. . . . The poet lived through whatever ordeal he was experiencing to write about *YHWH*'s answer to his prayers and the deliverance he received. In his case this verse means that his death was so valuable to the LORD that he delivered him out of it. . . .

As we reflect on . . . its hope, this fifteenth verse has larger meanings. Our death is so precious to the Father that he gave up his Son to take away its sting for us. Through the death of Jesus, eternal life has been made available to the saints. Therefore, we know that our deaths are highly valued by the LORD; they mark our entrance into the fullness of his kingdom. He cares intensely about every death because his desire is for "all . . . to be saved and to come to a knowledge of the truth" (1 Tim. 2:4). . . .

When everything hurts, when we face the terror of leaving our loved ones, it is hard to remember that our God's character is marked by . . . infinite graciousness, righteousness, and compassion. . . . He wants us to know that these traits are his, even in the midst of our suffering and sorrow. Only then can we be comforted by such words as those of Paul to the Romans, that the sufferings of this present time are not worth comparing to the glory that is to be revealed in us (Rom. 8:18). . . .

The preciousness is our comfort. We are helped by knowing that every concern in our dying matters infinitely to God.

Prayer
  Resurrected Savior, we trust that our life and death are precious to you . . .
  Amen.

I'm Lonely, LORD, pp. 141, 146-47.

"To the angel of the church in Laodicea write: These are the words of the Amen, the faithful and true witness, the ruler of God's creation. . . . Those whom I love I rebuke and discipline. So be earnest, and repent."

Revelation 3:14, 19

Christ, the "faithful and true witness," reminds us that he reproves and disciplines us out of his love for us. Therefore, we are challenged to respond with zeal and repentance. Christ himself is at the door and he is knocking. If anyone hears his voice and opens the door, he will enter into that person and will eat with her and she with him.

This is plain and simple: Jesus calls us to repentance. We must begin by recognizing that we have turned to false values and gods when we have mistaken human goods for the things of God, and we must recognize that we desperately need the Lord's discipline and instruction.

This text also gives great comfort for many reasons. First of all, the ones whom the Lord reproves are the ones he loves. The original Greek word for "reprove" means "to bring to light" in the sense of exposing or correcting, but because that reproof comes from love it is not an exposure that destroys us.

In contrast, the word for "to discipline" means "to educate, to bring up with training." That idea, too, offers comfort. . . . Out of their love, my parents brought me up to know how to do many things — not only for useful purposes, but also for enjoyment.

In the same way, the Lord instructs us not only in the things that we might do in his service, but also in the things that give our lives value and purpose and meaning. Therefore, knowing that his reproof and discipline are designed to develop our Christian character, we respond zealously and repent for whatever keeps us from loving him in all aspects of life. We know that we need to change our mind about many things in order to have the mind of Christ.

Prayer

Guiding God, tender Trinity, you bless us with loving discipline, which forms our Christian character. Forgive our failure to follow your teaching. Call us again to repent and change . . .   Amen.

Joy in Our Weakness, pp. 105-6.

Lift up your eyes on high
  and see who has created these [stars].
The One who leads forth their host by number
  He calls them all by name. . . .

                                                    Isaiah 40:26 (NASV)

Jesus asserts in John 10:3 that the Good Shepherd knows his sheep, calls them by name, and leads them out. In Isaiah 40 the Creator, who was also called a shepherd in verse 11, is pictured with the same specificity, calling out all the hosts of heaven individually, by name. . . .

They aren't just a vast array of meaningless bright fires or reflections, but they have a distinctive character, a quality all their own. If God is really God, after all, then he has called out each dimension of his creation personally. God is behind every process, every development, every change, every birth — and gives to each creation or body its nature, its function, its characteristics, its uniqueness.

How very specific God has been in creating each of us. Ponder the multitudes of planets and stars and then think about the billions of people inhabiting the earth — yet each one is distinct. You and I are each unique in name in the biblical sense, which means our character. God calls us forth uniquely and cares for us personally. In Isaiah 43:1, the LORD says, "I have called you by name, you are mine."

Finally, Isaiah 40:26 reminds us that God's plan is so perfect and his omnipotence so complete that never is anything missing. Jesus says, "Consider the lilies . . . and the birds of the air" (Matt. 6:25-34). Here we realize that even all the falling stars are counted. . . .

Do we really believe that? . . . How much more freely we would live if we trusted God's personal care for stars and lilies and birds. Jesus asks, "How much more deeply" does God care for us? Never is anyone missing — by the Lord's pure grace and great power.

Mother Teresa's Sisters of Charity model for us God's particular care through their ministrations to each dying person they encounter. How can we, too, be more involved in God's tender attention for each one around us?

Prayer
  Creator of all and each, as you love each one of us, specifically and personally, teach us also to love one another . . .   Amen.

                                          To Walk and Not Faint, pp. 155-58.

For the beauty of the earth . . .
For the joy of ear and eye . . .
Christ our Lord, to you we raise
This our sacrifice of praise.

Folliott S. Pierpoint, 1835-1917

Besides the beauty of the temple where we worship, of our homes, of litera-ture and art — the beauty of the larger temple of nature offers another way to enjoy Sabbath keeping. We must be very careful with this idea, however, for there is a dangerous temptation to worship the creation instead of its Creator. As long as we keep our perspective, Sabbath time spent enjoying the beauty of nature can be a very worshipful experience.

When I was a child, one of my family's favorite Sunday afternoon activi-ties in the fall was taking a hike along the Maumee River (in northwest Ohio) to enjoy the colors of the leaves. I was sure that every year was more beautiful than the last. The activity was especially wonderful because it took my parents away from the work that consumed most of their time, and it gave my two older brothers and me a memorably enjoyable afternoon to-gether with them. During my years in graduate school in Indiana, many happy memories came back to me on Sunday afternoons when I rode my ramshackle bike or walked through the fall splendor in the parks. When we build family memories of delightful Sabbath times together, those become part of the heritage of our children and not only give them ideas for their own adult Sabbath observances, but also flood observances with happy memories. . . .

In a larger sense, the whole practice of Sabbath keeping makes me feel more beautiful. As I spend the day reflecting on the character of God, I am overwhelmed by his love for me. As I feast upon his goodness in all its beau-tiful forms, I realize more profoundly that I am a special part of his creation and designed especially for his purposes in a uniquely beautiful way. . . .

May our Christian observances of the Sabbath be filled with light and loveliness, so that the radiance and Joy of the day can soften our griefs and trials and bring beauty to the other days of our weeks.

Prayer
   Lord of loveliness, may the beauty of our Sabbath observances enrich all our
   days and memories . . .   Amen.

Keeping the Sabbath Wholly, pp. 177-79.

The way the church "talks to itself" at worship ultimately constitutes its witness to the world.

Richard Lischer

We need great boldness to sing and preach the faith in a post-Christian society. Our worship and education must nurture in us the courage to sing of hope and love in a world short of both.

In a world characterized by gender wars, . . . we need the presence of God to give us courage to discuss the language of our worship so that it is inclusive of women, biblically faithful, and constructive for the community's unity.

In a racially divided and ethically fractured world, it is brave to sing of the unity of all people in Christ. . . . For our community life to *reflect* genuine unity will require new awareness, deeper intention, careful practice, worshipful expression. . . .

What provisions do we make in our sanctuaries for the hearing or visually impaired? . . . Are we preventing children from growing up in the language of worship by banishing their cries, relegating their songs to special programs, not involving them in the practices of worship? Do we provide transportation, hospitality, entrance ramps, and alternative seating so that no one is denied access to the community's gatherings? Do we educate well so that worship-illiterates can join in? . . .

How can we design our worship to be truly inclusive, not only in our language, but also in our welcoming of all races and all people whose lives have been broken? . . .

Worship requires the creativity and active participation of everyone in the community, and that can happen only if we all recognize that worship is indeed the work of the people. The participation of every single member of the congregation is eminently important, but even more important is the gathering of the whole. We must ask not only if we have the courage to sing the faith, but also if we can be selfless enough to be a community. . . . When God is the subject, the community has the courage to sing the faith — and then to live it.

Prayer

Jesus, barrier-breaker, give us courage to be the all-inclusive community you desire us to be as we worship and serve . . .   Amen.

Reaching Out, pp. 158-61.

In prayer — continuing steadfast!

Romans 12:12c (my translation)

The apostle Paul frequently mentions in his letters that every time he thinks about his readers he prays for them. We cannot discount that merely as an exaggeration, that Paul really couldn't do so much praying. Obviously, he had developed a careful habit, so that whenever a person's name entered his head he would immediately respond to the thought with intercession and praise. He was grateful for each person and church and had learned to appreciate in constant thanksgiving how God used individuals and communities to enrich his life. . . .

If we develop a total attitude of consistently placing whatever happens into God's safekeeping, then our actions will be more intimately connected at all times with his purposes and our relationship with him. . . .

Not until I learned the concept of "putting legs on our prayers" did corporate prayer make much sense. Complete prayer does not mean simply throwing words about someone's needs up at God. After all, God already knows what all our needs are, and his perfect will is what is best for each of us. However, if we pray about concerns and say, "Thy will be done," we are actually promising, "Yes, Lord, here we are. Use us in whatever ways you want for the effecting of your will in this matter." . . .

Praying about the world hunger situation drives us to action; we must rethink our stewardship of money and our participation in groups that raise awareness and gather funds. If God's will to care for the poor and oppressed is going to be accomplished, he needs people willing to be vessels for his purposes in the world.

Similarly, if we pray for someone ill, then we must be open to ways in which God might use us in his processes of healing. . . . This is why we want the whole community to pray about a matter: more people offer all they can to free the person for healing. . . .

As we prioritize our time to allow longer periods for structured prayer, our spontaneous prayers will become more frequent and our sense of the presence of God more constant. Both our verbal and our incarnated prayers — personally and corporately — will issue in lives of caring, deepened relationships and Hilarious love.

Prayer

Guiding God, may our faithfulness in prayer result in deepened awareness of
your purposes and in growing servanthood . . .　　Amen.

Truly the Community, pp. 199, 208-10.

Offer yourselves to God, as those who have been brought from death to life; and offer the parts of your body to him as instruments of righteousness.

Romans 6:13

Christian ethics is more than rules or goals.

An ethics of character has great advantages over the more traditional styles of ethics. An ethics of rules (deontology) in sexual matters often fails because of our natural human resistance to commands. If a parent lays down the law that her teenager is not to engage in sexual intercourse, the youth might rebel simply to provoke his parent. Though an ethics of character makes use of the same biblical commandments as part of the narratives which form our character, its focus is not on the rules themselves but on the kind of people we want to be. Moreover, the motivation lies, not in the rules as laws for behavior, but in the positive invitation of God's grace and in the delightful results of obedience.

The major disadvantage of an ethics of the end, or of goals (teleology), is that too many factors in our life's experiences lie outside our control. Furthermore, we can rationalize all sorts of means toward an end because of the desirability of the goal. . . . An ethics of character, in contrast, insists that the means must match the end, that we are concerned with who we are along the way in pursuing any particular goal. Moreover, we are concerned about how each action in the process affects the development of our character.

Deontological and teleological ethics are built primarily upon quandaries, real or imaginary. What should I do in a particular situation? What rule should I obey, or what goal will help me choose? Particular behavior is dictated by the issue of the moment. In contrast, an ethics of character emphasizes that our particular behavior arises out of the kind of persons we are. . . .

Our ethics of character for sexual matters, therefore, must ask what kind of people we want to be. The rules and goals of the Christian community are part of the narratives that help us ask this question, but our emphasis will be on the *persons* who live out their sexuality in certain ways because of the kind of people they are.

Prayer

God of genuine love, may all our behavior reflect that we are your people . . . Amen.

Sexual Character, pp. 32-34.

For you created my inmost being;
  you knit me together in my mother's womb.
I praise you because I am fearfully and wonderfully made....

Psalm 139:13-14a

Our importance is not determined by our own efforts; our Creator made us special because he is. Theoretically, we who know that should have no problem with our self-identity. Unfortunately, often our faith doesn't penetrate to our bad feelings about ourselves. In the struggle to like ourselves, we need again and again to listen to the Scriptures, like the promise in Romans 8 that nothing can separate us from the love of God, or like these verses from Psalm 139 which show us how that love was at work in creating us exclusively.

Anyone who doesn't know the Creator cannot appreciate as well the intricacies of his creation. Unless we trust the Designer we can't rejoice fully in the wonders of his design.

The setting of these words of encouragement is a wisdom psalm that recounts the greatness of God in terms of his omnipresence, omniscience, omnipotence, and omni-judgment — the truths that he is everywhere present, all-knowing, all-powerful, and perfect in his evaluations. The mood of the psalm is one of wonder that the poet can be in a relationship with this God who is so "all" about everything. That relationship is the foundation for our worth and significance.

The very first line of this section of the psalm underscores our specialness. The Hebrew text says graphically, "For you created my kidneys." The word *kidneys* is used to signify the most sensitive and vital part of a person. Figuratively, then, it refers to the seat of the emotions and affections. Thus, the Jerusalem Bible uses the rendering "inmost self" and the New International Version translates the word as "my inmost being." A contemporary paraphrase might be "the true me." Consequently, Psalm 139:13 offers this great comfort: when our loneliness is intensified because no one seems to know our deepest emotions, God understands every facet of them. After all, he put us together.

Indeed, we are known by God intimately (1 Cor. 8:3). When God originated our complex personhood . . . his plan was good, for God is good. The truth of God's declaration that the creation is good sets us free to accept our uniqueness, too.

Prayer
  Intimate Creator, we thank and praise you for uniquely designing each of us
  as good and precious in your sight . . .   Amen.

I'm Lonely, LORD, pp. 150-52.

"To the angel of the church in Laodicea write: . . . Here I am! I stand at the door and knock. If anyone hears my voice and opens the door, I will come in and eat with him and he with me."

Revelation 3:14a, 20

Revelation 3:20 is misused in Christian circles if, in evangelism programs, it is used to describe the relationship of Jesus to people who do not yet believe in him. I have heard many Christians tell nonbelievers, "If you just recognize that Jesus is standing at the door of your heart and knocking to get in, if you will just open the door, then he will come in, and he will remain with you and have fellowship with you." To use this verse in such a way is to read the passage improperly and to make ourselves (because *we* open the door) the agents of God's redeeming grace.

The first major rule for using the Scriptures is to keep them appropriately in their context. This verse is not addressing non-Christians, who need to repent and to come to faith. Instead, it refers to Christians who have failed to trust God for their wealth and health and covering. Believers are to repent and recognize that Christ is at the door in his desire to come into their lives more deeply. We shut him out when we succumb to the temptation to trust money and possessions and remedies for our happiness. In our failure to repent we miss his purposes for our lives. If we become zealous to choose God's ways more intentionally, then we will experience the presence of Christ more deeply. The promise of eating with him implies the kind of fellowship that Christians can enjoy in God's company. . . .

Awareness of our failures and the limits of our human weaknesses and appreciation for the riches of God's resources cause us to be more zealous to repent and to find his grace sufficient for all our needs. Truly he will give us gold refined in the fire, garments that are white and pure, eye salve that will enable us to see spiritually, and his very own presence to sustain us. Then we can . . . seek to serve the Lord with full commitment.

Prayer
> *Persistent and gracious Lord, you knock at the door of my heart, ready to meet my needs and guide my life. Forgive my lack of trust. Restore me to faithful discipleship . . .   Amen.*

Joy in Our Weakness, pp. 106-7.

Why do you say, O Jacob, and speak, O Israel,
  "My way is hidden from the Lord,
  and my right is disregarded by my God"?

Isaiah 40:27 (NRSV)

Together these two lines could be interpreted two ways. . . . In the first sense, the descendants of Jacob would be exulting, "God doesn't see our misbehavior. We don't have to worry because we can escape the sentence we deserve." In the second sense, they would be mourning, "God just doesn't see our lot; our rights are being disregarded by our God." . . .

Both interpretations offer us significant lessons concerning our attitudes about God's relationship with us and his action in our lives.

In light of the first interpretation, we know that it is impossible to hide from the Lord, and yet how often we think we do. We think we can escape his sentence and the judgment we deserve. . . . But our sin will find us out. . . . Ultimately, sin always produces its own destructive consequences from which we can't escape. We choose our own judgment.

On the other hand, the second possibility for interpretation of this text confronts us with our blind folly at those times when we judge God. We shout that he doesn't act toward us as we deserve, that life isn't fair. . . .

We can't change these foolish feelings merely by telling ourselves that we are wrong. We need instead to learn to know God better in order to trust more thoroughly his purposes in our lives.

Let us celebrate that God does not deal with us fairly, for, though we don't deserve it, he gives us the right of being his children (John 1:12). . . .

In the Christian community we can learn from those with a sure and mature faith, who know that God fully perceives our way, that all things do indeed work together for good to them that love God (Rom. 8:28). . . . It is not that all things *are* good, only that eventually God works them around to produce good — if our love for him makes us receptive to receiving that benefit.

Prayer
  Lord *of all good, how fortunate we are that you do not treat us as we deserve* . . . *Amen.*

To Walk and Not Faint, pp. 160-64.

"But when you give a banquet, invite the poor. . . ."

Luke 14:13a

The Sabbath day is for feasting, but feasting in the best sense of the word. In general, most of us don't know how to feast, because we don't know how to fast.

Sabbath feasting — celebration — draws its meaning because of the contrast to the fasting — the simple life — of the other six days. . . .

If we lived more simply most of the time, our feasts would be distinctive events. As it is, since most of us have all kinds of special things to eat every day, for many the only way to make Thanksgiving and Christmas feasts uncommon is by eating more. It would be good if we could restore the concept of feasting not as something to regret . . . but as a delight. . . .

It might seem silly, but eating oatmeal for breakfast every weekday and then enjoying English muffins or an omelet on the Sabbath has really been an important part of my Sabbath keeping during the past few years. That way, the very simple ritual of eating breakfast reminds me that this is a special day to be intentionally appreciated. . . .

One of the most important reasons for restoring a proper sense of feasting is so that we can be more responsible about caring for the hungry. If we are gluttons all of the time, we do not know what it means to go without luxury, much less the essentials. If we consciously choose to live more simply most of the time so that our Sabbath feasting is a holy celebration, then we are aware of how special those occasions are. Inevitably this will lead to a greater concern for those who are never able to feast, for those whose very lives are threatened by our gluttony. . . .

If we fast on behalf of those who don't have enough and share our plenty with them, our feasting will be much more meaningful.

The same is doubly true when we share our Sabbath with friends or strangers. . . . We do all that we can to make the feast special. We share our feast with those in need. And we look to God's surprises in the way he provides for us and in the poor guest who brings us his presence.

Prayer
   Holy Spirit, guide our feasting and fasting . . .   Amen.
                                    Keeping the Sabbath Wholly, pp. 180-88.

What language shall I borrow to thank thee, dearest friend,
For this thy dying sorrow, thy pity without end?
Oh, make me thine forever, and, should I fainting be,
Lord, let me never, never outlive my love to thee.

Bernard of Clairvaux, 1091-1153

I have heard it too many times — an unfounded assumption that should be rigorously questioned. . . . "Baby boomers don't like hymns. They want to hear music like they hear outside the church."

First of all, how can anyone be so sure? I know *lots* of baby boomers who *love* hymns. I am one of them. Furthermore, many of those who dislike hymns participate in churches that disdain hymns, don't teach them well, and sing them poorly. What would happen if they were exposed to good hymn singing and better education about the Church's musical heritage? What if they came as adults to a parish with a vital musical life including various styles of music sung with vigor and gladness? Furthermore, . . . should worship be simply what we want, and should the Church be like the culture surrounding it? . . .

So often discussions about worship contain the implicit assumption that if we just use the right popular sounds, people will flock to our services. Samuel Adler, a teacher of composition at the Eastman School of Music, unmasks the deception of this assumption when he complains, "The music of worship has been cast in the role of convenient scapegoat for all maladies afflicting the attendance at, participation in and comprehension of worship services."

Music often becomes the scapegoat after pastors have failed for years to train congregation members to evangelize in their daily lives. . . . Most conversions are the result of friendship, not worship style — but if such reaching out has not occurred over the years, sometimes churches suddenly switch music and worship styles in order to "attract" people. The music of the faithful Church is jettisoned to compensate for long-term failure to be the Church, inviting unbelievers by friendship and by active Christian life. . . .

Our primary questions should concern the place of God, the character of the believer, and the building of the Christian community. . . . Then we can consider questions of style and musical worth.

Prayer

> *Lord of your Church, may our singing and our inviting be done joyfully,*
> *faithfully, and well! . . .   Amen.*

Reaching Out, pp. 165-66, 169-70.

In the needs of the saints — sharing in common! The hospitality — pursuing it!
                                                    Romans 12:13 (my translation)

The word *saints* specifically designates members of the family of God. The name reminds us that God set apart each of us for special functions within the community and that the community is set apart from the world to be a blessing to it (as in Gen. 12:1-3). To fulfill our personal and corporate callings we need to be strengthened, equipped, and supported. . . .

The real power in the first phrase of Romans 12:13 lies in the participle "sharing-in-common," which is related to the Greek noun *koinōnia,* a term many churches use to describe their fellowship gatherings. The Greek root actually implies a sharing in something to such a degree that one claims a part in it for oneself. Thus, in verse 13 it involves being partners together in meeting the needs of the set-apart people of God. More than just a contribution to assist someone, more than just taking an interest in that person's need, *koinōnia* signifies actually becoming immersed in the other's situation. . . .

Because members of the Body of Christ are gifted with so many differing sensitivities, we are each more aware of certain kinds of needs and thus are more able to provide certain necessities for particular saints. Paul's exhortation encourages us to explore them and to find ways in which the call of this verse can be put into practical application in each of our lives.

What a wonderful picture the saints offer of the reality of God in our midst if those around us can see how deeply we love each other . . . as we minister to one another's needs! That takes commitment. To choose to be deeply involved with each other, even when we do not feel so eager to do so, throws us back again upon grace. God's perfect and thorough love for us is our empowerment and motivation and source of gratitude. Under his direction we can choose those needs to which we can contribute, those ministries for which we are gifted, those persons with whom we can share. Our Christian congregations will remain just collections of disparate people unless we learn more directly, specifically, and practically to enter into the needs of others.

Prayer
    O Christ, builder of your Church, we pray for a spirit of koinōnia *in our*
    congregations and in our hearts . . .   Amen.
                                                    Truly the Community, pp. 212-16.

Praise be to the God and Father of our Lord Jesus Christ. . . .

Ephesians 1:3a

The letter to the Ephesians begins with a wonderful doxology. . . . The word *doxology* comes from two Greek words meaning "glory" *(doxa)* and "word" *(logos)*. Thus, defined simply, doxology is words about the Glory, words that express praise, true praise. . . . Praise is not merely something uplifting or upbeat. Rather, it is the naming of attributes, character, and/or actions of the one being praised. To praise God does not mean only to say, "I praise you; I love you; I adore you," but to say why, for what reasons. The psalms frequently . . . cite the specific interventions of God that have inspired the praise; they declare how God has related to his people and therefore how he can be perceived in the world. . . .

The particular doxology that begins the letter to the Ephesians (1:3-14) circles around verses 6, 12, and 14, with their phrase, "to the praise of his glory." If we look closely, we discover that the subject of verses 3-6 is the heavenly Father, that verses 7-12 are about the Son, and that verses 13-14 concern the Holy Spirit. All that we learn about the Father in the first section is such good news that we can't help but live to the praise of his glory. Everything that the next section tells us about the Son and what he has done for us thrills us so much that we can't help but live to the praise of his glory. The confident assurance that we gain from the final section about the Holy Spirit floods us with such Joy that we can't help but live to the praise of his glory.

Part of the weakness of many churches at the beginning of the twenty-first century is that our doxology is not trinitarian enough. . . . For example, if I think only about the Holy Spirit and his empowerment, I take for granted the immense sacrifice of Jesus Christ that made my empowerment possible and lose track of the Father's infinite love in giving his Son for the world. . . . It is vital that our Christian communities invigorate genuine trinitarian thinking so that we can understand who we are and then be continually renewed and reformed in response to the Triune God.

Prayer

Triune God, we praise you that you are the loving, redeeming, empowering One . . . Amen.

The Unnecessary Pastor, pp. 32-33.

I praise you because I am fearfully and wonderfully made;
your works are wonderful,
I know that full well. . . .
When I was woven together in the depths of the earth,
your eyes saw my unformed body.

Psalm 139:14, 15b-16a

This picture in our text from Psalm 139 is compelling, for its verb, *wove*, implies great care and craftsmanship. The poetic parallel asserts, "You wove me together in the womb of my mother." God didn't just throw us together; he carefully chose all the threads and colors and then fashioned them together into the beautiful patterns that compose you and me. No two tapestries are ever alike, so we see personal tenderness and love in the crafting. . . .

The poet responds to this splendid creation by vowing, "I praise you because I am fearfully and wonderfully made." The Hebrew verb *to praise* is often used ritually to signify formal worship, but it is also used throughout the Psalms to declare personal thanks or adoration.

The two adverbs in this line are especially graphic. *Fearfully* comes from a verb that describes excellent and glorious things that are so awe-inspiring they cause astonishment. Truly we are amazed by the marvel of our creation — not with the fear of terror, but with the fear of reverence and honor. The form of the second adverb, translated *wonderfully*, stresses the accomplishment of something that surpasses everything or is extraordinary. In other places, its verb root signifies that which is beyond a person's power to understand. The word comes from the root for "wonder." The extraordinariness of our fabrication is vastly beyond our comprehension. . . .

The final word in the Hebrew text of this verse ("full well," NIV) is one that is often translated "exceedingly." . . . This is the same word used in the last verse of Genesis 1, where God . . . declares not merely that all that he has made was good, as he had said on the previous five days, but that it was "good exceedingly." In response, then, the poet of this psalm knows "exceedingly" that the works of the LORD are superb.

Prayer

Tender Weaver, help us, with the psalmist, to recognize and praise you for fearfully and wonderfully creating us out of your incomprehensible, bountiful love . . .   Amen.

I'm Lonely, LORD, pp. 150-54.

"You are worthy, our Lord and God,
     to receive glory and honor and power,
for you created all things. . . ."

Revelation 4:11

Revelation 4 points to the gift of life as one reason for praise. . . .

The seer John is invited into a new vision of that which lies on the other side of the door of heaven . . . where he becomes aware of the throne of God. . . . How vital it is for us to catch visions of that throne to restore our perspectives in life on this side of the door!

We cannot properly learn to praise unless we begin at the throne, for praise is the recognition that God is there, that he is the ruler of our lives and all that is, that he is worthy of our adoration. In other words, praise prevents us from focusing on ourselves. It is wonderfully theocentric. . . .

The piling up of images in Revelation 4 is intended to create an atmosphere of great awesomeness, . . . which culminates in the declaration of why God is worthy of such praise. . . .

God is indeed worthy of our adoration because by his will all things were created. The idea of his creation here at the end of the Bible reminds us of the pictures of his work of ordering at the beginning. This God who could bring existence out of the chaotic mass without form and full of nothingness is certainly worthy of our praising recognition of his power. Furthermore, the song goes on to declare that . . . by his will he sustains all life; by his grace he allows it to continue. . . . Everything, from beginning to end and everywhere in between, is totally under his perfect control. . . .

We each need this picture of the one on the throne, by whose will we are sustained, in order to put the gift of life into its proper perspective. . . . That is the first reason why we are invited by the seer to learn better to praise God.

Prayer
     Creator and Sustainer of the universe — and of each of us — we give you all
     the praise and honor and glory and thanksgiving . . .   Amen.

Joy in Our Weakness, pp. 110-11, 114-15.

Have you not known? Have you not heard?
The LORD *is the everlasting God,*
   the Creator of the ends of the earth.
He does not faint or grow weary;
   his understanding is unsearchable.

Isaiah 40:28 (NRSV)

Immediately after the indicting questions, *YHWH* is defined by his relationship to timelessness. The Hebrew form of the words actually means that the only "God of everlastingness" is *YHWH*, the covenant "I AM" of the Hebrew people. Then three pictures follow which enable us to observe how his everlastingness can be recognized.

   First, *YHWH* is the "Creator of the ends of the earth." Not only did this God create all the earth and everything in it, but he also set its boundaries. For the Israelites this meant that God created beyond what they knew. Now, . . . we still cannot fathom the limits of the cosmos, but we know that God is beyond those boundaries as their beginning and end.

   Second, "Not does he become faint or grow weary." As is obvious, and as later verses in Isaiah 40 will emphasize, others do become tired. . . .

   Finally, "Not is there to be searching of his understanding." . . . No searching can penetrate his comprehension. Both of these last two phrases begin with *not* in the Hebrew. Never will God grow tired; never will he be understood. *YHWH* grasps everything; we can only barely begin to imagine him because his love encompasses us. . . .

   God's purposes from before all of time extend into time and go right on through time on our behalf. Because the I AM is boundless, we can trust his plans to unfold without limits.

   Everlastingness in God's creation means that all things are under his control. By his great might and powerful strength (verse 26), nothing is missing, nothing escapes the LORD's notice. Surely our way cannot be hidden from the One who sees to the end of the earth.

   Furthermore, the LORD does not become faint or grow weary. Not only did he create the world, but he continues to preserve it. Not only did he save us, but he continues to work in us to transform us into his likeness and to fulfill his purposes through us. Not only does the LORD establish us, but he continues to care and to provide for us and to sustain us.

Prayer
   LORD *of everlastingness, we trust your eternal love to sustain and transform*
   us day by day . . .   Amen.

To Walk and Not Faint, pp. 165-68.

God is love. Whoever lives in love lives in God, and God in him. In this way love is
made complete among us. . . .

1 John 4:16b-17

One of the most terrifying aspects of the technological society is its loss of
intimacy. Many people in our culture are desperate for affection, and most
do not know how to give or receive it. Sabbath keeping offers us the possibility for learning to deepen our relationships and to embrace others with
godly affection.

Sabbath keeping offers us hope for relationships because of its emphasis on our relationship with God. . . . The intentionality of the day lends itself to a conscious enjoyment of our relationships with, and delight in, each
other as the outgrowth of our delight in Yahweh. . . .

This frequently used image is wonderfully true: our relationships are
like spokes of a wheel — the closer we draw to the center, which is God, the
closer we are to the other spokes. . . .

Worship offers a multiplicity of opportunities for feasting in relationships. We repent together for our failures and receive the forgiveness for
which the corporate body of Christ is responsible (John 20:21-23). We sing
together and join our hearts and voices in praise. We pray about the concerns of others and commit ourselves to continued support of them during
the week to come. We hear the results of our prayers, celebrate together the
answers that God has given, and weep together over the sadnesses of this
strange world. We pass to each other the handshake or embrace or kiss of
peace. We feast together in the Holy Supper that calls us to discern therein
the true body of Christ, which nourishes his Body, the Church. . . .

When we set aside a whole day to cease the work of the week, we accept
the gift of time for deepening relationships through visits and hospitality,
. . . for writing letters or making phone calls to distant loved ones, for thinking about others and spending extra time in prayer for them or making gifts
for them. . . .

Indeed, the Christian community has much to offer the world as an alternative society full of honorable affection and intimacy.

Prayer
> *Intimate God, may our Sabbath keeping draw us closer to you and to each*
> *other . . .　Amen.*

Keeping the Sabbath Wholly, pp. 189-93.

All things are lawful, but not all things are profitable. All things are lawful, but not all things edify.

1 Corinthians 10:23 (NASV)

On many of his compositions Johann Sebastian Bach inscribed the letters *I.N.J.* or *S.D.G.*, which stand for "In the name of Jesus" and "Soli Deo Gloria." All music is "for the glory of God alone," according to Bach, and for "the instruction of my neighbors." . . .

Many kinds of musical styles could be used for worship, but whatever we use must pass the test of theological soundness. . . .

Worship service planners dare not include . . . songs that are pretty but do not proclaim any message about God or faith, . . . texts that are theologically correct but shallow, . . . texts that reiterate how much "I will praise God" but never actually praise him or that prevent us from really knowing how to worship God because we spend too much time focusing on ourselves, . . . texts that muddle Christian doctrine, . . . or camp songs that are fun to sing and might be thoroughly true in their doctrine, but . . . are not appropriate to sing to God in the Church's primary worship settings. . . .

For the sake of believers' character, we would not continually use evangelistic music in worship. . . . Those who worship God already know him and know that he is worthy of their praise. Let us then concentrate on deepening that knowledge and praise. . . .

We must also specifically reject songs that add our efforts to God's saving work. Songs that stress our searching for God or our success at finding him ignore the total inability of our sinful selves to want or to find God and miss the immense searching of God's gracious love. . . .

Let our music convey the hope and sureness of faith, the virtues of Christian morality, the love of Christian relationships, and — most of all — the conviction that the God known in Jesus Christ is the only reliable reference point. . . .

Our goal is that worship practices will form the character so that believers respond to God with commitment, love, thought, and virtuous action. The Scriptures make it clear that God wants his people not just to feel good, but to be good.

Prayer

O Lord, worthy of our best praise, may our worship music always be to your glory and our instruction . . . Amen.

Reaching Out, pp. 170-75.

The hospitality — pursuing it!

Romans 12:13b (my translation)

Obviously, the assemblies of Christian congregations are too large for thorough hospitality, although much warmth and welcoming friendliness can be demonstrated in the gatherings of believers. Here in Romans 12, however, Paul is addressing the greater need to welcome strangers into our homes and lives. . . .

Paul says literally, "pursuing the kindness to strangers." The word translated "kindness to strangers" is built from the same root as the noun *philadelphia* or "friendship love." . . . Thus, the same kind of love we are encouraged to express in the Christian family with tender affection (v. 10) is the love God wants us to express toward strangers. . . .

Furthermore, we won't merely express hospitality casually, whenever we can't avoid it, once in awhile. . . . Rather, we will become burdened — not weighed down unduly, but motivated — by the needs of the strangers around us. . . .

Then, knowing full well that the world's needs will always be larger than we can handle, we will each select those ways in which we can serve most effectively and commit ourselves to the ministries to which we are called. . . .

How immense is the need for a strengthening of community life so that we can share in each other's needs (v. 13a) in order to set us all free to do what we each can do well in the ministry of hospitality to strangers. . . .

We might not be gifted to administer a soup kitchen, but we can prepare sandwiches for it or drive delivery trucks. We certainly cannot care for everyone who is lonely, but we can invite a stranger home for dinner after Sunday worship. Jesus didn't heal everyone who was ill in Galilee, but he cared gently for each person who came to him — one at a time.

We cannot pursue kindness toward everyone, but each of us can find specific avenues for caring. The world has so many needs that each one of us is vitally significant for the meeting of those needs. It takes the global Christian community to respond to them all and to fight the structural injustice that escalates oppression.

Prayer

> *Welcoming Lord, may hospitality become more and more the way we live out our faith, individually and corporately . . .   Amen.*

Truly the Community, pp. 212, 217-20.

Offer yourselves to God, as those who have been brought from death to life; and offer the parts of your body to him as instruments of righteousness.

Romans 6:13b, c

An ethics of character recognizes that life is a spiral. Certain behavior will arise out of a certain kind of character, and that behavior reinforces the character. If I want to be a kind person, I must be choosing kind acts that will develop habits and virtues. . . .

Church leaders, parents, youth directors, counselors — all of us who care about the sexual morality of the Christian community — must ask, then, what kinds of means we can use to develop certain traits of character in ourselves and in the youth of our congregations. Especially because we live in a milieu that bombards us with false notions about our sexuality, we must be very direct and careful to foster biblical perspectives. . . .

Moreover, all the factors of our environment affect our development. . . . If a fish swims in toxic water, it will die. Many of the youth in our society are growing up in a poisoned milieu of violence, rage, and sexual exploitation. How can young persons choose purity, celibacy, and faithfulness when they are bombarded constantly by false values in sexually explicit movies, grossly overt genital language, suggestive rock music, or pornographic magazines?

Those of us who care . . . dare not let the moral indifference of our society immobilize us! Our world desperately needs what the Christian community has to teach about sexual character. . . .

In the community's worship and Bible classes, we hear and study the narratives that teach us who Jesus is and what his people are like. In the community's fellowship we experience the incarnation of those virtues. In the community's discipline we are rebuked and warned and then instructed and loved when we choose values other than those of the kingdom of God. In the community's strength we are bolstered with courage to continue holding fast to the truth. . . . Because the Christian community is an alternative milieu, many facets contribute together to nurture godly character. But this will not happen automatically; it must be intentional and consistent and pervasive and strong and beautiful to provide an appealing alternative to our society's milieu.

Prayer

Holy Spirit, guide our community in nurturing the virtues we profess . . .
Amen.

Sexual Character, pp. 34-37.

All the days ordained for me
  Were written in your book
  Before one of them came to be.
How precious to me are your thoughts, O God! . . .
When I awake, I am still with you.

Psalm 139:16b-17a, 18b

The poet exults that all of the days preordained for him were written down in the LORD's book before any one of them yet existed. . . . The tense of the verb *to write down* here signifies an uncompleted action. God is writing them, but we have the chance to choose what he writes. Nevertheless, they are "preordained." . . . This particular form of the verb stresses that God's purpose is to establish the days in a certain way.

When we put these two concepts together carefully, we can better understand their paradox. God's basic plan for our lives is set in the unique combination of our gifts and personalities, but we have enormous freedom in choosing how to live out that creation. If we choose to serve God according to his designs, we will experience his best. Yet we have the free will not to choose God's ways, and then, because he loves us so much, God will forgive our rebellions. He is even able to bring good out of our worst choices (Rom. 8:28). We won't have God's best if we follow our own will, but God can turn whatever we choose into good for us. . . .

That is why the poet continues by declaring how precious God's thoughts have become to him. . . .

This final line also offers vast comfort: "When I awake, I am still with you." We can never fall out of God's thought and care. . . . As Jesus promises, no one can snatch us out of the Father's hand (John 10:29). We don't really know very many of the thoughts of *YHWH*, but this one we know for sure: he will always love us. . . . Truly this picture of ourselves, marvelously designed, made with his tender care, should fill us with dignity and self-worth. We don't have to win God's approval; we had it even before we were born. We don't have to prove our worth; he wove it together. We don't have to impress him with our goodness; he just wants to show us his.

Prayer
  Gracious LORD, you have given us freedom, and you offer us blessings and
  your constant love. We praise and thank you! . . .   Amen.

I'm Lonely, LORD, pp. 150, 155-56.

"You are worthy to take the scroll
    and to open its seals,
because you were slain,
    and with your blood you purchased [human beings] for God. . . ."

Revelation 5:9b

Near the magnificent throne described in Revelation 4 is a book sealed with the perfect number (seven) of seals. The book has been written on both inside and out, so that it is full of important messages, but no one is able to unlock its mysteries. . . .

The original Greek says that the seer was crying vehemently because there was no one worthy . . . and the task requires worthiness.

One of the twenty-four elders offers a comforting word: Indeed, there is one great enough to open the scroll, and that individual is described in terms of power and strength. He is named the victor, . . . the lion of Judah, . . . and the Root of David. . . .

We are not at all ready for the appearance of this one who is called worthy, for he comes as a lamb, and not only as such a gentle creature, but also as a lamb that has been slain. . . .

Because of the glaring contrast between the names . . . and their actual fulfillment in the Lamb who was slain, we are forced to recognize this major theme of the New Testament in its entirety and particularly in The Revelation: the victory comes through sacrifice. . . .

Think what would happen if we would get this straight in our churches: victory is won through sacrifice. Could we aspire to . . . providing shelter for the homeless and meals for the hungry, . . . investing ourselves more deeply in the lives of the poor and the dispossessed to teach them skills, to help them find health care and jobs? . . . What would happen if God's people would truly enter into the situations of our neighbors in order to bring peace and justice to the slums, tenement houses, ghettos, the emptiness of riches, the struggles of the physically or mentally disabled? . . .

Is our evangelism weak because we are not willing to submit our lives to the slaying and sacrifice that make true witness possible? To be followers of Jesus means that we are willing to suffer for others as he did.

Prayer
    O Lamb of God, may your sacrifice empower us to live sacrificially . . .
    Amen.

Joy in Our Weakness, pp. 116-18, 120.

Have you not known? Have you not heard?
The LORD is the everlasting God,
  the Creator of the ends of the earth.
He does not faint or grow weary;
  his understanding is unsearchable.

Isaiah 40:28 (NRSV)

Imagine how God works constantly, watching over everything, all at once, all the time.... We can call on him in the middle of the night. We can call on him time and time and time again, and all of us can call on him at once....

Even though we cannot figure out why God behaves toward us as he does, we cannot attribute it to his being tired or powerless to help. Rather, we must recognize that we cannot penetrate God's infinite wisdom. This ... enables us to have hope in our waiting. When God does not intervene as we wish, when things don't change as we hope, it is not because God is not able or does not will it. He has reasons infinitely beyond our understanding; many mysteries of God are not yet unfolded.

That the LORD's understanding is unsearchable gives a foundation for much of the rest of Isaiah 40. We don't comprehend why the grass is blown away. We can't unravel the problem of pain. But God knows, and we can trust that his character is to be just and gracious and righteous. We believe that his understanding is right, truly in accordance with genuine reality, even though we cannot decipher it. Consequently, we are driven to a deeper love for his infinite care. Without growing weary of us, the LORD is everlastingly devoted to us....

Yet we allow ourselves to be dominated by our worries and controlled by our anxieties. Why do I worry about God's provision when I should have known that he does not grow weary of caring? Haven't I heard that he knows my needs and understands (better than I do) what I am going through?

One of the most precious assurances for our humanity, certainly, is that Jesus has undergone every temptation and trial to which we are subject, so that he eternally understands (Heb. 4:15). Who can begin to comprehend how deeply he discerns — since he knows our feelings both from a human perspective and from God's everlasting wisdom!

Prayer

Lord Jesus Christ, although we cannot understand your ways, we know that you understand us and that we can absolutely count on your everlasting love ...   Amen.

To Walk and Not Faint, pp. 165, 168-69.

Celebration is the honoring of that which we hold most dear. Celebration is delighting in that which tells us who we are. Celebration is taking the time to cherish each other. Celebration is returning with open arms and thankful hearts to our Maker.

Sara Wegner Shenk

In August of 1964, Jean Vanier, a French philosopher, began the experiment of living in a covenant community together with some handicapped men. Since then, his continued creation of l'Arche (the Ark) homes for the mentally and emotionally handicapped in Europe, North America, and the Third World has captured the interest of many, for, in his experiences of sharing intimately with those considered incapable of normal human life, Vanier has discovered that the "deficient" ones serve profoundly as his teachers. One of the most important things that they know how to do is celebrate. Residents of l'Arche communities commemorate each other's birthdays, other important events in their lives, and special blessings that come to the home. And if there isn't a reason for merriment on a particular day, they make one up! . . .

The handicapped teach us this important lesson: We do not need to wait until suffering is over to celebrate, and the festivity itself deepens our communication with God. For this reason, to keep the Sabbath necessarily has involved celebration — even in times when the Jews were being persecuted. To continue to observe the festival of the Sabbath enabled many of them to maintain great courage in the death camps of the Holocaust. . . .

Our society has forgotten how to celebrate. It has associated celebration with dissipation. It has turned the festival of the birth of Christ into a gluttonous spending spree and the festival of the resurrection of Christ into a spring egg-roll and candy-hunt. These occasions now nurture in children not a sense of the holy God, but a selfish desire to possess. Such acquisitiveness can never lead to true celebration, for the latter is inherently turned outward. . . .

Sabbath keeping offers us a unique opportunity to celebrate, for what we commemorate is God's constancy and consistency, his order and faithfulness, the preciousness of life under his sovereignty. It is not like our birthdays, which we celebrate because they happen only once a year. Rather, we celebrate every seven days because God's grace happens always.

Prayer
> *Constant and faithful God, may our Sabbath keeping teach us truly to celebrate and cherish our blessings . . .   Amen.*

Keeping the Sabbath Wholly, pp. 195-97.

Train children in the right way,
   and when old, they will not stray.

Proverbs 22:6 (NRSV)

In a culture that is overloaded with information, but bereft of wisdom, Christian congregations need a piercing wake-up call to attend to the training of our children's minds. We need to give them a worldview that provides a framework for discerning and assessing what they hear and read, that gives them good reasons to be different from their peers, that gives them hope and motivation to make their lives count. Good worship is one key factor in developing such a worldview because it builds in them a sense of the meta-narrative, the master story of the creating/saving/empowering God, which frees them to develop their identity as the Trinity's beloved. . . .

However, worship needs to be filled with reasons for our children to be there. We have all heard the plaintive cry from kids, "Why do I *have to go* to church?" Here are some answers that I give them:

- We're not *going to church;* YOU *are* the Church — and we go to worship so that we learn how to *be* church. . . .
- You need the gifts of worship because you will learn things there that will make sense later. . . .
- If you pay close attention to the words of the songs and the Scripture readings and the liturgy, you will learn all kinds of new things about God. . . . All of life is an adventure in getting to know God better, but worship is especially rich with his presence.
- Attending worship will teach you skills for your Christian life — skills like how to pray, how to sit quietly in God's presence, how to study the Bible. . . .
- The congregation needs the talents you bring to worship — your singing voice in the hymns, your ability to learn new songs quickly, your ability to read Scripture lessons well, your help with the ushering, your warmth and friendliness in the "Passing of the Peace," the answers you give during the children's sermon, your modeling of reverence for the other children.
- Most important, God needs you there because he loves to be with you in his house.

Prayer
   Lord of your Church, we pray that all congregations will offer their children worship experiences that bring them honestly into your presence, nurture their faith, and enfold them in the Christian community . . . Amen.

A Royal "Waste" of Time, pp. 252-53, 256-57.

Be blessing the ones persecuting you; be blessing and do not be cursing.
                                            Romans 12:14 (my translation)

Persecution, violent opposition to our beliefs, will be the likely lot of all who genuinely desire to be God's people in the world. The description to son-in-the-faith Timothy of the rigors of persecution Paul had suffered is concluded with this striking warning: "Indeed all who desire to live a godly life in Christ Jesus will be persecuted" (2 Tim. 3:12, RSV). But the key lies in the phrase "godly life" . . .

We need one another in the Christian community to help us know when our expressions of faith are causing offense. On the other hand, . . . a lack of persecution might indicate our failure to stand up truly for our principles. . . .

One of the best results from times of persecution is the strengthening of our faith. When everything we hold dear is called into question, we will either recognize its utter supremacy or throw it overboard. In the face of pain we discover what is worth our devotion. Indeed, persecution is a purger and a pruner. It clears out of our faith whatever is nonessential and drives us back to the basic, absolute reality of God's love. . . .

[T]his truth has been evident on a large scale throughout history: the times of persecution have always been great deepening times for the Church. Not only are doctrines often clarified . . . but also relationships are deepened as persons cling to each other for support and survival. . . .

Persecution can also turn into a great benefit for the persecutors — if they can come to understand the significance of their actions. . . .

If persons react with hostility . . . when we speak the truth, their true character is revealed. If persons are offended by how we live as the people of God, then they are being convicted for their own lack of integrity. . . .

We must be careful that the stumbling block is genuinely the grace of God and not our offensive lifestyle. Nevertheless, we can be glad if the truth that we speak and live is convicting to others. Moreover, we will want to follow up on that conviction with a sensitivity and care that frees the one who hassles us to come to know and accept the truth.

Prayer
    O God of truth, may our witness convict and not offend . . .   Amen.
                                            Truly the Community, pp. 223-26.

Paul, an apostle of Christ Jesus by means of the will of God,
To the saints who are in Ephesus, the faithful in Christ Jesus.
Grace and peace to you from God our Father and the Lord Jesus Christ.

Ephesians 1:1-2 (my translation)

Paul writes "to the saints." How many of us think of ourselves as saints? . . .
Of course, Paul's description is not determined by whether we act like the
saints that we are. Consequently, Paul's saint-talk stirs up right away our
awareness of just how unnecessary we are, for none of us became a saint by
our own efforts. We became saints not by working hard, but totally by sheer,
unadulterated gift. Absolutely *all* of our efforts are unnecessary.

Only when we understand this can we go on to the next phrase in verse
1 — "the saints, the ones who are faithful." Our faithfulness, too, does not
arise because we work at it. It is a gift just as much as our holiness is. Most
people would probably assume that "faithfulness" describes how well we are
doing. Let us pause to consider, however, on what our faithfulness rests. Am
I faithful to God because I am a good "faith-er" or because God is absolutely
faith-worthy? God's immense and gracious faithfulness, which sets me free
to be faithful, and his mercy, which forgives me when I am not — these aspects of his character evoke whatever faithfulness I evince. I do not believe
because I am a good believer or good at believing. I believe because God is
believable. . . .

We do not manufacture our faith. We don't bulldoze up better believing, and we don't force ourselves into finer faithfulness. God gifts it in us
and gifts it through us.

Of course, I am not saying that you are irrelevant, for it is indeed *you*
whom God is pulling into faithfulness. However, it puts us into our proper
place to know that we are the blessed and beloved recipients of faith and
faithfulness.

Verse 2 enables us to know how that is possible — namely, because of
grace and peace, God's unmerited favor and forgiveness, his largess that liberates us from our sin and his *shalom* that releases us from our guilt over it.
What a wonder that we can be set free both from our fallenness and from
how bad we feel about its results!

Prayer

Believable God, we thank you for the gift of faith . . .   Amen.

The Unnecessary Pastor, pp. 41-43.

LORD, I call to you; come quickly to me.
  Hear my voice when I call to you.
May my prayer be set before you like incense;
  may the lifting up of my hands be like the evening sacrifice.
Set a guard over my mouth, O LORD;
  keep watch over the door of my lips.
Let not my heart be drawn to what is evil . . .

Psalm 141:1-4a

The struggle against being lonely is itself compounded by, and in its turn complicates, the problems of resisting temptations. . . .

So how can we find the resources for fighting the seemingly insurmountable odds . . . in the battles against temptations? I especially find helpful the encouragement from Ephesians 6, which lists the armor that we are to put on to defend ourselves against all the powers of evil. Prayer is emphasized as the most essential tool for the fight, as it is also here in Psalm 141. . . .

The gesture of raising hands in prayer illustrates the nature of our relationship with God and puts us into proper humility before him — stretching out our hands both to beseech him and to reach for his hand of care. . . . Though we join the poet in asking *YHWH* to come quickly, we also know that we must have proper respect and patience in our prayers lest we call in demanding ways or fail to acknowledge in propriety who we are before him.

We always need the poet's caution lest our speech be unbefitting before the LORD, . . . or come from wrong motives, or trivialize God. . . . Nor do we want evil to get in the way. . . . The poet asks that his heart not even be drawn in the direction of that which is evil. . . . The word *heart* . . . in Hebrew (and in New Testament Greek) refers specifically to inclinations, resolutions, and determinations of the will. We don't want our desires or intentions to be drawn to any wicked or immoral practices. . . .

Sin is rooted in the intentions, so the place where we want God's action to begin in helping us to fight temptation is at the very core of our being in our basic motives.

Prayer

Jesus, who resisted Satan's wiles, come quickly to help us face temptations. Strengthen us through prayer and a heart committed to your ways . . . Amen.

I'm Lonely, LORD, pp. 158-61.

"These are they who have come out of the great tribulation; they have washed their robes and made them white in the blood of the Lamb."

Revelation 7:14b

Two texts from consecutive chapters of The Revelation . . . illustrate the biblical concept of patience. The people of the church at Ephesus were commended for their perseverance, as were the folks from Thyatira. In those places the Greek word *hupomonē* is used. . . .

The original Greek word is composed of the preposition *hupo,* which means "below," and *monē,* which comes from the verb meaning "to remain." . . . *Hupomonē* carries this connotation of being able to remain under or continuing to bear up under difficult circumstances — not just a patience until things change, but a remaining-under perseverance made possible by the knowledge that the Lord stands with us. . . .

How precious this concept is when we minister to those with physical challenges or struggle with them ourselves! I do believe that at times God grants miraculous healing — and that we do not ask for his interventions enough. However, in many situations we are left with the "thorn in the flesh." . . .

Notice that when the fifth seal is broken (6:9-11) the ones having been slaughtered and waiting beneath the altar cry out to ask how long . . . and are told that they must wait. . . .

In the next chapter of The Revelation, we see these same persons from the other side, after the time of persecution is complete, . . . dressed in white robes and carrying palms of victory in their hands. . . .

In Revelation 7:10 the saints rightfully acknowledge that salvation belongs to God. The passage underscores the point once again that they are not being regarded for their expertise in being faithful, but that God is faithful to give them the gift of the crown of life. . . .

Someday we, too, will join those saints who have arrived at the other side. We have, indeed, already washed our robes and become dressed in garments of salvation, but that does not mean that our problems are automatically ended. The Lamb justifies us and creates our relationship with him in the washing of the robes, and the hope of eventually coming through the tribulation gives us courage for living in it.

Prayer
　　O Lamb, help us wait with patient endurance . . .　　　*Amen.*

Joy in Our Weakness, pp. 128-30.

He gives power to the faint,
    and strengthens the powerless.

Isaiah 40:29 (NRSV)

The prophet calls *YHWH* "The One giving to the faint strength." . . . To those not like him in their weakness, the LORD imparts a bit of himself. He confers upon them his strength.

The second phrase, "and to the one without might he increases vastness," . . . suggests multiplication or making more tangible. In other words, on behalf of the one lacking might . . . the prophet proclaims that God increases might to a limitless degree. . . .

That was demonstrated so clearly by my friend Clifford. . . . Clifford deeply understood other people, and his faith and zeal for evangelism were a constant inspiration for me. He knew so well how to draw his strength from the LORD.

I remember one day when, while pushing his wheelchair through the halls on our way to sing for other patients, I was thinking about what an exertion life was for him. He strained to breathe. He could barely hold on to my guitar lying on the table of his wheelchair, and he travailed laboriously to speak and to sing (though he still told everyone he met about the great love of his Savior Jesus Christ). As I was pondering his afflictions, he suddenly exclaimed to me, "You know, Marva, life is so wonderful down here it's hard to imagine that heaven will be even better. But it will be!" I was so ashamed. Clifford patiently endured all his sufferings, and he never gave up or grumbled. . . . His heart, mind, and spirit were so eternally fixed that the limitations of his body were surmounted with great struggle and greater Joy. . . .

What is stunning about verse 29 is the realization that we never do really begin to discover the power of God until we learn our own weakness. . . .

When we are weak, we no longer try to exert our useless power. It is brought to its end, and we become yielded vessels. Then God can really begin to exert his power *through* us to reach out to others. . . . "I will glory in my weakness then," the apostle Paul concludes literally, "that the power of God may tabernacle upon me" (2 Cor. 12:9). Oh, to have that kind of attitude!

Prayer

Giver of the only true power, may your strength shine through our weakness! . . . Amen.

To Walk and Not Faint, pp. 171-75.

How do our children develop a sense of identity that runs deeper than the latest fad? How can we give them a heritage with firmer roots than the current peer group? These are questions that go to the heart of what celebration is about.

Sara Wenger Shenk

There are many ways in which the Sabbath provides opportunities for festival celebration. Most important of all is the worship time. We celebrate each other as we gather together for corporate worship, but especially we celebrate the gifts of God in our thanksgiving and praise. In the Lord's Supper we celebrate his passion and death until he comes; then we will celebrate perfectly and forever the Joy of his presence. The Scripture lessons that are read celebrate the events in our history as God's people. We listen to the accounts of Yahweh's intervention in the lives of the children of Israel and of the early Christians, and these narrative reminders prompt us to remember our own history of redemption. We pay attention to Yahweh's instructions to us for living according to his wisdom, and we receive guidance for our daily lives. The promises proclaimed stir up in us eager anticipation of their fulfillment in the future and gratitude for God's faithfulness on our behalf. To hear the stories of God's care for his people gives us myriads of reasons to celebrate, so every worship service becomes a special festival of some specific aspect of God's provision.

Certain traditions of preparation make each Sunday a festival. Sunday was always special in my childhood simply because of the delight of anticipation in our family's customary Saturday-night tasks. . . . I wish every child could grow up with that sense of delight in expectation of holy worship. The very habits of my home imbued me with a sense of the holy.

Festival involves the paradoxical combination of tradition and creativity. Our Sabbath customs . . . become the framework of tradition into which we can pour all our creativity. Each Sabbath becomes its own unique celebration as we . . . plan new menus for the feasts, articulate new prayers, design new activities, discover new forms to express our affection, think new ideas about God — and do all these things to honor him and to experience his presence in a special way.

Prayer

Creator of joyful festivity, may our Sabbath traditions and creative celebrations provide our church's children and our own with lifelong practices that honor you and nurture their faith and ours . . .   Amen.

Keeping the Sabbath Wholly, pp. 196-99.

How often, making music, we have found
a new dimension in the world of sound,
as worship moves us to a more profound
Alleluia!

Fred Pratt Green, b. 1903

Does our choice of worship music increase or reduce our capacity to listen to theology or to think theologically? Does superficial music dumb down the faith? Does our music nurture sensitivity to God? . . .

Churches must teach congregants the distinction between music appropriate for private enjoyment and music suitable for public worship. . . . For the community's sake, we cannot restrict worship music to personal favorites. Neither side in the worship wars that pit traditional hymns against contemporary songs can be right if the basis for argument is merely a matter of individual taste. . . .

Furthermore, it seems unwise to me to create two different Sunday worship services utilizing two different styles of music because almost always that splits the congregation into two camps. Throughout the country I have seen how divisive that can become. . . .

The use of two different styles often reflects deeper problems in a congregation. It might indicate a greater concern for "people out there" than for the people in the pew — an attitude that demonstrates an inadequate understanding of what worship is for. Such a split also allows a congregation to escape talking about worship and types of music and precludes genuine communal conversation about the weaknesses and strengths of various styles. Thus a question we must always ask about our music is whether it unifies the congregation. . . .

Music that shapes community will use many styles to invite greater inclusivity, but when the gospel is heard therein and obeyed it will ultimately prove subversive to the wider culture. This is a good test for all the music we choose: Does its text have the subversive effect of Christian truth? Does it call the culture around the Church into question and strengthen the culture of the Christian community? At the same time, is the music in the vernacular, in language that worshipers will understand? We must think more deeply about the "distinctive talk" of the Christian community and how to educate people to participate in it.

Prayer

Holy God, worthy of our best praise, help us see clearly the implications for our whole community as we select worship music . . .   Amen.

Reaching Out, pp. 176-78.

Be blessing the ones persecuting you; be blessing and do not be cursing.

Romans 12:14 (my translation)

Paul urges us in Romans 12:14 to react to those who persecute us by bless-ing them, being a gift to them. The present imperative form of the verb com-mands us to make our giving of love a continual attitude and action. . . .

The Greek verb that Paul uses in this verse, . . . *eulogeō,* grew from a root meaning of praising or extolling others to signify "to ask God to bestow di-vine favor on," with the implication that the verbal act itself constitutes a significant benefit. To bless our persecutors, then, does not mean that we quietly wish them well within ourselves. Rather, we respond to them vocally with the desire that God would provide them with benefits. Thus the action is no mere empty formality; it demands a commitment of us. . . .

Paul's . . . exhortation invites us to assess very carefully our persecutor's needs. . . .

The experience of persecution gives us a chance truly to minister to the hurts and griefs of those who afflict us. It offers us the opportunity . . . to love the unlovable, to speak the peace of Jesus to those who are reconciled neither with God, nor with others, nor — usually — with themselves. . . .

That is not my human reaction, however. . . . My usual reaction to being hassled is to get angry and lash out bitterly. Paul knew that we would have a hard time accepting this exhortation, so he said it twice in the same verse. . . .

Romans 12:14 seems to say, "Bless those persecuting you. Yes, you heard me right; I really mean that you can respond to persecutions with the opposite of cursing — indeed, with praise and love." . . .

God's purposes can never be accomplished if we react to our own pain by inflicting pain on others. Nor can we continue growing as the people of God if we seek vengeance on others. That spoils our reconciliation, not only with them, but also with God and with ourselves. To curse our persecutors is surely always more destructive to us than to them.

Prayer
> *Reconciling God, for their sake and ours, help us respond to our persecutors*
> *with a godly, redeeming love, as befits your children . . .   Amen.*

Truly the Community, pp. 223, 227-29.

Finally, be strong in the Lord. . . . Stand firm then, with the belt of truth buckled around your waist. . . .

Ephesians 6:10, 14

Because we are God's people, the Christian community will ask careful questions about the kind of sexual character we want to nurture. How does God's Word guide us as we seek the truth about our sexuality and God's design for its expression? What has been revealed by the biblical accounts of God's people in their sexual choices, in their instructions to each other? What virtues are displayed? What commands are issued that we ignore to our peril?

Especially the narratives of both Testaments are valuable because they expose the sexual idolatries that have endured throughout human history. . . .

Moreover, the Bible gives us courage to deal with the sexual problems of our society. . . . Those forces which contribute to the sexual pollution of our world have been defeated already by Christ (Col. 2:14-15), and we have been given the weapons of the Spirit to stand against all the methods of the demonic (Eph. 6:10-20). Truth is listed first as a primary component of our armor, and that is exactly what our culture needs. . . . There are many who will gladly choose God's intentions for their sexuality over the patterns of our society's behavior — if only we who know the truth will proclaim it more boldly!

The main task of ethics is to enable us to ask better questions about the issues of our day. An ethics of character is especially helpful because it gives us tools to ask new questions out of its comprehensive inclusion of means and ends, rules and narratives, models and virtues, personhood and community. Especially important is the fact that an ethics of character enables us to ask new questions out of the grace of God. We seek virtues and behaviors, not because we ought to, should, or must, but because they are modeled for us in Jesus, whose Spirit empowers us to follow in his way. We choose to live according to the design of the Creator because he invites us to the delights of such truthfulness. Moreover, we can invite others to participate in those choices, too, because we know that thereby they will be happier, more fulfilled, more whole.

Prayer

God who desires our true Joy, help us stand firm in the truth we know, and enable us to proclaim it boldly for our neighbors' sake . . . Amen.

Sexual Character, pp. 37-38.

Let not my heart be drawn to what is evil,
  to take part in wicked deeds
with men who are evildoers;
  let me not eat of their delicacies.
Let [the righteous] strike me — it is a kindness;
  Let [them] rebuke me — it is oil on my head.
  My head will not refuse it.

Psalm 141:4-5c

We are more thoroughly equipped to fight sin when we remember that it is never ultimately satisfying. Always its pleasure will turn to dust in our mouths. . . .

Even so, the poet David specifically says, "Let me not eat of their delicacies." . . . The idea of "delicacies" or "dainties" comes from the Hebrew word for "pleasant" or "delightful." It implies something very genial on the surface that is poisonous in truth. To eat of the delicacies of evildoers pulls us into their traps. . . .

Consequently, David asks that he be kept from those temptations, and his plea makes the next verse all the more important. The poet continues by reminding us of our most precious aid for resisting seductions — the help of friends. . . .

David urges us to be grateful when members of the community who are supportive help us to combat temptations. If someone righteous smites me to correct me, he says, that is a goodness. . . .

Notice that David's response to such correction is simply the phrase that his head will not refuse that kind of oil. . . . God's purposes are being worked out through the rebukes of godly friends, so we would obstruct God's discipline and purification in our lives if we refused it. . . .

Finally, as we grow in our relationship with the LORD, we will more thoroughly know the resources of his care, not only to counteract the evil that would draw us aside, but also to reach out to help others who face temptations, too. More and more, we could become guardians of righteousness, bringing goodness and healing oil to the heads of others.

Prayer

Caring LORD, we thank you for the help of prayer and the guidance of godly friends when we face temptations. As a community, may we ever support each other . . .   *Amen.*

I'm Lonely, LORD, pp. 158, 162-64.

Therefore,
  "they are before the throne of God
  and serve him day and night in his temple;
  and he who sits on the throne will spread his tent over them."

Revelation 7:15

A very exciting biblical concept is introduced by the word *tabernacle* in Revelation 7:15. It reveals a vital aspect of a theology of weakness. . . .

Think about God's tabernacling (or the way he pitches his tent) in three different verb tenses: past, present, and future. . . . In the *past,* "the Word became flesh and tabernacled among us." . . .

In Revelation 7, we read that someday God will pitch his tent among us again. The verb is a *future* tense verb, . . . for this world still remains and saints still come through persecutions. . . . It is a promise of hope for the early Christians and for us.

The verb's *present* tense use is especially significant for our purposes here, for how God can tabernacle upon us in the present is a concept full of surprises. We read about it in Paul's second letter to the Corinthians. . . .

In three periods of asking the Lord to remove his suffering from the thorn in the flesh Paul received the answer (v. 9) that God's grace was sufficient for all his needs. The next phrase . . . could perhaps be better translated . . . "for power is brought to its end in weakness." Then Paul's next sentence would logically follow: "All the more gladly, accordingly, will I glory rather in my weakness, in order that the power of Christ [instead of my own feeble power which has ended] will take up residence/tabernacle in me!"

This translation . . . underscores more clearly why grace is sufficient for us in thorny times. When we give up our own feeble power and let it be finished in weakness, then God's grace can work more thoroughly on us, and in us, and through us. . . . We never thoroughly realize the power of God at work in us until weakness makes us incapable of doing what we would like to do; then we no longer struggle out of our feeble power. Then God can conform us to his will. Then we are a submitted vessel in his hands.

Prayer

  O LORD, our strength and song, we give up our feeble power so that you may
  work through us . . .   Amen.

Joy in Our Weakness, pp. 131-32.

He gives power to the faint,
  and strengthens the powerless.

Isaiah 40:29 (NRSV)

Do we take God up on his promise? Are we able to receive his strength? We can never know God's power unless we attempt the impossible. As long as we are doing things that are within our capabilities, things for which we are qualified and skilled, we can too easily trust our own gifts (forgetting that those come from God also). Only when we try to do things beyond us will we end our attempts at power, dependently turn to the LORD, and rely solely on him.

One of the reasons why we need the Christian community is to help us discover this truth together, to learn to receive the power of God that is available to us. Let us grasp the visions from *YHWH* that allow us to move out boldly in his name (that is, his character) and by his strength. Too often churches wait around until they gather all the kinds of resources they think they'll need to undertake certain tasks. By the time they begin the tasks, however, it is too often too late, and the crisis needing ministry is past or changed.

Individuals and churches could proceed so much more boldly with missions that they know to be the LORD's will. We can trust that God will multiply doubly the strengths we need to accomplish his purposes. Most of the churches that are truly growing today (that is, deeper, and not just fatter) are those that pursue issues boldly, creating ministries to match the needs they see and trusting that God will provide the strength of finances and personnel.

The key to it all lies in knowing the One who is the Giver and Multiplier of strength. We might be faint or lack the necessary might, but that is irrelevant. In fact, it is better that way, because then our power can be brought to its end and instead God's power can be multiplied through us on behalf of others. We are just "earthen vessels," Paul says in 2 Corinthians 4:7 (RSV), but in our old clay pots we hold an unspeakable treasure. The fact that we are weak is of great benefit. Then everyone can see that the transcendent power definitely belongs to God and not to us.

Prayer
  Giver and Multiplier of strength, make us bold to minister, relying on your
  power and not our own . . .   Amen.

To Walk and Not Faint, pp. 171, 175-76.

Since, then, you have been raised with Christ, set your hearts on things above. . . .

Colossians 3:1

Festival includes the paradoxical combination of memory and anticipation. We see this especially in the festival of the Lord's Supper, in which we "remember the Lord's death until he comes" (a wonderful combination of the past and the future in our present experience!). The Sabbath is an intentional day of remembering how Yahweh ordained the practice of Sabbath keeping by his own example at Creation, how the people of Israel observed it throughout their history, and how Jesus continued to practice it and honor it. . . . Moreover, to keep the Sabbath is also to look to the future, when we will finally know the perfect ceasing of all work, the ultimate resting in the completion of God's purposes, the total embracing of all God's best gifts, and the eternal feasting in the very presence of our Lord.

Sabbath keeping also involves looking ahead to the next festival and thereby causing everything that occurs in the week between to be oriented around our relationship with God. The movement from one climax of the Sabbath to the next enables us to set our minds on things above . . . without becoming so heavenly minded that we are no earthly good. A Sabbath focus . . . does not remove us from the world; it simply gives us a larger perspective for plunging into its needs and sufferings more deeply.

For example, our Sabbath feasting challenges us to become more involved in providing food for the hungry and economic possibilities for the oppressed. Experiencing God's peace in our Sabbath worship and listening to Scripture texts that proclaim God's purposes of peace motivate us to become more active in working for peace in the world — serving as agents of reconciliation in our offices and neighborhoods, voting for local and national political candidates who will work for global justice. Our celebration of the Sabbath festival gives us hope and strength and power for dealing with all the work and events of the week to come in worshipful ways. Most of all, Sabbath celebration gives us a deep sense of the Joy that is ours because of the resurrection of Christ, and that festival Joy equips us to glorify God in whatever tasks we might undertake in the following six days.

Prayer

God of the past and the future, may our Sabbath remembering and anticipation motivate all that we do . . .   Amen.

Keeping the Sabbath Wholly, pp. 199-200.

Do your best to present yourself to God as one approved by him, a worker who has no need to be ashamed, rightly explaining the word of truth.

2 Timothy 2:15 (NRSV)

It is essential that we think more accurately about how we handle not only the Word of truth in the Scriptures, but all words by which we wish to convey truths. . . . In a world in which "stupendous," "amazing," and "exciting" refer . . . to laundry soap and in which politicians routinely break their campaign promises or tell more and more lies to cover up earlier lies, it is essential that Christians take deep care to speak the truth as clearly as we can at all times. . . . Consider how words or phrases related to worship can be misused, confused, abused, or over- or underused in churches. . . .

For example, the words *contemporary worship* to most people mean one and only one style, although exactly what that style is varies. . . . What makes music contemporary? Much of what I have heard in "contemporary worship services" has been at least two to ten years old — sometimes including folk songs from the 1960s. The truth is that in a way all music is contemporary if we are engaging in it now.

Moreover, most people who use the term *contemporary* to define music mean by it songs that are played with guitars or folk/rock combos or tunes that are heard on the radio and are performed with backup tapes. However, there are numerous living composers who are currently producing music in a hymnic style and for organs, choirs, bell choirs, orchestras, or congregational singing. Is their music not contemporary? . . .

Let us be clear about what we mean when we discuss the issues raised by confusion over the word. When people say they want more "contemporary worship," let us ask them to what they are specifically referring. Do they mean writing a new order of worship each week, jettisoning the hymnal, signing up for CCLI licensing permission, putting screens in the sanctuary, or using guitars instead of the organ? Do they mean paying attention to new global music, commissioning poets and composers to produce new works for the congregation, learning new skills for instrumental accompaniment? Clarity would be worth working for and might keep a community from splitting.

Prayer

    O Word of God, guide our thinking and speaking for truthful communication about how we worship you . . .   Amen.

                                     A Royal "Waste" of Time, pp. 277-79.

To be rejoicing with the ones rejoicing; to be mourning with the ones mourning.
                                                    Romans 12:15 (my translation)

At first glance Romans 12:15 seems too easy, a simple instruction to be happy with folks when they are happy and sad when they are sad. However, the depth of Paul's exhortation and its implications for . . . our community easily escape us unless we pay closer attention to the obstacles that keep us from obeying it.

One difficulty with this text lies in its apparent contradiction with verse 9, which asserts that our love should be genuine. How can we be genuine in our ministry to others if we don't feel like rejoicing or mourning when they are happy or grieving? . . . We must recognize *agapē* as intelligent love, purposely directed toward the needs of the other. Thus, when we are trying to minister to others in their present emotions, genuine love will care enough to enter with them into their state of mind and psyche.

What an immense tragedy it is in our churches that jealousy and envy cause Christian brothers and sisters to become enemies! How greatly we could prevent that if we learned instead to be rejoicing in each other's blessings!

Equally tragic, many Christians think . . . that what we should do with persons who are sad is "cheer them up." In times of deep sorrow, it is profoundly aggravating when friends say such things as "Well, be happy" or "Come on, smile." Such roadblocks arouse our anger because they deny the reality of our emotions. They do not allow us to be ourselves, persons who at that point in time are sad and grieving.

Why are we so afraid of other persons' sadnesses and fears . . . ? Why do some believers think that the Christian remedy for sadness is to talk about all the promises of God and how we who suffer should just be able to lift ourselves right up out of that depression because, after all, God loves us? . . .

The major point of this verse from Paul is to encourage us to be real with our emotions and to be real about them together with others. . . . These two simple phrases (six simple words in Greek) show the reality of human existence with its ups and downs.

Prayer

Faithful Lord, help us minister genuinely and lovingly to those rejoicing and those mourning. . . . Amen.

                                        Truly the Community, pp. 231-33, 239.

*Blessed be the God and Father of our Lord Jesus Christ, the one having blessed us with
every spiritual blessing in the heavenlies in Christ. . . .*

Ephesians 1:3 (my translation)

It is important that we think of the Greek word *eulogētos* ("blessed be") in
terms of worthiness to be praised or commended. Otherwise we might find
it difficult to think about "blessing" God since God certainly doesn't need
our blessing. . . . But, in fact, what a Joy it is . . . to respond unpretentiously
and wholeheartedly to all that God is. How much it will change *us* to enter
forthrightly and unfeignedly into blessing God!

Could we ever get to the maturity of simply blessing God without needing to go on in verse 3 to remember how richly God has blessed us? . . .

We know the answer is NO, partly because the character of God is such
that he *must* bless us to be true to himself. Partly the answer is NO because
we will always be our sinful selves until the end of time. . . .

What sets us free . . . is the practice of doxology, the praise of God until
it becomes our habit, for it is the habit of God to be eminently worthy of our
praise and thanks. Indeed, Ephesians 1:3 reminds us that every single blessing we possess has come from God.

Some people might think that "every spiritual blessing" refers only to
theological or churchly things as opposed to material blessings. . . . Instead,
. . . imagine a great big circle of spiritual blessing, inside of which is the
smaller component of bodily gifts. . . .

Knowing that spiritual blessing is the larger category, we are helped to
understand better the various trials of our daily lives. . . .

No matter what is going on . . . it is inside the greater realm of spiritual
blessing. We can say, "Even in this conflict, God can produce spiritual gifts."
"Even in this shortage of money, God can generate other assets." "Even in
this time of much suffering, God can create Joy." . . .

All the blessings we receive derive their benefit by being signs of God,
whose presence is made known most clearly to us, as the verse concludes, "in
Christ." So we have moved from the blessings of God to the God of blessing.

Prayer
> *God of every blessing, you are ever worthy of our praise and thanks . . .*
> *Amen.*

The Unnecessary Pastor, pp. 44-46.

A father to the fatherless, a defender of widows,
  is God in his holy dwelling.
God sets the lonely in families,
  he leads forth the prisoners with singing. . . .

Psalm 68:5-6a

Psalm 68 celebrates God's provision for his people as one manifestation of his kingship. . . .

Specifically here his holiness is manifested on behalf of the solitary. . . . The New American Standard Version interprets this as saying that God "makes a home for the lonely." For the people in the procession that this psalm celebrates, the phrase might refer to the fact that the LORD had led them into a homeland. They had been exiles and friendless, but now God had given them the Promised Land.

The phrase is one of immense comfort, not only to the wandering Israelites, but also for those of us who are alone and isolated. God enfolds those who are lonely and gives us a place of security. . . .

God has called his people to participate in his purposes of providing for the afflicted ones, but we are not doing a very good job. . . .

In particular, what do our churches do for the lonely? How have God's people learned to love better so that we might be one of the primary families into which lonely persons are set? . . . Forty percent of the U.S. population is single, but very few churches include such a proportion in their membership. Consequently, I plead with you to be active, out of your own aloneness or out of your concern for a lonely person, to encourage deeper caring in your parish. Out of the healing that we experience can come a powerful ministry of sensitivity to the needs of others around us who also long to be enfamilied. . . .

The LORD wants to place us all into a home, to enable us to experience security in our aloneness, to change our loneliness into being enfolded by his grace incarnate in the Christian community. As a tender Father and righteous Defender he cares for us when we are orphaned or widowed. As Jesus promised, "I will not leave you as orphans; I will come to you" (John 14:18).

Prayer
  Father and Defender, help us all be family to each other . . .   Amen.

I'm Lonely, LORD, pp. 166-73.

For the Lamb . . . will lead them to springs of living water.
And God will wipe away every tear from their eyes.

Revelation 7:17

There is an immense danger in . . . merely saying that we can endure what troubles we have now because someday God will take us away from this vale of tears to a place where there is only Joy. To look *only* to the future without acknowledging the pain of the present is to dump an empty gospel on those who suffer. . . .

So how can this page from The Revelation help? The secret lies in grasping with patience that the eternal has already begun. . . .

As we wrestle with various problems in our lives, we realize again and again that our deepest needs are those that are satisfied by the present sealing of God. We long for the authenticating support of a God who values us, who urges us in his Word to do what we are capable of doing but sometimes doubt, who will stand beside us in the hard times. . . .

The fact that the end of Revelation 7 asserts that someday the saints will not hunger or thirst . . . indicates that now they might. . . .

The best way we can help each other in the suffering is to acknowledge its existence. . . . We are better enabled to fight the effects of sin if we are able to acknowledge its bitter reality more thoroughly. Then we are not so surprised and thwarted by the failure of our efforts to change things. . . .

Nevertheless, this requires a very careful tension. . . . If pain and suffering are always going to be the case, then why work so hard to change them?

Revelation 7 provides us with the balance necessary to avoid slipping into despair. Those who have passed through the tribulation assure us that indeed someday the pain will be no more. Someday the tears will be wiped away forever. Meanwhile, as we wait for that day, we can taste . . . moments of victory. . . . Learning to delight in those moments, not expecting them to last very long, we know they merely whet our appetite for the ultimate victory . . . when things *will* be different and evil *will* be destroyed.

Prayer

Lord of the future and the meanwhile, sustain us today with comfort and
hope . . .   Amen.

Joy in Our Weakness, pp. 135-38.

Even youths will faint and be weary,
  and the young will fall exhausted.

Isaiah 40:30 (NRSV)

Together these two lines declare, "Even those of whom we wouldn't expect it will become faint and grow weary . . . and the very best of those, the most vigorous, will surely stumble badly." . . . We think we can get by on our own strength, at least when we're younger, but this verse reminds us that everyone is subject to the same malady. . . .

We are all profoundly deficient and stumble badly spiritually. Even in our prime, we discover that we don't have all the energy and resources we need to face life and all its problems. . . .

This verse is especially appropriate now, in contemporary culture, when there is such a lauding of youthfulness. . . . Advertisements pressure us to . . . look young, to use the language of the young and adopt their fads. . . .

The threat to our society that this emphasis on youth poses is that many citizens are remaining adolescent in their attitudes, behavior, work habits, and family life skills. . . . In contrast, Isaiah 40 invites us not to immaturity but to weakness — availability to and flexibility with God, instead of undisciplined self-centeredness.

Our culture militates against a theology of weakness, for society is built upon seeking after power. We crave influence over others; we work hard to establish our reputations; we manipulate and exploit others to have our own way. The "original" sin was just such a longing for power. In contrast, God calls us to give up our efforts at control. In the truest weakness is seen the truest vision of the grace of God. . . .

Ephesians 3:20-21a praises God so splendidly in these words: "Now to him who by the power at work within us is able to accomplish abundantly far more than all we can ask or imagine, to him be glory. . . ."

Beyond our wildest desires, prayers, or hopes — what a promise! Far more abundantly than we could ever experience by ourselves, even in our youth — this is the kind of power that God makes available to us. But knowing that we are hopelessly weak is the first step toward receiving God's gift of might and strength.

Prayer
  O LORD *of might, truly even youthfulness is weakness; but your gift of*
  strength is true power for life . . .   Amen.

To Walk and Not Faint, pp. 177-81.

Rejoice in the Lord always. I will say it again: Rejoice!

Philippians 4:4

Hanging in my study is a picture of the laughing Christ. . . .

This painting especially captures for me the essence of Sabbath keeping. God certainly never intended the day to be one of boring rituals, empty rites, oppressive restrictions, or condemning legalism. . . . Jesus' humor usually escapes us, but many of the stories he told to describe the kingdom of God are absolutely hilarious. Imagine a smoking bedmat about to burst into flames because someone tried to hide a light under it! (Luke 8:16). Jesus no doubt enjoyed the children immensely when he touched them and blessed them and enfolded them in his arms (Mark 10:13-16). . . . As Jesus has shown us by his example, our relationship with God and, thus, with his people can be a great source of delight. Our Sabbath keeping is to be a great adventure of fun. . . .

Most of the days of the week we do what we have to do, what is expected of us. Sabbath keeping frees us to take delight in everything, to uncork our own spontaneity. Because there is nothing we *have* to do, . . . keeping the Sabbath invites us to have festival fun, to play, to enjoy our guests and our activities, to relish the opportunity for worship, to celebrate the eternal presence of God himself. We feast in every aspect of our being — physical, intellectual, social, emotional, spiritual — and we feast with music, beauty, food, and affection. Our bodies, minds, souls, and spirits celebrate together with others that God is in our midst.

I once thought that if I made every Sabbath day a festival, week after week of such celebrations would cause them to become routine and meaningless. However, to my great delight, that has not proved to be the case. Instead, each celebration has its own special characteristics, but the thread of the festival's weekly occurrence provides some unity and continuity. The result is that the Sabbath celebration carries over into the attitudes and spirit of the workweek. Truly . . . the whole week derives its character from the Sabbath day.

Prayer

> *O Lord of all goodness, we rejoice in the opportunity to celebrate each Sabbath day, and we pray that its refreshment will sustain and direct our weekday lives . . .   Amen.*

Keeping the Sabbath Wholly, pp. 197, 201-2.

So has the Church in liturgy and song,
in faith and love, through centuries of wrong,
borne witness to the truth in every tongue,
Alleluia!

Fred Pratt Green, b. 1903

Musical style in worship music is not a simple matter of taste, what we do or don't like; rather, it involves the appropriateness of a particular sound for the message expressed. . . .

Worship music should convey its message in an honest way and with integrity and internal coherence. . . .

We wouldn't use a light and airy melodic style to sing about the suffering of Christ on the cross. We wouldn't use a heavy, plodding hymn tune to capture the ecstasy of the resurrection.

Honesty must also mark the singing or playing of music during worship. I have seen music worship leaders act happy and tell worshipers to "get excited" simply for excitement's sake. The advantage of texts that focus on objective truths instead of subjective feelings is that we bring to them our own honest emotions. . . .

Style can best be evaluated by asking whether it disrupts worship. For example, sometimes feminist efforts to replace masculine language are disruptive of worship. . . . We must ask why such modification is necessary. For those who have sung the hymn since childhood and have memorized it, the modified version disrupts worship. . . . Why not create a new hymn, as Brian Wren does, with new feminine images for God, rather than disrupt a familiar hymn that means so much to so many Christians? . . .

Let us reach out in the Church and to the world with the best music we can offer from the Church's entire history, from the distant past to the present. The congregation can "sing a new song" not because we are trying to appeal to the culture, but because God is present in our midst in new ways. As we respond to God, the subject of our worship, our song will reach out to the culture surrounding the Church with the Church's best gifts — without dumbing down the faith.

Prayer

> *Praiseworthy God, as we select music for worship, help us choose not just what we like best, but what is best — to communicate what we want to say to you and about you . . .   Amen.*

Reaching Out, pp. 181, 189-91, 204.

. . . to be mourning with the ones mourning.

> Romans 12:15 (my translation)

One way to participate in the pain of persons who are mourning is by griev-ing with them. That is not phony because, in our genuine love for them, we know intelligently that what they need is not someone to dump God's love on them with trite pious platitudes, but someone to incarnate God's love for them so that they are not alone in their pain. Moreover, at appropriate moments, we can remind them . . . that God is there, too, and that ulti-mately his love will prevail. . . .

What enables us to be genuine about the "with-ness" is the realization that we each have certain areas of weakness in which we need to be sup-ported by the rest of the community. . . . Thus, our mourning with others is genuine because we mourn for ourselves, too, at the same time, and for all the pain people have suffered and do suffer and will suffer as long as we are human. . . .

Unquestionably, "with-ness" involves commitment to the other person. We can't know what an individual's . . . grief is about unless we spend the time necessary to listen. . . .

One of the best things that we can do, then, for persons who are in de-spair is to create for them an enfolding and safe environment in which they will know so deeply that they are loved that they are set free to do their mourning work, to discover that their grief can be enfolded within the wholeness of the community, that they are not alone in their pain. Some-times many months of caring are required to make a major breakthrough. Many people might invest many hours to let the grieving persons cry, to lis-ten to their sadness, and thus to bring God's healing. . . .

When Paul calls us to mourn together, he is urging us to make use of one of the means God has for bringing us healing. In the closeness and secu-rity of one another's love our mourning can be transformed into good grief.

Prayer

Jesus, who wept, empower us so to grieve with the grieving that they, and we, will find your comfort and wholeness in the midst of pain. . . . Amen.

> *Truly the Community*, pp. 231, 234-37.

Each one should use whatever gift he has received to serve others, faithfully adminis-trating God's grace in its various forms.

1 Peter 4:10

Genesis 1 invites God's people to live in relationship with each other in the mutuality of imaging God, with each person contributing his or her partic-ular gifts, which reveal facets of God's grace. That picture . . . enables us to place the marriage relationship and its contributions within the framework of the entire purpose of the Christian community. . . .

We know that the Scriptures challenge us to direct our marriage outside of itself. Its primary purpose is not merely to satisfy ourselves and rest com-fortably in each other's love. Rather, its major purpose is to be an agent of the kingdom of God, to bring God's reign to bear on the world around us. In most marriages, that happens not only through outside involvements, but especially through bearing children and passing on to them the heritage of the faith. . . .

Marriage needs a larger focus, a greater goal outside itself. An infinite goal (to live according to the purposes of God) is truly fulfilling — because it cannot be reached, but integrates the whole person and the couple in the constant desire for faithfulness. In contrast, a finite goal, even if it is reached, can never satisfy because it only integrates one aspect of life. . . .

To recognize larger purposes in marriage enables us to avoid the sexual idolatries that characterize our culture. We remember that God alone is to be worshiped. Our lives together in marriage empower us more thoroughly in that worship — not only because we support each other's involvements in the work of the kingdom, but also because our very sexual celebration is also an experience of worship and gratitude to a Creator who designed such a beautiful expression of our intimate bond in marriage. . . .

It is for the purposes of the community of God's people that marriage is so important — for nurturing children to carry on the faith, for reaching out to the world with the alternatives of the reign of God. The community, therefore, must provide the narrative in which we can understand marriage in the framework of these larger goals of loving and serving God.

Prayer
> *Triune God, bless all marriages, not only with love, but also with an under-standing of larger purposes: to nurture children in faith and to strengthen each other for service . . .   Amen.*

Sexual Character, pp. 47-52.

As the deer pants for streams of water,
  so my soul pants for you, O God.
My soul thirsts for God, for the living God.
  When can I go and meet with God?

Psalm 42:1-2

The poet compares his desire to that of a hart that longs for streams of water. . . . We must envision ourselves in the blinding desert wilderness of the Middle East in order to imagine the intense longing that the poet describes.

The poetic repetition underscores that intensity. The third line of the psalm announces again that the poet's soul, the core of who he truly is, thirsts not just for anybody, but for the living God, the one who alone is the vigorous fountain of life.

That longing leads naturally in the poem to the following question: "When can I go and meet with God?" . . . Children ask, "When are we going to have dinner?" or "When can we have some ice cream?" This poet begs, "When can I have some worship?" . . .

Quiet devotional time alone is vitally important; however, it is also necessary at times not to be alone in worship. Our spirits crave corporate worship, a throng of people celebrating together, a sense of the entire cloud of witnesses of God's people throughout all time and space.

The refrain of this psalm moves dramatically from despair and discouragement to the great *yet* of "Put your hope in God, for I will yet praise him, my Savior and my God." The poet realizes that one of the solutions for his being downcast and disturbed is to gather together with the people of God. Praising God with others will usher in again a time of hope. The rejoicing of God's people carries us — even when we are too discouraged to feel much of anything.

Surely that matches our experience. . . . Times of worship with an assembly or times of prayer with a small group are some of the greatest means for uplifting us. When the soul is thronged with doubts and despair, comfort is found in the fellowship of the throngs of the saints.

Prayer
  Lord of community, thank you for the blessings of meeting you in corporate
  worship . . .   Amen.

I'm Lonely, LORD, pp. 174-78.

When he opened the seventh seal, there was silence in heaven for about half an hour.
                                                                    Revelation 8:1

What a fascinating interlude! What did the seer John experience in that time? . . . And what is the connection of this silence with the next events, the channeling of the prayers of the saints to God and the preparation of the angels to sound their trumpets and initiate the plagues of hail and fire? . . .

No one can say for sure why this particular silence . . . occurred at this point in the heavenly vision. . . . However, all of us can meditate on this text and recognize in it a heavenly model that could fittingly be applied to our earthly worship. . . .

Moments of silence give opportunity for . . . the Spirit's teaching and inspiration. God enables us to understand the Bible much more deeply when there is plenty of time for God's work in our minds. . . . Silence helps us to give God the reverence he deserves. . . . In the silence we breathe in the magnificence that cannot be uttered. . . . Spending time at the listening end of prayer enables us to hear the answers God gives to our intercessions and the purposes he teaches.

If we give ourselves meditative space and time to understand God's Word, we can more accurately apply the truths of God to the circumstances we encounter. Our most important model for this is Jesus. . . .

We know from the words of Jesus that he intercedes for us (John 17) and from the apostle Paul that the Holy Spirit intercedes for us (Rom. 8:27). In Revelation 8:3 we are reminded of that great fact — that all our prayers are only supplements to those of the angelic hosts, the heavenly beings, and God himself. Moreover, our prayer is connected with the silence and with the action of God's wrath in response to the needs of the saints. We are invited by Revelation 8, therefore, to connect everything in our lives with our prayers — our gratitude for the deliverance from tears promised in Revelation 7, our awe at the majesty of God, our desire to be freed from the tormentings of our enemies. All these things are matters for our prayers.

Prayer

Triune Lord, we stand before you in silent awe, ready to be taught . . . Amen.

                                                    Joy in Our Weakness, pp. 142-46.

But those who wait for the Lord *shall renew their strength,*
   they shall mount up with wings like eagles,
they shall run and not be weary,
   they shall walk and not faint.

Isaiah 40:31 (NRSV)

The most important word around which this verse . . . is focused is the name *YHWH.* What kind of a God do we have? . . . We remember especially that he is a covenant God, a gracious and compassionate God, who wills the very best for us. Because he is that kind of God, he enables us to be "waiters-upon" of him.

The second theme is the waiting itself. We wait hopefully — with a hope that does not disappoint (Rom. 5:5) — because we know that, in his time and according to his perfect wisdom, the Lord brings all things together for good to those who love him (8:28). We often wait restlessly, so we need the community of faithful people to help us learn to abide with greater trust and confidence. The word *wait* implies absolute realization that the Lord is in control, that in his sovereignty God will accomplish his purposes, which are best for us. Therefore, thinking about the kind of God we have, envisioning the immensity of his power and love, and knowing that he alone is the God of everlastingness, we await his perfect will. . . .

What will happen when we wait in such a way? The third emphasis of this verse is that our strength will be renewed . . . or "exchanged." We don't just pep up our own strength; we don't merely supplement it. Rather, we turn it in for that which is truly strong, a power that is new. Our human strength is totally insufficient. . . .

When we exchange our strength, we don't receive the kind of power the world offers and fights for. We don't receive more blatant might, but we receive "a spirit of power and love and self-control" (2 Tim. 1:7, RSV). The combination of those three gifts enables us to understand the unique kind of potency God wants us to exert. His power is governed by love, intelligent and purposeful love directed toward the needs of others . . . and toward extending the kingdom of God.

Prayer
   Mighty and gracious Lord, *we rejoice in your gift of a spirit of power, love, and self-control . . .   Amen.*

To Walk and Not Faint, pp. 182, 185-86.

Observe the Sabbath day by keeping it holy, as the LORD your God has commanded you.

Deuteronomy 5:12

All the great motifs of our Christian faith are underscored in our Sabbath keeping. Its ceasing deepens our repentance for the many ways we fail to trust God and try to create our own future. Its resting strengthens our faith in the totality of his grace. Its embracing invites us to take the truths of our faith and apply them practically in our values and lifestyles. Its feasting heightens . . . the Joy of our present experience of God's love and its foretaste of the Joy to come. . . .

To develop the habit of Sabbath keeping requires some intentionality on our part, but ultimately it sets us free to be creative. . . .

First of all, it is foundational to *decide* that you want to keep the Sabbath. . . . The important beginning point is to be adamant about the day — that it *will* be set aside for ceasing, resting, embracing, and feasting. (However, don't forget that this is an ideal — and sometimes our circumstances prevent our being able to practice our vision. Moreover, . . . we dare not let our Sabbath keeping become legalistic. We are adamant about setting aside the day because we have freely chosen to observe it in response to God's grace, not because we have to fulfill an onerous obligation!) . . .

In order to set the day apart, it is important to establish a precise, deliberate beginning and ending. . . . We dare not legislate for others how to keep the Sabbath, but we must act decisively to establish the point at which this day . . . has started and the point at which we have again returned to the workweek.

One of the most important parts of Sabbath keeping is the involvement of the worshiping community. We cannot keep the day all alone. Rather, as we invite others to participate with us in honoring the whole day, they can support us in our intentions as well as provide companionship in our activities. Moreover, I have discovered that every time I explain some of my Sabbath practices carefully, it brings a gift to my listeners, because they then contemplate their own habits . . . for Sabbath keeping.

Prayer

O LORD our God, out of grace you command us to keep the Sabbath — a day full of blessings! . . .   Amen.

Keeping the Sabbath Wholly, pp. 203-7.

"You did not choose me but I chose you. And I appointed you to go and bear fruit, fruit that will last. . . ."

John 15:16

What would happen if everyone in our pews for worship on Sunday morning departed afterward with a deep understanding of all that Jesus meant by the sentences above? For that to happen, our worship would have to be remarkably filled with the sense that we did not choose to come, but that God . . . invited us here. Immersed in the wonder that God has chosen us for his purposes, appointed us specifically for our various ministries in the world, and equipped us to bear lasting fruit, we would depart with a vision for being Church the rest of the week. . . .

Mary Jo Leddy . . . reported that the playwright-president of the Czech Republic, Václav Havel, was asked why the "Velvet Revolution" against the communists in the former Czechoslovakia was successfully nonviolent. . . . Havel answered somewhat like this: "We had our parallel society. And in that parallel society we wrote our plays and sang our songs and read our poems until we knew the truth so well that we could go out to the streets of Prague and say, 'We don't believe your lies anymore' — and communism *had* to fall." . . .

The true Church must be a similar sort of parallel society. We gather together in worship to speak our language, to read our narratives of God at work, to sing the hymns, . . . and to pour out our prayers until we know the truth so well that we can . . . invite the world to share this truth with us. . . .

When our worship gives us continual hearing of and deep reflection on God's Word, songs and prayers that nurture discipleship, and new visions of God's appointment of us to bear fruit, then we will gain God's heart for our mission and ministry of communicating the Christian story, of enfolding our neighbors in God's love, of choosing deliberately to live out the alternative Churchbeing of the people of God's kingdom.

Prayer

> *Reigning Lord, give us a clear vision of being chosen and nurture us for fruit-bearing through the communal hymns, liturgy, lessons, sermons, and prayers of worship — so that we live daily our calling to be an alternative society, offering your gifts to the world . . .   Amen.*

A Royal "Waste" of Time, pp. 333-35.

Live in harmony with one another . . .

Romans 12:16a (my translation)

True harmony doesn't just happen; community must be intended. To work together as God's people requires a common commitment. . . .

We won't necessarily think alike on every matter, but our basic orientation in purpose is the same — to be God's people, followers of Jesus Christ, having his mind. . . .

The members of the board of Christians Equipped for Ministry (under which I do my freelance ministries) have learned the necessity of careful pondering together. . . . Sometimes we have to wrestle a long while before we come to the same perspective. . . . Much effort is needed to be "minding" the same thing, but when consensus is made a top priority in the Christian community we will . . . experience the resultant gladness in finding unanimity rather than mere majority in our decisions.

However, good intentions are not enough. . . . We are pulled back into dependence upon God's grace-gifting for our harmony. The truest unity is that which he creates . . . by his grace. We obstruct his plan when we do not enter into the community he has designed, when we fail to celebrate each other's gifts and to love as persons who belong to each other.

Thus, to be like-minded requires intentionality, but it is first of all based on the gifts of God's love. . . .

Similarly, the unity of the community requires practice. That practice might involve some confrontation, but that, too, is an important lesson about the unity of the Church that we must learn. Too often we think that unity is achieved by backing down on certain things in order to keep the peace. If peace in a congregation is achieved by people giving up their principles or being overly nice so that everyone can agree, then the community might as well not exist. . . .

Healthy unity is achieved by wrestling together until we come to agreement. God's Spirit is at work in us to make us into the community of Christ, as the sandpaper of our relationships grinds down the rough spots.

Prayer

Triune God of unity, empower us always to work diligently for "like-mindedness" as we serve in your name. . . . Amen.

Truly the Community, pp. 242-45.

Just as he chose us out in him before the foundation of the world, for us to be holy and blameless in his presence in love, in love he foreordained us for adoption as his sons through Jesus Christ, according to the desire of his will.

Ephesians 1:4-5 (my translation)

Those of us who have been Christians all of our lives perhaps don't recognize, as deeply as someone whose life has been acutely wounded, the wonder of this: no matter how dreadful our past, no matter how self-centered our present, still God has chosen us out! . . .

How amazing it is, then, that out of all the possible persons in the world, God chose you for the ministry to which he has called you, whatever that ministry might be. But he chose you *out* for much more than that — namely, to come *out* from this environment of sin into the relationship he creates in order for you to be holy and blameless in his presence in love. This is simply stunning, isn't it? We can hardly do anything but say, "Ah!"

Of course, for you to be holy and blameless is impossible — so give up all your efforts! . . . God is the one who sanctifies us and renders us irreproachable. We are declared righteous in the blood of Jesus Christ — and the Holy Spirit continually is transforming us so that we act more like the saints that we are. What amazing grace; you are chosen to be holy and blameless! . . .

Furthermore, God's eternal desire is that all would be saved, that all would come to the knowledge of the truth (1 Tim. 2:4). God longs for everyone to be his servants in the world.

God has foreordained that through Jesus Christ we should be adopted as sons, . . . to be trained to fulfill the Father's mission, . . . to be the agents of the Father and to do the Father's work. . . .

Not only does God prefer sonship for us; his will also effects it. We are back to grace again. Sheer, pure, undiluted gift!

Prayer
Adopting and sanctifying God, you call us out of sin into responsible sonship, into lives of service, made holy and blameless. We praise and thank you for this amazing grace, this gift of love . . .   Amen.

The Unnecessary Pastor, pp. 47-49.

> *. . . the* Lord *is enthroned as King forever.*
> *The* Lord *gives strength to his people;*
>   *the* Lord *blesses his people with peace.*

Psalm 29:10b-11

Psalm 29 offers immense comfort for all of us, no matter what kinds of deficiencies we might suffer. Perhaps you don't lack for strength, but you feel inferior to others in certain kinds of intelligence or in appearance or social finesse. Whatever our weaknesses, they cause a lack of wholeness, and certainly the latter is the greater problem. Into the insecurity of all that, this psalm brings a tremendous word of hope. . . .

Stop for a minute and read the whole psalm aloud from some version of the Bible that has set it up in poetic lines, and accentuate as you read the tremendous crescendo of power as the poem progresses. Altogether it creates a vivid picture of the immense strength of *YHWH* as he handles all of creation and all of history with his majestic voice. . . .

No wonder all the beings in the temple . . . respond, "Glory!" All the hosts of heaven and all the people in the temple at Jerusalem recall that *YHWH* has used his voice in these powerful ways. Therefore, all the dwellers in God's temple must shout out "the glory due his name."

When we worship in our earthly temples, we, too, respond to the recounting of God's actions in creation and history with "Glory!" Certainly we are astounded by the extent of the Lord's might. . . . All that he has accomplished by a simple word must fill us with amazement at the immensity of his total strength. . . .

Now what are the consequences of this tremendous strength? . . . We are reminded personally that this same *YHWH* chooses graciously to give that strength to his people. This is another sentence that we must frequently hear to realize the impact of its meaning: *YHWH does give strength* to his people. . . .

We can count on it now. The simple answer to that terrible question, "How can I find the strength to go on?" is this strong assurance: "*YHWH* gives might to his people."

Prayer

> Lord *of might, your strength is sufficient for all our needs . . .*   *Amen.*

I'm Lonely, Lord, *pp. 181-86.*

Then the seven angels who had the seven trumpets prepared to sound them.

Revelation 8:6

Revelation 8 and 9 raise a difficult issue: how evil in the world relates to God's sovereignty. In this picture, although the forces of evil are unleashed to do their destructive work, they cannot do it until God's angels sound their trumpets. God is not the author of evil. But he is sovereign over it.

God's control is suggested, first of all, by his deliberate confining of the destruction. . . . God's control is even clearer when . . . the seer declares that the locusts were *given* power; they had not usurped it for themselves. . . .

Furthermore the locusts could harm neither the plants of the earth nor the people who had the seal of God on their foreheads, nor were they able to kill anyone. . . . Those people who were not sealed by God were thereby given impetus to think about their lives. In seeking death (but it eludes them, v. 6), they will perhaps think again about the meaning of life. . . .

This was a crucially important message for the early Christians being persecuted. Because it must have often seemed as if evil was in control, they needed the reminder that God reigned supreme. . . .

Revelation 9 ends with the very great tragedy that, in spite of all the different woes God has allowed throughout history (and with his long-suffering patience) in order to warn people, human beings have still willed to go their own way. . . .

Thus, the vision of the first six trumpets encourages all of us to spend time asking ourselves what trials God has allowed in order to call us back to himself. Of course, he does not inflict pain — the evil and brokenness of this world after the fall are its cause — but in his infinite care he knows that sometimes those loved must be allowed to experience discipline. Furthermore, when we turn to him repentantly, he reminds us again of the blood of the Lamb and the shepherding of his salvation (see Rev. 7:14-17). . . .

The trumpets of Revelation 8 and 9 let us see God. His immense grace allows certain plagues to call human beings to repentance, but his sovereign control sets limits. His goal is to save.

Prayer

> *Sovereign Lord, help us recognize in afflictions the opportunity to turn to you . . . Amen.*

Joy in Our Weakness, pp. 149-52.

But those who wait for the Lord *shall renew their strength,*
   they shall mount up with wings like eagles,
they shall run and not be weary,
   they shall walk and not faint.

                                                        Isaiah 40:31 (NRSV)

When we wait before the Lord, it is not to receive power only for ourselves, but so that God's purposes can be accomplished for the building up of his Body and the renewing of his kingdom. . . . We wait for the renewing of our spirits by the gift of his. We wait to be transformed, to become more and more like the image of his son, Jesus Christ.

This leads us to . . . three inspiring images of the fullness, satisfaction, and completeness of life in the Lord. The first representation is that we shall mount up with pinions like eagles. . . . When we wait before *YHWH,* we, too, rise up above our troubles. . . . The storms of this life will continue to buffet us, but in the midst of them we find ourselves surmounting them or enduring them or transforming them. . . . Having his strength empowers us, in spite of obstacles, to experience his perfect grace at work in and through us. We shall mount up with pinions of strength; we shall be like the eagles in their freedom. . . .

We can see beyond the limits of our present existence into God's larger purposes, not only for our particular lives, but also for the whole Church and for everything by which he will be glorified.

The second picture in this verse is that we shall run and not be weary. . . . As we continue to wait before the Lord, he increases our endurance. . . . Verse 31 promises that the exchange of our strength for God's equips us for the long haul. . . .

The last picture is that we shall walk and not faint. This picture seems to imply steadiness; it suggests consistency of life. The word *walk* is often used in the Scriptures with the connotation of our daily behavior or course of conduct. If we walk continually in the Lord, we shall not lose the way or lose heart or become discouraged.

Prayer

   O Lord, *in gratitude we wait on you to empower us to live faithfully, no mat-*
   ter what we encounter, every day of our lives . . .   Amen.

                                   To Walk and Not Faint, pp. 182, 186-87.

Spread Thou over us thy shelter of peace. . . .

From a Jewish Sabbath hymn

The great benefit of good spiritual habits is that they enable us to practice the presence of God objectively — by reading his Word, spending time in prayer, worshiping, observing the Sabbath — even when positive subjective feelings are not there.

I am so grateful to my parents for instilling in me from earliest childhood the habits of regular worship and tithing. The result is that I never even have to ask myself on a Sunday morning whether I feel like going to worship or at the beginning of a month whether I feel like giving God a certain percentage of my income. Feelings never even enter the picture, and I don't ever have to waste time trying to make a choice. The habits are there — positively, constructively freeing me to live according to these "childhood" values that I have confirmed as mine in my adulthood. . . .

The habits of Sabbath keeping include calling to God even in his apparent absence. In obedience, we learn that God is always present, and that one of the places that he is especially present is in the day that he himself has hallowed. . . . Certainly that is one of the reasons that God ordained the keeping of the Sabbath day, for in that practice we will always know his presence, even in the dark nights of the soul when he seems to be absent. . . .

In the person of Jesus Christ, God has spread over us the shelter of peace as the Word tabernacled among us (John 1:14), and in our faith we anticipate the end of time when he will tabernacle among us forever (Rev. 21:3). Meanwhile, God counsels and directs us through the gift of the Holy Spirit. Out of his great love he sent us a Savior and continues daily to save us from all that would take us away from him. All these gifts we celebrate and know more deeply in the festival of the Sabbath. . . .

When the Sabbath is finally fulfilled, our divisions and weaknesses will *cease* forever. We will *rest* eternally in God's grace and love. We will *embrace* his kingdom and sovereignty ultimately and perfectly. We will *feast* unceasingly in his presence.

Prayer

Holy Spirit, inspire us to welcome and honor the Sabbath and God's presence therein . . .   Amen.

Keeping the Sabbath Wholly, pp. 208, 211.

So the name of the Lord *will be declared in Zion*
    and his praise in Jerusalem
when the peoples and the kingdoms
    assemble to worship the Lord.

Psalm 102:21-22

If the Word does not bear its fruit and if the Holy Spirit is not seizing control when pastors preach, it might be because they use the tools of our self-help society instead of introducing the God who changes lives. . . .

Sermons cannot form the character of believers when sin is treated merely as an addiction and redemption is only therapy. The believer's new life in Christ must be based on Christ's objective work of redemption, not on our experience of it, nor on a process of self-improvement or self-actualization.

All the gimmicks sermons use instead of sustained attention to biblical texts hinder the development of faithful life. . . .

Richard Caemmerer in his book *Preaching for the Church* insists that "the goal of preaching is always more than to inform, to relay fact. That preaching convey clear ideas and sound facts is important, but only as means to a further end. That end is meaning." He explains the difference between sense and meaning simply: "Sense is the shape of a fact. Meaning is the shaping of the hearer." Sense asks, "'Do you understand this fact?' Meaning asks: 'Is this fact doing to you what it is supposed to do?' Sense informs the hearer. Meaning strikes him."

Sermons should shape hearers by bringing the transforming Word to nurture the development of their character in the pattern of Christ. The sermon gives time for specific theological and ethical instruction, for painting the picture of the Christian life and community so that worshipers can enter into it. However, these overt calls to the life of following Jesus can be counteracted by the entire ambience of the worshiping milieu; therefore, everything else in the service must be cohesive with the message of the day. No matter how much the Scripture readings and sermons stress that God is gracious, congregations won't learn that truth and become gracious if worship is not grace-full.

Prayer
    Triune God, may your Word be preached and listened to, faithfully and effectively . . . Amen.

Reaching Out, pp. 209-11.

. . . do not be haughty, but associate with the lowly [or, give yourselves to humble tasks]. . . .

Romans 12:16b (my translation)

Romans 12b — literally "not the high things minding" — . . . reminds us that unity is broken when any group considers itself better than others in the community. . . .

In Paul's time the haughtiness in the house churches in Rome must have concerned the relations between Jews and Gentiles. Today we might apply his rebuke to relations between denominations or to factions in congregational arguments. . . . The divisions are very real and must be worked at carefully; haughtiness only exacerbates the tensions. . . .

Paul gives the other side of "high things" . . . as "associating with the lowly." Two possible interpretations for the phrase depend on whether "lowly" signifies tasks or persons. Paul might be urging us to share in doing what is humble. . . .

This does not suggest a fawning subservience that makes Christians into doormats. To think in lowly terms or to have true humility of mind requires courage and wisdom and strength of character — as those qualities are demonstrated in the attitudes of Christ. His was never the humility of wishy-washiness; rather, he chose to lay down his life for others. The complete control that is so often stressed in the Gospel of John (see, for example 10:17-18) underscores his total willingness to sacrifice himself for our sake. Undoubtedly we need this humble mind of Christ in our contemporary communities. . . .

The second possible interpretation of Paul's exhortation — to associate with humble people — . . . can't be done without first purging from ourselves any sort of sense of superiority. . . .

We all — rich or poor, laborers with muscle or mind, athletically fit or physically challenged — have wonderful things to teach each other. Paul's exhortation to associate with the humble people invites us all to care about each other without pretensions, to become more involved with all those who can help us become more like Christ. We would all benefit if our communities were more directly associated with rescue missions, shelters for the homeless, ministries to the lowly and the outcasts of society.

Prayer
> *God before whom all are equal, help us accept, with Christ-like humility and*
> *a willingness to serve, any people or tasks that come to us . . .   Amen.*
>
> Truly the Community, pp. 242, 246-49.

For this reason a man will leave his father and mother and be united to his wife, and they will become one flesh.

Genesis 2:24

The loving Creator of our human sexuality instructed us to celebrate sexual union only with our spouse. He graciously warned us of the dangers and the consequences of fornication and adultery, of promiscuity and betrayal. To ignore the Designer's instructions is to rupture our spirits and souls, to destroy the possibility for that union to carry the significance and delight for which it was intended.

After many years of counseling and observing, I write this with great anguish. How I long for young people in our society to enjoy the exquisite gift of sexual intercourse as a special sign of covenant promising, of permanent commitment to one and only one person! . . .

I long for them to understand that the common slang expression "to make love" does not accurately describe what happens in the sexual union of committed marriage partners. Love is *made* all the time in a marriage — when together we clean up the kitchen, sing a hymn, . . . talk on the porch swing about the day's work, play a game, plan for the future, or remember the past. Love grows when, apart from each other, we speak lovingly about our spouse, work at our jobs with a sense of the other's support, or plan surprises. The way the phrase "to make love" is used in our society, it might rather show some of the emptiness of trying to invent love for a partner for whom there is not such a consistent investment in love-generating and with whom there is no protective framework of covenant promising. . . .

The greatest gift of sexual union is its truth — the assurance that this man is committed to me for life, the divine call that our marriage is to be a sign of God's grace, the security that love does not depend upon our attractiveness or sexual prowess.

There is enormous security in knowing that our marriage isn't built on the single pillar of sexual pleasure. . . . Because the many supports of all kinds of intimacies hold up our marriage, our sexual relationship doesn't have to prove anything. It can simply tell the truth — and that alone is overwhelmingly beautiful.

Prayer
    Creator and Designer, help us make love by daily caring practices and faithful intimacy . . .   Amen.

Sexual Character, pp. 54-57.

313

The LORD gives strength to his people;
  the LORD blesses his people with peace.

Psalm 29:11

The culmination of this overwhelmingly encouraging psalm is the poetic
parallel to the promise of strength. Not only does *YHWH* give us the might
that we need, but, moreover, he blesses us with *shalom*. . . .

The noun *shalom* carries with it immense connotations in the First Testament. We do the word an injustice if we limit it to the idea of peace, although that is where it begins. First of all, *shalom* commences with reconciliation with God. Then, because of that peace, God's people can be at peace
with themselves — and because they are at ease with themselves they can
work for peace with their neighbors, not only in the sense of absence of war,
but more broadly in regard to positive relationships. Such peace issues in
both health and wealth — health because the body is spared from the psy-
chosomatic effects of anxiety and discord, and wealth because the self is free
to enjoy the richness of blessings received.

These truths lead, in turn, to benefits of tranquility, satisfaction, contentment, and fulfillment. All of these results of *shalom* are summarized in
the word *wholeness*, which is what we long for most deeply as we search for
healing and freedom from loneliness.

Finally, the word *shalom* contains within it the promise of commitment.
If we say *shalom* to someone and mean it sincerely, we are binding ourselves
to that person so that whatever we might have that he or she needs to be
whole we will gladly give. . . .

YHWH creates for us reconciliation with himself, and, consequently, the
peace with our neighbors and with ourselves that leads to healing, abun-
dance, serenity, enjoyment, fulfillment, and completeness. God is committed to all of that in us, so that, when he gives us the strength to go on, he
also gives us the courage to overcome whatever hinders our strength.

He gives us not only the physical power but also the spiritual and emotional ability to continue. The fullness of his *shalom* frees us to accept our
limitations and rest in his sufficiency. After all, his voice can make the
whole forest of Lebanon dance. Certainly that strength will enable us to
dance again too.

Prayer
  O LORD, you bless us with your shalom. Teach us to share that blessing with
  our neighbors, so that none of us is alone or powerless . . .   Amen.

I'm Lonely, LORD, pp. 181, 186-87.

Then the angel... said, "There will be no more delay!... [T]he mystery of God will be accomplished...."

Revelation 10:5a-7b

If we were to outline the whole book of The Revelation together, we would notice a cyclical pattern.... A closer look... reveals an interruption both between the sixth and the seventh seals (the two visions of Revelation 7) and then, when the trumpets follow the seals, the same kind of interlude between the sixth and seventh trumpets. The two visions of 10:1–11:13 make up this interlude.

Both of these interruptions serve a literary purpose — in this case to focus on two significant questions: "How long?" and "What is the role of the people of God in the meanwhile?" ... These two questions form the backbone of The Revelation. God teaches the saints that their first question is not answered in terms of how long the suffering must yet go on, but with God's reversal of this question to them: "How long will it be till the Church goes about its duty in the meanwhile?" Furthermore, the duty of the Church in the meanwhile is revealed as this: to witness to the sovereignty of God that seems to be hidden in this meanwhile. These are still the primary issues for God's people today. This is the challenge for each of us personally: how can my life manifest God's lordship?

For several years my daily meditation focused on the Psalms, and in this project I was repeatedly encouraged to become more theocentrically focused, to turn around that question "How long?" in order to ask instead, "Who is God in the midst of this?" This is the lesson of true biblical patience, which does not mean waiting until things change, but learning to wait because of who God is even when things don't change....

Revelation 10 seems to underscore this lesson because at first we are told of a message from the thunders that the seer was not allowed to reveal. Immediately thereafter, however, the angel does make it plain that there will be no more delay.

We simply cannot understand all the mysteries of God,... perhaps because we can't handle them; but this message is unquestionable: there is no more delay. God's purposes must be accomplished now.

Prayer

> *O Lord, even when we don't understand, keep us faithful in manifesting your Lordship...   Amen.*

Joy in Our Weakness, pp. 154-55.

... to the praise of the glory of his grace, which he graciously gave us in the beloved ...

Ephesians 1:6 (my translation)

Here is that great theological stacking of Paul! Though the subject and verb are not specified here, the phrase can be understood to emphasize that God means for us to live this way. . . . Our adoption as sons will be lived out in and as adoration of God for the fullness of his relationship with us.

The word *glory* will be richer for us if we think about it in First Testament terms. Remember that extraordinary story in which Moses wants to see God's glory, but the LORD responds that, though he will show Moses his character, Moses cannot see the LORD's face, for no one can see God and live through it (Exod. 33:18-20). However, the LORD condescends to hide Moses in the cleft of the rock and to cover him with his hand until he has passed by. When the LORD removes his hand, Moses will see his back, but his face will not be seen (vv. 21-23). The LORD keeps his promise, passes in front of Moses, and proclaims who he is — "the LORD, the LORD God, compassionate and gracious, slow to anger, and abounding in lovingkindness and truth . . ." (34:6, NASV) — and Moses' response is to "make haste" to bow low toward the earth to worship.

That splendid account makes me think that Moses got what he asked for — to see God's glory — but on God's terms (for the sake of protecting Moses' life) of seeing only the LORD's back. Let's be lyrical with that picture and suggest that the glory of the LORD is his back, that we can't see God's face, but we can see where he has been, what he has done, how he has intervened in — and left his mark on — the world. We know who God is by the fruits of his being. Since his character is elusively, endlessly beyond our grasp, we can only know him by the result of his having been there. If our lives are actively committed to the praise of his glory, then they will offer others the visual manifestation of God's grace at work through and in us. How can our ministries help people to notice God's back?

Prayer

O LORD, our LORD God, may our witness help others see your glory . . .
Amen.

The Unnecessary Pastor, pp. 49-50.

Blessed art Thou, O LORD our God, King of the Universe,
  who hast sanctified us by Thy commandments
  and commanded us to kindle the Sabbath lights.

Opening prayer of the traditional
Jewish home service for Sabbath eve

Here are a few suggestions for rituals to begin and end the Sabbath day. At the beginning of the Sabbath day (Saturday evening), light two candles (since the Exodus account of the Sabbath commandment says "Remember" and the Deuteronomic says "Observe"). While lighting the candles recite the prayer above. . . .

Then the Sabbath prayers can continue in whatever manner the Spirit moves. It is especially valuable to pray
  • for the Church,
  • for pastors, congregational musicians, and anyone else who will assist in worship
  • for the worship service and your participation in it,
  • for Christians all over the world as they worship, and
  • for the unity of the global Church.

You might also pray for the activities of your Sabbath day — that they might be restful and that you might cease from all work, worry, anxiety, productivity, needing to be God, striving to create your own future, and so forth. Pray also that your Sabbath might be a time of embracing people and Christian values, of feasting and intimacy, laughter and delight.

End the Sabbath welcoming with these words: "Blessed art Thou, O LORD our God, King of the Universe, that you have commanded us to observe the Sabbath day and keep it holy."

At the close of the Sabbath day (Sunday evening), begin with a lighting of the candles and the kindling prayer above. . . . The Havdalah or farewell prayers include thanking God for all the gifts of the special day — the worship, relationships, fun activities, special foods, and other special things that you have enjoyed during the day. The prayer closes with an expression of longing for the next Sabbath day to come and yearning for the day when Christ will come to take us to his perfect rest. This ceremony, like the Sabbath welcoming, ends with these words:

Prayer
  "Blessed art Thou, O LORD our God, King of the Universe, that you have commanded us to observe the Sabbath day and keep it holy." . . .   Amen.

Keeping the Sabbath Wholly, pp. 212-13.

Great God, in Christ you set us free
your life to live, your joy to share.
Give us your Spirit's liberty
to turn from guilt and dull despair,
and offer all that faith can do
while love is making all things new.

Brian Wren, b. 1936

We must understand that the work of the Church is to teach people the language, the habits, and the practices of Christianity, so that people are both formed by the canonical texts of Scripture at the heart of the language of faith and then sent out to bear the fruit of discipleship thus nurtured. The rules of doctrine are the grammar, to guide our first-order speech of worship and life, so that we know how to converse as a people in this culture....

We can learn some lessons about being a community that teaches to others the languages and practices of faith from Bernice Johnson Reagon, a founder of the singing group "Sweet Honey in the Rock," a gifted *a cappella* ensemble that performs mostly music from African-American traditions....

On her "Good News" album she confesses these words from a traditional African-American song: "It was good news to lay down the world and shoulder the cross of Jesus. It's not a good time, but it is good news."

Are our congregations conducting worship that is deep enough to equip people to lay down the world's follies and shoulder the cross, or do we simply seek a good time? Does our worship welcome us into the community and its way of life, its willingness to learn more difficult songs for the sake of Churchbeing? Does it equip us to be hospitable, welcoming the strangers into our songs so they feel that if they don't sing they will really miss the goodness of this way of life? Does our worship thereby strengthen us to be friends with our neighbors? Does it fill us with such Joy from the good news that we can bear the not-so-good times?

Prayer

Suffering and risen Christ, may our worship instruct, sustain, strengthen,
and call us, "your life to live, your joy to share"... Amen.

A Royal "Waste" of Time, pp. 340-41.

. . . never be conceited.

Romans 12:16c (my translation)

This phrase says literally, "Do not be wise according to yourselves." It gives two significant directions for our consideration and obedience.

First, the phrase warns us against any sort of conceit. . . .

Once again, two sides in tension force us to look for a biblical balance. Godly ambition has stirred those who attempt great things for God, and the result has been powerful ministry. On the other hand, too easily we who think we are serving God might really be attempting great things for ourselves.

The Christian community is a society in which we can be asking each other critical questions all the time. Are we engaging in certain activities as genuine service or for the sake of our personal reputations? How easily our motives can become impure. We constantly need the admonition and encouragement of other believers to push us back to a balance, to fight temptation to mix up our work and God's grace-gifts, . . . to use our gifts with freedom and godly ambition within the unity of the whole community.

Second, besides admonishing us for our self-evaluation, this final phrase of verse 16 also invites us to recognize that wisdom cannot come to us individually but must instead develop in community. . . .

Solo efforts are terribly destructive to our functioning together as the community. Gifts are given to each person for stewardship to build up the . . . whole Church (1 Pet. 4:10).

Often in the Church we copy the "rugged individualism" of our culture and think that plans can be made faster and more effectively if certain people just do things alone. Nevertheless, to act this way is to forget that God has given gifts to each member of the community and that, when all those gifts are working together in harmony, a much richer manifestation of God's love can be experienced and demonstrated to the world. The attaining of wisdom cannot be a solo effort. Always the insights of another will modify our own and draw us both more closely to the center of truth.

Prayer

Grace-gifting God, keep us centered in our communities, so that our corporate wisdom and faith guide us all . . . Amen.

Truly the Community, pp. 242, 250-52.

. . . for the purpose that we, the first ones to hope in Christ, might exist to the praise of his glory. . . .

Ephesians 1:12 (my translation)

Whenever I read the Greek word for transgressions, *paraptōmatōn*, I remember my confirmation teacher stressing that it connotes all the ways we "miss the mark" in transgressing God's will. The very next year at high school I took archery class. . . . One girl got her bow so cockeyed that her arrow not only missed the target entirely but flew over to the track . . . into the very bushy tail of a dog that was running around. The dog wasn't hurt at all, but in its confusion it sprinted all over the field, . . . a graphic image of the fatal wanderings of our sinfulness. Our wrongdoing doesn't merely miss the mark; it often hits someone else.

The deep symbol of sin is one we often trivialize by terming it merely a mistake. Many sins we euphemize; for example we label fornication "sleeping together," which sounds so nice and cozy. We call it "fudging on our income tax" when we cheat the government or a "little white lie" when we do violence to the truth. Since in our culture we do not name sin for the despicable *sin* that it is, we rarely recognize how truly *dead* we are (see Eph. 2:1-3).

We are enslaved to sin. There is no escaping it, as Martin Luther pointed out. . . . This slavery to my sinful self even makes it impossible to come to faith. . . . In his explanation of the Third Article of the Apostles' Creed Luther taught "that I cannot by my own reason or strength believe in Jesus Christ my Lord or come to him. . . ." Only because God calls, delivers, enlightens, frees, and graces us can we be set free for and into faith. . . .

All these graces God lavishes upon us with perfect wisdom, insight, or capacity to understand. Never does God pour out his mercy in ways that are not good for us. . . .

We live, we sing, we *ARE*, to the praise of God's glory. Our lives become a sign of what God is, where he has worked, how he graces. We demonstrate our hope by living as praise.

Prayer

Triune God, help us acknowledge sin, repent, receive forgiveness, and live as praise to your glory . . . Amen.

The Unnecessary Pastor, pp. 53-56.

"But now, Lord, what do I look for?
  My hope is in you. . . ."

Psalm 39:7

The poet of Psalm 39 continues to hope, even though everything seems to be against him. Perhaps only Psalm 88 is darker. . . .

Why should we consider such gloomy psalms? . . . First of all, because they help us to know that we are not alone. Other believers have struggled against seemingly insurmountable odds and yet have been able to continue to believe.

However, that would not be sufficient comfort without another truth and another gloomy psalm. Psalm 22 begins with this shriek: "My God, my God, why have you forsaken me?" . . .

Because this psalm was cried out by the One who changed our lives and destinies for us, we can find comfort in the despairing psalms. . . . We can trust, knowing the character of Jesus and what he has done to deliver us from this world's suffering.

Consider these verses from the letter to the Hebrews: ". . . let us hold firmly to the faith we profess. For we do not have a high priest who is unable to sympathize with our weaknesses. . . . Let us then approach the throne of grace with confidence, so that we may receive mercy and find grace to help us in our time of need" (4:14-16).

As he carried all our sin on himself, Jesus, in his extreme pain of body and soul, called out to the God whom he couldn't find. And because he bore that total forsakenness for us, . . . we may speak out of despair, but we never have to speak out of abandonment. The psalmist recognizes God's chastising, but he also realizes that his sin and human brokenness have caused his state of woes.

You might be saying at this point, "But I haven't sinned. I'm the victim." . . . Yet, in the recognition that we are sinners in a sinful world and that God is God, we can finally come to peace. It might not be our particular fault that we are undergoing our present suffering, but human sinfulness brought all this evil into the world — and we bear undeserved consequences because we can't escape our basic humanity. . . .

Wounds are deep, and despair can be profound. Yet our hope is in the Lord.

Prayer

O Lord our God, in our despair, help us recognize that you are always beside
us . . .   Amen.

I'm Lonely, Lord, pp. 189-92, 197.

". . . the mystery of God will be accomplished, just as he announced to his servants the prophets." . . . Then I was told, "You must prophesy again about many peoples, nations, languages and kings."

Revelation 10:7b, 11

The aura of mystery that surrounds this text is wonderfully captured by the composer Olivier Messiaen in his . . . "Quartet for the End of Time," . . . written while he was imprisoned by the Nazis in 1941. . . .

Messiaen himself and three other inmates first performed the quartet on damaged instruments in the prison camp at Görlitz in Silesia. . . .

That God's mystery will be accomplished is an incredibly important message for the Christian community in our times. We might not have all the answers, but because of those that we do have, we must certainly get on with our task of manifesting to the world the undeniable reality of the sovereign lordship of Christ. . . .

When we do not know the answers to all of life's questions, we can ask different ones — questions of how we can best be stewards of this time in the meanwhile. How can we fulfill the purposes of the kingdom with the information that we do have? . . .

Speaking the Word is the church's task. . . . There can be no delay. God's people must be faithful now to proclaim his message, . . . to speak truly the Word God gives us to proclaim. . . .

What is the witnessing task of the church today? We proclaim the sovereignty of God, not of the nations. Perhaps that might take the form of speaking against the pretensions of the nations that would seek to control the world by means of a nuclear arsenal. . . . Perhaps our task is to proclaim to kings the judgment — and hope — of God. Most of all, our task is to live faithfully the ethics of God's kingdom in our own communities, to stand as a witnessing people against the lifestyle of a world that wears the mark of the beast on its forehead and right hand. We are to be a people marked instead with the Father's name. . . . Then, even if we are killed in the process of such a witness, we will be called to come up to heaven, and the world will be astonished at the greatness of the sovereign God (Rev. 11:12-13).

Prayer
> *Almighty Lord, empower us to be faithful witnesses to your sovereignty over all of life . . .   Amen.*

Joy in Our Weakness, pp. 155-60.

All your works shall give thanks to you, O Lord,
    and all your faithful shall bless you.
Your kingdom is an everlasting kingdom,
    and your dominion endures through all generations.

                                        Psalm 145:10, 13 (NRSV)

We are the people who practice God's reign. . . . It is this dominion of God
into which we invite our neighbors; God's sovereignty is our good news. In
our culture, which is enslaved to other powers, it is good news indeed.

> The Lord upholds all who are falling,
>   and raises up all who are bowed down.
> The eyes of all look to you,
>   and you give them their food in due season. . . .
> The Lord is just in all his ways,
>   and kind in all his doings.
>   (Ps. 145:14-15, 17, NRSV)

What an elegant list of ways in which the faithfulness and graciousness of
the Lord are manifested — in emotional, physical, and spiritual ways; with
justice and kindness and generosity; with support and answers and presence!

These stanzas take us into the responsibility for our way of life, for if
our Lord is like this, then we, his people, will want to be just and kind and
generous also — supportive of our neighbors, listening to their cries, and incarnating for them the love of God.

Our testimony to God's character and conduct is thus given credence if
we embody who he is in who we are becoming, and what he does in how we
live. The more we observe God (the great gift of our worship and educational practices and community life), the more we are transformed into his
likeness, from one degree of glory to another (2 Cor. 3:18). . . .

> My mouth will speak the praise of the Lord,
>   and all flesh will bless his holy name forever and ever.
>   (Ps. 145:21, NRSV)

Prayer
    O Lord, covenant God, we want to tell your praises so that everyone will
    know your character and bless you . . .   Amen.
                            A Royal "Waste" of Time, pp. 350-51.

323

If believers are conscious of the liturgy, they have missed the presence of God. Ritual be-
havior works precisely because it draws attention away from the self and allows people
an opportunity to greet God.

Patrick R. Keifert

Many churches who want to make their worship reach out to nonbelievers
think that to do so they must "throw out the liturgy" — as if that were possible! Even congregations that do not practice specific forms outlined in
hymnals or service books usually follow some kind of ordering of worship
elements. . . . Unless the service is entirely a performance by musicians and
preacher with no involvement at all by the people, every worship service has
a liturgy. The question is whether it is a faithful one. . . .

We worship by God's invitation and not by our own concoction. Using
God's own words in liturgical responses helps to remind us that worship is
God's gift to us before it can be our gift to God. Liturgical pieces that highlight the reading of the Scriptures and the Eucharist as the central moments
of the worship service also reinforce the awareness that God is the subject
and object of whatever we are doing.

Losing God as the subject can turn liturgy into performance rather
than sacrament. This results in a modern form of a medieval notion . . . that
liturgy's power and effectiveness depend on the priest's worthiness. The
modern version insists that liturgy must be performed well in order to be effective, and its potency is determined according to the criterion that every
participant must have had some sort of emotionally satisfying experience. . . .

However, the point of liturgical form is to receive God's self. The recipients are not private individuals relating to God in their own cozy way; they
are the corporate Body of the Church that experiences God's presence
through public worship, the means by which God gives God's self. . . .

Liturgy should stir new thoughts about God — new insights into God's
character, which will result in a transformation of our own character. . . .

Out of concern for character formation, churches must think very carefully in planning the liturgy. . . . We must not ask, Is this liturgy attractive?
but always, What kind of character does this nurture?

Prayer
> God who invites us to worship, may our liturgies on the Sabbath lead us into
> your transforming presence . . .   Amen.

Reaching Out, pp. 242-49.

"Pastor, that was a wonderful sermon," said the parishioner. . . .
"That remains to be seen," said the preacher.

Richard R. Caemmerer

The community itself is destroyed as *Christian* community if preaching does not hold before the people the decisive Word of God that makes those who follow Jesus different from the society around them. . . .

The preacher's words must emerge from the Church's life and go forth to nourish that life. As Richard Lischer explains, if the sermon is not theological — that is, if it does not offer words about God and the life to be found in Christ — "it suffers the same fate as the seed sown on rocky soil. But in this case, its rootlessness derives from the preacher's rather than the hearer's lack of depth." . . .

My favorite sentence for years has been, "The Christian community is an alternative society." That thesis requires all sermons to ask, How does this text form us to be the people of God? What do we learn from this text that cannot be known apart from the community of faith? How can we offer this alternative understanding to the world? . . .

When we come to faith in Christ, we enter a new world. Our eyes are opened to the beauty and wonder of God's creation and the immense gifts of God's grace. We enter into a community trying to live wholly in the character of Jesus and faithfully in the virtues the Scriptures describe. We speak the forgiveness of God and God's total acceptance of us through Christ. In the face of the great sufferings in the world, we know that God is at work to fulfill his purposes of justice and hope and that God is with us as we seek to do his will. . . .

The ultimate test of sermons is whether they turn the hearers into theologians and activists. Do they grapple with texts and teach the people how to question? Do they wrestle with faith and invite the listeners to know that victory is assured? Do they struggle against the world's pain and challenge believers to create justice? Above all, do they bring us all into God's presence to hear his Word to us?

Prayer

O Christ the Word, we pray for our preachers. May their sermons nourish our faith and strengthen us as an alternative community . . .   Amen.

Reaching Out, pp. 212-15, 238-40.

To no one repaying evil for evil . . .

Romans 12:17a (my translation)

Literally, this phrase says, "To no one evil against evil recompensing." . . .
Paul's placement of "to no one" at the beginning of the phrase underscores
his point that in our relations *with no one* should we ever resort to repaying
evil for evil. . . .

Furthermore, this verse commands us to recompense to no one evil *in
exchange for* evil. We would have preferred it if Paul had written, "Be careful
that your just retribution does not escalate." . . .

Jewish laws were unusually just for the historical period in which the Israelite nation developed to its peak. The Hebrew Scriptures demand this
equality of response: "But if there is a serious injury, you are to take life for
life, eye for eye, tooth for tooth . . ." (Exod. 21:23-24). That law prevented the
terrible avenging which characterized Semitic societies. God was requiring
that punishment of offenders could only be equal to the crime. . . .

But then Jesus came along and took God's work of creating a people of
peace one step further. Remember that he said this:

> "Do not resist an evil person. If someone strikes you on the right cheek,
> turn to him the other also. . . . Love your enemies and pray for those who
> persecute you. . . . [I]f you love only those who love you, what credit is that
> to you? . . . No, you will be perfect even as your Heavenly Father is perfect.
> (Matt. 5:38-45, NIV, and 46-48, JBP)

The form of the final Greek verb in Matthew 5 is a simple future. Rather
than holding a club over our heads by translating this passage as the command, "you must be perfect" (TEV and RSV), J. B. Philips more fittingly
translates it as "you will be perfect." . . .

Not profoundly enough do we recognize how radical Jesus was. . . .

If we recompense to no one even evil to match the evil we've received,
then the question of what a person deserves does not at all enter the picture
any longer.

Prayer
> *God of grace, help us resist retribution and choose instead to love even our en-
> emies, in Jesus' name . . .   Amen.*

Truly the Community, pp. 254-57.

. . . I urge you to live a life worthy of the calling you have received.

Ephesians 4:1

Many times in the First Testament, especially in the story of the prophet Hosea, God illustrates by means of human sexuality his faithful covenant love for Israel and her infidelity. The sexual lives of God's people, therefore, are always judged by this question: Are we symbolizing God's fidelity or imitating Israel's faithlessness?

The question is critically important for those of us who deeply desire to be the agents of God's purposes in the world. Only with integrity of character can we invite the world to witness the faithfulness of God.

The intertwined relationship of sexuality and spirituality is emphasized throughout the Scriptures by the frequency with which God uses sexual images to admonish Israel. Rebukes for "going awhoring after other gods" occur almost twenty times in the First Testament, revealing the interconnection between making sexual intercourse an idol and giving our love promiscuously to any of a multiplicity of other gods.

The profound damage that is done to life and faith and the witness of the community when God's design for sexual union is violated is suggested by the severity of the punishment called for in Israel. Fornicators and adulterers were to be stoned. If one cannot live in a holy way, one should not live.

It is imperative in our reading of such severe passages that we do not put the cart before the horse. Such proscriptions in the Scriptures are not given so that God's people avoid adultery merely out of fear of punishment. Rather, the canonical construction (and God's grace!) invites us first to appreciate God's design, and only afterwards are we told about the consequences of failure. To emphasize only the law without the gospel undergirding it is to miss the intent of God's Word. Even the foundational commandments do not simply say "Thou shalt" and "Thou shalt not." Instead, they begin with the words, "I am the LORD your God, who brought you out of the land of Egypt" (Exod. 20:2, RSV). This is the God who created us, who saved us, who set us free from the Egyptian bondage, who led us out of captivity to other gods. Now here are the instructions for living fully his creative design, in response to his saving interventions on our behalf.

Prayer

> *Loving Creator and Father, we pray that our lives will reflect your design with integrity — and thereby witness to your faithfulness . . .   Amen.*

Sexual Character, pp. 58-59.

"Will the LORD reject us forever?
  Will he never show his favor again? . . ."
Then I thought, "To this I will appeal:
  the years of the right hand of the Most High."
I will remember the deeds of the LORD;
  yes, I will remember your miracles of long ago.

Psalm 77:7, 10-11

As the psalmist mourns some unknown distress, he pauses to put his troubles into a larger framework so that he can trust God to rescue him from the trial he is presently undergoing.

He deals with his gloom and anxious spirit with a firm discipline of mind, . . . focusing his thoughts on the past, the previous ages in which God's love had been clearly seen, and . . . searching for the truth.

This offers us a wonderful model. . . . By the grace of God we can prevent ourselves from becoming so overwhelmed by our emotions that our faith is incapacitated. With the support and encouragement of others in the Christian community, we can deal with ourselves in our grief by putting things into God's perspective and, thereby, finding comfort and hope. . . .

Could God forget to show favor — God? That would be a contradiction in terms. No! he hasn't forgotten. No! this can't last forever. No! he hasn't closed up his compassion toward us.

The poet discloses how ridiculously obvious the answer to these rhetorical questions are when he continues with an appeal to many "years of the right hand of the Most High." This . . . phrase refers to all the time the poet has spent in the place of intimacy and fellowship with this highest and only God.

We worry about loneliness or grief in terms of months or even years; in contrast, we need to learn the habit of remembering the LORD's love in terms of scores of years and aeons. . . .

Whenever we review the past we have to come to this same conclusion. . . . Grief put into historical perspective is bearable. When we ask, "How can I go on?" the answer is the same as last time: "The LORD will give you the strength." We know that he will; we have seen it happen time and again.

Prayer

  Steadfast LORD, we trust your faithful love to sustain us in times of grief or despair . . .   Amen.

I'm Lonely, LORD, pp. 198-201, 205.

A great and wondrous sign appeared in heaven. . . .

Revelation 12:1a

After the announcement that the third woe is coming and the sounding of the seventh angel's trumpet (11:14-15), loud voices remind us that Christ is the Lord and that he will reign forever and ever. The elders worship God because his reign is beginning; the nations are going to be judged and the saints rewarded. Meanwhile, the temple in heaven is opened, the ark is revealed (to remind us of God's covenant faithfulness), and the usual signs of God's theophany (lightning, rumblings, thunder, earthquake, and hailstorm) occur. . . .

Then the seer proclaims that a great sign appeared in the heaven (12:1). In both The Revelation and John's Gospel, the word *sign* carries important connotations. . . . Signs should be accepted as true in themselves — that is, the miracles really did happen — but they are of secondary importance. Most essentially, we notice to whom the sign points.

Think, for example, of a sign to the beach. . . . We wouldn't park our car at it and enjoy only the sign. . . . This understanding is essential for reading the fantastic accounts of The Revelation: the signs point to something beyond themselves, to which we should pay primary attention.

Our attention in chapter 12 should primarily be focused on the two major opponents: Satan and Christ. . . . The most significant aspect . . . is that Satan is overcome by the blood of the Lamb and by the word of the saints' testimony and by their willingness even to die. . . . By this reference to the saints . . . John encouraged his original readers as they faced the persecutions of the emperor.

Similarly, as God's people today struggle with various physical or spiritual setbacks or challenges, we can also be greatly comforted. . . . Sometimes in our personal trials we think that we are being overcome by the powers of evil instead, but this chapter offers us genuine hope. Though we undergo sufferings, these, too, can be the means for God's purposes to be accomplished. Consequently, we can join the heavens and all who dwell there in their rejoicing (12:12). . . . The dragon (Satan) cannot get us. God's love and grace will always protect us.

Prayer

Overcoming Lord, may we see in your victorious resurrection a sign of our eventual victory — and rejoice . . .   Amen.

Joy in Our Weakness, pp. 161-66.

The fear of the LORD is the beginning of wisdom,
  and knowledge of the Holy One is understanding.

Proverbs 9:10

One of the disenchanting goals of our present society is the accumulation of information. . . . The society that surrounds us . . . is overloaded with useless or contextless (though often interesting) information. Thus, we have learned to receive data without learning from it or acting on it. . . . Ponder how . . . we know the sufferings of the poor in our world but do not change our consumption habits in order to change the inequities, or how we in the Church . . . learn about the grace of God but do not live as a community that embodies it.

To those who chase after more and more information, . . . a vital Christian community has great gifts to offer in introducing them to the One who alone can appease their yearning . . . and immersing them in a Life that acts on the information of faith, in a Way that brings wisdom out of knowledge, and in Truth that infuses everything with meaning and hope.

Part of the reason why so many people in our society chase after information is that they think accumulating data will help them to be more in control of their lives — and perhaps the lives of others. Society has fostered the idolatry of autonomy, that all individuals pursue their own personal happiness without much concern for the common good. . . . Never before in the history of the world has there been such a visionless repudiation of the wisdom of elders, of the past, of traditions (in the best sense of that word). . . .

Yet many people in our society do not realize that the very thing they need — trustworthy authorities beyond themselves who will nurture their moral and character development — is what they have with blind prejudice disdained. . . .

Contrarily, the authentic Christian community enfolds seekers in a gracious narrative, the story of God's loving care that has been passed on by a people ever since Sarah and Abraham. This is a Word that enables persons to find themselves truly by giving themselves first to God and then to others.

Prayer
  Loving Lord, fill us with a desire to seek you and your will for our lives, and
  empower us to act in response to what we learn . . .   Amen.

A Royal "Waste" of Time, pp. 245-47.

I keep asking that the God of our Lord Jesus Christ, the glorious Father, may give you the Spirit of wisdom and revelation, so that you may know him better.

Ephesians 1:17

If we skimmed through Ephesians to survey all the passages that deal with formation, we would be surprised at their extent. The second half of Ephesians 1 . . . is Paul's prayer for the saints at Ephesus, and it includes, after his thanksgiving for their faith and love, his petition that God's wisdom, God's revelation would form them. What is indispensably important for us here is to notice how so much of the prayer is about God.

It is urgent in our humanly centered times that we see how extensively Paul's prayer names God. If we pay attention to God, we will gain God's wisdom, receive God's revelation, and be formed to be more like God. . . .

All shaping of the spiritual life takes place in the midst of the entire Christian community throughout space and time. . . . But we must always be vigilant against thinking that we can grow ourselves in faith and faith-life, or that we . . . are "necessary" to the faith formation of others. . . .

One of the most severe failures in churches today is that so often preaching has become therapeutic instead of proclamatory. The point of sermons should not be to tell listeners how to pull themselves up by their own bootstraps, or how to fix their lives and adjust their attitudes. Rather, sermons should paint so beautiful and compelling a vision of the kingdom of God that . . . hearers are enabled to inhabit it.

I don't think it is possible to overstate this point. . . . It is the revelation of God that forms us. . . .

I am not advocating, of course, a proclamation that does not connect to the daily lives of people. We are not speaking about God in the abstract, but yet the focus remains on God and not on us.

Prayer

Triune God, we pray that all preaching of your Word every Sabbath will instill in us such a desire to know more about you that your Revelation can truly be formative in our faith and lives . . . Amen.

The Unnecessary Pastor, pp. 149-51.

Come, thou long expected Jesus,
born to set thy people free;
From our sins and fears release us;
let us find our rest in thee.

Charles Wesley, 1707-1788

At an Interim Ministry Network conference a few years ago Chuck Olsen suggested that the Christian life has a rhythm of anticipation or yearning, celebration of a high point of fulfillment, and proclamation or practice. . . . How helpful his notion is for understanding the complete church year.

At the beginning of the church year, we observe a season of yearning in Advent as we imagine the longing of the Jews for their Messiah, as we hunger for Jesus to come more deeply into our own lives, and as we thirst for his coming again. The culminating celebration is Christmas, of course; and then the proclamation, the going out into life, is observed in the season of Epiphany . . . and the subsequent spread of God's grace to the Gentiles through all the ways in which Jesus is the Light of the world.

After the Epiphany season, we return to yearning with Lent, . . . meditating on all that Christ did for us, lest we take for granted the enormous gift of Easter. After the festival celebration of Easter, the proclamation or practice happens in the season of the forty days, during which time Jesus trained the disciples in the meaning of his resurrection and its promise of fulfillment in the final recapitulation of God's cosmic reign.

Ascension is again a time of yearning, for it initiates the disciples — and us — into the ten days of waiting for the outpouring of the Holy Spirit and for Christ's coming again. We celebrate the high festival of Pentecost, after which the entire season of "ordinary time" ("the Sundays after Pentecost") is a practicing of Christ's presence through the power of the Holy Spirit.

The three high festivals are actually trinitarian, though most would think there are two celebrations of Christ. It seems to me that we would be able to avoid the overly romantic sentimentalizing of Christmas if we remembered that it is more fully a festival of the Father, the One who gave us the unfathomable gift of his Son. . . . The other two festivals are obviously those of the Son at Easter and the Holy Spirit at Pentecost.

Prayer
    Triune God, bless us through the rhythm of our church year . . .   *Amen.*
                         The Unnecessary Pastor, pp. 145-46.

To no one repaying evil for evil; giving attention to doing what is good before all persons.

Romans 12:17 (my translation)

In this verse Paul chooses the word *kalos* for the style of life we want to exhibit before all other persons. . . . *Kalos* in the Scriptures carries a whole range of meanings, and Paul probably uses it here quite comprehensively. Fundamentally it means beauty or quality, in the sense of accordance with the purpose of something. From this basic meaning of good and useful, it stresses appropriateness with such concepts as moral goodness and noble praiseworthiness.

Various translations of verse 17 demonstrate this diversity. The RSV urges us to "take thought for what is noble in the sight of all," while the Jerusalem Bible invites us to "let everyone see that you are interested only in the highest ideals." J. B. Phillips's paraphrase urges us to "See that your public behavior is above criticism."

Such injunctions are too large for us; trapped in our sinful human nature we find the challenge impossible. We know we don't always act nobly; we can't always live above criticism. Consequently, this verse drives us once again to the forgiveness and empowerment of God's love. . . .

The responsibility for living so nobly in public is made much easier by the realization that if we live together in the Christian community as the rest of Romans 12 has exhorted, then the Spirit-empowered outpouring of such caring into the wider sphere of the world will surely be honorable. . . .

Only by demonstrating God's character in tangible ways do we gain credibility for our message about his love. . . . When we manifest God's love publicly under the Lordship of Christ, others will ask us to account for our hope (1 Pet. 3:15-16).

Sharing our faith happens not only because of what we won't do — that is, to recompense evil for evil — but also because of what we will choose to do instead — to aim for the highest ideals in manifesting the meaning of the gospel.

Prayer

O Lord Christ, empower us to exemplify the loving behavior that truly witnesses to our faith. . . . Amen.

Truly the Community, pp. 254, 258-60.

. . . [the beloved], in whom we have liberation through his blood, the pardon of [our] false steps, according to the riches of his grace, which he lavished upon us using all wisdom and understanding. . . .   Ephesians 1:7-8 (my translation)

We have made redemption much too small. We have turned the deep symbol of salvation into a comparatively little thing by relegating it to the future. . . . God's liberation gives us plenty of room — breathing space, deliverance from our tight anguishes and confining bondages. Moreover, God is continually doing this for us now, not only in a far distant future. Do we recognize his gracious snatching as he rescues us and delivers us from our various enslavements in life?

This emancipation happens through the blood. . . . The blood of Christ represents all of his sacrifice on our behalf — not just his final surrender to death on the cross, but the sacrifices of his entire life on earth.

We have put the comma in the wrong place in the Apostles' Creed, with the result that we have reduced Christ's travail for us to only one piece (though the major one) of its entirety. We say,

> born of the virgin Mary,
> He suffered under Pontius Pilate,
> Was crucified, died, and was buried.

We should say,

> born of the virgin Mary,
> He suffered,
> under Pontius Pilate was crucified,
> died, and was buried.

Do you notice the immense difference it makes? Jesus didn't suffer only under Pontius Pilate. He suffered from the very beginning — even in the womb, where his life was threatened with future marginalization and poverty if Joseph decided to "put Mary away quietly." Jesus suffered when he was born and laid in a manger, . . . no doubt a stinky, scratchy, mucky, wretched place. He suffered the crowds and their pushiness, the Romans and their oppressions, the impossible disciples and their phenomenal inability to get things right. And he suffers *you!*

Therefore, when we say that we are delivered through the blood, let us remember that God is always suffering in order to liberate us.

Prayer
   Jesus our Savior, your suffering for us is rich grace beyond measure . . .   Amen.
                                          The Unnecessary Pastor, pp. 50-52.

Trust in the Lord and do good;
  dwell in the land and enjoy safe pasture.
Delight yourself in the Lord
  and he will give you the desires of your heart.

Psalm 37:3-4

The poet urges us to trust in the Lord, . . . and then he exhorts us to do good. The significant order here reminds us that we don't do good out of our ability to accomplish it, but out of our trusting. Our relationship with YHWH enables us to produce what is morally good and of benefit to others. . . .

The second poetic line invites us to inhabit the land and enjoy safe pasture. . . . This gives us a picture of hope. When the Israelites entered their Promised Land, they were counseled that . . . their pastures would be safe if they continued to be faithful to God's call and commands for justice and compassion.

Another implication of the text is that those who dwell in the land are able to observe, in the seasons of rain and sunshine and in every harvest, the faithfulness of YHWH. Thus, the safety of the pasture is more deeply enjoyed by those who recognize the Lord, who makes it secure.

For us these words can continue to convey a sense of security. . . . As long as we are trusting God we will be empowered to do good, to dwell wherever he has called us, and to enjoy being nourished by his steadfastness.

This ties in very closely with the psalm's next point: . . . security in the faithfulness of the Lord is much more available to those who supremely delight in him. . . . That idea challenges us to grow so close to the Lord that . . . we will delight in him thoroughly. . . . When we do, he will give us the desire of our hearts. That is because our intentional desires will be his. The closer we are to God the more we will want only what he wants. . . .

We will come to the point someday of resting in that truth and finding our longings stilled with the deepest *shalom*.

Prayer

  Faithful Lord, help us to trust and delight in you in ways that empower us to do what is good and to will what you will as the delight of our hearts . . . Amen.

I'm Lonely, Lord, pp. 206-9.

All inhabitants of the earth will worship the beast — all whose names have not been written in the book of life belonging to the Lamb that was slain. . . .

Revelation 13:8

Spiritually, we have to be born a Christian through the Holy Spirit *and* be educated into the values of the kingdom of God to know the difference between what is true and what is a corrupted imitation. . . .

The powers of evil take what was originally good in God's design and twist it into the opposite. . . . You know that quite well already. What we don't as readily recognize is the very perversion of the powers of evil themselves. . . .

The most gruesome of all the parodies in Revelation 13 and 14 is the fact that the second beast gives a mark to all the inhabitants of the earth who follow him. . . .

In Hebrew thought the number 6 signifies what is less than perfect and, therefore, that which is corrupted or evil. . . . To put three 6s together, then, is to . . . make sacred what is marred or imperfect. Thus, anything in our thoughts or lifestyle that elevates to the position of a god things that are merely human or actually evil is marked as the work of the beast. The number 666 symbolizes all our allegiances to the gods of this world. . . .

We do not have to be afraid of how this imagery of the mark of the beast might be fulfilled someday. . . . Rather, we should be afraid of how that imagery is being constantly fulfilled whenever . . . we let that which might have been good become corrupted and beastly/demonic.

How do things become gods to us? . . .

The idolatries of our culture, symbolized by the mark of the beast, beckon us with illusions of wealth, power, position, and success. All these things parody the abundant life that Jesus promised us. . . .

In contrast, the Father's love in Christ frees us from the control of these and other gods. . . . The Holy Spirit empowers us to live in those ways that stand against the mark of the beast. In our limitations we learn the Joy of total dependence on the triune God, whose mark of ownership is on our foreheads.

Prayer
> *Dependable Trinity, empower us to display the mark of your presence in our lives . . . Amen.*

Joy in Our Weakness, pp. 168-75.

And you, being dead in your wrongdoing and sins . . .

Ephesians 2:1-3 (my translation)

One big problem in churches these days is that members don't know how dead they are.

We human beings have a great aversion to naming sin SIN. We want to euphemize it with terms like "brokenness" which make people feel cozy because it seems not to be their fault. Something else caused them to be "broken."

Now it is true that many outside forces do break us, but if we never take responsibility for our own self-centeredness, faults, missteps, and more blatant evils — in other words, if we never acknowledge that we are *sinners* — we can never get forgiven. . . .

This is why we are so refreshed when we admit with the apostle Paul that we cannot do what we want to do and that we keep on doing what we wish we didn't do (Rom. 7:15-20). . . . Truly the announcement of forgiveness is the greatest gift the Church offers to the world. I hungrily eat up those words of forgiveness because I cannot forgive myself. Can you?

We can't forgive ourselves because we always hedge it. We turn back and wallow in our despair, or we excuse ourselves too easily, or we put a penance on ourselves and try to earn forgiveness, or we assume we are far too unworthy to be forgiven.

That is why it is such a Joy in worship to be able to confess our sins and sinfulness and to hear forgiveness and to taste it in the Lord's Supper. Forgiveness is a fact, a gift that needs to be proclaimed, shouted from the rooftops, heralded, and declared gently to our burdened neighbors. When we know how dead we are, we comprehend, too, how desperate we are for forgiveness. . . .

Ephesians 2:4 offers one of the most beautiful contrasts in all of Scripture: "but God, being rich in mercy, because of his great love with which he loved us, and we being dead in wrongdoings, he made us alive together with Christ." Its introduction — *"but God"* — then picks up steam, rolling on into the liberating passage of verses 4-9. As you read these verses, observe their comprehensive emphasis on gifts, riches, mercy, lavishing, God pouring out on us exactly the grace that we need.

Prayer

Forgiving Lord, thank you for your blessed gifts of confession and absolution . . .   Amen.

The Unnecessary Pastor, pp. 152-54.

"Salt is good; but if salt has lost its taste, how can its saltiness be restored?"
                                                            Luke 14:34 (NRSV)

Sociologists recognize that any alternative way of life that is substantially different from the larger society around it and that wants to maintain itself needs a language, customs, habits, rituals, institutions, procedures, and practices that uphold and nurture *a clear vision of how it is different and why that matters.* Are we as Christians committed to the alternative way of life described in the Scriptures and incarnated in Christ, so that we are willing to invest ourselves diligently in order to transmit this valued way of life to our children and neighbors? If so, our worship cannot be too much like the surrounding culture, or it will be impossible to teach this alternative. . . .

What, then, does it mean to participate in *Christian* worship? . . . One wrong turn . . . is to blur our unique identity as the people of God, instead of accentuating it with loving commitment. . . .

Why is there such panic and confusion in churches these days over what it means to be the Church? Jesus never told us that we had to be big, successful, attractive to nonmembers, or like the culture in which we live. In fact, he said the opposite of all those things — that the way was narrow (Matt. 7:13-14), that the first shall be last (Mark 10:31), that we would be persecuted (Matt. 5:11), that we would be hated by all because of his name (Luke 21:17) — and he wondered whether, when the Son of Man comes, he would find faith on earth (Luke 18:8). . . .

On the other hand, Jesus also never said that we should hide ourselves away from the world, ignore our neighbors' needs, keep silent about what we know, or be purposely elitist. Instead he told his disciples to let our light shine before others (Matt. 5:14-16), to heal the sick and announce the kingdom (Luke 10:1-9), to sell what we have to give to the poor (Luke 12:22-34), to proclaim repentance and forgiveness and to be witnesses (Luke 24:44-49). How, then, will we equip congregational members with a vision for this mission?

Prayer

> *Jesus our Lord, as we prepare to keep the Sabbath, open our eyes to the mission before us — to be your Church, faithfully different from the culture around us . . .   Amen.*

A Royal "Waste" of Time, pp. 335-36.

From [Christ] the whole body, joined and held together by every supporting ligament, grows and builds itself up in love, as each part does its work.

Ephesians 4:16

Besides influencing profoundly the development of Christian character, liturgical forms — even the smallest elements — promote the sense that we who worship are a whole community, belonging to our Head, Jesus Christ, and to each other. Liturgy serves its purpose best when it enfolds worship participants in the *life* of God's people. Faith is not the work of an isolated self but God's gift, passed on by the community or "household of faith." . . . Tragically, many contemporary congregations do not convey the sense of the global and universally timeless Church. We have forgotten, as Hebrews 12:1 reminds us, that we "are surrounded by so great a cloud of witnesses" (NRSV). . . .

The Church into which worship enfolds believers is a community of people who have, throughout the ages, *participated*. . . . We must do the best job of education we can so that, ideally, everyone can be included in what we do in worship. We will train the children and untutored adults in the actions and habits of worship and in their meanings. . . .

How is it that congregations have failed so miserably to teach the beauty of liturgy, to incorporate new believers into its splendors? Why have we not instructed children so that they may gain from its insights a deeper understanding of their place in the story of the faith community? Couldn't we teach in Sunday school the biblical roots of the liturgy so that children know when they are participating in it that the salutation comes from the story of Ruth and Boaz, the *Agnus Dei* from John the Baptist, the *Sanctus* from Isaiah, the *Magnificat* from Mary, and the *Nunc Dimitis* from Simeon? What a rich web of witnesses we call to mind when we enact the liturgy! . . .

The purpose of any liturgy, no matter what we use, must be to carry God's presence and the faith of the community. . . . Our liturgy's style may vary. . . . What is important is that the liturgy give a sense that the whole Church is present in it. We never worship alone in just this locality, age, or language.

Prayer

Eternal Lord, may worship root us in the past, present, and ongoing community of faith in the world . . .   Amen.

Reaching Out, pp. 250-51, 255, 264.

If it is possible, as far as it depends on you, live at peace with everyone.

Romans 12:18

"If it is possible." Those words set us free from self-recrimination because they enable us to accept the fact that sometimes we cannot be reconciled with everyone. . . .

We bear no guilt if we have done the best that we can to restore broken relationships. If another party is not willing to relate, then we need the courage to move on in life without carrying around vestiges of that pain. . . .

The challenge to try again, however, predominates in Paul's exhortation. The second phrase, "as far as it depends upon you," emphasizes that efforts to restore relationships should be continued, continued some more, and still continued even more until we are thoroughly convinced that reconciliation is not achievable. Then, if we finally have to give up, the phrase "If it is possible" acknowledges the reality of human barriers that we cannot break. . . .

As followers of Jesus, furthermore, we are enabled to go beyond what is humanly reasonable in attempting to create peace. As Paul writes to the Corinthians, "The very spring of our actions is the love of Christ" (2 Cor. 5:14a, J. B. Phillips's paraphrase). Our human motivations don't create sufficient potential for peace, but . . . our faith gives us trampoline springs under all of our actions. Our ability to seek peace and pursue it has all the resources of God's love and grace at its disposal.

Furthermore, we remember that Jesus said, "If someone wants to sue you and take your tunic, let him have your cloak as well. If someone forces you to go one mile, go with him two miles" (Matt. 5:40-41). These words carry us beyond mere interpersonal relations and into the political realm. The Jews in Jesus' day were required to carry the packs of the Roman soldiers for one mile upon demand; Christ was encouraging the oppressed Jews to be willing to carry the soldiers' packs twice as far as required. Jesus invites us to surprise our enemies by responding with more than they demand.

Similarly, in Romans 12:17 Paul began widening his instructions to the Christian community to include "all persons," and here that widening out into the world is repeated. Paul encourages us to be cultivating peace with everyone.

Prayer

> *Prince of Peace, empower us to become peace-builders in every part of our lives . . . Amen.*

Truly the Community, pp. 262-64.

But the fruit of the Spirit is love, joy, peace, patience, kindness, goodness, faithfulness, gentleness, self-control.

Galatians 5:22-23, NASV

The Scriptures show us the real and tragic consequences of choosing sexual behaviors outside of God's design for human sexuality, and they offer a true and promising vision of what life can be like if it is lived faithfully.

How desperately our world needs the biblical visions! In our chaotic culture, many persons yearn for hope that their sexual lives could be more meaningful, that relationships could be permanent, that lasting happiness wouldn't constantly elude them.

The task of the Church, then, in sexual matters is to proclaim the visions of God, to invite the world around us into the values of God's kingdom, to model lives of faithfulness. What kind of persons should we be to support the mission of the Church?

As in all other aspects of life, to fulfill the purposes of God and to accomplish the mission of the Church in sexual matters, we need to be persons like Jesus. All the character traits exhibited by him in the Gospel accounts are virtues that we pray will be formed in ourselves. As the apostle Paul writes to the Philippians, we want to be persons who have the mind of Christ (2:5). Lest that be too overwhelming for us to think about, however, let us focus our attention on a representative sampling of the virtues of Jesus.

One of the best pictures of the virtues necessary to be persons able to live out the visions of God is given by Paul's listing in Galatians 5:22-23 of the fruit of the Spirit. We cannot live as God intended us to live without the empowerment of the Spirit at work in our characters.

It is necessary to note that in Galatians 5:22 both the noun *fruit* and the verb *is* are singular. There is only one fruit of the Spirit — the life of Christ formed in us — but it has many manifestations. . . .

These virtues, formed by the Spirit, can issue in behavior that is different from that manifested by those who are controlled by their own corrupted natures. . . .

The more we allow the Spirit to work in us the more truly we will reflect the life of Christ and the more thoroughly our lives will express the fruit of the Spirit.

Prayer
  Holy Spirit, form in us the virtues of faithful followers of Jesus . . .   *Amen.*
  Sexual Character, pp. 61-64.

Commit your way to the Lord;
   trust in him and he will do this:
He will make your righteousness shine like the dawn,
   the justice of your cause like the noonday sun.

Psalm 37:5-6

"Commit your way to the Lord," is, in the Hebrew, a very graphic image — "Roll unto *YHWH* your way." To roll it as one rolls stones into a groove puts our way firmly into place. . . .

If we roll our way unto the Lord, then he will act. . . . He will take care of everything that is associated with our "way." When we trust him, we can do good because he is the one doing it through us. . . .

Specifically, one of his good purposes will be to make our righteousness shine like the dawn. . . . As Isaiah 58:7-8 promises, when you work to "share your food with the hungry and to provide the poor wanderer with shelter — when you see the naked, to clothe him, and not turn away from your own flesh and blood, then your light will break forth like the dawn, and your healing will quickly appear; then your righteousness will go before you, and the glory of the Lord will be your rear guard." . . .

The Jerusalem Bible renders "like the noonday sun" in this way: "making your virtue clear as the light, your integrity as bright as noon." The words *virtue* and *integrity* stress the character, the goodness and wholeness, of righteousness and justice. God will certainly vindicate us . . . so that his truth will be clear to everyone.

Notice, finally, that again it is the Lord who accomplishes this, for indeed it is he who is doing the acting. He will exhibit our righteousness as a light to the world. The verb in this verse especially accentuates that he publishes the justice of our cause.

The accent in all this is on the invitation to us to keep on keeping on — doing good, being righteous and just, committing our way to *YHWH,* and trusting that the publishing, the vindicating, and the results of all our efforts are up to him. All we need to be concerned about is that we are thoroughly delighting in the Lord so that the deepest desires of our being are tied up with his faithfulness.

Prayer
   Righteous Lord, help us "roll our way" firmly into the groove of your good
   purposes . . .   Amen.

I'm Lonely, Lord, pp. 206, 210-11.

I saw in heaven another great and marvelous sign: seven angels with the seven last plagues — last, because with them God's wrath is completed.

Revelation 15:1

The book of Revelation is not trying to teach us how the world will end. Rather, it seeks to comfort us in our struggles with the hope that, in the end, evil will ultimately be vanquished forever.

This emphasis is reinforced by the seventh plague, which is depicted with all the elements from the First Testament for a theophany, an appearance of God — flashes of lightning, peals of thunder, and severe earthquakes. . . . These images reinforce that the end of the world is not going to be brought about by any warring between the kings of the earth, but by the mighty coming of God. Furthermore, the warring of the kings is not the cause of anything that happens, for the loud voice from the temple has already said that "it has come to pass" (16:17), and the Greek verb tense emphasizes that what has already come to pass remains. God's justice and righteousness have already had their way. Evil was destroyed at the cross, and now we will see effected what Christ already accomplished there.

The images of the next few verses reinforce this point. . . . However, the scene ends (v. 21) with this tragic declaration that the whole picture was meant to make more poignant to us: even though all these elements happen to warn human beings and to call them to repentance, still they respond only with more blasphemy. . . .

How terribly disturbing it is if Christians rejoice over a coming Armageddon, almost giddy because God will punish all the evil people in the world. No, instead we must leave this chapter with subdued hearts. How easily we, too, blaspheme God and do not repent. How have I failed to heed his warnings? What call is he giving me now to which I'm not paying heed? In what areas of my life am I being rebellious? . . . How can this be, that in my failures and weaknesses and doubts and sinfulness his grace still enfolds me? How can I spread the message of that grace more effectively? How can I urge my neighbors to repent and learn God's love?

It drives me to my knees in gratitude — this overwhelming grace of God!

Prayer

Gracious God, may The Revelation comfort, convict, and challenge us! . . .
Amen.

Joy in Our Weakness, pp. 180-81.

I will extol you, my God and King,
  and bless your name forever and ever.
Every day I will bless you,
  and praise your name forever and ever.

Psalm 145:1-2 (NRSV)

Notice the different words for speaking about God — extolling him to others, blessing God himself, praising him — and all of this speaking is due to God's character, which is too immense for us ever to capture sufficiently. Our witness is not for the purpose of making our congregation grow; it is simply because God is worthy of our praise and witness.

> One generation shall laud your works to another,
>   and shall declare your mighty acts. . . .
> They shall celebrate the fame of your abundant goodness,
>   and shall sing aloud of your righteousness.

(vv. 4, 7)

Again, the reason for speaking is the greatness of God. . . . Several important new themes are introduced.

One of the first responsibilities of our witness is to our children. By telling the youth of the Church how God works in our lives and in the world, we invite them to share our faith and to participate in the community of God's people. If we continue to meditate on God's splendor in his demeanor and deeds, then we will have more to proclaim and declare. The result will be that others ("they") will join in the celebrating and singing of God's grace and justice.

> The LORD is gracious and merciful,
>   slow to anger and abounding in steadfast love.
> The LORD is good to all,
>   and his compassion is over all that he has made.

(vv. 8-9)

These lines are a Hebrew creed. . . . We invite our children and our neighbors and strangers into this language of faith. We derive our identity from such testimony about God.

Prayer

> *Our God and King, your splendor is beyond our telling, but we try nonetheless. We want all the world to know you — our children, our friends, and everyone we meet — so that they may also rejoice in your greatness . . .   Amen.*

A Royal "Waste" of Time, pp. 349-50.

For by grace you have come to be and remain saved through faith, and this not from yourselves, the gift [is] of God, not from works, so that no one might boast.

Ephesians 2:8-9 (my translation)

We didn't do anything to become saved, and we continue in God's salvation through no effort or merit or worthiness on our part. Coming to faith is a gift; remaining in it is also sheer grace. How could we ever stop being altogether amazed by this grace? Surely such lavish mercy on God's part forms us into thankfulness, wonder, freedom, commitment, eagerness, and dedication to the praise of God's glory. . . .

Moreover, the following understanding of the nature of our lives underscores the grace once again:

For of [the Triune God] we are the workmanship, having been created in Christ Jesus for good works which God appointed beforehand, in order that we might walk in them. (Eph. 2:10, my translation)

Once again we are astounded by the vision, this entirely new perception of our daily existence, of what we are and how we live as a result of God's incomprehensible, mysterious, overwhelming grace. What bliss it is to discover that since God has dealt with our deadness (totally because of his character!), we are, therefore, a work of art! It is such an unfathomable change: from casket to fresh creation, from colorlessness to craftsmanship, from deadness to great deeds, already planned by God for us to fulfill. God has choreographed the ballet and set us free to dance. Oh, the ecstasy of dancing when Someone has given us new feet and formed them in his steps! . . .

In Matthew 5:14-16, Jesus calls us the light of the world. We are the lamp. No one, he says, lights a lamp and puts it under a bushel basket. Rather, a lamp is put on its stand from which it can give light to all in the house.

If we are the lamp in this parable, let's be consistent. We don't light ourselves, do we? Nor do we set ourselves on the lampstand. Nor do we invite the people into the house. God sets us on fire by grace, appoints us to our places of ministry by grace, brings the people into our lives by grace — and by grace liberates us simply to shine!

Prayer

Creator God, by grace you have fashioned us to be light for others. Help us to truly shine . . .   Amen.

The Unnecessary Pastor, pp. 154-55.

On Sunday all are gathered together in unity. The records of the apostles or the writings of the prophets are read for as long as time allows. The presider exhorts and invites us into the pattern of these good things. Then we all stand and offer a prayer.

From the Apology of Justin Martyr (c. A.D. 150)

Many complain that old liturgies are dead, and they're often right. In many places they are dead, for churches have turned them into mere traditionalism, which Jaroslav Pelikan calls "the dead faith of the living." Those who advocate using the Church's historic liturgies are searching instead for what Pelikan calls "the living faith of the dead" — that is, worship within a tradition that enables us to be actively conscious of the Church's past as well as of its eschatological future in Christ. As Pelikan insists, tradition has the capacity to develop while still maintaining its identity and continuity. . . . It places us into the story of God's people and stirs our sense of belonging to a continuing fellowship that stretches throughout time and space. . . .

As Graeme Hunter observes, "To repudiate one's past has consequences in the search for meaning in life. To find meaning in our lives is to see them as fitting into a larger story, which implies projecting them against the backdrop of some culture." Especially as the Church seeks to convey to its members the meaning of following Jesus and to incorporate them into the community of those who live in that discipleship, our liturgies must bear that larger story by sustaining the culture of worship. . . .

Instead of throwing away the past, we can update, renew, reform, revive it. We can use new melodies, fresh instruction, thorough education, gentle reminders of what we are doing and why. . . .

When we are careful not to let them become mindless habits, these worship practices subtly but powerfully over time affect the development of our character. . . . For example, our bowing at the altar can influence us to bow to God's will in our daily choices; our telling the creed to each other in worship invites us to share our faith more easily with our neighbors and work colleagues and family. Those who discard ritual as outmoded tradition do not understand its profound effects on character formation.

Prayer
>   *Lord of your Church, may our rituals connect and direct us in faith . . .*
>   *Amen.*

Reaching Out, pp. 256-59, 268.

If it is possible, as far as it depends on you, live at peace with everyone.

Romans 12:18

A strategy for peacekeeping suggests that we must not merely displace conflict. . . . Rather, knowing God's grace and peace, we must reduce violence, need, bondage, and anxiety at all levels. . . .

To respond to a hateful remark with a gentle answer minimizes *violence* between individuals. A person can be an agent of small group reconciliation on the job or in congregational arguments. Some people will become mediators to decrease violence on a worldwide scale, but such large contributions ought not to eclipse the fact that every individual effort to minimize any sort of violence on any level contributes to the calming of the world as a whole. . . .

Our Christian communities significantly minimize *need* when we work in soup kitchens, bring groceries to food banks, shelter the homeless or help to build them a home, contribute to agencies that bring medical aid to the poor, vote for legislation to combat poverty, question the use of government funds for disproportionate military spending, or "live more simply so that others may simply live." . . .

The people of God can participate in minimizing *bondage,* for that evil takes many forms in our world. Not only do we want to free the political prisoners of various totalitarian states, but we also want to deliver our friends and neighbors and enemies from the bondage of fear or loneliness, the slavery of ideological illusions, the prisons of despair and meaninglessness.

Similarly, the followers of Jesus can deliver others from a multitude of *anxieties* on various levels of society. Simple notes to those under stress to remind them of our concern, a kind word to someone in a difficult leadership position, the fervent prayers of the Church on behalf of world rulers — these are just a few ways in which Christians can serve to minimize anxiety and thereby build peace. . . .

Because we know that God himself always is at work (ultimately successfully) to bring the world to *shalom,* to wholeness, we can have hope as we pursue our own unique part of the whole — even when it seems that our efforts are not effective. . . . God is at work through each of us — and all of us together — to build peace!

Prayer

> *God of Shalom, use us to bring peace by reducing violence, need, bondage, and anxiety wherever we are able . . .   Amen.*

Truly the Community, pp. 262, 266-70.

347

For this reason a man will leave his father and mother and be united to his wife . . .
                                                                Genesis 2:24a

It seems to me that keeping a marriage alive is very much like keeping myself alive. The three main ingredients are a reason for living, intense self-discipline, and, most importantly, the grace of God. . . .

Christian marriage exists above all to symbolize the mystery of God's faithfulness to his people. That reason to live gives marriage a profound motivation . . . that enables us to decide before we ever enter into marriage that this WILL be permanent. Conflicts and confusions will end in resolution and repentance and reconciliation, not rupture. How could there be an end to God's loyalty and constant love? We are challenged to live accordingly. . . .

A second goal in Christian marriage is to raise children in a way that passes on to the next generation the traditions of the faith. . . .

Another goal . . . is for the couple to be strengthened by their union to reach out beyond themselves to others. . . .

A fourth goal for Christian marriage . . . is that a union in Christ is both a source and a sign of hope. . . . Our belief in God's provision for our future together, no matter what things might go wrong, can be a sign of hope to those around us. . . . Christian marriages boldly declare that the sovereign God is in control of the future and therefore can be trusted to lead us through the present. . . .

These four goals are prime examples, to which we could add particular goals specific to each marriage, which give the partners courage and grit, motivation and sustenance for practicing the personal and mutual disciplines necessary to maintain a vital marriage. How can our churches help members, especially young people and married couples, to accept and live by these goals? . . . We do not have to let the society around us convince us that our biblical goals are old-fashioned and naively idealistic. Rather, our visions are the true realism, the way God designed things to be, and we are bearers of the hope that God is at work to bring his design into existence.

Prayer
> *Christ, your Church's Bridegroom, implant these goals, and the discipline*
> *they call for, in the hearts of all marriage partners . . .   Amen.*
> *Sexual Character,* pp. 110-15.

Be still before the LORD and wait patiently for him;
  do not fret when men succeed in their ways,
  when they carry out their wicked schemes . . .

Psalm 37:7

Usually in our agitations we are not very quiet. When we cannot be restful, we are not very able to wait patiently before the LORD. The result is that we miss many of his gifts because we are too frantic to hear his voice.

I like to call my devotional practices "quiet time," to remind me that this block of time is set apart for being still before the LORD in order to hear God, so that my ways are not my own devising. This verse from . . . Psalm 37 deals with the need for those who are struggling against the wickedness of evil to learn to rest in the LORD. . . .

We live in the in-between times — days and years between the moment or progression when Christ became the center and focus of our existence and the time when he will come again or we will die and go home to be with him. So how do we live in the meanwhile? Christ didn't call us to any easy Christianity, a comfortable "I'm saved" lifestyle that isn't intensely wrapped up in the work of his kingdom. Rather, as we wait for our LORD to come back, we wait with eager longing and anguish, for often what surrounds us is corrupted. . . .

Our frustrations with the wickedness around us must serve only for kindling purposes, to encourage our active involvement in fighting evil, not to start a huge fire of vexation that burns out of control and immobilizes us. Our efforts to combat evil will become overwhelming and hopeless if we forget that ultimately God is in control of the world. . . .

If we can learn to be silent before *YHWH*, he will not be thwarted in his purpose to guide us and firmly root our ways. . . . Then we will experience this hopeful sequence from Paul's second letter to the Corinthians:

We are hard pressed on every side, but not crushed; perplexed, but not in despair; persecuted, but not abandoned; struck down, but not destroyed. (4:8-9)

Prayer
  Sovereign LORD, when the world around us seems evil indeed, keep us focused
  on listening to you for guidance, trusting that you are in control and that we
  will not be crushed . . .   Amen.

I'm Lonely, LORD, pp. 213-16.

"They will make war against the Lamb, but the Lamb will overcome them . . . and with him will be his called, chosen and faithful followers."

Revelation 17:14

Five essential items of the description that closes Revelation 17 must be noted. First of all, these kings and powers all receive their authority from someone else (v. 12). They serve one purpose, and that is to give power to the beast. All the evil influences in our world serve one end — to contradict and destroy the work of God and to draw humankind away from God. . . .

Second, none of these . . . are going to be able to accomplish anything in the end (v. 14) . . . because, let us never forget, the Lamb is Lord over every lord and King of all kings and everything else.

Third, wonder of wonders! We are named right there with him . . . the "called and chosen and faithful." . . . We are not going to be left behind. He has called us; he has chosen us; and by the power of his Spirit, we are faithful in response to his grace.

Fourth, . . . no place on earth escapes the demonic working of the forces of evil.

However, none of this is out of God's control. Verse 16 reminds us of this final point: the powers of evil betray and destroy themselves. . . . God's righteous wrath and punishment allow evil eventually to annihilate itself.

From the perspective of Christ's victory, evil is indeed already destroyed. . . . God's purposes of good cannot be thwarted — the last enemies were exposed and defeated in the cross and resurrection of Jesus. That is why chapter 18 begins with the declaration that Babylon *has* fallen. . . .

Perhaps our age has made up so many interpretations of The Revelation because we have not wanted to face how much its eighteenth chapter condemns us. In a world of gross inequities, *we* are reproached for our accumulation of silver and silks and spices. *We* are rebuked for our enculturation into a society that has fallen to the power of Mammon. We dare not read The Revelation to find out whom to blame as having ten heads. We can only read it to know our own sin and repent for it with humility and grief.

Prayer

    Conquering Lamb, we anticipate your ultimate victory with repentance and rejoicing . . .   Amen.

Joy in Our Weakness, pp. 186-88.

Every unwholesome word — let it not be proceeding out of your mouth, but if any [word is] good for building up what is needed, [speak it] in order that it might give grace to the ones hearing.

Ephesians 4:29 (my translation)

Paul is not merely giving rules here. Rather, he is inviting us into the design God has for his people. He teaches us the language of what it means to follow the Christian community's way of life.

I know that the above rendering of verse 29 is awkward, but I wanted to accentuate as the Greek text does the importance of our staying alert. . . . As God's people we are invited to make sure that all our words are ones that will build others up, provide what they need, offer grace to every single person who hears us. . . .

It will cost us to live this way because the world around us does not expect grace. People could think we're not too smart, might take advantage of us. . . . But imagine what the world could be like if everyone lived according to God's design for language that uplifts, that imparts grace! This is not a rule to spoil our fun, but a great invitation to live together kindly and truly and well. . . .

If we are living according to these instructions, we will also corporately pay the price. Our churches could grow, but they might not grow larger (or fatter) if we are truth tellers and grace speakers. However, they will certainly grow deeper if we will be what we are called to be. Meanwhile, people might suspect that we are being radical — but what better word could there be for the nonconformity of the gospel? . . .

Our world needs us, the Church, to be formed by the Word of God, to be immersed in its instructions — if it is indeed a suffering immersion, . . . if we are willing to bear the cost of really living true to God's instructions.

Can we let Paul woo us with the goodness of these instructions? He summons us to alternative attitudes, alternative words, alternative behaviors, alternatives of our whole being personally and corporately. What he wants is for our character to be formed into a certain kind of person, the image of God.

Prayer

Graciously speaking God, may your Word form us so that our words honor you and uplift others . . .   Amen.

The Unnecessary Pastor, pp. 157-59.

Praise the God of our salvation;
hosts on high, his pow'r proclaim;
heav'n and earth and all creation,
praise and glorify his name.

"Foundling Hospital Collection" (1796), alt.

If worship stays well focused on the Trinity, our children will become better equipped to be God's witnesses to their diverse worlds. . . .

Of course, it will be extremely difficult to form strong Christian character if the worship hour is the only time the Church has to nurture it, but worship's subtle influence on character dare not be misdirected. . . . With so much quality contemporary as well as traditional music to choose from, why does so much of the new music used in many congregations lack theological depth, biblical images, motivation to be about God's purposes of witnessing, justice building, and peacemaking in the world? What kind of people are our worship services forming?

Second Timothy 3:14-17 speaks about Timothy being trained throughout his childhood in the Holy Scriptures — trained to *know* them and be formed by them and not just to "believe" as if that were a leap in the dark, to have habits and not simply to make a single choice. Our offspring — and perhaps we — need that kind of training much more than our parents did, since the society no longer supports it and since so many cultural forces alien to the gospel impinge on our lives and urge our conformity. . . .

This is a wonderful description of worship for us and for our children: that by God's gracious invitation and Christ's intercession and the Spirit's enabling we are welcomed to learn of the Trinity through the biblical narratives passed on by faithful witnesses. Gathered in the community of saints, we are formed by the truth taught in worship music and Word and ritual so that out of our Christian character will flow the witness of our words and deeds.

Growing up in the postmodern world that surrounds us, our children deeply yearn for stability, morality, security, fidelity, faith, hope, and love. These deep needs can only be met through the One who meets our deepest need for Truth. Let us make sure that the worship services we plan and conduct present to them that Truth in all its clarity and beauty and goodness.

Prayer

Faithful Trinity, direct our choices concerning worship, so that all attending will encounter your truth and be formed thereby into witnesses in word and deed . . .   Amen.

Is It a Lost Cause? pp. 64, 81-82, 86-87.

Every Service, whether elaborate or spare, sung or said, should be within the framework of the common rite of the Church, so that the integrity of the rite is always respected and maintained.

Lutheran Book of Worship (1978)

The point of liturgy is to give the service shape and flow . . . so that worship is not a string of unrelated items. The services outlined in denominational hymnals fundamentally respond to three different rhythms in Christian life with basic formats and many variations. The rhythm of the week breaks out of time with Sabbath/Sunday worship involving the Word and Supper, lessons, sermons, hymns, offerings, and blessings. The rhythm of the day is observed with the morning and evening prayer and the eight offices in between. Worship liturgies for the rhythm of life celebrate baptisms, confirmations, weddings, commissions, and burials. . . .

The Lord's Supper in all its fullness . . . has multiple meanings and moods. . . . In Lent, the Supper is more mournful (sharing the grief of the apostles at its institution), humble (to think that our sins sent Christ to the cross), and focused upon the past. In the Easter season, the Eucharist is more joyous (Christ is risen indeed!) and looks to the future and the heavenly feast after we arise. Pentecost concentrates more on the present through discerning the Body of Christ, who, in our midst, calls us by the Spirit's power to be a community without barriers. . . .

Liturgy elements surrounding the focus on the Word are equally dramatic. These gathering pieces prepare us for the Word: confession and absolution remove all barriers between us and God; . . . the invocation places us under the sign of the cross; an opening hymn sets the tone for the day; the *Kyrie* asks for mercy for all the congregation's needs; the *Gloria in Excelsis* or the new "This is the Feast" both join in the angels' praises; the collect prays about themes to be sounded in the Scripture lessons. Then the lessons are introduced or summarized with psalms, choir anthems, or versicles; the Gospel is spotlighted by responses as the service's first high point; and the hymn of the day prepares for, or responds to, the sermon. The creed joins all the worshipers together in declaring the whole substance of this faith community, and the prayers unite us in concerns for God's will to be done.

Prayer

Thank you, Lord, for liturgies! . . .   Amen.

Reaching Out, pp. 262-64.

Never take your own revenge, beloved, but leave room for the wrath of God, for it is written, "Vengeance is mine, I will repay," says the Lord.

Romans 12:19 (NASV)

Of course, Paul realizes the difficulty of resisting our human impulses to seek revenge. We are comforted by his insertion at this point of a term of affection for his readers. . . .

Paul evidently intends this . . . as extra encouragement for the Roman Christians in the difficult task of giving up their rights to justice. Holy anger against injustice has its place, and the Scriptures — especially the Hebrew prophets — exhort us to work for the rights of others. However, in cases concerning ourselves we are urged not to seek retribution. That injunction is terribly hard to follow. . . .

Paul's next phrase doubles the difficulty. Choosing the stronger of two Greek conjunctions for *but,* he tells us "greatly to the contrary" what should characterize us instead of avenging. Paul's point is accentuated by the fact that here he puts the verb in the imperative, . . . which signifies a decisive once-for-all action that we should undertake.

What we should do, he writes literally, is "give place in the wrath." J. B. Phillips's paraphrase underlines this point: "Never take vengeance into your own hands, my dear friends; stand back and let God punish if he will."

We are to give place, once and for all. That means to give the outworking of wrath over to another, to give up with finality our desire to inflict punishment on one who has wronged us, and to NEVER GO BACK!

Then, to convince us further, Paul adds a quotation from Deuteronomy, which he introduces with the standard formula "for it stands written." This formula . . . asserts that whatever God has caused to be written in the Scriptures will continue always to apply and can be counted on as an authority for our lives.

That phrase is very encouraging and a source of security. When all else passes away, we can know that God's Word abides forever.

Precisely what "has been written" in this instance is the fact that vengeance belongs to the LORD; he himself will do the recompensing. . . .

Therefore, we can confidently leave all matters of vengeance in his hands and trust that whatever is appropriate will happen.

Prayer
> *Merciful Lord, thank you for directing us away from wrath . . .   Amen.*

Truly the Community, pp. 271-74, 278.

Oh, blest the house, whate'er befall,
where Jesus Christ is All in All!
For if he were not dwelling there,
how dark and poor and void it were!

                              Christoph C. L. von Pfeil, 1712-1784

My favorite story about discipline concerns Yehudi Menuhin, the great concert violinist and conductor. When an awed listener praised his exquisite performance by insisting, "I would give my life to play like that," he gently replied, "I have."

That story demonstrates a critical truth that has been lost in our culture — that disciplines (such as the disciplines of practicing the violin or building a marriage) produce freedom and delight. . . . They enable us truly to live and give our best. . . .

What personal and mutual disciplines are needed to strengthen marriages? . . . Let us simply reflect on ways in which our focus on an ethics of character and on the Christian community as the locus for nurturing virtues gives us extra insights into the process. . . .

Our communities could promote the disciplines of respect, habits of courtesy, and deeds of kindness that build marriage. . . .

Our congregations could make better use of the marriage models that are available in our midst in order to strengthen other marriages and foster disciplines. . . .

Probably the most important discipline for Christian marriages is that of mutual confession and absolution. . . . We could make it a constant practice to confess our faults and forgive each other's errors before the day's end. . . .

Various other disciplines for marriage come out of the fact that we are created and called to image God. For example, a God willing to sacrifice his own Son for the salvation of his people invites us to be willing to sacrifice our own interests for the well-being of a spouse. . . .

A final discipline that is essential to the strength of both the Christian community and marriage . . . is the fact that we nurture faithfulness by consciously upbuilding each other. . . . How full is the happiness when we do so.

Prayer

Heavenly Father, strengthen in all marriages the life-long, life-sacrificing commitment it takes to build a faith-filled and faithful, lasting relationship . . . Amen.

                                   Sexual Character, pp. 116-19.

The Lord delights in the way of the [strong] man
  whose steps he has made firm;
though he stumble, he will not fall,
  for the Lord upholds him with his hand. . . .

Consider the blameless, observe the upright;
  there is a future for the man of peace.

                                                                Psalm 37:23-24, 37

Psalm 37 tells us *why* we can know for sure that we will not be destroyed, though we might have to suffer. *YHWH* upholds with his hand the one whose steps he is establishing. The verb *upholds* encourages us with the promise that we can lean or rest on God, who will always support us. . . .

In these pictures the Lord is both capable of healing us and perfectly willing to do so. . . .

The poet of Psalm 37 has had ample time to observe these qualities of the Lord. He notes in verse 25, just following our section, that he is now old and has never seen the righteous forsaken. Then, in the next several verses, he continues his words of wisdom to the young and advises them to turn away from evil and to watch out for the wicked.

The last line of our excerpt, verse 37, summarizes well the message of the psalm. The poet urges us, "Watch the complete one and see the upright, for there is a posterity to a man of *shalom*." There will be a future not to the warrior but to the one who seeks peace instead. . . .

A person of *shalom* lives in right relationship with God, and, therefore, in right relationship with him- or herself and with others. That kind of person — one who is tranquil and contented and fulfilled and whole — does indeed have a posterity. . . .

For this reason the poet urges his listeners to "consider the blameless." . . . The ones we are to watch are those who are complete — the morally innocent, the ones having integrity. . . .

The more we observe those who have integrity, the more we will follow their example and rest in the wholeness that *YHWH* delights to establish for us.

Prayer
  Healing Lord, you have promised us support and a future. Help us learn
  from the role models around us the way to live in peace and wholeness . . .
  Amen.

                                                    I'm Lonely, Lord, pp. 213, 217-19.

After this I heard what sounded like the roar of a great multitude in heaven shouting:

"Hallelujah!
Salvation and glory and power belong to our God" . . .

Revelation 19:1

All of this noise in chapter 19 proclaims a momentous change of perspective. For several chapters The Revelation has focused on the corruption of Babylon and the way she has corrupted the earth. Anyone not in touch with the reality of sin will grasp it easily if he or she pays attention to the evil described in these chapters. Now, in 19:2-4, the fall of Babylon is announced and praised. . . .

Revelation 19:5-10 ties together several main points of the New Testament. The passage talks about praise, celebration, equality, blessedness, rejoicing, the righteous deeds of the saints, and the purity of the bride who is . . . dressed in white linens (v. 8), which are defined as the righteous deeds of the saints. We must read that description in the light of the whole chapter, lest we think that those righteous deeds earn her salvation. . . . Rather, the true church is obedient in her faith, and a submissive church is faithful in that obedience. Verse 8 does not deny justification by grace, but it stresses instead that a transformed life is the proper response to the call of the bridegroom. . . .

How blessed to participate, then, in the marriage feast. . . . All are made welcome except the one who has refused to accept the wedding garment. . . .

Once again the importance of our own weakness is emphasized. God doesn't invite us to the feast because we are worthy; . . . rather, we truly come to the wedding supper when, out of our helplessness, we joyfully receive the gifts of God's gracious banquet. . . .

This is the attitude that prevails in a theology of weakness. In spite of the sufferings of the present moment, in which all of us are reduced to equality before the Lord whom we worship together, we have tasted of the final victory. And that gives us courage to put up with the pain of the meanwhile.

Prayer

Gracious Lord, unworthy as we are, you have offered us salvation as a gift.
We respond with joy and thankfulness, desiring to live obediently, faithfully,
and patiently in this already but not yet time . . .   Amen.

Joy in Our Weakness, pp. 190-94.

But you did not so learn Christ!

Ephesians 4:20 (my translation)

That verse ought to be underlined, circled, or starred in our Bibles and put up in our churches on broad, brilliant banners to help us keep remembering that the Christian community is an alternative society. We practice a way of life radically different from the ways of the world with its . . . estrangement from the life of God . . . (Eph. 4:17-19). In immense contrast, we have learned Christ — and continue to be formed in his ways! . . .

If faith is a language to be taught and practiced, then we spread it not by translating, but by immersing newcomers in it. The learners submit themselves to it and exercise its skills. Think about how children learn a language — by hearing it and imitating it. . . . Similarly, the way to help our neighbors know Christ is to live his resurrection life so that they realize how Christ makes a difference and want to participate in his life too.

Church members find themselves powerless in the world and not able to invite neighbors into the faith because Christians often don't live in ways that give any warrant for belief. Observers don't seem to be saying, "Oh, you Christians have a superb attitude about time. I can see that in the way you observe the Sabbath." They don't say, "Oh, you Christians have a great perspective on money; you are so generous and don't seem to be scrambling after it like the rest of society," or "It amazes me that you Christians never try to pull power plays." The best evangelist I've ever known was a dear man who spoke English so poorly that he was painfully shy. . . . Yet his grace and goodness were evident to all his peers. Anyone who ever needed any help went to Peter, for the people knew that he loved them.

God's love through us is the language we speak, the way of life in which we are engaged. The Trinity's grace undergirds our customs and practices and habits of faith, which show how we have learned Christ. The Holy Spirit uses Scripture and the community of faith and the risen Christ within us to train us in those traditions and disciplines and language. By these means God draws the world to himself.

Prayer

Holy Spirit, help us live what we have learned as an open invitation to everyone to know Christ . . .   Amen.

The Unnecessary Pastor, pp. 160-62.

Praise the Lord! For he is glorious;
never shall his promise fail. . . .

"Foundling Hospital Collection" (1796), alt.

What we need in worship is the Truth. . . . We must help our offspring understand the whole truth that we remain sinful and fallible. We do that in worship with genuine confession (and the announcement of forgiveness). We also proclaim in worship what the Scriptures thoroughly teach us about our nature being helplessly sinful, hopelessly lost. That fact forces us to see that we cannot know the Truth entirely, that our eyes are blinded by sin, that our understanding of God is only partial. But that does not negate the Truth of God we confess, nor our recognition of Christ who is the Truth, the Life, and the Way.

Against the postmodern rejection of meta-narrative — that is, of the possibility that there is any universal, overarching Truth that is true for all people in all places — I believe that we Christians can humbly and gladly celebrate with our children in worship the non-oppressive, all-inclusive story of a triune God who creates, redeems, and unifies as manifestations of his perfect love for the whole world. The Christian meta-narrative, specific parts of which are declared in our worship each week, and the whole of which is proclaimed in our worship over time, is the account of a promising God who always keeps his promises — a Truth clearly seen in the First Testament history of Israel and most clearly seen in the history of Jesus of Nazareth, who died and rose again in fulfillment of God's promises. We believe that this meta-narrative will reach its ultimate fulfillment when Jesus comes again to bring God's promised gracious reign to fruition — and thus the meta-narrative of God's kingdom already initiated and celebrated in worship gives us all that our children most deeply need of hope, purpose, and fulfillment in this present life. . . .

Furthermore, our worship must contain nothing but the Truth. Music, songs, Scripture lessons, sermons, liturgical forms, architecture . . . are all means by which God invites, reveals, and forms us. . . .

Our children's young minds — and our finite minds — cannot begin to grasp all that there is to learn about God, but every time the community gathers we have the opportunity to add to our total store of truth.

Prayer
Triune God, thank you for teaching us your truth as we worship you . . .
Amen.

Is It a Lost Cause? pp. 64, 78-80.

359

O God of earth and altar, in mercy hear our cry;
our earthly rulers falter, our people drift and die;
the walls of gold entomb us, the words of scorn divide;
take not Thy thunder from us, but take away our pride.

G. K. Chesterton, 1906

Every week more than 53,000 people leave churches and never come back. The percentage of active Christians in the world has fallen from 29.0 percent in 1900 to 23.3 percent of today's population. Losses in the Western and formerly Communist worlds slightly outweigh Christian growth in the Two-Thirds World. . . .

Something is seriously wrong if so many people do not find it worthwhile to continue participating in the Church! . . .

If worship is fulfilling its subversive role, it will present to church members and visitors alike what C. Welton Gaddy calls *"a confrontation with reality."* . . .

How often does this happen? Does our worship regularly turn us upside down? If it occurred often, we would probably be much more intent on inviting everyone we know to participate in such worship, too. Even as the Samaritan woman left her water jar and ran back to the village to get her neighbors (see John 4), we would set aside our other, mundane concerns in our eagerness to share the water of life with our world. . . .

If worship only attracts and does not disturb or quicken, it will leave visitors and regular participants unchanged. For worship to be subversive, however, does not negate the possibility that it will be attractive to outsiders. . . . Worship that is planned with . . . essential guidelines in mind can welcome strangers with exactly what they need and most profoundly desire. . . .

The key to true worship is for God to be its subject. In his *Exit Interviews,* William Hendricks discovered that many stopped participating in worship because of boredom. He summarizes, "It was not just that these gatherings were not interesting; they were not *worshipful.* They did little to help people meet God." . . . Music style and liturgy type won't matter if God is not found in them, if they do not incarnate God's self-giving or enable us to respond to God's grace.

Prayer
> *God of earth and altar, help all who plan worship services to keep them worshipful — full of opportunities for worshipers to meet and honor you . . .*
> *Amen.*

Reaching Out, pp. 205, 280, 286-88.

"But if your enemy is hungry, feed him, and if he is thirsty, give him a drink; for in so doing you will heap burning coals upon his head."

Romans 12:20 (NASV)

We need to . . . recognize the close connection between this verse and the preceding three. Showering our enemies with love and kindness is one way to put the right behavior before others rather than to recompense evil for evil (v. 17), one way to do all that we can to cultivate peace (v. 18), and one way to avoid seeking revenge (v. 19). Paul offers excellent directions for fulfilling the previous three exhortations by quoting Proverbs 25 (especially vv. 21-25). . . .

As Peter Cotterell and Max Turner assert in their book *Linguistics and Biblical Interpretation,* an explanation of this difficult passage . . . may be found in

> an Egyptian text . . . from which it appears that a penitent would go to the individual he had wronged, bearing on his head a clay dish containing burning coals. The meaning of the metaphor as it is used in Proverbs then becomes clear: if a man acts generously towards his enemy he may bring him to repentance. And if this is the sense of the metaphor as Paul understood it, then he is telling us that if a Christian has an enemy, and instead of threatening him forgives him, he is likely to bring his enemy to the point of repentance; metaphorically the Christian is himself putting the clay bowl of burning coals on the man's head and starting him on his way to repentance.

The wise man's instructions to minister to our enemies in practical ways requires a good job of assessing their needs. For each enemy we can surely find certain needs about which we might do something. . . .

The point is that our actions are specific and intentional and directed. . . .

The whole metaphor in Proverbs, therefore, promises that when we react to our enemies by caring for them, Yahweh will make us more whole. That summarizes well what we have learned in Romans 12:19-20. To be vindictive does not lead to wholeness for ourselves or for our community. Rather, to give up our desire for revenge and to work instead toward meeting the needs of our enemies is a means by which Yahweh can bring us back to *shalom.*

Prayer
God of shalom, teach us to love and serve our enemies . . .   Amen.

Truly the Community, pp. 280-85.

Do not be overcome by evil, but overcome evil with good.

Romans 12:21

This last verse of Romans 12 . . . emphasizes that each of us as individuals must do our own overcoming of evil, or else we as particular persons will be overcome.

This final emphasis on the singular is not meant to take us out of the community and set us off by ourselves. . . . Rather, in the framework and with the support of the whole Body of Christ, we are encouraged for the battles that we have to fight alone; but ultimately each of us must deal with our own particular attitudes. . . .

Our attitudes are the key factor in fulfilling this final verse in Romans 12. Either the evil we must constantly face in a world governed by darkness will seem too large for us and we will give in to despair, or we will remember that Christ has already conquered the principalities and powers and that he shares his triumph with us. To choose the latter will give us the motivation and the power . . . to overcome evil with good. We especially need each other in the Christian community for reminders of Christ's victory and for encouragement to keep fighting faithfully against the powers of evil that we encounter in our daily lives and work. . . .

Evil doesn't just hit us generally. It comes to each of us in particular temptations, specific trials, individual difficulties and persons and things. We are not to be conquered by any of those unique forms of evil. . . .

The fact of life is that evil exists. But we don't have to be overcome by it; instead, we have the power to overcome. . . . We know that at the cross Christ defeated all the powers of evil and death arrayed against him, and someday all the forces of evil will be ultimately overcome. . . . The assurance of that ultimate victory gives us the courage to keep battling. . . .

With our eyes wide open to the mercies of God, we can live as a community of God's people amid the challenges of the evil of the world that surrounds us.

Prayer

    Merciful God, empower us in our daily struggle with evil that we might overcome it with good, and give us hope in your ultimate victory . . .   Amen.

Truly the Community, pp. 287-91, 294.

I waited patiently for the Lord*;*
   he turned to me and heard my cry. . . .
He put a new song in my mouth.
   a hymn of praise to our God.
Many will see and fear
   and put their trust in the Lord*.*

Psalm 40:1, 3

Out of my loneliness came ministry. . . . God kept turning around things that caused me pain and continued to use them as vehicles for witness and service. That is also the message of Psalm 40. This psalm includes a lament, . . . but it also includes a hymn of praise as the poet's response to all the good things that God brought out of his trouble. When David declares that he had waited patiently for the Lord and that *YHWH* had turned to him, heard his cry, and lifted him out of the pit, he sets the scene for the praises that follow. . . .

The opening phrase, "I waited patiently," . . . stresses the hope and patience involved, until the waiting ended in deliverance. The result of the deliverance, in turn, was witness. . . .

The poet declares that *YHWH* "put a new song in my mouth, a hymn of praise to our God." Notice that *YHWH* places the song in his mouth. . . .

Next, David tells us that from a new song of praise, "many will see and fear and put their trust in the Lord." . . . In so many ways God can use things we would never expect as vehicles of praise to draw people closer to himself. . . .

When the poet assesses what God has done, he realizes that the latter has accomplished many . . . deeds that fill a person with awe because they are so extraordinary. . . .

This gives us tremendous confidence as we seek to share with others the good news of faith. . . . If we see a friend after being apart for a long time and have to catch up on everything, words just come pouring out. In the same way, our witness to the wonders of the Lord's doing comes out of the overflow of our lives. As we observe his glorious works, we proclaim them with joy because their magnificence overwhelms us.

Prayer
   Trustworthy Lord*, grant us patience, deliverance, and a new song! . . .*
   Amen.

I'm Lonely, Lord*,* pp. 220-25.

The Spirit and the bride say, "Come!" And let him who hears say, "Come!" Whoever is thirsty, let him come; and whoever wishes, let him take the free gift of the water of life.

Revelation 22:17

Truly, when we are burdened and persecuted, we learn the depth of the word *come*. When we are defenseless, we must ask our Defender to come; when we struggle endlessly with the simple tasks of life, we look forward eagerly to the invitation to come to rest. Sometimes if we lack the human resources to meet our basic needs, we become more aware of the thirst that yearns to be satisfied and waits to be bidden to come. . . .

We are eager, therefore, to respond to the Spirit's invitation to come. God's people have continued throughout the ages to be the bride saying, "Come." We enter into her tradition and join "all the ones who hear" in passing on the summons to others. We respond both by coming and by swelling the chorus of those saying, "Come." . . .

We each accept God's invitation as individuals, yet we come together as a community. We need each other for the coming, though no one can receive God's gracious gifts for another. . . .

To offer us the gift of the water of life was costly for God; it required the sacrifice of the Lamb who was slain. The gift had to be purchased, but its cost to us is free. We dare never take it for granted, therefore, as if the gift were worthless, nor do we dare get all caught up in our own efforts to earn the gift or deserve it or pay God back for it. . . .

We might refuse to listen to the bride's calling, . . . we might refuse to acknowledge our thirst, . . . we might refuse to drink the only water that will quench our thirst. . . . All these are our own choices for response. On the other hand, if we accept the gift of life-giving water, it is through no merit on our own, . . . for this ability, too, is a free gift from God. That is why the word *come* is so precious. It simply invites us into Christ's waiting and welcoming arms.

Prayer
>   *Gracious Trinity, how precious, indeed, is your invitation — come! . . .*
>   *Amen.*

Joy in Our Weakness, pp. 212, 215-16.

364

'Tis grace has brought me safe thus far,
and grace will lead me home.

John Newton, 1725-1807

The most important ingredient in Christian marriage is the grace of God. Grace brings us together and holds us together. The more we are aware of the giftedness of it all, the more thoroughly we can delight in it.

But we Christians are not very good at living under grace. Instead, we put ourselves under what Robin Scroggs calls "performance principles," both in our relationship with God and with each other, and as a result we lose the possibility for living out of freedom and response rather than necessity and obligation. . . .

One essential habit in my marriage with Myron builds its gracefulness. When something goes wrong, or the other person does something wrong, we both try to be quick to say, "I love you." Myron's constant love is pure grace — a gift I can't earn or deserve or repay, an incarnation of God's grace — and his assurance of its permanence frees me to confess my fault or to hope in spite of a new physical setback.

Another habit that enfolds us in grace is the farewell prayer at the end of our Sabbath day together. In this Havdalah we thank God for all the gifts of the special day, especially for the gift of each other. This happens in other prayers, too — frequently at mealtimes — but Sabbath prayers particularly build the sense of grace in our marriage because one of the major purposes for celebrating the day is to become more aware of the grace of God. . . .

What a great preserver of marriage it is to know that even when our life together is not "happy," especially because of outward circumstances that are inflicted upon us, we can still experience the Joy of knowing that God is good and that these evils which befall us can indeed work together for our good. The basis is grace, manifested undoubtedly for us in the cross of Jesus Christ and affirmed by the testimony of God's people throughout the history of the believing community.

Prayer

> *God of Grace, keep us mindful of your special gift of grace, which redeems our failures and protects our relationships, even as it offers us eternal life . . .*
> *Amen.*

Sexual Character, pp. 119-21.

Therefore, be noticing accurately how you are walking, not as unwise, but as wise, re-deeming the time, for the days are evil.

Ephesians 5:15-16 (my translation)

Our faith is not simply intellectual agreement, nor is it an expression of universal religious emotions. These ways of understanding faith won't lead us to serving others and loving our neighbors. Rather, faith is a "walking," a language, a way of life. . . .

I love the old King James phrasing for verse 15, "Walk circumspectly." . . . It captures well Paul's emphasis here that we are to look all around (Latin *circum*) carefully as we walk/live. . . .

We look all around us as we go through life to observe what is happening in the places where we walk, so that we remain culturally concerned though not culturally conformed — not necessarily relevant in the world's terms, but relational. . . .

To walk circumspectly requires a more thorough look at the issues, not only with regard to wars and politics and economics, but also with regard to theological and ecclesiological controversies. . . .

To walk circumspectly is to recognize the complexity of issues instead of reducing them to two polarized options. . . .

We get a wider perspective concerning the whole world, because the Church is found throughout the world. We can learn more deeply the affairs of nations by listening to our brothers and sisters who live in them. Moreover, being Church keeps us from drowning in despair over the world's catastrophes, because we remember that Christ is still Lord over the cosmos, that someday God will wipe away these sorrows and struggles forever, and that the Holy Spirit empowers us to be agents of justice and healing and peacemaking in the world now. . . .

Walking circumspectly both keeps us from being formed by the culture . . . and enables us to minister to our neighbors. . . . To walk circumspectly is to live within the framework of interpretation established by the canonical narrative of our promising God. If we are seeking formation by that narrative, then we don't change the Scriptures to fit in with the world; rather, the Scriptures redescribe the world for us. By means of that biblical redescription we understand more truly our neighbors, our milieu, and the gifts we offer.

Prayer

Promising God, help us "walk" our faith in service to others, seeing the world through your eyes, directed by the Scriptures, with hope . . .   Amen.

The Unnecessary Pastor, pp. 162-66.

Meditations for Special Days

The First Sunday of Advent

*"Prepare the way for the Lord,
    make straight paths for him."*

Mark 1:3, quoting Isaiah 40:3

No doubt a huge proportion of people in our culture will be disappointed in this year's Christmas if all it means to them are material elements of cards, decorations, gifts, and parties, or if they are trying to recapture some romantic magic from exaggerated childhood memories. The Church, in contrast, offers a great gift — which counteracts such disillusionment — in the season of Advent. Advent teaches us to long for a Messiah, who never disappoints us!

Advent wreaths teach us to wait and hope. When I was a child, our wreath had candles for every day of the season — tall purple ones (for repentance) and pink ones (for Joy) for the Sundays, short red ones (the liturgical color of the saints) for all the weekdays, and two large white ones for Christmas Eve and Christmas Day. Every evening we lit candles for however many Sundays we'd already celebrated and the weekday candles for only the particular week we were in. Then we had our nightly Advent devotions with hymns sung in four-part harmony. Each night anticipation grew for Christmas Eve, when all but one of the candles would finally be lit at once to celebrate that the Christ Child, the Light of the world, had come to our house.

Advent also teaches us alternativity. Since we await a Messiah who came in poverty and gave his life to serve others, the season helps us ponder ways to keep our Christmas celebration simple.

Here are a few suggestions of ways to prepare for Christ's coming: participate in special Advent worship services; invite neighbors for Advent devotions rather than giving presents; spend the season preparing homemade gifts; channel time and money to care for those in need — for example, by assisting in local programs for the poor or by giving gifts in honor of others to such agencies as MAP International, Heifer Project, or Habitat for Humanity . . . ; invite foreign students to share your home when their universities close; join carolers in visiting shut-ins; spend extra time in prayer for peace and hope in the world.

Prayer

Coming Christ, in this season of waiting, repentance, and hope, enable us to prepare our hearts for your indwelling by imitating your generous sacrificing and suffering on our behalf . . .   Amen.

Adapted from materials prepared for a congregational Advent
workshop and from a "Pastor's Perspective" column in
The Olympian [Olympia, Washington], December 1982.

Christmas Eve

For to us a child is born, . . . and he will be called . . . Prince of Peace.

Isaiah 9:6

How much we need the gift of the Christ Child, the "Prince of Peace"!

Certainly we all observe the lack of peace in our culture and world — even in our churches. Indeed, I readily see "unpeace" in myself. I violate peace not only in hasty words or angry attitudes but also in failing to be the reconciler Jesus calls his followers to be.

So much of our culture's unpeace arises because of greed, our proliferating needs and wants. How easily, especially at Christmastime, we and our children concentrate on all the "stuff" we want.

No matter how many presents we accumulate, there is always something *else* to be had — better toys, newer models, fancier clothes, faster computers. As time goes by, toys break, the excitement wanes, and we discover the truth of the Preacher's words "All is vanity" (Eccles. 1:2b, NRSV).

If we prepare for the true gift of Christmas in Advent repentance and Joy, we discern the source of our yearnings in our profound thirst for God. That awareness frees us from our need to accumulate and grooms us to participate in our Prince's reign, which he continues to establish and uphold "with justice and righteousness" (Isa. 9:7).

How much we need the Christ Child! We cannot free ourselves from all the unpeace — the subtle forms of violence against neighbors near and far, the injustices entrenched in the wealth of our nation over against the rest of the world.

That consciousness prevents any romanticizing of Christ's birth. He came into, and himself experienced, exactly such darkness, poverty, oppression, and confusion. And to all of us "people walking in darkness" he has brought "a great light" (Isa. 9:2).

Moreover, because "the light [of his salvation] has dawned" upon us, we are transformed by his Spirit's power into a new people who join in his work of peacemaking and justice building — always knowing that "the zeal of the LORD Almighty will accomplish this" (Isa. 9:7c), and not our own efforts. The LORD, the covenant God, will accomplish the reconciling of the cosmos and embrace us in Christ's reign to embody his purposes!

He is the "Wonderful Counselor, Mighty God, Everlasting Father, Prince of Peace" (Isa. 9:6) who defeated the powers of darkness that threaten, hinder, usurp, and destroy the world's peace. Now, in this in-between time before God's reign comes to total fruition, "His authority shall grow continually," and consequently "there shall be endless peace" (Isa. 9:7a, NRSV).

Prayer

> *Come, Lord Jesus. Reign in us to bring your peace . . .*   *Amen.*

Abridged and modified from Marva Dawn's "Faithways" column in *The Lutheran,*
December 2000, p. 6.

Christmas Day

"Ceaseless My Rejoicing" (A Carol of Paradox)

Gentle comes the might of God:
Poor, the gen'rous Savior —
All of God wrapped in a child,
Mystery forever!

Humble shepherds angels call —
Magi at a manger,
Promised Rescuer so small,
Peace in spite of danger!

My frail heart can't take it in,
All is wrapped in splendor.
Once so captured, lost in sin,
Now I'm free to render

Praises! Praises burst my soul;
Songs, my gladness voicing.
Oh, the Christ Child makes me whole —
Ceaseless, my rejoicing!

Alleluia!

A Royal "Waste" of Time, p. 316; first written for the adult choir of St. John Lutheran Church, Vancouver, Washington, as an anthem (set to music by David Hendricksen) for Christmas 1992.

The angel said to me, "These words are trustworthy and true. The Lord, the God of the spirits of the prophets, sent his angel to show his servants the things that must soon take place."

Revelation 22:6

Immediately after the angel's words about truth and trustworthiness, the Christ himself speaks and promises that he is coming quickly. How blessed are the ones who heed the words of the prophecy of the Revelation! As we wait for his coming, our time is not to be spent in useless speculation about how and when he will come or how to literalize the thousand-year reign and the tribulation. Rather, we are to be busy keeping the words of the book — following the warnings sent to the seven churches and still applicable to situations in our times; recognizing the presence of evil in this world but praising God for his lordship anyway; faithfully enduring with biblical patience the tribulations we must suffer in order that we might participate in the suffering work of the kingdom; and serving as priests for the world.

The trouble throughout the centuries has been that Christianity has not found the proper balance between heaven and earth in its perspectives. To be too heavenly minded is to be no earthly good. If all we do is speculate about what it might be like when we finally get to the holy city, we will not be involved in the present work of the kingdom. The question must rather be how we are to *be* the holy city now.

In our day perhaps the threat is greater to err on the other side, to get so involved in trying to remedy the situation of this world (which will someday pass away anyway) that we lose track of the heavenly city for which we are headed. If our relationship with God does not motivate our present service, then it will not last, for we will have lost our first love. However, if we serve out of adoration and genuine worship of the Lord God Almighty and the Lamb that was slain, then our hatred of false doctrine and our patience and our works will be commended.

Blessed are those in the process of keeping the words of the Revelation — those who faithfully live according to the kingdom as they wait for its grand fulfillment.

Prayer

O Lord, keep us both heavenly minded and earthly good, as we serve your kingdom and wait for its fulfillment . . . Amen.

Joy in Our Weakness, pp. 209-10.

New Year's Day

Blessed and holy are those who have part in the first resurrection. The second death has no power over them, but they will be priests of God and of Christ and will reign with him for a thousand years.

Revelation 20:6

Too often the number 1,000 is understood in a literalistic sense. All the other numbers in the book of Revelation are symbolic numbers, and surely this one is too. . . . We simply must understand this properly because otherwise we forfeit the Joy that can be ours in experiencing in the present Christ's sovereign reign already begun. We can delight in it now already, even though there is still pain and suffering in the world. . . .

Christ's present reign will last for the perfect length of time — completion (10) times itself a divine number (3) of times. It began at the cross and the empty tomb, where Christ defeated the powers, and will continue until the final assault and defeat of Satan. In the meanwhile, however, we manifest Christ's reign to the world by living out the purposes of his kingdom. . . .

I want the reign of Christ to dominate the way I choose the values I espouse, the behaviors that characterize my lifestyle, the methods that I use to build peace in the world. I want to participate in the thousand-year, divinely perfect reign as much as possible. Moments when that reign is not evident in my life are my fault.

Those Christians who focus on a literal thousand-year reign of Christ at some time in the future — . . . though Christ tells us we can't know anything about the future calendar — miss the whole message. . . .

To understand his reign as a present (though not completed) reality makes a huge difference in our perspective on life. . . .

Such a perspective will influence the way we handle all of our daily affairs. . . . Everything that we are and do becomes an important indication of whether or not the lifestyle of the kingdom characterizes our existence and choices.

Most important, Christ's present reign enables us to be overcomers in our times of suffering and trouble. . . . We will cherish the unfailing hope that someday this old order will have passed away. Someday our tears will be gone, so in the meanwhile we can carry on.

Prayer

Sovereign Christ, help us participate fully in your reign — throughout this new year and always . . .   Amen.

Joy in Our Weakness, pp. 196, 202-3.

As with gladness men of old
Did the guiding star behold;
As with joy they hailed its light,
Leading onward, beaming bright,
So, most gracious Lord, may we
Evermore be led by Thee!

William Dix, 1860

In the Christmas season we witnessed the glory of the heavenly hosts, the brilliance of the light of God. Perhaps we ourselves reflected that glory in the splendor of our worshipful singing. But as we move on into the Epiphany season we need a larger understanding of glory, for it means the entire reflection of God's presence.

The season begins with the coming of the Magi, beckoned by the natal star. The festival of their adoration reminds us that God's gifts in Christ are intended for the whole world and that we respond to the immensity of Triune grace with our best gifts.

The season continues with weeks of remembering ways in which Jesus manifests his divinity, the fullness of God. Christ, our bright Morning Star, perfectly reveals the holy glory of God, yet his lowliness also shows us the glory of God's infinite compassion and listening heart. The immensity of the Son's glory lies in his willingness to enter our human estate, to conquer sin and death for us forever.

Let all the heavens and earth reply with praise!

The gift of worship, in this and every season, is the constant invitation to renew afresh our commitment to following Jesus, the Light of the world. What a privilege is ours — to give up ourselves and our agendas, to walk instead as children of the light, in the guidance of the One in whom there is no darkness whatsoever!

The book of Revelation promises us that someday we will need no lamps at all, for the Lamb who was slain will himself be the Light of the city of God. Then there will be no sorrow or mourning, no pain or trouble. Meanwhile, however, the eternity of God has already shone into our world, and the Lamb himself shepherds our journey.

Prayer

Jesus, our only true light, shine in our lives that we may reflect your glory . . .
Amen.

Adapted from Marva Dawn's commentary for "Walk as Children of the Light," a hymn festival for the Symposium on Worship and the Arts, Calvin College, Grand Rapids, Michigan, on January 10, 1997.

Ash Wednesday

Lent seems these days to be a season of the church year in which worship services are often flimsy, if not flippant. The season was designed by our forebears to give us ample time to consider all that Christ did for us in his entire life of suffering, as that culminated in his death on the cross. Indeed, we cannot appreciate the immense triumph of Easter if we don't recognize the enormous cost it required.

In two forty-day seasons of exploring various churches, I've run into the following mistreatments of Lenten worship: an introduction and Ash Wednesday service that suggested that we observe a "joyful Lent" this year; sermons that spoke about our journey and our temptations without once mentioning Christ's; chancel dramas that told stories of biblical figures not at all related to Christ's work of atonement or anything else Lenten; a reading of the story of Bel and the Dragon (from the apocryphal book of Daniel) as the main message; songs that were happy and uplifting on Good Friday; the sharing of "our stories," again without any reference to Christ; a discussion that focused on our feelings about people and how we can crank ourselves up to love them; and a children's sermon on burying the Alleluia during Lent without a single statement as to why. . . .

What has happened to LENT?

Can we be formed as a people willing to suffer if we do not reflect upon the willingness of Jesus to bear our sufferings? Are we able to refrain from making grace cheap if we do not pause to remember the agony of Good Friday and the days that preceded it? . . .

I certainly do not want to advocate an overly morose Lent and funeral dirges similar to those some of us might have experienced as children in excessively sober Scandinavian or German congregations. But we *need* Lent! Our forebears were wise to put its forty days into the calendar to keep us mindful of the great sacrifice of Christ and the immense love of the Father, the overwhelming grace-full — and grotesque — suffering of the Trinity. In these postmodern times, sin and failure are almost universally unacknowledged, though everyone experiences or is aware of disillusionment and despair. In response to this anguish, Lent and its fulfillment of the Promising God's forgiveness are great gifts the Church can offer the world around it.

Prayer

Jesus, in this Lenten season, remind us of the immensity of your love, evidenced in your Passion on our behalf, and free us by that grace to be willing to suffer for the sake of others . . .   Amen.

A Royal "Waste" of Time, pp. 279-80.

I have not written meditations for Maundy Thursday and Good Friday because these days' events are too immense, the love of the Triune God too far beyond my imagining, the meaning of it all unfathomable.

Ponder instead these accounts from the earliest believers:

Matthew 26:17–27:66
Mark 14:12–15:47
Luke 22:7–23:56
John 13:1–19:42

Ponder and pray some of these hymns from wise saints of the Church:

"When I Survey the Wondrous Cross" (Isaac Watts, 1707)
"Jesus, I will Ponder Now" (Sigismund v. Birken, 1653)
"Go to Dark Gethsemane" (James Montgomery, 1820)
"Christ, the Model of the Meek" (Lukas of Prague, 1460)
"What Wondrous Love Is This?" (African American Spiritual)
"O Dearest Jesus, What Law Hast Thou Broken?" (Johann Heermann, 1630)
"A Lamb Goes Uncomplaining Forth" (Paul Gerhardt, 1643)
"Were You There?" (American folk hymn)
"O Sacred Head, Now Wounded" (Bernard of Clairvaux, died in 1153)
"Alas! and Did My Savior Bleed" (Isaac Watts, 1707)
"There Is a Fountain Filled with Blood" (William Cowper, 1771)
"Come to Calvary's Holy Mountain" (James Montgomery, 1819)
"Lamb of God, Pure and Holy" (Nikolaus Decius, 1531)
"Jesus, Refuge of the Weary" (Girolamo Savonarola, 1563)

Easter

But Christ has indeed been raised from the dead, the firstfruits of those who have fallen asleep.

1 Corinthians 15:20

Everything hinges on the resurrection. If there is no resurrection, we might as well give everything up. . . . But if there is a resurrection from the dead, then all heaven breaks loose. . . .

Let us look carefully at the progression of Paul's argument in 1 Corinthians 15:12-20, so that its good news can surprise us again with the wonder of it all.

In a more literal rendering of the original Greek, verse 12 begins, "But if Christ is being preached as having been raised from the dead, how can certain ones among you say that there is no resurrection from the dead?" Do people understand the implications? . . . Earlier in 1 Corinthians 15, verses 1-8 list all those who saw Jesus after his resurrection, and Paul noted that many who saw the Christ were still alive and could testify to the accuracy of Paul's list. . . . How, then, can you doubt your own resurrection?

Now Paul embarks on a spiraling progression: "and if there is no resurrection from the dead, neither has Christ been raised" (v. 13). If you don't believe God is capable of raising the dead, then do you doubt that he raised Jesus?

Furthermore, "if Christ has not been raised, then also our preaching [is] foolish (v. 14a) — without result, without purpose, untrue, vain. If we doubt that Christ has been raised, then our preaching makes no sense — it is ludicrous, pointless, meaningless, worthless, downright false.

Moreover, "foolish [is] your faith" (v. 14b). It, too, is without result, without purpose, untrue, vain. Why be deceived? Why believe illusions? Why bother? Why come mess with this Christianity stuff if Christ has not been raised?

In addition, "we are [then] found also [to be] testifying falsely of God, for we testified of God that he raised the Christ, whom he did not raise if it be true that the dead are not raised" (v. 15). This is getting even worse: we are caught lying about God! Everything we understand about God hinges on his fulfillment of the promise to raise Jesus — all of God's promises to his covenant people culminate in this one.

Again, "if the dead are not raised, neither has Christ been raised" (v. 16). Paul repeats this phrase, with a slight variation, to lead us into the next round of the spiral.

"And if Christ has not been raised, your faith — groundless, fallacious; you are yet in your sins" (v. 17). The absence of a verb in the description of our faith stresses that not only is your faith without foundation, not only is it false — but if Christ has not been raised, you are stuck with yourself, with your inability to be who you want to be, with your not being able to say, do, or think what you wish you could. If Christ is not raised, you cannot be delivered from yourself.

"Consequently also the ones having fallen asleep in Christ have perished. They are utterly destroyed" (v. 18). The repercussions are getting more and more dire. Think about the implications if those who have died are not with God, as we have thought.

All these phrases Paul has stacked up, all these spiraling ramifications, culminate in this last remark of the case: "If for this life only we have been brought to hope, we are of all human beings most to be pitied" (v. 19). If we hope only for what good we can experience in this life, then how wretched and miserable we are, for this life is full of inconveniences, frustrations, bad experiences, blatant evil, undeserved suffering, profound tragedies. Does our faith invite us only to those? Is there no greater hope? . . .

Are we left only with the warnings and exploded promises? . . . Is there no good news?

"BUT NOW," Paul says. Those are two of his best words in the biblical vocabulary; they signal a dramatic change. . . . "BUT NOW, Christ *has* been raised from the dead, the first fruits of the ones having fallen asleep" (v. 20). . . . That changes EVERYTHING! Christ is risen

so we do know that we, too, shall be raised;

we do know that our preaching is not meaningless;

we do know that our faith is not in vain;

we do know that what we have learned about God can be trusted;

we do know that those who have died are alive in Christ;

we do know that suffering and sorrow are not the last word;

we do know that there is a solid foundation to our faith;

we do know that there is a joyous reason to be here worshiping to celebrate our resurrection;

we do know that we are not wretched or pitiable, but instead we have the best news to share, the best news in all the world: we are home free.

we do know that, no matter who or what we are, God welcomes us into this story, this hope, this forgiveness, this new life, this resurrection, this Joy!

Prayer

Glorious Christ, please help us never to lose the wonder that you are indeed raised from the dead. Fill us with Joy and eagerness to share this good news with the world . . . Amen.

A Royal "Waste" of Time, pp. 161-63.

Ascension Day

Therefore God exalted him to the highest place
and gave him the name that is above every name,
that at the name of Jesus every knee should bow . . .

Philippians 2:9-10

Why should we celebrate Ascension Day? . . . The most obvious gift of the ascension is that otherwise . . . we would have to go to Galilee to find Jesus. Because he returned to the Father, he . . . can be found by all of us, everywhere. He is present with you now as you read. . . .

The second glory of Christ's ascension is that by it God affirmed Christ's total obedience and the completion of his work on our behalf. In the ascension Jesus took up again the fullness of his God-self, his deity; he ended the *kenosis,* his self-imposed self-limitation. . . .

The Philippians hymn also hints at another gift in that Jesus was given the name at which every knee shall bow. Other texts in the New Testament (for example, 1 Pet. 3:22) expand this notion to specify that all the powers have become subject to him. . . . The resurrection of Jesus signaled the final defeat of the last enemy, death (1 Cor. 15), just as his exaltation to God's right hand indicates his rule over all other powers. . . . From that position of power Jesus will come again. The greatest Joy of the ascension is its promise that someday Christ will come to reign eternally, to end all sorrow and pain, to take us to be with him. . . .

Meanwhile, at that position of power and relationship with the Father, Christ stays to intercede for us (Rom. 8:34; Heb. 8:1-2). . . .

Jesus himself gave us yet another reason for the ascension when he told the disciples that unless he went away, the Holy Spirit would not be sent to them (John 16:5-15). Peter proclaims this reason on Pentecost in Acts 2:33. . . .

The result of that pouring out of the Spirit, furthermore, has been all God's gifts to the Church (specified in Eph. 4:7-11). . . .

This gifting of the Church . . . emerges in another astonishing consequence, that we the Church shall do greater works even than Christ. As Jesus foretold in John 14:12, "the one who believes in me will also do the works that I do and, in fact, will do greater works than these, because I am going to the Father." Can we even imagine such a stunning result of the ascension? Moreover, our works in Jesus' name are even greater because . . . they include all Christians throughout time and space. Imagine the incredible possibilities!

Prayer

Ascended Lord, reign in us and work through us . . .   Amen.

The Unnecessary Pastor, pp. 140-44.

Suddenly a sound like the blowing of a violent wind came from heaven. . . . All of them were filled with the Holy Spirit and began to speak in other tongues. . . .

Acts 2:2, 4

The scene in Acts 2 is dramatic. The pouring out of the Spirit has caused bewilderment and astonishment in the city (vv. 6-7). In reply to the sneering and amazement (vv. 12-13), Peter has given his extraordinary account of . . . God's foretelling of the Messiah and its fulfillment in Jesus (vv. 14-36). The people are "cut to the heart" and urgently entreat the disciples, "what should we do?" (v. 37). Peter calls them to repentance and baptism, to the gifts of forgiveness and the Holy Spirit (v. 38). He assures everyone that God's promise is for them, for their children, for all, whether near or far (v. 39), but particularly he urges them, "Save yourselves from this corrupt generation" (v. 40).

The whole occasion is a startling combination of God's power and human weakness: the fire of the Spirit poured out in the power of courage and languages; the weakness of the disciples, not understanding how they could speak so forcefully and in divergent tongues; the dominion of God, whose "deeds of power" (v. 11) are the subject of their speech; the belittlement when the apostles are scoffed for being drunk; the sovereignty of God whose ancient promises are fulfilled; the weakness of Jesus (as narrated by Peter), who accomplished those sovereign purposes by being handed over to the crushing contradiction of crucifixion; the crowning glory that "the entire house of Israel [could] know *with certainty* that God has made him both Lord and Messiah, this Jesus whom [we] crucified" (v. 36); the humbled weakness of being "cut to the heart" (v. 37); the glorious power of forgiveness and Holy Spirit giftedness; the utter frailty of Christians in the midst of a corrupt generation (v. 40).

How, then, did they live . . . in response to the powerful outpouring of the Holy Spirit? . . . Inextricably connected to the Lord's calling, they all lived ardent lives . . . as they continually devoted themselves . . . to these seven practices:

1. the apostles' teaching
2. fellowship
3. breaking of bread
4. prayers
5. many signs and wonders
6. being together, having all things in common, selling their property and possessions, distributing the proceeds to all as any had need
7. day by day, being devoted with one mind in the temple praising God and also worshiping/breaking bread from house to house.

Pentecost

The results of this way of life were that . . . the Church grew — not because of the power of these believers, but because "the Lord added to their number day by day those who were being saved" (v. 47b).

Prayer

Holy Spirit, fill us, in our weakness, with your power . . . Amen.

Powers, Weakness, and the Tabernacling of God, pp. 79-80.

382

Do all things without murmuring and arguing. . . .

Philippians 2:14 (NRSV)

One night the airplane on which I traveled was full of "murmuring" — about boarding delays, mechanical problems, take-off postponements.

During the flight I watched the glorious sunset and pondered our murmurings. Why, instead, were we not grateful that the mechanical defect was discovered so we could fly safely? Why did we bemoan our late arrival instead of acknowledging the privilege of flying?

As the rainbow band of colors grew more dazzling, I realized with shame how full of complaints I've become. Why has it become my habit to mutter and gripe instead of recognizing blessings? Why is this such a cultural habit, reflected even in our language? My computer thesaurus gives only seven alternatives for the verb *thank,* but nineteen possibilities for *complain!* We have lots of ways to be grumpy but are not so skilled at appreciation.

And why is murmuring a congregational habit? Just before flying I'd been leading a clergy conference and had encountered there the same low morale I often discover. *Many* pastors are very discouraged because no matter what they do someone in the congregation complains.

As I continued to ponder, the sunset outside my window was gradually replaced by stars, luminous against the surrounding night. In the same way, thanksgiving can be luminous in a culture of complaint, as is evident in the Philippians 2 context of the verse above.

> It is God who is at work in you, enabling you both to will and to work for his good pleasure. Do all things without murmuring and arguing, so that you may be blameless and innocent, children of God without blemish in the midst of a crooked and perverse generation, in which you shine like stars in the world. (vv. 13-15)

Paul's injunction against complaining in verse 14 is part of his guidance for an entire way of life that keeps in mind Christ's "emptying" of himself in his life, suffering, death, and glorification (vv. 5-11). Because God is actively working in us, we are enabled to want and to do God's good will (v. 13).

What a remarkable thanksgiving gift to the world this faithway could be! Remembering in our attitudes and actions all that Christ's incarnation has accomplished for us and rejoicing in his ascension to the full glory of his exalted name (vv. 5-11), we live his Spirit's rays of light in the darkness of our times (v. 15).

Thanksgiving Day

Prayer

Triune God, may our thanksgivings, in will and word and work, shine like stars . . .   Amen.

Abridged and modified "Faithways" column in
The Lutheran, November 2000, p. 6.

For by the grace which has been given to me, I say to each one who is among you not to be thinking more highly [of yourself] than it is necessary to think, but rather to be thinking for the purpose of sane thinking, as God has assigned to each one a measure of faith.

Romans 12:3 (my translation)

"Think for the purpose of thinking sanely," Paul says literally. . . . We are challenged to undertake a process of critical analysis to know appropriately our capabilities and how God might use them. . . .

Unfortunately, . . . I know very few Christians who are delighted with who they are.

Of course, not one of us is satisfied with our spiritual progress. . . . Truly, as our spiritual sensitivities get more and more refined, we know all too precisely how much we fail to be the people God designed us to be.

However, our . . . society is desperately searching for people with a sense of adventure and Hilarity, those who feel good about themselves and delight in their own capabilities and visions and gifts. Truly, we who are God's people are the only ones that have the potential to be so delightfully free. With sane judgment we discover that we are specially created, which should fill us with Hilarity, rather than overwhelm us with a weighty burden. . . .

Why isn't the Christian community more characterized by the FUN that could be ours as we delight in the exquisite creation of God? Why are we so afraid to go full tilt into life? Where is the Hilarity of sane thinking?

Of course, the Christian life is not without strain and suffering and hard work and difficulties. Nevertheless, when we learn to have a healthy appreciation of who we are, life will certainly never be boring. God will constantly be unfolding to us new dimensions of the mysteries of ourselves.

Perhaps we don't delight in ourselves because we assess our own worth by comparing ourselves to others. . . . Yet what a freedom it is not ever to have to be like anyone else! We can honestly pour ourselves into being who we are within the whole of the community because we know that no one else can do the particular ministry to which God has individually called us.

Prayer
> *Calling and gifting God, on my birthday I thank you for making me special. Let me rejoice in who I am, and free me to live full tilt for your glory . . . Amen.*

Truly the Community, pp. 65, 69-70, 74.

Extra Meditations

Then the angel showed me the river of the water of life, as clear as crystal, flowing from the throne of God and of the Lamb. . . .

Revelation 22:1

Revelation 22 begins with the picture of the river of life, the tree with its twelve months of fruit and its leaves for the healing of the nations, the presence of God to remove the curse, and the constant ministering of those who are his servants. They are able at last to see his face, and they carry his name on their foreheads, as they reign forever in his light.

All these images work together to create a tremendous hope and to stir up longing in us for the abundant life, a life thoroughly nourished, well watered, and healed. All the conflicts of the past are over, and now people live together equally, serving God in his presence. Pictures such as these inspire our work in this present world. Since this is what the kingdom is going to be like when we experience it fully in God's own presence, then our lifestyle now, which is to be a reflection of the reign of Christ at this time, must seek the same ends. Our work as the people of God, in our present imperfect service, is to bring healing to the nations, to be counteracting the curse, to be reaping the nourishment of God's living water and fruitful tree of life. . . . Certainly it is right for us to look forward to the day when we will know Jesus face-to-face, but in the meanwhile there are many ways in which we can participate in his purposes to bring healing to the nations. Nourished by his present reign in our lives, we are challenged to be ambassadors of his kingdom and bearers of its reality.

What aspects of our present world urgently need our witness to principles of his present kingdom? . . . Our words about God's grace are more easily perceived as true when our lives seek to manifest that grace faithfully. . . .

When the kingdom of God determines our priorities, we are empowered to live the gospel, . . . for the reign of Christ is not some far-off future event. It begins to take place now in the reign of the servants.

Prayer
> *Reigning Lamb, empower us to be faithful witnesses and servants of your gospel today, in all we do . . .   Amen.*

Joy in Our Weakness, pp. 208-9.

"Going, make disciples of all nations, baptizing them in the name of the Father and of the Son and of the Holy Spirit, teaching them to be observing all things whatsoever I have commanded you; and behold! I myself am with you always until the consummation of the ages."

Matthew 28:19-20 (my literal translation)

Since . . . the confusion of worship and evangelism that characterizes much contemporary discussion in churches . . . violates the biblical directives which form the Church, . . . let us look at this biblical text in order to sketch some principles for faithful evangelism. . . .

Being Church means following a way of life, rather than resorting to techniques. Evangelism is not something that we strategize or plan to do in a certain way — although studying ways of talking about faith are certainly helpful. Rather, as the text above from the final scene in Matthew's Gospel notes, evangelism happens *as we are going.* As we go about our daily lives — to work, to the grocery store, to school, to the neighbor's house for tea — we live the gospel. We speak it freely. We incarnate it. We display a Joy in following Jesus and his Way that invites our neighbors to consider the Truth of his Life in us.

We possess that Joy because of the "behold!" in the Matthew text. Let this wake us up: Jesus is always with us, and someday he will bring to their consummation all the ages. Living in the light of that eternity, we have an entirely different perspective on everything — on the meaning and purpose of our lives, on our sense of identity and its place in a master story, on how and to whom we are beloved and how we therefore cope with the struggles of this life, on the values of this world, and on our hope for the future and its effect on our meanwhile.

And we do not live this way alone. The only verb in the text above is plural. We make disciples as a community demonstrating this way of life by being Church — and thereby our corporate witness gives the neighbor warrant for belief. The task is making disciples — which we do while we go and which is followed by immersing them in the triune Name and instructing them in the triune life.

Prayer
Triune God, we offer our daily lives; use us as your witnesses . . .   Amen.

A Royal *"Waste"* of Time, pp. 345-46.

. . . but in your hearts sanctify Christ as Lord. Always be ready to make your defense to anyone who demands from you an accounting for the hope that is in you; yet do it with gentleness and reverence. Keep your conscience clear, so that, when you are maligned, those who abuse you for your good conduct in Christ may be put to shame. For it is better to suffer for doing good, if suffering should be God's will, than to suffer for doing evil.

1 Peter 3:15-17 (NRSV)

The third chapter of 1 Peter gives very precise instructions for evangelism. . . .

1. "In your hearts [which means in biblical language not simply one's feelings, but one's intentional, deliberate will] sanctify [or reverence] Christ as Lord." . . .

2. "Always be ready." . . . Simply, we will be ready to talk about Christ if we honor him as Lord of everything in our lives. Love is always ready to tell of the one loved. . . .

3. Constantly be prepared "to make your defense." . . . We can easily promote the gospel, for the kingdom is its own warrant for belief. . . .

4. Make your defense "to anyone who demands from you an accounting." . . . This phrase should at least prod us to consider whether our life provokes any questions about the hope we display.

5. Give an answer to those who ask "an accounting for the hope that is in you." . . . Christ as the *Logos* or Word of God . . . is sufficient for our accounting. He *is* our hope. . . . When many possess only wishful thinking, Christians rejoice that our hope is a fact that never disappoints (Rom. 5:5). . . .

6. "[Y]et do it with gentleness and reverence." . . . The bearing with which we speak our hope is essential, for the tone of the invitation determines its reception. . . .

7. "Keep your conscience clear." . . . Whenever we suffer evil it is easier to bear the troubles if there is no guilt and regret mixed in.

These seven themes from 1 Peter 3 form us to be witnesses without coercion, evangelists without condescension, apologetes without animosity. Most important, they nurture mission that arises out of . . . worship, which leads to being Church, which leads to witness for the sake of the world.

Prayer
Christ our Lord, prepare us for true evangelism . . .   Amen.

A Royal "Waste" of Time, pp. 346-49.

"I hate divorce," says the LORD God of Israel, "and I hate a man's covering himself with violence as well as with his garment," says the LORD Almighty. So guard yourself in your spirit, and do not break faith.

Malachi 2:16

Many of us grew up in churches which taught (mostly implicitly) that divorce is the worst sin on the face of the globe. . . . How terrible that God's gracious warnings have been turned into condemnation of those who suffer the great tragedy of broken oneness. For many of us, experiences of rejection, betrayal, and abandonment confront us with the critical need for bringing grace to any discussion about the issues of divorce.

On the other hand, bringing grace back dare not mean making it flabby. In total rejection of churches' former condemnations, the pendulum often swings too far in the opposite direction and accommodates too readily our culture's easy divorce. In the middle of these extremes, the Church could recognize that divorce is a great tragedy and sometimes necessary (as Jesus said, because of adultery), but it is certainly to be avoided if at all possible by supporting marriages as couples try to work things out. . . .

For example, we can avoid extremes by saying that divorce is usually not so much a sin as it is the result of sin and brokenness. Often it is not so much the breaking of the marriage bond as it is the decisive declaration that the marriage has already been irretrievably broken. . . . Sometimes in our violent world, divorce, though certainly not God's best, is critically necessary for the preservation of life.

The biblical picture is intense. God does not say he hates the person who is divorced, but he does say, "I hate divorce." It violates his design for marriages to be permanent, so he warns and rebukes the children of Israel; but he does not disown the persons involved, as churches often do. To imitate God in this matter would be also to hate divorce, to see it as the rupture of God's plan that it is, and then to do everything we can to prevent it and to bring healing to those who have been broken by it.

Prayer

Forgiving LORD, in our churches help us strengthen marriages, encourage and support couples experiencing trouble, and bring healing to persons who have suffered divorce . . .   Amen.

Sexual Character, pp. 125-26.

"Blessed are those who wash their robes, that they may have the right to the tree of life and may go through the gates into the city."

Revelation 22:14

We live in a world that makes a god of strength and power, of being most important and best. Tragically, so many churches have become so caught up in our society's success and victory philosophy that U.S. Christians rarely speak a prophetic word to the world. We do not stand as an alternative community, offering a model of a different lifestyle under Christ's lordship. . . . We have forgotten that God's Word still applies today, to be lived and proclaimed. We are called, as were the earliest Christians, to live by depending only on God, resisting the idolatries of the world around us, and yet compassionately offering the citizens of that world a message of hope. . . .

The Revelation offered to the believers of the first century the profound assurance that, in spite of all appearances to the contrary, God was still in control of world history. We desperately need to recover that assurance and confident hope in our time. The secret to its recovery lies in . . . becoming again, like the saints of old, a people characterized by theocentricity. . . .

We must be vigilant against all forms of evil and be conscious in our daily decisions so that we choose . . . the purposes of the kingdom of God. . . .

Because Jesus is Lord in spite of the powers of evil, we yearn for a greater willingness to endure suffering patiently. . . . Because biblical patience invites us to look for the presence of the Lord even in our own contrary circumstances, we do not ask merely how long it will be till things are different, but we seek to learn who he is and how he enables us to respond in the midst of our suffering.

We have learned, therefore, . . . to depend on the sufficiency of God's grace. We have recognized that . . . we are called to a new gentleness, a submissive humility, a gracious integrity that enables us to stand true to the principles of the kingdom of God . . . in the compassionate offering of a . . . lifestyle that awaits its eventual vindication.

Prayer
> *Cosmic Lord, be the center of our lives, so that we always live by your grace . . .   Amen.*

Joy in Our Weakness, pp. 218-20.

Worship, honor, glory, blessing, Lord, we offer as our gift;
young and old, your praise expressing,
our glad songs to you we lift. . . .

Edward Osler (1836), alt.

The worst thing churches can do about worship for the sake of their children is to choose music and worship forms according to *their* taste — when their tastes are not yet biblically formed. . . .

I often wonder how it came about that churches began to sacrifice their identity in an attempt to please people. The Boy Scouts or 4-H clubs or sports associations do not change who they are to appeal to people. . . . It is commonly known that these organizations serve purposes that people want to participate in, so when a young person wants to join, he or she is grateful for the opportunity and learns how the program works. Similarly, if we want to learn an ethnic dance, those who have practiced it do not change the steps for us. We practice with them so that we can develop the habits of the art. Why do churches throw away their habits and arts — and more deeply, their identity as the parallel, alternative community — instead of welcoming our children and neighbors into the dance and helping them to learn it? . . .

I have observed that, if they are taught, young people enjoy a wide range of music. . . . Furthermore, I have noticed invariably that the youth who love to sing in worship are the children of parents who sing with gladness. . . .

Instead of changing its music and worship forms to please the young people, a congregation should teach its youth why the older members value certain songs and hymns, why each part of the liturgy is meaningful, how the various things we do in worship contribute to keeping our focus on God and to nurturing us, individually and corporately, in the life of discipleship. Similarly, we should also encourage the youth to continue to bring to our worship planning group new music that does the same. . . .

What is appropriate to bring us all together, young and old, as a community? What will appropriately nurture us corporately and personally for being the church?

Prayer
   Worthy Lord, forgive our using worship to attract or please, rather than to
   honor you . . .   Amen.

Is It a Lost Cause? pp. 65, 71-74.

Acknowledgments

The material in these devotions is taken from the following books by Marva Dawn:

I'm Lonely, Lord—How Long?: Meditations on the Psalms (Eerdmans, 1998).

Is It a Lost Cause?: Having the Heart of God for the Church's Children (Eerdmans, 1997).

56 selections (pp. 10, 11, 13-26, 29-31, 35-41, 43-55, 57-73, 76-79, 82-84, 86-93, 95-108, 110, 111, 114-120, 128-132, 135-138, 142-146, 149-152, 154-166, 168-175, 180, 181, 186-188, 190-194, 212, 215, and 216) are adapted from *Joy in Our Weakness: A Gift of Hope from the Book of Revelation.* © 1994 Concordia Publishing House. Used with permission of CPH.

Keeping the Sabbath Wholly: Ceasing, Resting, Embracing, Feasting (Eerdmans, 1989).

Reaching Out without Dumbing Down: A Theology of Worship for This Urgent Time (Eerdmans, 1995).

A Royal "Waste" of Time: The Splendor of Worshiping God and Being Church for the World (Eerdmans, 1999).

Sexual Character: Beyond Technique to Intimacy (Eerdmans, 1993).

To Walk and Not Faint: A Month of Meditations on Isaiah 40 (Eerdmans, 1997).

Truly the Community: Romans 12 and How to Be the Church (Eerdmans, 1997).

The Unnecessary Pastor: Rediscovering the Call (Eerdmans, 1999).